Roman Religion in the Danubian Provinces

Roman Religion in the Danubian Provinces

Space sacralisation and religious communication during the Principate (1st–3rd century AD)

Csaba Szabó

OXBOW | books
Oxford & Philadelphia

Published in the United Kingdom in 2022 by
OXBOW BOOKS
The Old Music Hall, 106–108 Cowley Road, Oxford, OX4 1JE

and in the United States by
OXBOW BOOKS
1950 Lawrence Road, Havertown, PA 19083

Paperback Edition: ISBN 978-1-78925-783-0
Digital Edition: ISBN 978-1-78925-784-7

A CIP record for this book is available from the British Library

Library of Congress Control Number: 2022930862

This book was supported by the Postdoctoral Research Grant PD NKFI-8 no. 127948 by the National Research, Development, and Innovation Office of Hungary (2018–2021). See also: *www.danubianreligion.com.*

Printed in the United Kingdom by Short Run Press

Typeset in India by Lapiz Digital Services, Chennai.

For a complete list of Oxbow titles, please contact:

UNITED KINGDOM
Oxbow Books
Telephone (01865) 241249
Email: oxbow@oxbowbooks.com
www.oxbowbooks.com

UNITED STATES OF AMERICA
Oxbow Books
Telephone (610) 853-9131, Fax (610) 853-9146
Email: queries@casemateacademic.com
www.casemateacademic.com/oxbow

Oxbow Books is part of the Casemate Group

Front cover: Roman Mithraic relief from Dacia (Dragu, Sălaj county). Photo in custody of the National History Museum of Transylvania, Cluj-Napoca, Romania (inv. no. 15812).

Contents

List of illustrations vi
List of abbreviations ix
Foreword xi

1. Introduction 1

2. Emerging Roman religion: the beginnings 27

3. Lived religion and its macro-spaces in the Danubian provinces 89

4. Space sacralisation in meso-spaces 152

5. Religious experience in micro-spaces: housing the gods 190

6. Conclusion: beyond the materiality of Roman religious communication 198

Appendices

1. Sanctuaries in the Danubian provinces 208
2. Divinities in the Danubian provinces 225
3. Diagrams 234

Bibliography 247
Index 294

List of figures

Fig. 1.1 General map of the Danubian provinces. (Source: Glomb 2021 open access with the special permission of the author). https://doi.org/10.1371/journal.pone.0256356 3
Fig. 1.2 Political map of the Danubian region. (Source: https://danube-region.eu/about/). Open access. 6
Fig. 1.3 Danube river basin. (Source: https://www.eea.europa.eu/). Open access.
Fig. 1.4 Taxonomy of space sacralisation. (Source: the author) 18
Fig. 1.5 Materiality of religion used in space sacralisation. (Source: the author) 20
Fig. 2.1 Map of Roman Raetia showing the settlements discussed in Chapter 2. (Source: https://dh.gu.se/dare/). Open access. 30
Fig. 2.2 Plan of Magdalensberg showing the district of sacralised spaces. (Source: after Wikicommons). Open access. 37
Fig. 2.3 Funerary inventory of Luna Sol. priestess in Nagyberki-Szalacska. (Source: Tóth 2015, 23, Fig. 3) 39
Fig. 2.4 Map of Roman Noricum showing the settlements discussed in the Chapter 2. (Source: Țentea 2011, 229, pl. 1 with the special permission of the author) 50
Fig. 2.5 Plan of the Noreia sanctuary in Hohenstein. (Source: Áron Hegedűs and the author after Trunk 1991, 193, Fig. 136) 51
Fig. 2.6 Plan of the sanctuary in Burgstall in St Margarethen in Levanttal. (Source: author after Groh-Sedlmeyer 2007, 31, abb. 1.) 54
Fig. 2.7 Plan of the sanctuary in Frauenberg. (Source: Áron Hegedűs and the author after Schrettle 2016, 189, Fig. 5) 55
Fig. 2.8 Plan of the sanctuaries in Celeia. (Source: Áron Hegedűs and the author after Krempus *et al.* 2007, 41, abb. 3) 57
Fig. 2.9 Map of Roman Pannonia showing the settlements discussed in the Chapter 2. (Source: Țentea 2011, 229, pl. 1 with the special permission of the author) 58
Fig. 2.10 Capitoline triad in Scarbantia, Pannonia. (Photo: Bolodár Zoltán, with the permission of Museum of Sopron, Hungary) 59
Fig. 2.11 Relief of Silvanus in Aquincum. (Source: Lupa 10482, photo of Ortolf Harl, with the special permission of the directorate of Aquincum Museum, Budapest) 64

Fig. 2.12 Relief of the Nutrices in Poetovio, Ptuj. (Source: Lupa 8763, photo of Ortolf Harl, with the special permission of the Pokrajinski muzej Ptuj – Ormoz) 66
Fig. 2.13 Lead votive plaque representing the so-called 'Danubian Riders'. (Photo: Manfred Clauss, EDCS-44200062) Open access. 74
Fig. 3.1 Genius of the *publicum portorii Illyrici* in Apulum. (Source: Lupa 12238, photo of Ortolf Harl, with the special permission of the National Museum of Union Alba Iulia) 91
Fig. 3.2 Altars discovered in the sanctuary of the *beneficiarii* station in Sirmium (Source: after Mirković 2008 with the permission of Nadežda Gavrilović Vitas). 95
Fig. 3.3 Relief of a Genius *nautarum* in Apulum. (Source: Lupa 19332-3, photo of Ortolf Harl with the special permission of the National Museum of Union Alba Iulia) 97
Fig. 3.4 Map of Roman Moesia Superior. (Source: Țentea 2011, 229, pl. 1. with the special permission of the author) 100
Fig. 3.5 The Iseum of Savaria. (Source: author) 101
Fig. 3.6 The Roman spring and sanctuary of Germisara. (Source: after Szabó 2018b, photo of Aurora Pețan with the special permission of the author) 104
Fig. 3.7 Urbanity and citification in religious communication. (Source: author) 110
Fig. 3.8 Geographic distribution and density of votive inscriptions in urban centres of the Danubian provinces. (Source: author). 113
Fig. 3.9 Urban plan of Aquincum with the most important sacralised spaces attested. (Source: author from the DAS map) 114
Fig. 3.10 The so-called 'Symphorus Mithraeum' in Aquincum. (Photo: author) 119
Fig. 3.11 Representation of an emperor (probably Septimius Severus) with Jupiter Heliopolitanus. (Source: Lupa 11574, photo of Ortolf Harl with the special permission of Archäologisches Museum Carnuntum) 119
Fig. 3.12 Frontiers of the Roman Empire depicting the legionary fortresses. (Source: https://www.univie.ac.at/limes) Open access. 124
Fig. 3.13 The plan of the forum in Virunum. (Source: author) 129
Fig. 3.14 The plan of the forum in Sarmizegetusa. (Source: author after Piso 2017b) 131
Fig. 3.15 The plan of the forum in Oescus. (Source: author after Kabakchieva 2014) 133
Fig. 3.16 Isis-Sothis relief in the Iseum of Savaria. (Source: with special permission of the Museum of Savaria) 134

Fig. 3.17 Itinerary of Titlus Iulius Capito in the Danubian provinces. (Source: author after Țentea 2011) 136
Fig. 4.1 Life cycle of small group religions – a model. (Source: author) 156
Fig. 4.2 Altar dedicated to Glykon in Apulum. (Source: Lupa 11284–1, photo by Ortolf Harl with the special permission of the National Museum of Union Alba Iulia) 157
Fig. 4.3 Statue of Glykon in Tomis. (Source: Lupa 21360–1, photo by Ortolf Harl with the special permission of the National Museum of History and Archaeology in Constanța) 158
Fig. 4.4 Mithraic altar in Poetovio. (Source: Lupa 9330–1, photo by Ortolf Harl with the special permission of Pokrajinski muzej Ptuj – Ormoz Museum) 159
Fig. 4.5 Statue of Jupiter Dolichenus from the Dolichenum of Porolissum. (Source: Lupa 20363, photo by Ortolf Harl, with the special permission of the Museum of Zalău) 163
Fig. 4.6 Statue of Turmazgades Hero Romula, Dacia. (Source: Lupa 21951, photo by Ortolf Harl with the special permission of the National History Museum of Romania, București) 164
Fig. 4.7 Mithraic inscription, memorialisation of an initiation. (Source: Lupa 9348, photo by Ortolf Harl with the special permission of Pokrajinski muzej Ptuj – Ormoz Museum) 168
Fig. 4.8 Statue of Asclepius from Iuvavum, Noricum. (Source: with the special permission of Salzburg Museum – Domgrabungsmuseum) 170
Fig. 4.9 Representation of the rain miracle at the column of Marcus Aurelius. (Source: Wikicommons) Open access. 172
Fig. 4.10 Funerary relief representing Perseus and Andromeda Hero Moosburg, Noricum. (Source: Lupa 1069, photo by Ortolf Harl, Pfarrkriche St Michael und St Georg) Open access. 175
Fig. 4.11 Mithras Tauroctonos from Apulum. (Source: author, after Szabó 2013) 177
Fig. 4.12 Victoria (Niké) killing the bull, Rome, Villa of Antoninus Pius. (Source: British Museum, cat. no. 1805,0703.4.). 178
Fig. 4.13 Mithraic relief in Dragu, Dacia Porolissensis. (Source: after Szabó 2012 with the special permission of the National Museum of History of Transylvania, Cluj-Napoca) 180
Fig. 4.14 Cautes with bucranium in Apulum. (Source: author photo after Szabó 2015b) 181
Fig. 5.1 Apollo statuette from Roman Dacia. (Source: Kunsthistorisches Museum Wien, Antikensammlung) Open access: https://www.khm.at/objektdb/detail/66805/. 192
Fig. 6.1 Roman monuments integrated in the Orthodox Church of Densuș, Transylvania. (Source: author) 207

List of abbreviations

AÉ — L'Année Épigraphique.

ANRW — Haase, W. – Temporini, H. (eds), *Aufstieg und Niedergang der römischen Welt/Rise and Decline of the Roman World. Geschichte und Kultur Roms im Spiegel der neueren Forschung.* Berlin-New York, 1972–???.

BBRD — Boda, I. – Szabó, C., *Bibliography of Roman Religion in Dacia.* Cluj-Napoca, 2014.

CCID — Hörg, M. – Schwertheim, E., *Corpus Cultus Iovis Dolicheni, Études préliminaires aux religions orientales dans l'Empire romain 106.* Leiden, 1987.

CIGD — Ruscu, L., *Corpus inscriptionum Graecarum Dacicarum, Hungarian Polis Studies 10.* Debrecen, 2003.

CIL — *Corpus Inscriptionum Latinarum. Consilio et auctoritate Academiae Litterarum Regiae Borussicae editum.*

CIMRM — Vermaseren, M. J., *Corpus Inscriptionum et Monumentorum Religionis Mithriacae I–II.* The Hague, 1956–1960.

Clauss-Slaby — Epigraphik Dantebank Clauss-Slaby.

CSIR — Corpus Signorum Imperii Romani.

DAS — The Digital Atlas of Roman Sanctuaries in the Danubian Provinces.

DMA — Digital Map of Apulum.

EDH — Epigraphic Database Heidelberg.

EPRO — Études préliminaires aux religions orientales dans l'Empire romain (founded by M. J. Vermaseren).

HA — Scriptores historiae Augustae.

IDR — *Inscriptiones Daciae Romanae I–III.* București/Paris, 1975.

IG — Inscriptiones Graecae.

IGLN — J. Kolendo – V. Božilova (eds), *Inscriptions Greques et Latines de Novae (Mésie Inférieure).* Bordeaux 1997.

IGUR — *Inscriptiones Graecae Urbis Romae I–IV.* Rome, 1971–1990.

ILD — Petolescu, C. C., *Inscripţii latine din Dacia* (*Inscriptiones Latinae Dacicae*). București, 2005.

ILJug — Šašel, Anna – Šašel, Jaroslav, *Inscriptiones latinae quae in Iugoslavia inter annos MCMII et MCMXL repertae et editae sunt.* Ljubljana, Situla, 1986.

ILS — Dessau, Hermann, *Inscriptiones Latinae Selectae.* Berlin, 1892–1916, 3 vols.

IMS Papazoglou. Fanoula – Mirkovic, Miroslava, *Inscriptions de la Mesie Superieure*. Beograd, Centre d'Études epigraphiques et numismatiques, 1976–.

LIMC Lexicon Iconographicum Mythologiae Classicae, Zürich, München, Düsseldorf, 1981–1999 and 2009.

LTUR Steinby, E. M. (ed.), *Lexicon Topographicum Urbis Romae*. 1993–2000).

Lupa Ubi Erat Lupa Bilddatenbank zu antiken Steindenkmälern (lupa.at).

MMM Cumont, F. V., *Textes et monuments figurés relatifs aux Mystères de Mithra: pub. avec une introduction critique*. Bruxelles, 1894–1896.

OPEL Lorincz, Barnabás – Redo, Franciscus (eds), Onomasticon Provinciarum Europae Latinarum. Budapest-Wien, 1994–2002.

RIU Barkóczi, L. – Mócsy, A., *Die römischen Inschriften Ungarns*. Amsterdam, 1972–1991.

Tit. Aq. Kovács, P. – Szabó, Á., *Tituli Aquincenses I-III. Vol. 1.* Tituli *operum publicorum et honorarii et sacri*, Szabó, Ádám (ed.) ... [*et al.*] – *Vol. 2.* Tituli *sepulcrales et alii Budapestini reperti*, with the help of Fehér Bence – Borhy, László (eds)... [*et al.*] – *Vol. 3.* Tituli *instrumenti domestici*, cura Fehér, Bence. Budapest, 2009–2011.

Foreword

During the course of my doctoral studies, I have participated in numerous international conferences, workshops and meetings focusing on Roman religion or the materiality of religion from antiquity. At most of these events, there were few – usually two or three – participants from Central-Eastern Europe. Very often, these scholars came from a classical archaeological background and had a very poor opinion of scholars of religious studies. Two worlds were meeting in these spaces: the world of classical, often outdated positivist and Kossinna-type archaeology of the provinces, and the highly theoreticised and often too-abstract field of religious studies searching for the obscure notion of material religion. Their theoretical conflict and methodological incompatibility were very provocative and appealing for me: I realised that uniting Roman religious studies with provincial archaeology represents one of the most innovative scientific methods – one that can unite Western and Eastern European scholarship and create a lived academic dialogue, perhaps ultimately attracting more young scholars from Central-Eastern Europe to the discipline.

The Danubian provinces have long occupied a well-established position in Roman provincial archaeology. These include the century-old *Limesforschung* (study of Limes) in this region; the historical link between Central-Eastern European scholarship and the Austrian and German archaeological traditions; the visits and infrequent but impactful connections between Sir Ronald Syme, Sheppard Frere, John Wilkes, Andrew Wilson and others in the Danubian region; and the general contemporary dialogue between archaeologists from this region of Europe. All of these provide a good start for the development of new methodological perspectives.

My previous work, which focused on the sacralised spaces and religious communication in Roman Dacia, was the result of an early attempt to unite these two often conflicting disciplines and to open a dialogue between religious studies and provincial archaeology in Romania and Hungary, where this tradition is still in its infancy. The work was received surprisingly well, although the interest came especially from Western scholars: from the 11 known reviews, just four were published in Central-Eastern Europe. Until recently, this book was one of just a few case studies in which the innovative methodology of lived ancient religion approach of Jörg Rüpke and his team from Erfurt was tested against the materiality of religion from the Danubian provinces of the Roman Empire.

A year and a half after the publication of my doctoral defence and having had numerous temporary jobs outside academia, I was lucky to receive a postdoctoral research grant from the Hungarian state (NKFI Postdoctoral Research Grant 127948) in autumn 2018. The project, entitled 'Roman religious communication in the Danubian provinces during the Principate' was hosted by the Department of Religious Studies at the University of Szeged under the supervision of Professor András Máté-Tóth. The stated aim of the project was to collect and map all the archaeologically attested sanctuaries (sacralised spaces) of the Danubian provinces in macro- and meso-spaces. I had been preparing this idea for many years and being able to finally work on it was a dream come true for a young researcher. Furthermore, I believe that continuing the work of great and unparalleled scholars of the Danubian region – such as Géza Alföldy, András Mócsy, István Tóth and John Wilkes – by writing a book on Roman religion in the Danubian provinces was an urgent necessity.

With this historiographical burden, I announced my work and sought the help of my colleagues from Central-Eastern Europe at the wonderful *Limescongress* that took place in Serbia in September 2018. At this coming-together of numerous scholars of Roman religion from the Danubian area, a small, ad hoc think thank formed, led by Professor Martin Henig. During the course of our discussions, we decided that a long-term collaboration was necessary in order to establish a new academic network and to renew the study of Roman religion in this region. This collaboration resulted in an international conference being organised in mid-October 2021, which focused on the latest archaeological results from religion and sanctuaries in the Danubian provinces. The hope is that such events will continue in the future with similar, productive initiatives.

My work – as is the case for many others worldwide – was overshadowed of course by this unusual pandemic. It has been a complex time of despair, digital transformation and the rise of dehumanisation, which on a micro-level has separated researchers from libraries, conferences and fieldworks. Prior to the onset of the pandemic in 2020, I was lucky enough in 2019 and the early months of 2020 to visit several important research libraries in Rome, Budapest, Oxford and Berlin, where I have amazing friends and colleagues, who helped me in this hard endeavour. This period proved just how hard the work of Central-Eastern European scholars is, since there are so few big research libraries east of Vienna. Without the existence of well-known online and open-access resources, our work during the pandemic would have been completely paralysed.

In the last three years, despite such hardships, I have published several works focusing on space sacralisation and the taxonomy of sacralised spaces, as well as on glocal aspects of Roman religion in the Danubian provinces. Some of these studies are included in this book.

During the course of this project, I have read and learned a lot, and my work is based on the canon of great scholars, many of whom helped me with my research. It is hard to list all of them – literally hundreds of scholars and colleagues, friends and relatives have helped me. However, in brief, I am very grateful to all my colleagues from the University of Szeged; the students of Lucian Blaga University in Sibiu; the archaeological institutes in Belgrade and Vienna; and my colleagues from Cluj, Alba

Iulia, București, Pécs, Budapest, Berlin, Rome, Oxford, Erfurt, Frankfurt, Mainz and the many other cities in which I have lived, studied or researched in the last 10 years.

I am fully aware that this book is far from being a complete and comprehensive work on Roman religion in the Danubian provinces. I am not even sure if it is possible to write such a work. My aim with this modest, but unusual contribution is to shake the comfort zone of Roman provincial archaeology in Central-Eastern Europe and to create a new academic arena in which scholars of religious studies, archaeologists, sociologists of religions, and epigraphists can discuss the materiality of religion in a new, transdisciplinary way.

Time will tell whether or not this ambitious attempt will be followed by others.

Szeged
October 2021

1

Introduction

Caius Bruttius Goutus, son of Caius, from the tribe of Claudia, died at the venerable – almost Saturnian – age of 80 in the legionary *canaba* of Novae, in modern-day Svishtov, Bulgaria. Upon Goutus's death, his tombstone was laid down by Caius Vibius Therapo, a Greek-speaking friend of his, in accordance with an agreement the pair had probably made long before the event. Thus Goutus was prepared for the Afterlife, and fulfilled his last important duty as a solider, as a citizen and as an old man, far away from his homeland.

Caius Bruttius Goutus was born a Roman citizen 1,200 km from Novae, in Virunum, the capital city of Noricum, probably in the time of Tiberius. The region was in the process of becoming a province at that time, although the Romans and especially their itinerant merchants and soldiers were already familiar with the Noricans. It is possible that Caius's father, also called Caius, was born outside of Noricum, but we don't know for sure since only his name has been preserved on a fragmentary and badly damaged tombstone far away from Virunum. Whatever his father's origins, Caius Bruttius Goutus spent his childhood in Virunum in the age of Tiberius and Caligula and was recruited as a solider in the Legio I Italica, in the time of Nero or Vespasian. History didn't preserve the adventures and major events of his unusually long life, but it seems that as a solider he was much luckier than many of his fellow legionaries, who died in the turmoil of wars, revolts and campaigns of the I Italica legion between 58 and 70 AD, when the legion was moved by Emperor Vespasian to Novae.

Our hero – a man who had probably had a fairly standard military career during the peak of the Roman Empire[1] – represents the voice of thousands from antiquity and survives as a name from 1,900 years ago thanks to the action of a loyal friend. The same is true of countless other the Roman citizens who had the will, the financial ability and the luck to immortalise their names on stone monuments. History was also kind to Goutus: his tombstone survived the vicissitudes of time and the turbulent history of Central-Eastern Europe.

By the time Caius Bruttius Goutus finally departed this world, the Roman Empire was radically different – and certainly much bigger – than it had been upon his birth

80 years previously. Close to the moment of his death, he perhaps marvelled at the new coins bearing the triumphal figures of Emperor Trajan, the Alexander of his age. What might he have seen during his long life in Virunum, Carnuntum or along the banks of the Danube in Novae? Did he have friends among the local population of Noricum or Moesia? How did he meet his Greek-speaking friend, Therapo? What gods did he evoke during his long life? How did the sacralised spaces he knew in Virunum from his childhood change during his lifetime? Did he have a *lararium* in Novae and what were the names of the gods whom he asked for help? How did the landscape of Novae, Virunum or other cities visited by him or by his fellow legionaries change in this period?

In a broader context, during the course of Goutus's lifetime, major changes occurred around the world – changes that defined the history of Central-Eastern Europe not only for the period of classical antiquity but also today, having a long-lasting impact on modern urban structures, cultural heritage, linguistic specificities and cultural identities. During the course of those 80 years between about 30 AD and 110 AD,[2] the Roman Empire expanded significantly, englobing the Alpine provinces (Raetia, Noricum), the middle part of the Danubian area (Pannonia) and the lower Danubian region (Moesia, Dacia). While Goutus experienced a regular Roman childhood in the mountainous area of Virunum, the adventurous, dynamic and highly mobile lifestyle of a Roman legionary and the peaceful retirement of a veteran 1,200 km from his home town, the Roman Empire went through 11 emperors. In addition, due to its rapid expansion, it also assimilated a significant number of people and brought about long-lasting population mobility and mass migration in the form of dislocations of the army, organised colonisation and opportunist migrations.

These structural, demographic and political changes radically reshaped not only the life of millions in Central-Eastern Europe and the Mediterranean, but also the world of the gods. New divine agents, new sacralised spaces and new strategies of religious communication were used at micro-, meso- and macro-levels of individuals and groups. Indeed, it is almost impossible to present in a single book the major religious transformations that occurred in the first three centuries AD, during the Principate. Hundreds of sacralised spaces were formed in both pre-Roman and newly established settlements – whether urban or rural. Thousands of objects (altars, statues, statuettes, ceramic material, reliefs and small finds) produced in this period in the seven provinces analysed in this work served the successful maintenance of the newly established sacralised spaces and transformed the already existing ones, often resulting in the obliteration of the pre-Roman religious landscapes and languages of divine communication. New divine agents, such as Mithras, the cult of the so-called 'Danubian Riders' (*Domna et Domnus*) or reinvented traditions with attractive visual narratives reshaped the visual culture of Goutus's generation.

This book cannot hope to answer all the questions raised above regarding the details of his daily life and his religious experiences, although these will constitute the guiding principles of my work. Good, provocative and in-depth questions will always guide the historian through the mute and silent history of materialities, revealing fragments of both local and global stories. Instead, this book will focus on three major aspects of Roman religion: 1) lived religion and strategies of religious communication; 2) forms of space sacralisation; and 3) glocalisation of Roman religion. These will be analysed using material evidence from seven provinces, commonly known today as the Danubian provinces: Raetia, Noricum, Pannonia Superior, Pannonia Inferior, Moesia Superior, Moesia Inferior and Dacia.

To highlight the importance of this region in the macro-history of the Roman Empire and beyond, however, it is necessary to first clarify some of the most frequently used notions of this book and to contextualise my work in the larger theoretical and historiographic framework of Roman religious studies.

Danubian provinces: history of a notion[3]

The Scottish physician and poet William Beattie in his classical book on the Danube from 1844 describes the second-longest river of Europe as a 'dark rolling

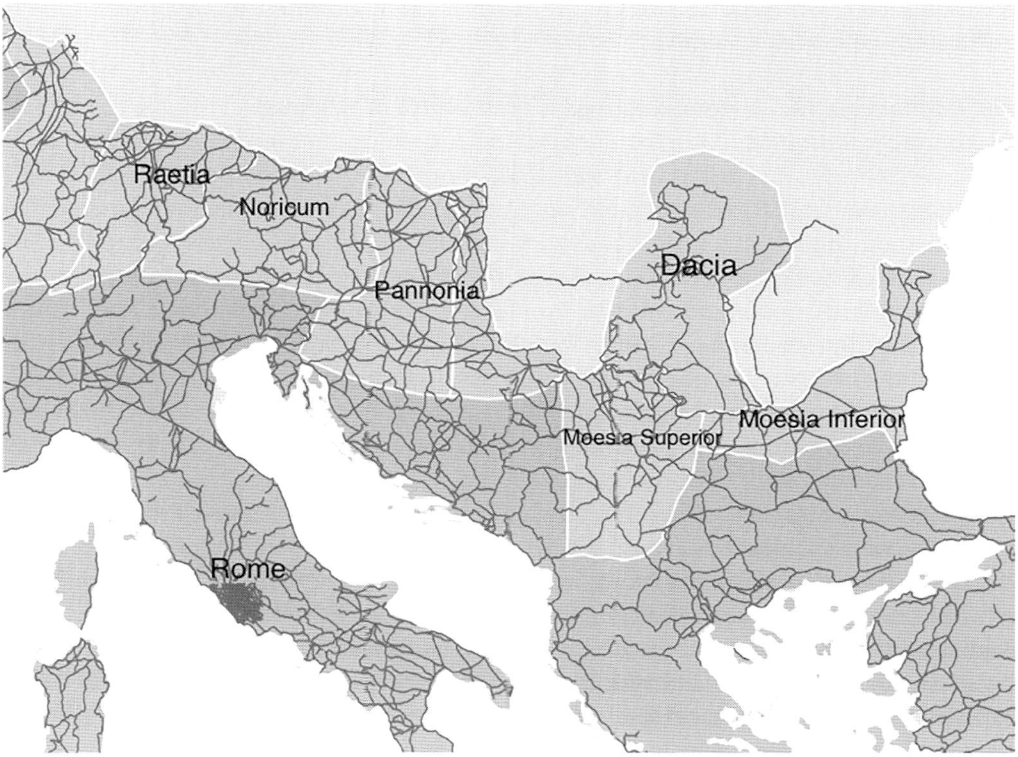

Fig. 1.1 General map of the Danubian provinces. (Source: Glomb 2021 open access with the special permission of the author). https://doi.org/10.1371/journal.pone.0256356

Danube of the poet, which rivets the attention and conjures up a thousand associations. The Danube, the second river of Europe receives the tribute of sixty others in its course and rolls its majestic tide through empires, kingdoms and principalities. Its banks monumented with the glorious deeds of old and rich in magnificent scenery have been hitherto reserved as a free and open field for the pencil of the illustrator'.[4] In his beautifully illustrated book, written during the age of Western intellectual travellers discovering Central-East Europe,[5] Beattie thus created the ultimate version of the Danube and the Danubian region, described by him as the mystical, exotic and ancient part of the continent. This vision of the Danube and its region became highly influential not only in terms of 19th-century cultural tourism, but also in various intellectual and even academic works. Indeed, the longevity of Beattie's romanticised view and his notion of the cultural 'unity' of the Danubian region persists even today in numerous books, essays and travel guides.

So, just how did this romantic picture of the Danube and the surrounding region became the standard literary and scholarly view and how did this idea enter Roman studies and Roman provincial archaeology in the 19th century (Fig. 1.1)? To try to unpick this, we have to look at the meta-histories related to this notion from antiquity until modern times.

The Danube and the surrounding region in ancient Latin sources

The Danube (Danubius, Danuvius, Δανούβιος, Δανούιος , Δάνουβις)[6] was well known by ancient Greek and Latin authors long before the age of the Principate (14 BC–285 AD).[7] Most of the Latin texts mention very briefly just the name of the river in their ethnographic descriptions of the Barbaricum and the 'northern people' (*i.e.* north of the Alps): the laconic passages mention the river and its hinterland in connection with historical – mostly military – events, its populations and ethnic groups (Dacians, Germans, Sarmatians), and its monumentality.[8] Probably the first mention of the Danube in an administrative context of the Empire and the Roman world[9] appears on the monumental inscription detailing the life of Emperor Augustus, the Monumentum Ancyranum[10]: '*... protulique fines Illyrici ad ripam fluminis Danuvi (μέχρι Ἴστρου)*'.

The Danube in the age of Augustus had become a symbol of boundaries, represented more and more often in Roman Imperial propaganda as a bearded old river god. Pliny the Elder in his *Natural History* mentions 60 tributaries of the Danube[11] and considered the Danube to be a cultural and administrative division between the Roman and Barbaric worlds[12]. The strategic military and commercial importance of the Danube was also mentioned in numerous literary sources, most famously *Buildings* 4.5.2. by Procopius. The name of the river also appeared in iconographic and epigraphic sources: 'Danuvius' appears on the column of Trajan, on a relief from Carnuntum and on votive inscriptions from Aquincum, where a possible shrine dedicated to the river has also been identified.[13]

With the exception of the Monumentum Ancyranum inscription, none of the ancient authors associated the Danube with an administrative unit of the Roman Empire, although its important role as *fines* and *limes* (the northern end of the Empire) can be interpreted as a cultural and administrative boundary that united these provinces.[14] The notion that was used much more often as an administrative, fiscal and economic unit for this region was Illyricum or the *publicum portorii Illyrici*, the customs system of the north-eastern provinces of Rome.[15] The entire region was united in the divine form of the *genius publici portorii Illyrici*, known from votive inscriptions from Poetovio or Porolissum[16]. However, although the inscriptions from the *stationes* and customs centres suggest a strong economic macro-unit within the Roman Empire, there are no traces in literary or epigraphic inscriptions of a common macro-regional identity. Indeed, the intense mobility of the legions along the Danube was mentioned numerous times by Roman historians, especially in the context of 192–193 AD, when Septimius Severus became emperor, helped by the 'legions of Illyricum'.[17]

Donauländer, Donauprovinzen *and the invention of a notion: the 18th–19th centuries*

Europe was reshaped after 1648 in the aftermath of the Peace of Westphalia. Now, the Central-Eastern European area came to be dominated by the Habsburg Empire and was often called a *Donaumonarchie*, a monarchy of the Danubian area.[18] The new political formation established in Central-Eastern Europe created not only a systematic unification of industry and German-speaking culture, but also influenced the evolution of classical studies and early examples of Roman archaeological research in the 18th century. It was this new type of political, administrative and cultural 'unity' in the region that created the notion of *Donauländer*, the Danubian countries. The Danube in this case became a geographical thread uniting the territories of modern Bavaria, Austria, Slovenia, Croatia, Hungary, Slovakia, the Czech Republic, Serbia, Romania and Bulgaria as well as serving as an important commercial channel, especially in light of the major political and infrastructural competition between the Habsburg, Ottoman and Russian empires for control of navigation on the Danube.

In fact, it was the more than 200-year-old military and political conflict between the Habsburg Empire and the Ottomans that gave a cultural legitimacy to the separation of the Upper and Lower Danubian areas – regions that were also divided by geographical specificities (especially at the Iron Gates gorge between Serbia and Romania). This geographic and cultural duality of the Danubian areas was present in 18th-century travellers' literature as well as in the first papers on the Roman Danubian provinces, which appeared in German historical works by, for example, Johann Hübner, Johann Baptist Schels, Eduard Duller or Ferdinand Stiefelhagen (Figs 1.2 and 1.3).[19]

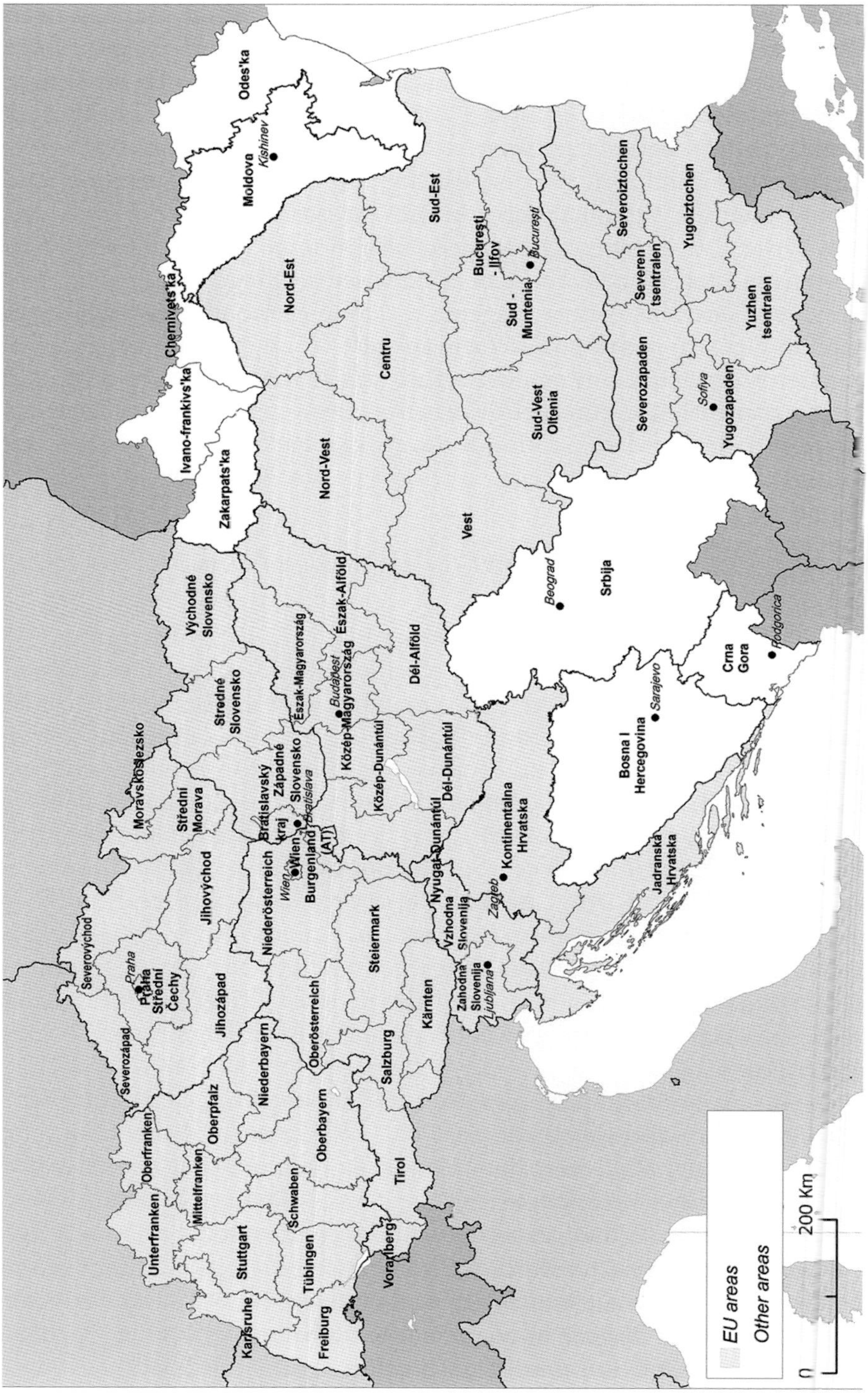

Fig. 1.2 Political map of the Danubian region. (Source: https://danube-region.eu/about/). Open access

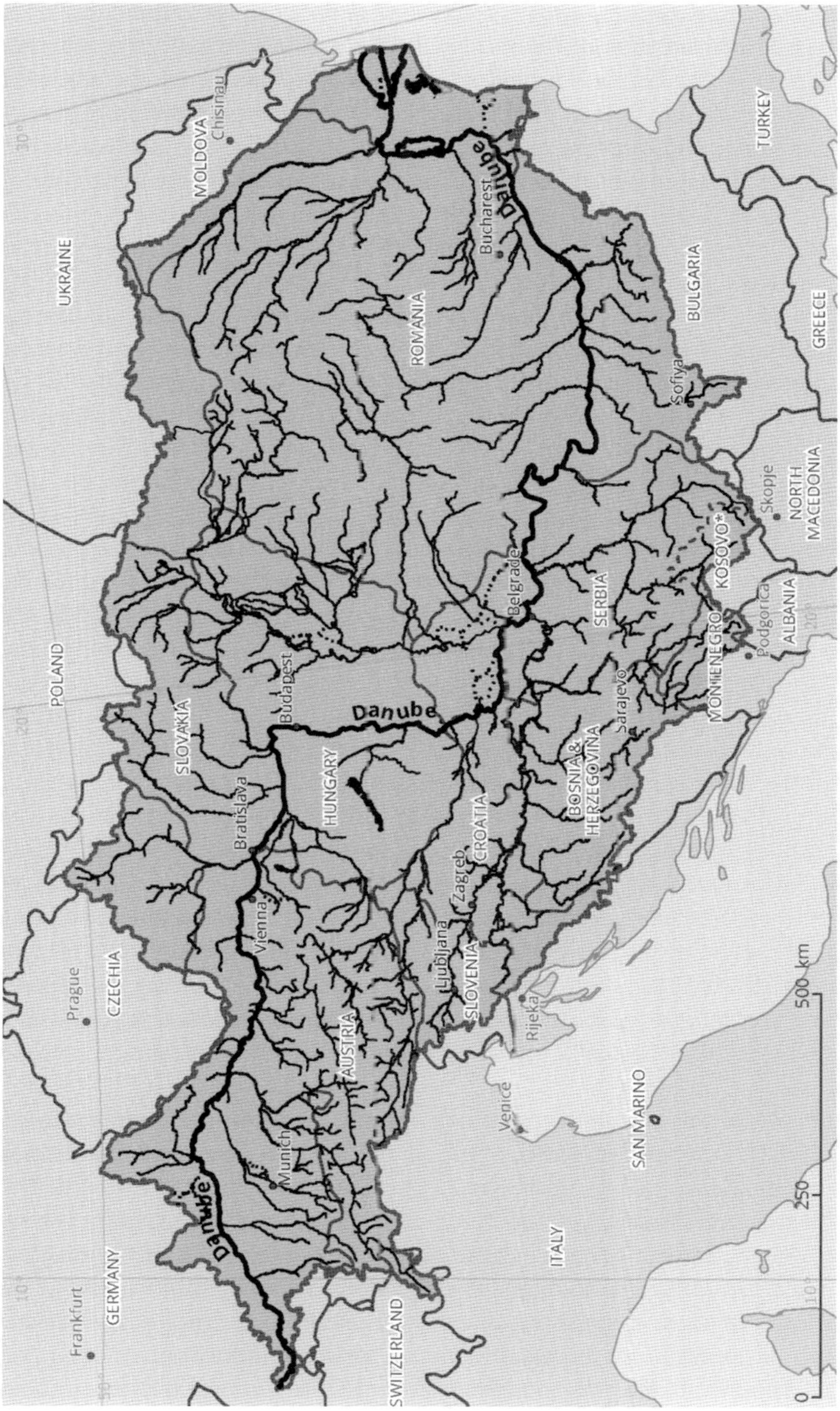

Fig. 1.3 Danube river basin. (Source: https://www.eea.europa.eu/). Open access

It was thus following an early 19th-century encyclopaedic tradition[20] that Johann Jakob Herzog in 1861 used the notion of *Donauländer* in the context of the Augustan-Tiberian expansion of the Roman Empire in this region.[21] This can also be interpreted as a historiographic manifestation of the *translatio imperii*, the imitation of Rome by the Habsburg dynasty and Imperial self-representation. The notion also appeared in the title of the first book on the area by Eduard Robert Rösler in 1864, although not exclusively in a Roman context.[22]

Friedrich Kenner was among the first to dedicate an entire book to two provinces of the Danubian area, and he also used this geographic denomination in the title of his important work on Noricum and Pannonia.[23] Followed by the paradigmatic work of Theodor Mommsen on epigraphic studies in Central-Eastern Europe,[24] Julius Jung, the famous professor of classics from Prague, published an important synthesis in 1877, in which he presented for the first time the importance and enduring impact of Roman provincial administration in the Danubian area.[25] Indeed, the Danubian provinces as an administrative, political, cultural and military macro-unit of the Roman Empire was 'canonised' by the work of Theodor Mommsen, who in 1885 in his volume focusing on the provinces of the Roman Empire dedicated an entire chapter to the Danubian provinces (Raetia, Noricum, Pannoniae, Dalmatia, Moesiae and Daciae[26]), presenting the area as '*das Werk des Augustus*'.[27] Mommsen's writing established the major methodological frames and facets that would go on to characterise the study of the Danubian provinces in the following century of research: the area represented the edges of Empire; the provinces were highly militarised (the beginnings of *Limesgorschung*); and the region served as an a intermediary between the Western provinces and the Near East that united Latin, Greek, Celtic and local cultures.

A few years later, in 1890, Wilhelm Drexler used the notion of the Danubian provinces for the first time in the title of a monograph focusing on Roman religion in this region.[28] Although the intense military mobility between the Lower and Upper Danubian provinces was well known from literary sources, the emerging discipline of epigraphy and prosopographical studies and art historical approaches at the end of the 19th century stressed the regional networks between the Danubian provinces. In this period, the common denomination of the region also appeared in Anglo-Saxon literature, especially in historical, epigraphic and military studies.[29]

The exotic area of the Empire: between centre and periphery in the 20th century

The Danubian provinces as a macro-unit of the Roman Empire was briefly mentioned in the first half of the 20th century, mostly in the paradigmatic works of Andreas Alföldi and Michael Rostovtzeff. The school of Alföldi – a leading figure of Hungarian classical archaeology in the interwar period[30] – was the first to analyse the Central-Eastern European classical antiquity and its material evidence in a holistic, supra-national view, focusing on global aspects and macro-units within the Roman Empire. As a result of this new vision based on archaeological evidence, several important doctoral theses were born. An important one was written by Árpád Dobó, who published a book on the *publicum portorii Illyrici* , one of the first comprehensive analyses of the customs system of this region.[31] The book was well received by the Anglo-Saxon academic community, especially because the major works on the economic history of the Roman Empire completely ignored the Danubian provinces in this period.[32] The same topic was presented in French in a much more cited and appreciated work by Siegfried De Laet.[33] The Danubian provinces as a macro-unit within the Roman Empire thus became a legitimate field in Roman studies after the publication of these two major works, followed later by several others, in particular the important monograph by Peter Ørsted.[34]

The so-called *Limesforschung*, the study of the military history and dislocations of the Roman army in this region, contributed enormously to the inclusion of the Danubian provinces in the global contextualisation of the Roman Empire. The works of Nicolae Gudea and Zsolt Visy are paradigmatic in this sense. From the Anglo-Saxon literature, the most relevant papers on prosopography, military and political history were collected in the volume by Ronald Syme in 1971.[35] His influential Danubian papers represented not only the rich connections of the local elite with the rest of the Empire but also instigated an academic network between Western and East-European scholars.[36] Commonly considered as the 'second founder of Roman History',[37] Syme's Danubian papers influenced the works of Géza Alföldy and John Wilkes, both of whom also contributed to the study of the Danubian provinces in a global context.[38] Géza Alföldy, András Mócsy and John Wilkes wrote individual monographs on some of the provinces from this region that serve as major references for the provinces of Noricum, Pannonia and Dalmatia.[39] The studies of G. Alföldy from 1988 and 2004 contextualised the Danubian provinces within the social history of the Roman Empire,[40] while Wilkes contributed with three major works on this topic, focusing especially on the major archaeological sources of the region.[41] The influential work of G. Alföldy in the second wave of the *Corpus Inscriptionum Latinarum* in Central-Eastern Europe (mostly Austria, Hungary, Romania and Serbia) also established numerous epigraphic schools, where the study of the Danubian provinces or *Großillyricum* (Lower and Upper Danubian provinces) follows his holistic and inclusive view on this area of the Empire.

Today, several contemporary projects and institutions are focusing especially on this area of the Empire.[42] Recent international collaborations are primarily concerned with Late Antiquity and the transformation of the Roman world in the Danubian area,[43] and feature various *limes* projects as well as seeking the integration of the archaeological heritage of this region in EU sustainability projects.[44] Future projects will need to focus on the creation of academic networks of Roman studies in the Danubian provinces and the integration of this region in international trends and academic discussions.

Roman religious studies: past, present and perspectives[45]

Although the material evidence of Roman religious communication represents almost half of the complete epigraphic, iconographic and architectural heritage of ancient Roman history and has been researched systematically in the last two centuries, producing thousands of important works on the various aspects of Roman religion, there is still no systematic summary of the historiography of Roman religious studies.[46]

The first major works on Roman religion were published in the 19th century and adopted the positivist and legal approach – dominated by Mommsen and Georg Wissowa – that culminated in the paradigmatic work of Wissowa.[47] The work of Wissowa and most of the authors in the 19th century focused on Roman religion as a civic/polis religion, formed in an urban environment, controlled by religious specialists and a strict legal tradition. The major force in the communication between divine and human agents was the Roman law, although time, state and the divine agents also played a significant role in Wissowa's work. These are important aspects, which were approached differently by Franz Cumont, who challenged the notion of *sacra peregrina* ('foreignness'), and came up with a new terminology: 'oriental cults'.[48] This approach and the doctrinal influence of Cumont changed the major currents of Roman religious studies and created a strong dichotomy between the 'state religion' and '*sacra peregrina*' of Wissowa.[49] Thereafter, few individuals tried to think outside these two major categories. One of them was William Warde Fowler, whose book on the religious experiences in Roman religion remained for a long time one of a kind.[50]

The first half of the 20th century saw the production of numerous syntheses on Roman religion from Anglo-Saxon, French and German writers. Some of these were highly influential, in particular the large synthesis by Franz Altheim.[51] During the 1960s and 1970s, two major book series marked the discipline of Roman religious studies. The first was the almost 100 volumes that were published in the series by M. J. Vermaseren (*Études préliminaires aux religions orientales dans l'Empire romain* or *The Imperial Cult in the Latin West*[52]), who continued the work of Cumont on the so-called oriental cults, but focused his research on the archaeological evidence. A slightly different, more classical approach to Roman religion (in which the concepts of *Reichsreligion* and *Provinzialreligion* played a key role) was established in the monumental *Aufstieg und Niedergang der Römischen Welt* (*The Rise and Decline of the Roman World*) by Hildegard Temporini and Wolfgang Haase. These two series comprised thousands of pages and represented a systematic analysis of the archaeological, epigraphic, literary and historiographic sources of Roman religious communication. However, what they didn't do was radically change the major theoretical currents that had been established in the end of the 19th century.

It wasn't until the 1998 publication of the paradigmatic work by Mary Beard, Simon Price and John North that there appeared a radically new approach to Roman religions – one that pluralised the narrative of the official *Reichsreligion* and polis-religion and integrated domestic religion, magic, monotheistic tendencies and the followers of Christ in this topic. Price and his team also questioned the dichotomy of oriental religions and the 'official' Roman religions, opening the door to a flood of literature on the reinterpretation of orientalism in religious studies.[53]

In the last 10–15 years, the work of Jörg Rüpke and the so-called Erfurt School on Roman religion has introduced a paradigmatic new research methodology and approach, especially through the lived ancient religion project.[54] Thanks to the publication of numerous books, Rüpke and his school have now become one of the leading voices in Roman religious studies, especially in Europe, but also in the USA. Several other important currents and approaches also coexist on the academic market, creating a methodological heterogeneity.[55] In contrast to these Western academic trends, however, the study of Roman religion in Central-Eastern Europe shows a radically different history.

The material heritage of the provinces of Illyricum is one of the richest among the main areas of the Roman Empire.[56] Thanks to the material artefacts produced by the Roman presence in this area, the largest part of this evidence is related to various religious experiences and sacralised spaces. Despite this, the Danubian provinces as a research unit in Roman archaeology and ancient history has been strictly limited to military, political and, rarely, economic investigations.[57] Studying Roman religion of the provinces of Illyricum has two major lacunas: 1) it was researched either as a footnote example in the major Western works of Roman religious studies; and 2) it remained a research field of peripheral, local schools.[58] Although the study of Roman religion is one of the most dynamic sub-disciplines of Roman studies and ancient history,[59] the major projects that have shaped our view on Roman religion in the last decade were operating mostly or exclusively with the materiality of the Western and Eastern (or rarely with the African) provinces.[60]

Studying Roman religion in Central-Eastern Europe: a short historiography of the last decade

There is no comprehensive study focusing on the century-long history of research of Roman religious studies in the Danubian area. In the seminal work of Wilkes on the Roman Danube, the great scholar made a very short summary of the research, focusing exclusively on the latest publications (1990–2005) and major discoveries in this area of the Empire.[61] From Wilkes's summary we can observe a traditional Cumontian approach to Roman religion, separating clearly the indigenous, 'Roman', 'oriental' and Christian cults and religious manifestations. He also emphasised some of the new currents in the research, especially on the problematic notion of religious continuity, Christianisation and local appropriation of Roman divinities, without contextualising these religious phenomena in a larger, global scale of Roman religious studies. Since Wilkes's summary was published, local scholars have produced numerous important works and discoveries that need to be mentioned, along with the recent currents of research and the major shifts in research history in the Danubian provinces.

Raetia

Raetia was researched mostly as a military province, thanks to the history of the *Limesforschung* from Bavaria and Austria.[62] Around 230 votive inscriptions have been identified in the province, mostly from the greater urban centres, which material has been systematically published in recent years.[63] Yet despite the presence of this meticulously published archaeological material, there are very few studies that focus on Roman religion in Raetia.[64] Most concentrate on the local specific aspects of the military religion,[65] others on religious syncretism, provincialism or local religious appropriations.[66] Several studies and books have also been dedicated to the study of the *Brandopferplätze*, which were attested in a large quantity in this region, serving as one of the main reasons for the development of Alpine archaeology and mountain archaeology in Bavaria.

Noricum

The case study of Noricum is well researched, due to its rich archaeological material (more than 600 votive inscriptions) and the intriguing case study of religious appropriation and indigenous religious aspects.[67] A catalogue containing the most relevant finds and short summaries of the recent research was published in the 2010s.[68] And yet in his more recent book focusing on the problematic notion of Romanisation,[69] M. Zimmermann mentions only sporadically the archaeological evidence of Roman religion as part of this cultural/material process.[70] Most of the studies on religion in Noricum instead focus on Celtic divinities and their epigraphic evidence, often with new, provoking, but perhaps overly sophisticated analysis.[71]

Pannoniae

Pannonia Inferior and Superior have provided some of the richest archaeological evidence of Roman religious communication in the Danubian provinces. The area contained several interesting indigenous groups, whose religious material was inherited and appropriated during the Principate. The proximity of the Amber Road and the commercial networks with the Po area (especially Aquileia) also contributed to the local appropriations attested in Roman religious communication here. Although there is no comprehensive synthesis on the religion of Pannonia, the seminal work of I. Tóth from 2015 gives a detailed analysis in some of the relevant fields of the research, as well as marking the lacunas within it.[72]

Pannonia is remarkable for its well-documented sanctuary excavations, especially in Carnuntum (IOM Heliopolitanus) and Savaria (Isea, Mithraea).[73] Important studies focusing on priests,[74] bronzes,[75] magical practices[76] and urban religion have also been published.[77] There is also a paradigmatic project concerning the early Christian artefacts from the province, reinterpreting their chronology and historical context, which might be a model for other future provincial studies.[78] Further research might focus on the archaeology of sanctuaries, domestic religion, small-group religions and religious networks within the Danubian area.

Moesia Superior

The most well known and still the most cited work on Moesia Superior was written by Andras Mócsy.[79] Since the publication of his seminal work in 1974, however, numerous important studies have focused on the local particularities of Roman religion in the province. Studies have concentrated particularly on the figurative-sculptural material of the province in numerous important books.[80] While in some works focusing on settlements (especially well-excavated Viminacium, Sirmium and Singidunum) religion is mentioned only briefly, recent studies have been concerned with individual divinities,[81] and economic[82] and iconographic aspects.[83] Some case studies have also tried to identify some indigenous cults and their appropriation during the Principate, mostly in the so-called cult of the 'Danubian Riders' cult, which has recently been identified with the cult of *Domna et Domnus*, which might have been formed and spread in Moesia Superior.[84]

There have also been numerous studies that have produced important, unpublished materials focusing on the so-called oriental cults, although methodologically, they follow an old concept that is questioned and regularly contested in Western scholarship.[85] Numerous sporadic finds of lead tablets identified recently on the black market seem to have come in large numbers from the area of Sirmium, which was probably one of the regional centres of this cult. Elsewhere, important studies have been published on the extensively known cemeteries in Viminacium, which makes Moesia Superior one of the best places in which to conduct case studies on funerary religion.[86]

Moesia Inferior

The province of Moesia Inferior has a very long and continuous Roman history. It is divided into two main areas – the Ripa (the fluvial *limes* of the Danube) and Dobrudja – which were radically different due to their cultural and historical background. The province is also divided between the Bulgarian and Romanian scholarship, the latter focusing especially on Dobrudja. Studies have focused on individual sites – especially larger urban and military centres and Greek cities[87] – and numerous studies are concerned with the so-called oriental divinities and numismatic iconographies, often in comparison with those of Thrace and Dacia.[88] Short studies have been made focusing on Roman magic,[89] and extensive studies on the early Christian archaeology of the region. Beside some aspects of the public Roman religious communication,[90] indigenous religion has been mostly discussed only briefly in onomastic studies and with an emphasis on Thracian and 'Danubian Riders' (*Domna et Domnus*) cults. There have also been important studies published on local iconography.[91]

Dacia

With more than 1,500 votive inscriptions, hundreds of figurative monuments and around 160 sanctuaries (54 identified archaeologically),[92] the case study of Dacia has been well presented in the last couple of decades.[93] Dominated for a long time by the seminal work of M. Bărbulescu,[94] Romanian and international research on Roman religion in Dacia has given rise to more than 500 titles in the last two decades. This period was important not only because of the emergence of new theoretical works focusing on religious syncretism,[95] military religion,[96] priesthood[97] and the problem of the so-called oriental cults,[98] but also thanks to the publication of important monographs on divinities[99] and sanctuaries.[100] There have also been numerous works published by foreign scholars, focusing on the material from Dacia[101] as well as on the problem of the indigenous Dacian religion,[102] magic[103] and early Christianity.[104]

Aims, sources and methodology: lived ancient religion, space sacralisation and glocalisation

As the historiographic synthesis shows, most works focusing on Roman religion produced in Central-Eastern Europe have presented the material evidence of religion in descriptive catalogues or site monographs, using provincial or urban limits for their analysis. Macro-spaces or thematic approaches that break the traditional spatial limits of the scholarship are rarely used, although – as hopefully this book will argue convincingly – Roman provincial limits didn't in fact represent a valid and relevant delimitation in religious communication, mobility and transformations.[105]

This work aims to break the traditional spatial, theoretical and chronological limits used in the analysis of Roman religion in Central-Eastern Europe, which have until now been focused on individual divinities, settlements or provinces in a short period of time. Roman religion here is analysed as a complex, living and glocal language, dependent on the demographic realities, legal framework and political existence of the Roman Empire, having numerous 'dialects' – forms of strategies and manifestations that marked the social fabric of the Empire. These 'dialects of religious communication' have universal (global) and local variations and the Danubian provinces serve with numerous, often ignored or rarely analysed, case studies for such a radically new approach.

Roman religious communication produced a rich material evidence in the Danubian provinces: almost 30 per cent of the total amount of known inscriptions from the seven provinces are votive inscriptions,[106] while the quantity of the non-epigraphic material used in religious communication is almost impossible to estimate (Fig. A4 in the Appendices). Similarly, the number of people involved in Roman religious communication over the course of three centuries can possibly be measured in the millions, although only a few thousands of them contributed to the materiality and the maintenance of the sacralised macro- and meso-spaces of religion.[107]

The materiality of Roman religion preserved in this region has several local specificities, which are analysed in Chapters 2 and 3, which focus on local transformations, reinvented religious traditions and the major macro-spaces that also played an essential role in religious communication. The sources used represent a subjective and, by the nature of such synthetic works, painfully incomplete kaleidoscope of archaeological sites and materials. However, the analogies used in the book reflect the current state of research in each of the modern countries that inherited the materiality of Roman religion from the Danubian provinces. Most of the sacralised spaces or material evidence (both epigraphic and non-epigraphic) are from the few well-researched and systematically excavated case studies found in this macro-region. For despite the mass of material evidence and impressive number of sacralised spaces that have been attested, there are very few case studies that have been systematically excavated, documented and published.[108]

Following the above-presented aims of the book, in the analysis of this greatly heterogenous and complex material evidence I have used three major theoretical notions and approaches, which require terminological clarification.

Lived ancient religion

The concept of 'lived ancient religion' is now an almost canonised methodological and theoretical approach used in Roman religious studies and beyond.[109] The concept developed by Jörg Rüpke and his team changed radically the current academic discussion on ancient religions, having a significant impact in Western European and American scholarship.[110] The approach also received a few critical comments[111] and it is not commonly used in Central-Eastern Europe, where new theoretical approaches in Roman provincial archaeology are rarely adopted.[112]

The methodological concept of lived religion was used long before it was applied to ancient religions, especially in American anthropological and religious studies.[113] Jörg Rüpke's concept of lived ancient religion tried to explore new dimensions of religious communication that go beyond the descriptive method of archaeology, the classical philological tendencies or the polis-religion approach, whereby religion is interpreted as a controlled language of an elite or else is marginalised because of the problematic nature of the primary sources.[114] The innovative aspects of the approach (religious embodiment, local appropriations, a special focus on religious individualisation, various facets of religious communication, the concept of religion 'in the making') were tested on numerous case studies in Rome, Egypt,[115] Syria,[116] urban contexts, magical practices and many other examples predominantly in the Western provinces.[117] This approach also united the study of early Christianity, ancient Judaism and Roman religion in the same theoretical framework.

Lived ancient religion therefore represents not only a unique and provocative opportunity to analyse the materiality of religion in the Danubian provinces in a radically new manner, but as the case study of Roman Dacia has shown, peripheral case studies also reflect the limits of adaptability of these highly innovative approaches.[118] One of the arguments for why this radically new approach did not reach the Central-Eastern European scholarship is the lack of literary sources on Roman religion for this region and the problematic, often non-existing dialogue between classical archaeology (which commonly adopts a descriptive, object-fetishist approach) and the contemporary religious studies used by the lived ancient religion approach. As J. Bodel argued, this new current initiated by J. Rüpke indeed often represents a far too superficial methodology for archaeologists, who are used to discussing the micro-changes of space sacralisation and the stratigraphy of archaeological sites and buildings or object biographies.[119]

The problem of disciplinary and methodological differences, especially in case studies where archaeological material dominates, are partially resolved in some of the latest works of the lived ancient religion approach, which focus on North Africa and the Near East, or particular case studies, such as that of the Mithraea.[120] As the following chapters will hopefully show, these case studies are useful analogies for the Danubian provinces, where numerous case studies of local religious appropriations, individuations and strategies of space sacralisation in an urban context can be observed.

Space sacralisation[121]

Humans have presumably since the beginning of prehistoric times been in constant communication with beings endowed with superhuman forces, known as gods, or not unquestionably plausible divine agents.[122] The past of the objectified religion(s) and figurative divine agents goes far beyond the temporal dimensions of written history and institutionalised religion.[123] Establishing and maintaining religious communication needs not only a constant interaction between human and divine agents,[124] but also shows an interdependent relationship between space and its materiality.[125]

Space only became a research field in religious studies in the 1970s, although Gerard van der Leeuw introduced in the 1930s a phenomenology of sacred sites.[126] In 1974, Henri Lefebvre coined the term 'space production'. In his works, space is dependent on human interaction: it is created, maintained and reproduced by social interaction and is dependent on human actors.[127] Following this idea, in 1986 Michel Foucault developed the idea of simultaneity in space, whereby spatial transformation coexists in the human body as well as political and social spaces.[128] Jonathan Z. Smith was the first scholar in religious studies to continue the French social theory on space and argued in 1978 that space sacralisation is more than the Eliadian duality of 'sacred and profane' and emphasised the imaginary and interconnected aspects of space in religion.[129] He also stated that the sacralised produces meaningful places, which he termed 'sacred spaces'.[130] J. Z. Smith's theory of *homo faber* created a human agent who, through dialogue with the divine world, 'sacralises' the profane space via an active, dynamic, transformative process.[131] The sacralisation of space is therefore not possible without the active role of the human agent: there is no 'sacred space' without the creative act of human devotion, verbal transmission, habitual repetition or reinvented traditions.[132]

However, space sacralisation does not end with the creative act itself: its aim is to provide a successful and possibly long-lasting space for the dialogue between the human and divine worlds, thus the divine agent also plays a key role in transforming and sacralising the space. This process takes place by means of a number of tools and strategies.

Based on these theoretical models and the paradigmatic works of Veikko Anttonen[133] on the corporeal and territorial boundaries in religion, K. Knott developed a complex spatial theory and methodological approach that focuses on five major features: 1) the body, as a source of space; 2) dimensions of space (physical, mental, social); 3) properties of space (simultaneity, extension); 4) aspects of space (perceived and lived); and 5) dynamics of space.[134] The spatial theory of religion developed by Smith and continued by Knott focuses almost exclusively on space itself: the attention is on the multidimensionality and lived, transformative aspect of space, where human agency, as the transformative force, is the crucial element. Materiality of religion and the macro-spaces of larger clusters (cities, states, economic routes, climate, environmental aspects) are neglected in this theoretical model. Their model also retains the dichotomy of 'local' and 'global',[135] although globality as a methodological tool in historic narratives was recently reinterpreted and introduced a more fluid approach going towards glocality.[136]

New approaches on the spatiality of religion are derived from prehistoric and cartographic narratives.[137] Understanding prehistoric religion involves analysing the interconnectivity of nature, climate, long-distance mobilities and the locality of small groups, and there is a special focus on the material agency of religion, which is the exclusive source of religious communication from this period.[138] Peter Biehl and François Bertemes developed a complex space taxonomy of religion that included not only the human and material agency of religious communication, but also large geographic and natural clusters, such as rivers, commercial routes and social hierarchies.[139] This model was unfortunately neglected by scholars of classical archaeology or religious studies, where knowledge production on religious spaces often fails in disciplinary meta-histories.[140] Traditional narratives in classical archaeology and Roman religious studies instead analysed the spatial aspects of religion through their architectural, functional and visual (art-historical, decorative) aspects.[141] In rare, exceptional cases, material and human agency of religion were interpreted through a complex spatial theory, such as the one established by Hubert Cancik, whereby objects and their users are perceived in the physical, social and imagined simultaneity of landscapes.[142]

Combining the lived ancient religion approach with David Clarke's space archaeology and systemic model of past societies[143] evokes the theoretical framework proposed by Biehl and gives a complex framework that goes beyond the previous space models in religious studies (Fig. 1.4).[144] Biehl's and Cancik's models have shown that space sacralisation is not only a product of human interaction, but is also interconnected with material agency, natural landscape and socio-political and economic structures. A systemic model of space sacralisation – similar to the paradigmatic deep maps in cartography[145] – aims to unite hierarchies of spaces with levels of religious intensity, appropriations and simultaneity where human and material agencies are interconnected and in constant dialogue with divine powers (gods).

In this active, living, transforming and creative act of dialogue between human and divine, materiality of religion and their hierarchy plays a very important role. The inner dynamics of the four major components of space sacralisation (divine agency, human agency, space itself and the materiality of religion) is also influenced by macro-spaces, such as the city (citification of religion), climate changes, economic routes, military interventions, medical and public health issues (such as pandemics) and larger administrative or financial units, such as provinces, routes or customs systems. Within this network, accessibility, personal choice and the intensity of religious experience are crucial: they reflect the simultaneous coexistence of private and public, sacred and profane and the three major spatial categories, which often overlap, as the following case studies will show.

The most intimate dimension of space sacralisation is the human body itself: signs marked on the skin surface (tattoos, writings, figurative marks, wounds, cuts, mutilations), dances, songs and outdoor processions, along with neurobiological processes caused by religious ecstasy, all transform the human body into a living

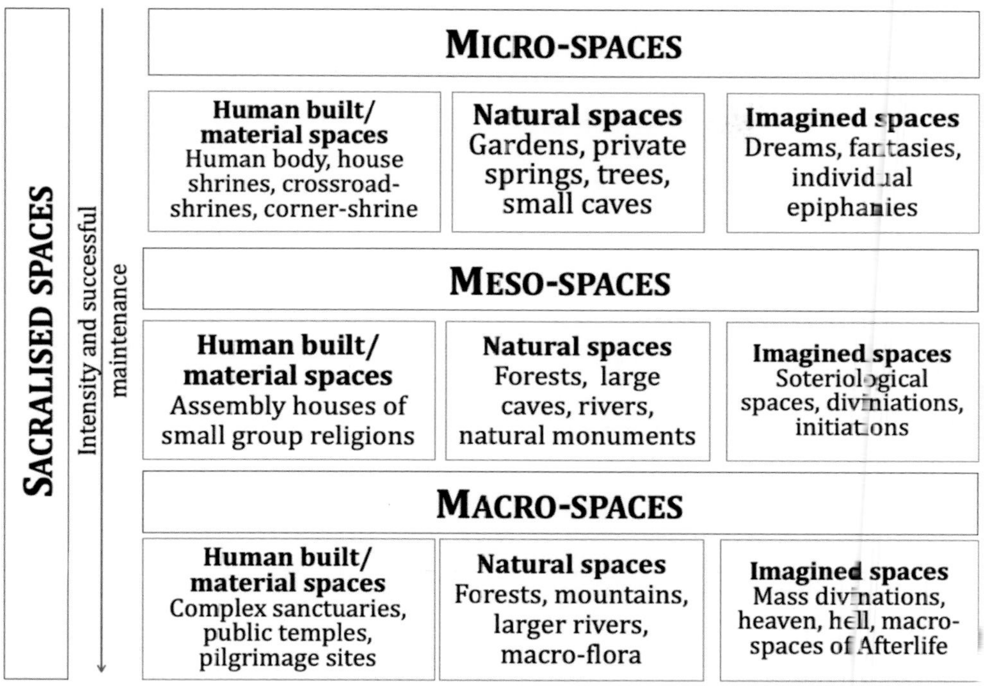

Fig. 1.4 Taxonomy of space sacralisation. (Source: the author)

sacralised space.[146] Space sacralisation also results in a high degree of religious individualism in the so-called domestic spaces (house shrines, corner shrines, rooms, corridors, private gardens, cellars, etc.). I have called these spaces 'micro-spaces', breaking with the now much-discussed 'private-public' dichotomy.[147] These micro-spaces provide for the participant a high level of religious individuality,[148] creativity and spatial coherence. In these cases, religious experience and the various aspects of lived religion can be much more easily observed.[149] The material evidence of religious communication in micro-spaces also shows a personalised aspect, with a high level of individuality in visual narratives, too. The dense network of sacralised micro-spaces and their close intertwining with the diverse world of meso-spaces has already broken the 'private-public' duality in contemporary works on spatial theory.[150]

Meso-spaces (assembly houses, synagogues, small-group religious meeting places, *spelaeum*/caves, Mithraea, springs) have a much stronger social coherence, uniting numerous individuals in the same place, serving as a dynamic physical, visual and imaginary agent (third space) in religious hierarchies and new social structures.[151] Architectural atmosphere and visuality play a secondary part in these spaces, although the inner geography of assembly houses could play an important role in the social cohesion of small-group religions.[152] These places also have a short existence, spanning just one or a few generations, which means that their longevity and maintenance is dependent on the charismatic religious leaders and the so-called 'critical phase' of small-group religions, when they expand from familial and personal networks into larger groups and social clusters.[153] Most of them fail before they reach this phase of expansion.

Macro-spaces (complex sanctuaries, healing shrines, pilgrimage sites, mountains, forests, etc.) represent the most successful case studies. These places are maintained by investments consisting of intense financial and human resources and represent a concentration of religious experience, knowledge and personnel.[154] Sacralised macro-spaces also have a *longue durée* existence, and their success is maintained by religious pilgrimage, monopolisation of religious knowledge and divine agencies (central sanctuaries, temples, shrines of religious founders, oracular sanctuaries). In these cases, architecture, visual narrative and monumentality, religious traditions and the memory of the sacred play a crucial role in religious space production and maintenance.[155]

The successful survival of these sacralised spaces is interdependent of the ongoing human and divine communication and the materiality of religion used as tools in all the above-mentioned locations. These spatial categories are highly interconnected in natural, rural and urban environments, each of them having a direct impact on the dynamics of religious transformations (Fig. 1.5).[156] Larger spatial units, such as provinces or even macro-economic, political or geographical clusters (the Amber Road, Silk roads, maritime routes, *publicum portorii Illyrici*) also have an indirect but visible impact on space sacralisation and the movement of objects and religious groups.[157]

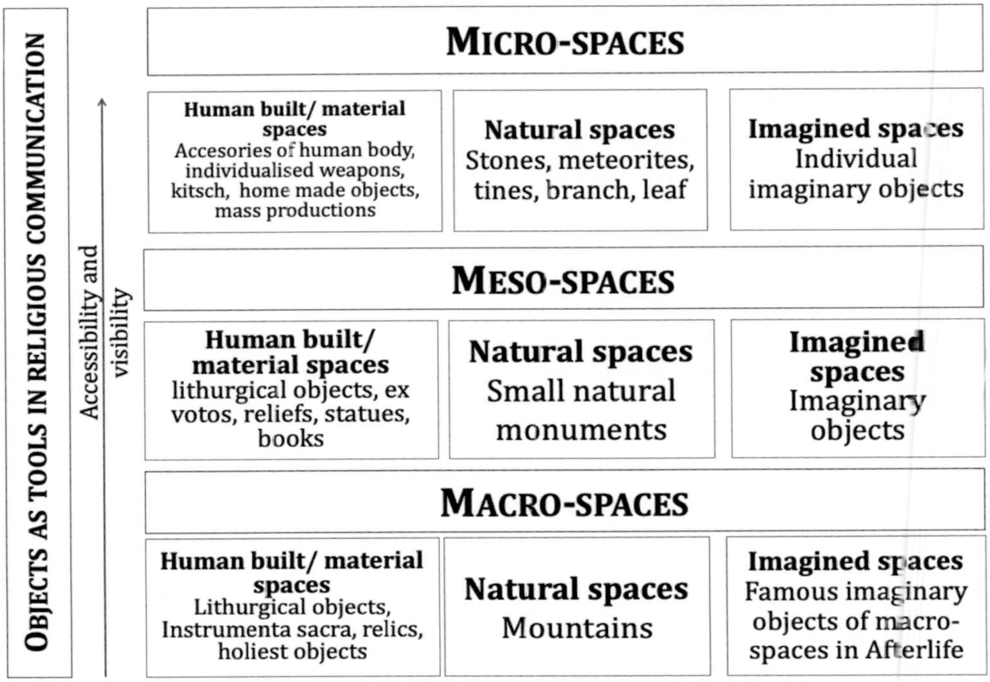

Fig. 1.5 Materiality of religion used in space sacralisation. (Source: the author)

In this theoretical framework of a new space taxonomy of religious communication, the material evidence of Roman religion in a provincial context can no longer be deemed 'peripheral' or 'local': the interconnectivity of individuals in micro-, meso- and macro-spaces and their omnipresence in larger clusters within the Roman Empire instead creates a glocalised spatial network.[158]

Glocalisation

The notion of glocalisation travelled from economic studies into the various fields of social sciences and was also recently adopted by historical studies. The origin of the concept is problematic: according to some authors, it comes from the economic studies that focus on the revitalisation of the Japanese economic system in the post-war period.[159] In this definition, glocalisation is defined almost exclusively in the context of globalisation studies as an opposition or alternative for cultural, social, historical phenomena, where globalisation does not offer a satisfactory theoretical and methodological tool. Although globalisation theories are intensively used nowadays in Roman studies, these recent works highlight the importance of the local and global (universal) dichotomy to replace the notion of 'native' and 'Roman', which is interpreted as an uncomfortable, derogative, colonial approach to Romanisation.[160]

Martin Pitts and Miguel Versluys argued that 'the main strength of globalisation theories is that they concern a world of disjunctive flows, which produce problems that manifest themselves in intensively local forms, but have context, that are anything but local'.[161] This duality of 'local' and 'global' was also used in the chapter of Ray Laurence and Francesco Trifiló on Roman urbanisation.[162] Interestingly, their approach was rarely adopted by Roman religious studies and there have been few studies until now that have focused on the local-global dichotomy, going beyond the old-fashioned, ethicised archaeological approach, which is basically a heritage of the Kossinna type of metahistorical narrative.[163] Such attempts were concerned especially with the global connectivity of local religious groups[164] or the global mobility of objects used in religious communication.[165]

The lived ancient religion approach, by contrast, produced few studies focusing on mobility, connectivity and the spatial aspects of Roman religious communication and the transformations of spaces, especially in the context of Roman globalisation.[166] This field therefore has important potential and a notion of glocalisation can offer a useful tool to understand the complex relationship of the local and global in the context of religious studies.

The first issue with the notion is its definition itself: in the last three decades, there have been numerous attempts to define glocalisation, however none of them has been universally accepted. In 1995, Roland Robertson argued that glocalisation is 'a twofold process involving the interpretation of the universalization of particularism and the particularization of universalism, the so-called paradox of globalization or the local-global nexus'.[167] Then, in 2007, Melanie Smith argued that glocalisation 'represents the intersection of political economics and sociocultural concerns, with its emphasis on the local and community impacts of global structures and processes'.[168]

Nevertheless, glocalisation has recently become a popular theoretical concept in religious studies, especially in the works of Victor Roudometof and many others.[169] The concept is not clearly defined in Roudometof's work; however, he did stress the importance of transnationalism and the glocal-religious nexus, especially in contemporary religions. As a continuation of his work, David van Alten used probably for the first time the notion of glocalisation as an analytical tool in the study of Roman religion.[170] He argued that religion is a cultural communication system, as Clifford Geertz presented in his paradigmatic work, therefore religious changes can be understood through communication studies and theories: as contemporary individuals, small groups and macro-groups adopt new linguistic strategies and change their vocabulary in local contexts, influenced by global factors, religion can also be interpreted as a communication system in constant transformation, whereby individuals, small groups and macro-societies adopt new language forms and strategies in order to maintain divine-human communication.[171] This relativisation of 'religiousness' gives endless possibilities to the interpretation of religious communication on the level of the individual and beyond: in this chapter, van Alten uses a similar argument to the one posited in the lived ancient religion approach, which stated that not all the ancient people were religious in the same way or manner.[172]

Amid these myriad possible religious experiences, glocality is a useful tool: some of the strategies (linguistic methods) used in religious communication are developed by the individual and never leave the locality, whereas others have a global outreach and well-established connectivity involving numerous individuals and macro-societies beyond the provincial limits. Localities meeting globality is particularly present in the Danubian provinces, which represents one of the most divided and culturally heterogenous regions of the continent. The transformations caused by the Roman conquest occurred in every single locality but at a different speed and via a different method, creating various languages of religion(s).

This book will present several case studies in which religious glocalisation, space sacralisation and lived religion can be attested in the Danubian provinces. These three major foci will offer a new methodological insight of the already known archaeological material that goes way beyond the ethnicist (Kossinna-type) and descriptive (art historian, classical archaeologist) approaches so deeply rooted in Central-Eastern European scholarship.

Notes

1 AÉ 1939, 0121= IGLN 079 = AÉ 2006, 1203: *------?] / C(aio) Bruttio C(ai) f(ilio) / Cl(audia) Gauto Vir(uno) / vet(erano) leg(ionis) I Ital(icae) vix(it) / ann(os) LXXX h(ic) s(itus) e(st) / C(aius) Vibius Therapo / amico bene merenti / secundum formulam / testamenti / f(aciendum) c(uravit).* See also: Conrad 2004, 235, No. 404; Taf. 121.

2 The date of the inscription is under debate: while Kolendo argued for a chronology in the first half of the 2nd century AD (100–150 AD), Conrad – based on the paleography of the inscription – argued that the funerary monument was erected at the end of the 1st century AD. In both cases, the most probable dating is Trajanic: IGLN 079, Conrad 2004, 235. See also: Matei-Popescu 2010, 79, footnote no. 535 for further bibliography.

3 See also: Szabó 2020a.

4 Beattie 1844, 1.

5 Katsiardi-Hering-Stassinopoulou 2017, 1–24. See also: Diaz-Andreu 2020, 31–57 although with few analogies from Central-Eastern Europe. More detailed analysis on this topic: Spiridon 2019; Zimmermann 2019.

6 See Danubius, Danubius in TLL Online. O.3.36.20–3.37.25.

7 Pețan 2012.

8 Mela 2.8, Sall. Hist. fr. 3.79, Caes. Gall. 6.25.2.

9 Kovács 2008, 243, footnote no. 2. for full bibliography on the topic.

10 Res Gestae Divi Augusti 5.47.

11 Pliny the Elder, *Natural History* 4.79.

12 Idem 4.80.

13 Mráv 2017, 102.

14 Campbell 2012, 291–298.

15 Dobó 1940; Laet 1949; Zaccaria 2010; Kritzinger 2015.

16 AÉ 1988, 977, AÉ 1988, 978.

17 HA, Vita Sept. Sev.5.3-4. The wars during the age of Marcus Aurelius (*bellum Germanicum*) or Septimius Severus are often called *Donaukriege* in German literature: Mitthof *et al.* 2019, 309–316.

18 Knittler 1993; Rady 2017.
19 Hübner 1746; Schels 1820; Duller 1849; Stiefelhagen 1854.
20 Ersch-Gruber 1836, 221.
21 Herzog 1861, 304.
22 Rösler 1864.
23 Kenner 1870.
24 Alföldy 2004.
25 Jung 1877, I–VIII.
26 The contemporary list of Danubian provinces often also includes Thracia. Other lists focus only on Raetia, Noricum, Pannoniae, Moesiae and Dacia.
27 Mommsen 1885, 125.
28 Drexler 1890.
29 Haverfield 1889, 99 for use of the phrase 'Danubian provinces'.
30 Szilágyi 2015.
31 Dobó 1940.
32 Heichelheim 1942.
33 Laet 1949.
34 Ørsted 1985.
35 Syme 1971.
36 For more on his role in Roman studies in the Balkans, see: Szabó 2020b.
37 JRS 1990, XI.
38 Vivas Garcia 2017.
39 Alföldy 1974; Mócsy 1974; Wilkes 1969.
40 Alföldy 1988; Alföldy 2004.
41 Wilkes 1996; Wilkes 2005; Wilkes 2006. See also: Szabó 2020c.
42 Zerbini 2010; Zerbini 2015.
43 See the project of Dominic Moreau: DANUBIUS Project Ecclesiastical Organisation and Christian Topography of the Lower Danube during Late Antiquity (3rd–8th centuries AD).
44 ARCHEODANUBE Archaeological Park in urban areas as a tool for Local Sustainable Development Interreg EU project.
45 See also: Szabó 2019a; Szabó 2020b.
46 Phillips 2007; Rives 2010. See also: bibliography in footnote nos 4 and 5 in Szabó 2017a, 152.
47 Wissowa 1912.
48 Cumont 1906. See also: Bonnet 2005.
49 The last one was analysed by Wissowa in less than 30 pages in his book: Wissowa 1912, 348–379.
50 Fowler 1911.
51 Altheim 1931–33.
52 The series was continued as *Religions in the Graeco-Roman World* at the BRILL, Leiden.
53 Versluys 2013.
54 The most important works of Rüpke's and his team are: Rüpke 2007; Rüpke 2012; Raja-Rüpke 2015; Rüpke 2018; Albrecht *et al.* 2018. See also: later in this chapter.
55 Scheid 2015a.
56 For a comparative example, the provinces of Raetia, Noricum, Dalmatia, Pannoniae, Moesiae, Daciae and Thracia have more than 18,000 inscriptions, almost the same amount as the so-called Western provinces: EDH.
57 Wilkes 2005. See also: Szabó 2016a, 480–483.
58 Nemeti 2012; Nemeti–Marcu 2014, 9–20; Szabó 2014a, 195–208.
59 Phillips 2007, 10–29; Rives 2010, 240–299.
60 In their seminal work on Roman religion – which changed the paradigm of research in this discipline – M. Beard and S. Price used one single inscription from Roman Dacia and very

few other references for Pannonia. They also used the chapter by Edith Thomas on Roman religion from the most cited manual, *Roman Archaeology of Roman Southern Pannonia*: Beard-North-Price 1998, 320, 327–328 (citing: Thomas 1980, 177–206). Similarly, in the last companion on archaeology of Roman religion, there are few case studies cited by Western scholars from Pannonia and one sanctuary from Dacia: Raja–Rüpke 2015, 389, 421, 445; there are few exceptions from the Western scholarship: Dészpa 2012; Scheuermann 2013; Zerbini 2015.

61 Wilkes 2005, 175–180.
62 Farkas 2015.
63 Czysz 1995.
64 Ardevan 2015, 23–24 with further bibliography focusing on the problematic notion of *interpretatio Romana*.
65 Kemkes-Willburger 2004; Farkas 2015.
66 Spickermann 1997, 145–167; Scheuermann 2013.
67 Ardevan 2015, 24–25 with an introductory bibliography. Szabó 2010 for the summary of the priests and official religion in Noricum. Tóth 2015 also deals with the indigenous Norican religion. See also: Šašel-Kos 1999.
68 Leitner 2007.
69 See also: Versluys 2014, 50–64; Woolf 2014, 45–50.
70 Zimmermann 2017.
71 Hainzmann 2020.
72 István Tóth 2015. See also: Szabó 2018a. The volume edited by Fitz J. from 1998 also remains an important reference: Fitz 1998.
73 Kiss 2011, 183–192; Kremer 2012; Sosztarits *et al.* 2013.
74 Szabó 2006.
75 Bartus 2015.
76 Barta 2015.
77 Lazar 2011. For Poetovio, see: Mišić 2013.
78 Nagy 2015, 19–36.
79 Mócsy 1974. See also: Mirković 2007; Mladenović 2012; Ardevan 2015.
80 Srejović 1987; Tomović 1992. A part of the material has been digitized by O. Harl in the Ubi Erat Lupa project.
81 Pilipović 2009; Gavrilović-Vitas 2014; Plemić 2015.
82 Petrović 2015, 323–332.
83 Jovanović 2007.
84 Szabó 2017b.
85 Gavrilović-Vitas 2020. See also: Bricault *et al.* 2015, 431–432.
86 Golubović 2015, 483–496.
87 Aparaschivei 2010. Ardevan 2015, 29–31 for a good introduction on recent bibliography focusing on religion in Moesia Inferior.
88 Gočeva 1992, 183–189; Iacob 2000–2001, 355–371; Covacef 2001, 373–386; Nemminger 2006, 199–212; Shopova 2017, 419–421; Ştirbulescu 2010, 463–492; Boteva 2011, 84–105; Bozhkova 2012, 9–19; Panaite 2013. See also: Velkov 1989, 1317–1361 with the previous bibliography. For numismatic sources, see: Peter 2005, 107–114.
89 Nemeti 2013a, 145–156.
90 Aparaschivei 2007, 91–100.
91 Lungarova 2012.
92 Szabó 2018b.
93 A brief history of the research: Marcu-Nemeti 2014; Szabó 2014. See also: Boda-Szabó 2014.
94 Bărbulescu 1984.

95 Nemeti 2005. See also: Nemeti 2012.
96 Popescu 2004.
97 Szabó 2007.
98 Carbó-Garcia 2010.
99 Sicoe 2014; Antal 2016.
100 Gudea-Tamba 2001; Benea 2008. See also: Diaconescu-Schäfer-Haynes 1997, 195–218; Fiedler-Höpken 2010, 319–333; Piso-Țentea 2011, 111–121; Piso-Țentea-Marcu 2012, 119–123. See also: Szabó 2015(2020).
101 Schäfer 2007; Dészpa 2012.
102 Varga 2019.
103 Németh 2015, 169–175.
104 Timotin 1998, 43–172. For a nationalistic approach, see: Gudea 2011; Gudea 2016. A new corpora and history of Christianisation in Roman and post-Roman Dacia is yet to be created.
105 For more arguments, see: Woolf 2004.
106 Of 18,200 inscriptions from the seven provinces introduced in the EDH there are 5,724 votive inscriptions.
107 The population of the Danubian provinces is almost impossible to estimate and there are few case studies of macro-estimations from this region: Scheidel 2001.
108 See the list of the sacralised spaces in the Appendices.
109 The impact of this approach can be measured by the large number of studies in which the notion has been used in the last decade (2012–2021): almost 440 books, studies and mentioned the notion in their title or text as a core theoretical approach. The success of this new methodological current can also be measured by the numerous references of the notion in both the European Association for the Study of Religions (EASR) and the International Association for the History of Religions (IAHR) congresses. The citations of Jörg Rüpke, who coined the notion and directed the European Research Council (ERC) Advanced Research Project focusing on this radically new approach, increased from 230 in 2012 to 830 in 2018 (after Google Scholar). The project can thus be considered as one of the most successful ERC advanced grants focusing on ancient studies and classical antiquity.
110 Most of the authors who now use the notion are former fellows of the Max Weber Kolleg and collaborators of the institution in Erfurt, although this new approach has since also gained significantly in popularity in Germany, Italy, the UK, Brazil, and the USA.
111 Scheid 2015a; Bremmer 2018.
112 See also: Țentea-Olteanu 2020; Deac-Simion (forthcoming).
113 McGuire 2008. For a historiographic overview, see also: Rüpke 2019a; Knibbe-Kupari 2020.
114 The major theoretical features of his concept were published in numerous paradigmatic studies, the most important ones being: Rüpke 2012; Albrecht *et al.* 2018.
115 Weiss 2015.
116 Rieger 2020.
117 See also: Raja-Rüpke 2015; Gasparini *et al.* 2020.
118 Szabó 2018b, 1–10.
119 Bodel 2020, 585–586. See also: the limits of the lived ancient religion approach in regard to the archaeology of religion in: Andringa 2015.
120 Gasparini 2015; Raja-Weiss 2015; Dirven 2015.
121 See also: Szabó 2020d.
122 Abraham 2017, 1–18; Rüpke 2020, 90.
123 Renfrew 2007, 109–122; Hodder 2018, 111–122.
124 Rüpke 2018, 5–24.
125 Knott 2005.

126 Van der Leeuw 1986, 5.
127 Lefebvre 1991, 405.
128 Knott 2005, 160–161.
129 Smith 1978, 308–309.
130 Smith 1987.
131 Idem, 28.
132 Chen-Jeung 2012, 3.
133 Anttonen 1996, 36–64.
134 Knott 2005, 156.
135 Knott 2009, 154–160.
136 Conrad 2016.
137 Bodenhamer *et al.* 2013, 170–175.
138 Renfrew 2007.
139 Biehl-Bertemes 2001, 11–24; Biehl 2012, 133.
140 Meier-Tillessen 2014, 11–247.
141 Maschek 2016, 131–147.
142 Cancik 1986, 250–265.
143 Clarke 1977, 9; Bintliff 2014, 258–259.
144 Biehl 2012, 133–134.
145 Szabó 2020d, 183–195.
146 See Chapter 5.
147 Ando-Rüpke 2015, 1–5.
148 Rüpke 2015, 437–451.
149 McGuire 2008.
150 Rüpke 2015, 74.
151 See Chapter 4.
152 Nielsen 2015, 279–293; Dirven 2015, 20–50.
153 Beck 1996, 176–185.
154 Szabó 2018b, 47–78.
155 Moser-Feldman 2014, 1–12.
156 Rüpke 2020, 90.
157 See Chapter 3.
158 Van Alten 2017, 1–20.
159 Robertson 1994, 36; Khondker 2005, 184–185.
160 Pitts-Versluys 2015, 5–6. For the discussion of Romanisation as a concept and problematic notion, see also: Verlusys 2014; Woolf 2014.
161 Pitts-Versluys 2015, 7.
162 Laurence-Trifiló 2015, 100–101.
163 Curta 2014.
164 Collar 2013; Woolf 2016.
165 See also: Chapter 3, large-scale mobilities.
166 Rüpke 2018, 55–62 and 196–200; Arnhold 2020, although in this work the author only modestly used the methodological approach of the lived ancient religion project. See also: Raja-Rieger 2021.
167 Robertson 1995 cited by Van Alten 2017, 3.
168 Smith 2007, 1–2.
169 Roudometof 2018.
170 Van Alten 2017.
171 Idem, 4–5.
172 Albrecht *et al.* 2018, 568–569.

2

Emerging Roman religion: the beginnings

Pre-Roman religious communication and local appropriations

The territory of the Danubian area, later known in Roman literary traditions as Illyricum[1] and since the 18th century as *Großillyricum* or the Danubian provinces,[2] was never heterogeneous. The region has numerous cultural, historical, political, geographic and climatic localities and specificities, which make it a provocative case study for a glocal approach.[3] This area from Raetia to the Black Sea was connected by the Danube, a strong economic network that has existed since the Bronze Age, between the micro-regions of this macro-area of Europe. Since the 4th/5th centuries BC, the region had been the site of constant cultural interconnectivity between the Celtic and the Greco-Roman worlds. Despite these common features of the area as a whole,[4] however, the micro-regions of the Danubian provinces show a great variety in terms of forms of pre-Roman religious communication: each later province had several regional specificities. These need to be presented in detail in order to understand in depth the pre-Roman religious landscape, religious knowledge and cultural memory, the latter of which was an important agent in the formation of the later province and its forms and strategies of religious communication.

In most cases, the pre-Roman religious landscape is marked by Bronze Age or Iron Age cultural reforms and structures. While some regions – especially in the Upper Danubian area (Raetia, Pannoniae, Noricum) had already been integrated into the Roman world in the time of Augustus and the Julio-Claudian dynasty, other regions such as Dacia became part of the Roman Empire much later. This fact also played an important role in the formation of religious landscapes and modes of religiosity in these regions.

Raetia

The population and the social history of the region that later become the province of Raetia has an ethnographic and metahistorical tradition from antiquity that rarely correlates with the archaeological sources of the Late Iron Age of the northern Alps. The Roman literary traditions on the region follow the major ethnographic traditions of Latin literature and the collective mentality on the 'Barbaric' people outside of the Roman world.[5] The sources are blurred when it comes to the origins, linguistic and ethnic variety of the area. They instead mostly highlight some economic aspects such as the famous wine of Raetia praised by Cato and Virgil and favoured by Augustus;[6] the commercial routes and the major Alpine passages that connected the Po area and the northern territories beyond the Alps that were used by important families, such as the Laecanii, for their amphorae trade;[7] and the origins of the pre-Roman population. Livy claimed that the *Raeti* (Raetians) were originally from Etruria and related to the Etruscan people,[8] whereas Pliny the Elder argued that most of the Raetian population moved from the Po area in the Alps during the Gallic (Celtic) invasion in the 4th–6th centuries BC:

> it is supposed that the Rhæti are the descendants of the Tuscans, who were expelled by the Gauls and migrated hither under the command of their chief, whose name was Rhætus. Turning then to the side of the Alps which fronts Italy, we have the Euganean nations enjoying Latin rights, and of whom Cato enumerates thirty-four towns. Among these are the Triumpilini, a people who were sold with their territory; and then the Camuni, and several similar tribes, each of them in the jurisdiction of its neighboring municipal town. The same author also considers the Lepontii and the Salassi to be of Tauriscan origin, but most other writers, giving a Greek interpretation to their name, consider the Lepontii to have been those of the followers of Hercules who were left behind in consequence of their limbs being frozen by the snow of the Alps. They are also of opinion that the inhabitants of the Grecian Alps are descended from a portion of the Greeks of his army, and that the Euganeans, being sprung from an origin so illustrious, thence took their name. The head of these are the Stœni. The Vennonenses and the Sarunetes, peoples of the Rhæti, dwell about the sources of the River Rhenus, while the tribe of the Lepontii, known as the Uberi, dwell in the vicinity of the sources of the lhodanus, in the same district of the Alps. There are also other native tribes here, who have received Latin rights, such as the Octocurenses, and their neighbors the Centrones, the Cottian states, the Ligurian Vagienni, descended from the Caturiges, as also those called Montani; besides numerous nations of the Capillati, on the confines of the Ligurian Sea.[9]

In the list, Pliny also mentions the tribes of the Alpine area who were known from the famous inscription of the Tropaeum Alpium,[10] which lists 46 tribes:

> *Imperatori Caesari Divi filio Augusto / pont(ifici) max(imo) imp(eratori) XIIII trib(unicia) pot(estate) XVII / senatus populusque Romanus / quod eius ductu auspiciisque gentes Alpinae omnes quae a mari supero ad inferum pertinebant sub imperium p(opuli) R(omani) sunt redactae / gentes alpinae devictae Trumpilini Camunni Vennonetes Venostes Isarci Breuni Genaunes Focunates / Vindelicorum gentes quattuor Cosuanetes Rucinates Licates Catenates Ambisontes Rugusci Suanetes Calucones / Brixentes Leponti Viberi Nantuates Seduni Veragri Salassi Acitauones Medulli Vcenni Caturiges Brigiani / Sogiontii Brodionti Nemaloni Edenates (V)esubiani Veamini Gallitae Triulatti Ectini / Vergunni Egui(i) Turi Nemeturi Oratelli Nerusi Velauni Suetri*[11]

The exact location and habitat of these pre-Roman tribes have not yet been established,[12] however in many cases (the Vindelici, Brixentes, Estiones peoples) the population continuity from the Late Iron Age to the Roman conquest can be identified through the first *civitates* of Raetia.[13] Strabo and Ptolemy also provided important additional information on the territorial distribution of the pre-Roman population.[14]

Based on the literary traditions, linguists and historians accepted the Livian tradition for the Etruscan origins of the Raeti. However, in the last few decades, the very notion of the *Raeti* (*Raetus/Raeta* in singular) has been contested as an ethnic-linguistic marker and it is instead now considered as a regional, cultural and super-ethnic identity of the Roman era.[15]

The population of the Alpine area that later became Raetia et Vindelicia province contained two major linguistic groups: a Tyrrhenian (Rhaetic) group and a Celtic group, the latter becoming predominant by the end of the Second Iron Age (*c.* 475 BC).[16] The Etruscan influence can be attested in the proto-urban settlements in the Early Iron Age period[17] and in the epigraphic material from the pre-Roman era.[18] From the 5/4th centuries BC, the Celtisation of the region intensified, and this can be attested especially in the new type of materiality (Fritzens-Sanzeno culture[19] and the early Roman Heimstetten group[20]), though rarely in the epigraphic evidence (onomastic and theonymic aspects).[21] The infiltration of Celtic materiality and presumably a significant change in social and religious interconnectivities after the 5/4th centuries BC produced new Celtic visual narratives in religious communication and also changed the strategies of space sacralisation in pre-Roman Raetia.

After 113–101 BC, Germanic tribes arrived on the northern bank of the Danube, which increased the cultural interactions and economic relationships between the Po area, the Alps and the northern parts of the mountains, creating an intense connectivity between the Gallo-Roman koine in the south and the Celtic-Germanic world in the north.[22] The attack of the Cimbri after 113 BC and the following war also introduced the military presence of the Romans in this area.

Alpine religion before the Roman conquest

The Raetian area is a predominantly mountainous, barely accessible and sparsely populated area, where the Lech, Rhine (later the *Via Claudia Augusta* along the River Etsch),[23] Seez and Inn rivers created the major valleys and passages in the 2,000–2,500 m-height Alps (Fig. 2.1). The Raeti thus had a clearly delimited geographic area, and also a specific materiality (houses,[24] pottery,[25] epigraphy) that was created and constantly appropriated by the interactions with the northern Celtic world and the southern sub-Alpine groups, commonly known as the Gallo-Roman koine (Magrè group, Veneti).[26] The three main regions had been the sites of continuous, substantial human and animal migration since the Mesolithic era, with a much more intense material mobility since the early Bronze Age.[27] This *longue durée* connectivity created several interesting case studies where spatial, functional and mnemohistorical continuities and appropriations were formed. The major routes, which had been used constantly since the Bronze Age, produced not only isolated, local strategies of religious communication, but also glocalised, interconnected features that linked the northern Celtic (Vindelici) and southern Gallo-Roman koine, both of whom interacted with the Alpine Raeti people, who occupied a strategic and unavoidable geographic position in the road and commercial networks between Italy and the vast regions north of the Alps.

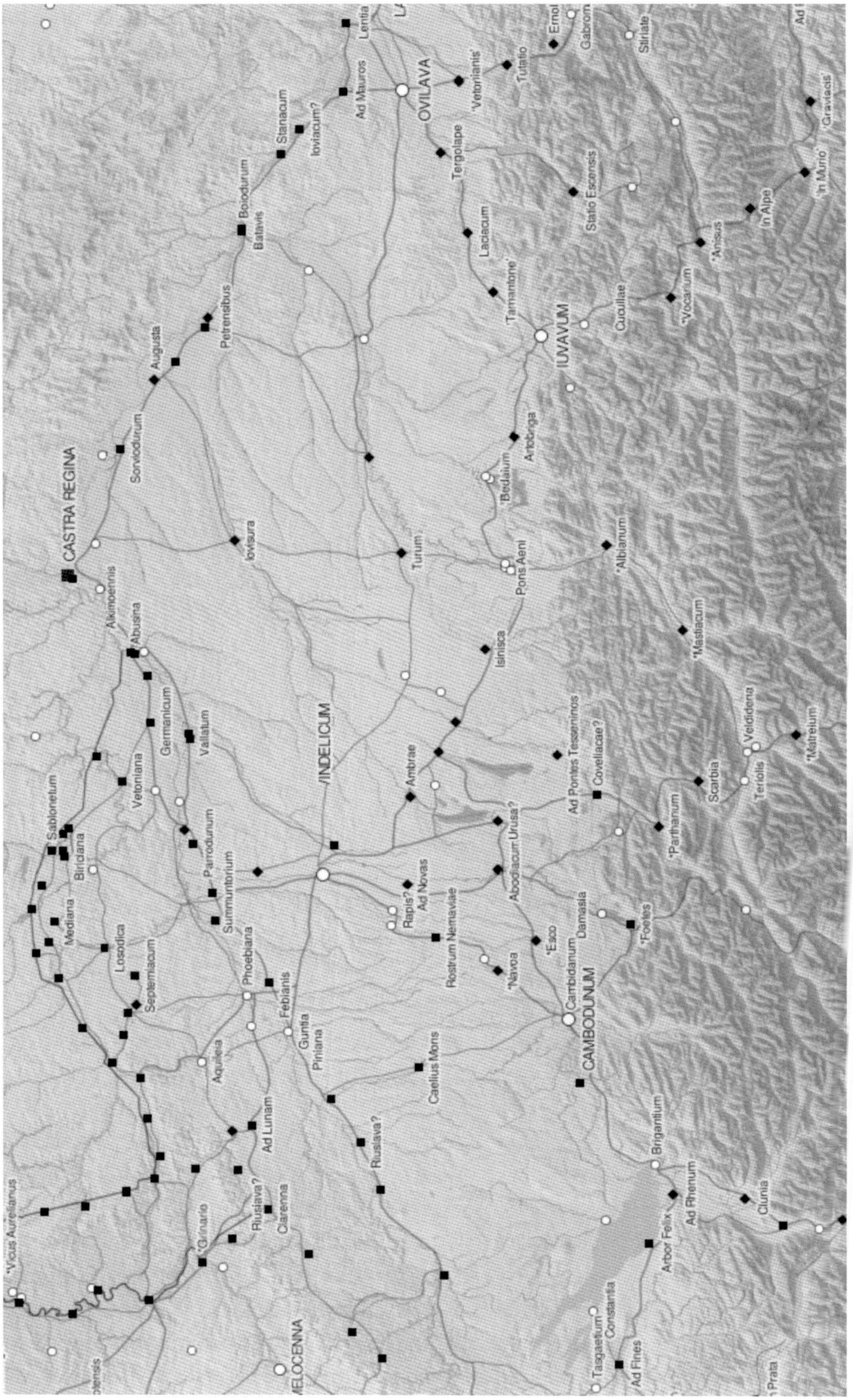

Fig. 2.1 Map of Roman Raetia showing the settlements discussed in Chapter 2. (Source: https://dh.gu.se/dare/). Open access

This area featured two major types of space sacralisation following the Bronze Age: the deposition of single bronze artefacts and the so-called *Brandopferplätze* (sites for burnt offerings).[28] The region of the later province Raetia before the 1st century AD was predominantly a sparsely populated, mostly rural area with several local specificities: in the south, near the major passages (Furka, St Gotthard, St Bernardino, Splügen, Julier, Septimer, Reschen Scheideck, Brenner, etc.), important commercial routes were formed that served especially the short-term mobilities between the Gallo-Roman koine and the Alpine Raeti, most specifically, the Calucones, Rigusci, Saevates, Breuni and Vennonetes. Such short-term mobilities of humans and transhumant animals created a persistent rural system of settlements in the Early Iron Age, which was identified with the Fritzens-Sanzeno culture.[29] This cultural horizon in the southern part of the later Roman province correlates with the major concentration of Raetian inscriptions[30] and domestic constructions found there.[31]

Furthermore, three major regions of Raetia contained not only domestic and epigraphic materialities, but also a significant number of pre-Roman sacralised spaces, commonly known as *Brandopferplätze.* More than 200 such complex places and 163 single bronze object deposits have been identified[32] there. These areas are also notable since they represent the essential commercial routes and communication networks of the later province: the route from Curia to Brigantium and the vicinity of the Brigantinus lacus, the Via Claudia from Tridentium as far as the Reschen Scheideck passage, and the central valley of the Inn River.[33] The topography and chronology of these sacralised spaces and memories of religious communication in a hostile geographic area reflects the importance of the mountain passages and the commercial routes: these were not only economic passages, but also religious channels and third spaces, where the divine agency was embodied with the mountains and the memory of religious traditions became a habitus.[34] Both traditions – the single bronze depositions and the complex open-air *Brandopferplätze* – have a strong aspect of temporality: in the case of individual, occasional and non-repetitive ways of religious communication (single object depositions), temporality is strictly related to a constant transfer of religious knowledge, a habit that is in a permanent state of interaction and interdependency with the ritual of passing the mountain. However, the materiality and the large variety of objects discovered show no 'ethnic' or cultural indications of this habit.

The ritualisation of depositing bronze or other type of objects (often small lead or terracotta figurines and even wooden pieces[35]) was created by a strong temporality and habitual continuity where the strongest agent is the mountain and the route itself from one side to another of the mountain. The necessity of memorialising this event through a religious act transformed the passages and the mountain roads themselves into a religious third space. Because these deposits were made in inaccessible, remote sites (*Höhenfunde*), there were no human-built structures and the spatial dimension of the religious communication was thus interdependent with the natural landscape (the mountains, the passages, the river valleys) and also the route – the movement (mobility) itself. For this reason, this religious habitus was correctly termed by David Fontijn as a 'sacrificial landscape'.[36] In contrast with cemeteries and large, complex sacralised spaces – such as *Brandopferplätze* – individual depositions are invisible to the later viewer and visitor. The transformation of the landscape into a space of memory and a religious agent therefore is not dependent on the materiality of these acts (which are mostly invisible or disappear in the moment of the deposition), but becomes instead a religious knowledge and habitus that is impossible to trace by archaeological methods.[37]

In contrast with these occasional and non-repetitive strategies of religious communication, the *Brandopferplätze* are much more complex spaces, where temporality, the continuous use of the place and the visual markers (stone structures, altars, roads, road-marking milestones, hilltops) represent a much more intense form of space sacralisation. It also presumes there was a material investment and repetitive actions to maintain the site. It is difficult, however, to understand exactly how these sites were used: the literature usually avoids the notion of sanctuaries in relation to these sites, arguing that they didn't necessarily require a permanent human agency to maintain the place.[38] Indeed, the maintenance of these places relied on a strict relationship with the settlement networks that had formed in these narrow valleys since the Bronze Age: similarly to other Danubian provinces, where communal sacralised spaces were attested (especially on hilltops in Pannoniae, for example[39]), these sacrificial sites were probably used regularly by various mobile and local groups too, creating a much more intense and vivid cultural memory of the sacralised space.[40]

A specific problem of these Alpine sacrificial sites is the presence of large quantities of animal bones, some of which were extremely rare in the Alpine area (pigs, large cattle, sheep[41]). The mobility of these animals and the exact process by which the bone collections were created is still under debate: recently, a symbolic sacrificial act was suggested, which argued that the animals were not sacrificed on the spot, but that the bones were transported there after the event as a votive deposition and to memorialise the religious act.[42]

Some of the well-documented and complex *Brandopferplätze* had a ceremonial road leading to them, which were marked with various-sized stones, a circular building or a place where the sacrifice or deposition could take place. Moreover, in several cases (the so-called Alpine ash altar sites or Rungger Egg-type conic altars) a pyramidal, conic form was created, which represented a strong marker in religious memorialisation and space sacralisation.[43] Recent analysis of the archaeobotanical material also suggests that these sites contributed not only with a strong visual marker (the pyramidal form, the stone altars) but also with ceremonial movements and sensescapes (smells, tastes) to the successful maintenance of the sacralised space.[44] Occasionally – probably during rare and extraordinary moments in the history of a community – evidence of human sacrifices have been produced, which correlates once again with some case studies from pre-Roman Pannonia and Dacia.[45] Inscribed votive plates and personalised brooches were also used as votive dedications in some of these complex sanctuaries, many of them having a remarkable chronological continuity with the Neolithic period.[46] The case of Demlfeld, Ampass is one of the most well-documented case studies, where a great concentration of brooches dating from 600–400 BC[47] were discovered, along with a beautifully decorated bronze lamellae.[48]

The Raetian groups also had a very vivid and intense cultural interaction with the Celtic world. This is well attested in the few pieces of epigraphic evidence of the southern region, which began to have direct contact with the Celtic world around the 5th–4th centuries BC. A particular case study was discovered in a Raetic house in Tesero, Sottopedonda, in the Fiemme Valley (Trento).[49] A small fragment of polished horn carried a few lines in Raetian letters and the name of the Celtic god Tarani(s). Although the archaeological context is part of the local, Raetian group and their domestic environment, the cited divine agent probably served as a protective divinity for the user and owner of the horn, and was a religious appropriation from the Celtic world.[50] Furthermore, material and human mobilities provoked a more intense exchange of religious knowledge, which manifested in new figurative forms and epigraphic interpretations, such as the graffiti of Taranis in the Raetian language.

In the north, the Celtic Vindelici are represented by their monumental *oppida*, the most significant of which was in Manching. This had probably been a regional capital and centre since the Neolithic era, and certainly since the late Bronze Age period.[51] This Celtic proto-urban centre – which represents one of the largest pre-urban settlements of pre-Roman Raetia – was built on prehistoric (Neolithic, Bronze Age) settlements and was a strategic point on the Danubian road that connected with the large-sized *oppidum* of Heidengraben bei Grabenstetten and Kelheim, east of Manching. A special particularity of the settlement is its long-lasting sanctuary, which was built in three phases. The last of these occurred around 105 BC and ended in the period of the conquest of the region by the Roman army (15–6 BC).[52]

The sanctuary was the mathematical and cosmological axis mundi of the settlement: the space sacralisation was not only maintained by the local elite through votive depositions (bronze objects, weapons, helmets), repetitive or occasional feasts (amphorae finds) but also by its central position and urbanistic impact, which marked the evolution of the settlement itself.[53] The site might be one of numerous examples of Iron Age space sacralisation where astronomy and cosmological space orientation played a significant role. Similar analogies of archaeoastronomy have been identified in the Mediterranean world and in the Danubian provinces, too.[54] Similarly to the case studies of the valleys and southern areas of the later Raetia province, the Celtic world had also had intense material interconnectivity with the Roman world since 200 BC.[55] In the 1st century BC, the settlement began a slow decline that probably ended one or two decades before the arrival of the Roman army in 15 BC and was likely due to various population mobilities, mostly attributed to Germanic tribes.[56]

Regnum Noricum: *Celtic religion before the Roman conquest*

The history of Noricum was well documented by G. Alföldy in his seminal work on the province, which is considered to be one of the best provincial syntheses from the Danubian provinces.[57] Between 400–200 BC,[58] the local, pre-Celtic population – commonly known as the Venetici and the Illyirici[59] – came into contact with the Celtic population. The epigraphic evidence shows that the Illyirici and Venetici lived in the south-west area of the later province (Drau, Isel and Möll valleys), whereas the majority of the population in the 2nd century BC consisted of various Celtic tribes (Ambidravi, Saevates, Laianci, Ambisontes, Uperaci, etc.)[60] known mostly from literary and epigraphic sources. These included the Taurisci and Norici: both denominations are Roman creations, but with Celtic origins.[61] The Taurisci represented a conglomeration of Celtic groups from the south and south-eastern part of the later province, while the Norici were the central and most powerful Celtic group, possibly named after a divinity (Noreia) or their central settlement. This tribe contributed to the political and military alliance of the central Celtic tribes and formed the kingdom of Noricum around 200 BC.[62] From 100 BC, intensive trade and commercial networks are attested between the Regnum Noricum and the Roman Republic, which changed not only the material landscape, but also influenced several aspects of space sacralisation and religious communication of the Norican kingdom.[63]

From the 4th–3rd centuries BC, the most common sacralised spaces from the later territory of Noricum were similar to the Raetian *Brandopferplätze.* The case study of the Celtic weapon deposition in Förker Laas-Riegel shows that these sanctuaries were usually separated from the civilian settlements, and were very inaccessible.[64] In addition, similar to most of the hilltop sanctuaries, the one in Förker Laas-Riegel shows evidence of continuous activity over several generations, which proves that the people were successful at maintaining the sacralised space. The case of the Gurina sanctuary, with its rich Hallstatt material evidence (more than 350 kg of pottery shards), also reveals the first evidence for small bronze statuette ex-votos – an unusual habit for the Celtic pre-Roman sanctuaries.[65] The 5 cm-long statuette is just one of the thousands of material tools used in the *longue durée* maintenance of the sacralised space. However, the role of such statuettes in religious communication goes beyond the simple role of a material tool: as a financial and emotional investment, the statuette represents a personalised metahistory that was used as a direct agent between the human and the divine world.

Gurina played a central role in the Gail valley as one of the famous metal-producing centres of the Norican kingdom (cat. no. II.14). Its economic importance and strategic location are among the reasons for the extraordinary quantity of material used as ex-votos and the shards discovered at the site. The pre-Roman population even used a rare type of Celtic (Venetic) inscription, which demonstrates that there was an intense commercial relationship with the southern Alpine area.[66] The strategic geographic position of the Gurina sanctuary might be one of the reasons why this place was continuously used in Roman times, too. This is not unprecedented: a Celtic, pre-Roman sacralised space was recently identified on the Hemmaberg, in the vicinity of several important late-antique, early Christian churches, which gives an interesting insight into the temporal and cultural memory of space sacralisation in this region.[67]

Elsewhere, other small hilltop settlements, such as Guggamoar near St Lorenzen bei Knittelfeld, also served as religious and economic centres in the kingdom of Noricum.[68] As was suggested recently, this sacralised space – where water and animal sacrifice played a very important role – was probably dedicated to the Celtic goddess Iouenat (Iouvenat).[69]

A very interesting and well-documented case study that helps us to understand in particular the economy of religious communication in the region in the Late Iron Age is the sanctuary and so-called 'temple district' of Sandberg Roseldorf.[70] This sanctuary was used for a very long time, as is evidenced by the 14 sacrificial pits where a large quantity of archaeobotanical material has been identified. The 14,000 seeds that were analysed show that there was abundant agricultural activity and that there was a commercial network that served the maintenance of the sanctuary and the community around it. Some of the plants identified (such as sorbus) were associated with the mythical fauna of Celtic folklore and religious knowledge, although it should be noted that this remains a metahistorical association.[71] The case of Sandberg Roseldorf also demonstrates the economic aspects of sacralised spaces in urban and, especially, rural environments. It can serve as a possible analogy for the case study of Sarmizegetusa Regia, too, where similar issues were raised recently on the functionality of late La Tène sanctuaries.[72]

As the society of the *regnum Noricum* reached a more complex level, the major Celtic *oppidum* of the Norici tribe was transformed into the capital of the kingdom, although its role and political 'unity' has recently been questioned. What's more, the existence of a well-established kingdom dates only to the period between Caesar and Augustus.[73] Known today as Magdalensberg[74] (falsely associated with Noreia in older literature[75] and often called 'Alt-Virunum'[76]), the Celtic *oppidum* had already been attested in the D2 La Tène period in the 2nd century BC. The settlement is located on a majestic hill (1,058 m) that dominates the surroundings and the lower Gurk valley. The physical landscape and the strategic position of the settlement both contributed to the formation of the Republican economic settlement (*emporium*) 200 m below the Celtic *oppidum*. In addition, it played an important role in space sacralisation and the maintenance of the sanctuaries of Magdalensberg.[77] The integration of the Norican commercial and social elite within the Roman economic trading network is well attested in the amphorae,[78] and the numismatic[79] or epigraphic[80] material from the late Republican and early Imperial period. Although the Republican *emporium* has been extensively researched in the last six decades, the Celtic *oppidum* and its possible sacralised space on the hill is still under debate.[81]

In the mid-1st century BC, the Roman *emporium* became a flourishing commercial centre, with a trading network that included Rome, Aquileia and the island of Delos.[82]

These connections were monopolised by several Italic trading dynasties, such as the Barbii, Fundanii, Poblicii and Postumii.[83] The favourable economic environment played a significant part in the creation of a major sacralised space for the Roman community living in the *emporium*. Their financial state was well reflected in the unique monumental temple building, which was begun in the second half of the 1st century BC and finished just before the kingdom of Noricum was conquered. Indeed, the Late-Republican-Augustean podium temple (hexastyle prostylos type) in Magdalensberg (cat. no. II.30) is the earliest Italic type of podium temple north of the Alps and in the Danubian provinces (Fig. 2.2). It reflects the economic and strategic importance of the Aquileia-Magdalensberg route, but also the financial capabilities of the local elite from the *emporium*.[84] Details of the creation and maintenance of the sacralised space and its environment were affected by the late antique and Medieval constructions: a church was built on the site of the Roman temple.[85] The centrality of the building within the Roman settlement and the imposing dimensions of the temple (26.2 × 17.4 m), as well as the lavish decoration that have been preserved and were discovered in the mid-20th century on the site, suggest that the sacralised space indeed played a central role in the settlement and even beyond.[86] However, the cult image (or images) of the sacralised space was not identified, although the Austrian literature speculated on the Capitoline nature of the temple.[87] It was also interpreted as a 'Noric-Roman central sanctuary' or a Vitruvian '*loco excelsissimo*'.[88]

The most intriguing question, however, regarding the nature of this *emporium* and the monumental, sacralised space of the Roman community within the quasi-independent kingdom of Noricum at the end of the 1st century BC is the relationship of the local, indigenous communities with this temple and its Roman worshippers. The Roman *emporium* was probably formed in the second half of the 1st century BC when the Celtic *oppidum* had already been fortified and might have been one of the major royal settlements of the kingdom. The relationship of the local, indigenous population with the temporary or long-term Roman traders can be justly presumed, based especially on the presence of Celtic pottery and brooches that have been discovered on the site.[89] However, most of the materiality of this Roman *emporium* has nothing to do with the local Norican culture and elite: the epigraphic and figurative material dated from before the conquest and instead suggests a cultural enclave within the Norican kingdom of Italic settlers and traders, most famously the Barbii family. Their Roman houses, lavishly decorated public buildings, Italic-type tombstones and exquisite figurative monuments transported probably directly from Imperial workshops all reflect a fully Roman identity and cultural landscape.

The most famous of the figurative monuments is the bronze statue, the Youth of Magdalensberg,[90] which was discovered in 1502 near the centre of the Roman *emporium*[91] and represents a young male figure in heroic nudity bearing a shield and a bard or axe.[92] The statue and the shield are inscribed with the names of the donors, all of whom were Roman *liberti* with oriental or Italic origins.[93] The statue represents a supreme piece of art from the Roman Republican workshops, imitating the Polykleitan statues of classical Greek art.[94] Representing a significant financial investment by the donors and having remarkably high artistic value, the statue was certainly meant to be displayed in a public, highly visible and accessible place within the Roman *emporium* of Magdalensberg. At several points in the past, the piece was considered as the cult statue of the Augustan temple of the settlement and was identified with Mars Latobius. Alföldy Géza also suggested that because one of the donors – Marcus Gallicinus, son of Vindilus – was probably a local Celtic person from Noricum,[95] the statue must also represent a case of *interpretatio indigena*. However, this interpretation was abandoned a long time ago, as the inscription was reinterpreted, and the reading of Mars is no longer accepted.[96] Other theories suggested that the statue was an offering to the Celtic divinity Belenus,[97] or a local Mercurius, or else that it represents a priest of the Noreia cult.[98] Older theories interpreted the statue as a mythical, founding hero of Old Virunum (Heros Virunus).[99]

All of these approaches united the ethnographic accounts of the literary sources on the pre-Roman religion of Noricum, in an attempt to identify a 'national god' of the Norican kingdom and to associate this important statue with a local divinity.[100] Yet the laconic information on the archaeological context and its discovery doesn't give us the opportunity to identify the functionality of the statue and its relation with the late Republican temple of Magdalensberg. The inscriptions on the statue, however, suggest a later, probably local carving, which might represent a secondary use of the statue within the new *emporium* context.

Although the interconnectivity of the local Norican elite and the royal family with the Roman *emporium* is not clear, the economic and cultural impact of this small Roman community in Noricum can be attested in several settlements, where the architectural landscape or 'atmosphere' was changed rapidly, using Roman

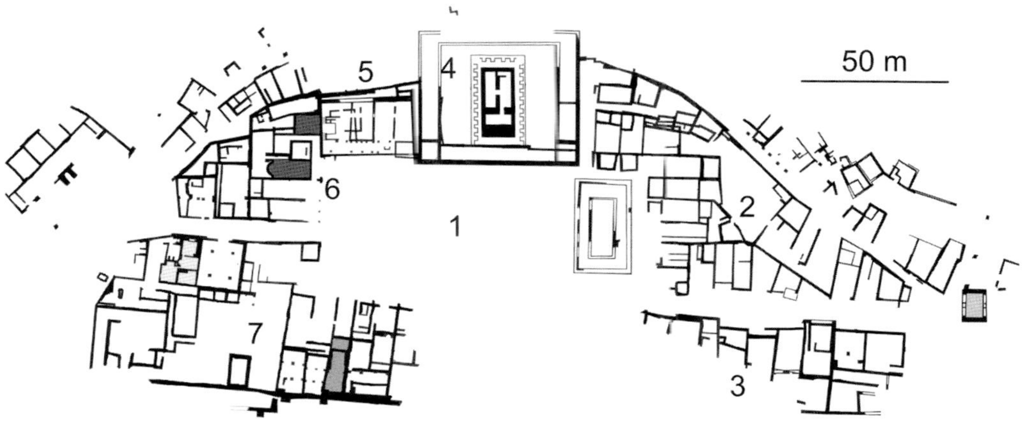

Fig. 2.2 Plan of Magdalensberg showing the district of sacralised spaces. (Source: after Wikicommons). Open access

architectural features. These serve as strong elements in the political, cultural and sensorial landscape as markers of a new, emerging age.[101] The Augustean settlement near St Michael and the later Italic temple in Zollfeld are products of these slow changes in the Norican cultural and religious landscape.[102] Several other important sacralised spaces from the La Tène period were also attested on the major economic and trading routes and in the central settlements of Celtic tribes. While in Raetia, Pannoniae and Dacia the pre-Roman sanctuaries were abandoned after the Roman conquest and provincialisation, Noricum seems to have been at least in the traditional classical archaeological narratives an exception, with numerous indigenous sacralised spaces used continuously in Roman times, too. The rich literature on the sanctuaries of Frauenberg, Burgstall and Celeia and the passage sanctuaries, such as Hochtor, focus on the functional continuity of the sacralised spaces, presenting this topic in the methodological framework of a 'peaceful' Romanisation[103] and social continuity. This narrative will be reconsidered in the following chapter.

Regionality in the pre-Roman religious landscape: the case of Pannonia

The history of the territories of the later Roman province of Pannonia – a territory between the Danube (north and east), the Sava River (south) and the Amber Road (west)[104] – has been discussed in detail by several paradigmatic works in the last 50 years or so.[105] However, although the archaeology of the second half of the La Tène period is well documented,[106] the cultural, linguistic and religious transformations between the 3rd and 1st centuries BC are still problematic.[107] András Mócsy argued that three major linguistic groups were in constant interaction in this area: 1) the Venetic groups in the south-west; 2) the Illyirians and the Pannonians in the area of the Sava (later South Pannonia); and 3) the Celtic groups along the western bank of the Danube.[108] As D. Dzino presented with convincing arguments and sources, the Illyrians didn't represent a united, pan-Illyirian group, but were a culturally and linguistically mixed and complex group of people who have often been reinvented as a metahistorical notion by Latin (Roman) and modern historiography.[109] Likewise, the Pannonians were also a very heterogenous group of people, comprising several tribes with multiple regional centres and with a glocal cultural and economic network.[110]

The later territory of Pannonia had a very dynamic history in the late La Tène period, which gave rise not only to military conflicts between pre-Celtic (Pannonian), Celtic (Boii, Eravisci) and Roman powers, but also an intense cultural interaction, which can be observed in the glocality of religion in this area.[111] István Tóth identified three major regions with different religious specificities in this later territory of Pannonia: 1) the western part (concentrated around the Amber Road – *Via succinea*[112]); 2) a smaller, predominantly Eraviscan area in the north-eastern part of the Danube; and 3) a large south and south-western part where there were numerous pre-Celtic populations (Scordisci, Pannonii).[113] These three regions had different cultural backgrounds and historical evolutions, and correspondingly different forms and strategies of religious communication.

The first region (Western Pannonia, a large part of the later Pannonia Superior) was dominated by the Amber Road, which served not only as an economic route and connection between northern Europe and the Mediterranean world, but also as the major route for the military campaigns of the Scordisci, Dacians and later the Pannonians in the region.[114] These features marked the religious landscape of Pannonia Superior in the late La Tène period. Archaeological evidence of sacralised spaces before the Roman conquest is scarce. In Szalacska, a large Celtic *oppidum* in modern-day Hungary that was home to an important coin mint, which has been identified as having glocal religious features: the coins imitate the Macedonian tetradrachmae, although their iconography is interpreted as a local appropriation of religious visual language, with several astronomic symbols and a possible connection with a local cult of Hermes.[115]

Elsewhere, I. Tóth presumed that the famous funerary inventory of a Luna Sol priestess from Nagyberki-Szalacska reflects a pre-Roman religious heritage and proves the presence of a solar cult in this region (Fig. 2.3).[116] The first part of the rich material was found in 1899 in the private garden of Vigyázó Sándor, but there was no further archaeological investigation.[117] At the time, the find was associated by Melhard with the nearby pre-Roman *oppidum*, although the date of the objects (especially the Norican type fibulae and the bronze vessels) is clearly from the Roman period.[118] The importance of the *oppidum* in Szalacska was documented especially in the second half of the 20th century and although no traces of sacralised spaces were discovered, the relationship between the Sol-Luna priestess and the pre-Roman settlement seems to be plausible.[119] Traces of the cult of the 'Celtic Ianus', a two-faced male divinity attested in numerous statuary representations in Celtic Europe,[120] had also been identified

Fig. 2.3 Funerary inventory of Luna Sol priestess in Nagyberki-Szalacska. (Source: Tóth 2015, 23, Fig. 3)

in pre-Roman Pannonia at the site of Badacsonylábdihegy.[121] However, since it was unfortunately discovered without an archaeological context, sacralised spaces cannot be associated with the find.

The second area – where there was a much more complex and dynamic ethnic and cultural interconnectivity between the Celtic and pre-Celtic populations – is the southern part of contemporary Hungary and the large area between the Drava and Sava rivers. Archaeological evidence is also very laconic in this area when it comes to pre-Roman sacralised spaces, but the epigraphic sources indicate the presence of a rich divine agency that was worshipped between the Drava and Sava rivers.[122] River cults (Sava, Drava, Danube) and spring cults (Aquae Iasae) are well documented in Roman times, although their pre-Roman presence in archaeological evidence is missing.[123]

The same problem is present in the Taurisci area between Emona and Poetovio: the rich epigraphic material suggests that numerous indigenous divinities were worshipped in pre-Roman times, but their sacralised spaces and pre-Roman archaeological sources have not yet been clarified.[124] I. Tóth presumed there were numerous 'sacralised mountains', hilltops worshipped by Celtic populations, and the cult of various animals (boars, pigs) in the southern region.[125] Given that this presumption was based exclusively on a few figurative monuments and especially on later Roman iconographic representations and epigraphic sources, his thesis remains a romantic hypothesis and is often criticised now.[126]

The third region with specific, mostly Celtic (Eravisci) settlements and environments offers several important case studies of space sacralisation before the Roman conquest. The region is also an example of Celtic and Illyrian (Boii, Eravisci, Azalii) interconnectivity. It is the only one where statuary representations of pre-Roman, Celtic divinities have been attested (for example, a statuette of Artio in Szentendre).[127] Furthermore, an important sanctuary from pre-Roman period was identified in 1969–1971 in Pákozd.[128] The small sacralised space contained several sacrificial pits (often called *favissae*, although the notion was contested even for the Roman contexts[129]) along with animal and human osteological material. The sanctuary was interpreted as a site of human sacrifice and a place for the head cult of Esus.[130] Based on the discovery of a single Roman brick in one of the sacrificial pits alongside the remains of a sacrificed dog,[131] Éva Petres argued that the Pákozd sanctuary was also used in the Roman period.[132]

Even if the continuity of the sacralised space is uncertain, the large number of sacrificial pits reflects a successful religious communication that was maintained and performed by multiple generations. Similar archaeological contexts were identified in the large cemetery in Pilismarót-Basaharc from the Late Copper Age that was also used in the Iron Age.[133] Elsewhere, the pre-Roman cult of Cernunnos was associated with the large amount of osteological material from stags found in Keszthely-Fenékpuszta, Szakály, Sé and Balatonőszöd-Temetői dulő.[134] In the case of Balatonőszöd, the well-documented archaeological context helped the author to identify the period when the unique, non-repetitive sacrificial act happened.[135] Horváth presumed that some of the sacrificial pits correlate with the Celtic *Lughnasadh* festival that took place in early August. Such important archaeological finds need to be centralised and contextualised as glocal sources of Celtic religious communication following the well-known Celtic calendar and religious traditions that were also represented on the Gundestrup cauldron.[136]

The osteological material discovered in the domestic environment in Sé, Vas country (today Hungary) in a house indicated the same forms of religious communication in private, micro-spaces as well as in public, mezzo-spaces.[137] Similarly, with regard to the so-called *pseudokernos* vases from the Late Bronze Age and the Hallstatt period in the later territory of Pannonia, such domestic sacrifices and osteological evidence can be both 'profane' or 'religious', too: without clear evidence and arguments, the functionality and agency role of these objects in religious communication can be justly presumed.[138] These examples in many senses put in context the literary sources and help us to deconstruct both the Roman ethnographic layers and the contemporary historiographic interpretations of pre-Roman, Celtic religion in provincial contexts [139]

For a long time, the Gellérthegy near Aquincum (today the hills of Buda) and the Pffafenberg (near Carnuntum) were considered to be the main Celtic sanctuaries of pre-Roman Pannonia, dedicated to the local supreme gods: Teutanus and the sky god of the mountain Karnuntinus (cat. no. III.50).[140] However, careful archaeological excavations and reanalysis of the old historiographic data call into question the pre-Roman cultic activity on the Gellérthegy, which remains only a hypothesis.[141] The 17 Roman altars dedicated to Teutanus discovered at Bölcske in 1980s were also associated with this 'central' sanctuary, but there are no direct links between the two discoveries.[142]

Identifying pre-Roman religion in Late Iron Age Moesia

The Late Iron Age (commonly associated with the Hellenistic period) history of what would later be called Moesia Superior recently underwent a research renaissance. As a result, numerous important studies focusing on the mobility of objects and cultural interconnectivities in the northern Balcanic and southern Danubian area offered a better understanding of the region and its integration in the Hellenistic and, later, Roman world.[143] The military and commercial dislocations and mobilities created not only well-established routes in the Balkans, but also new forms of reappropriation of Hellenistic materiality, architecture and cultural habits in the southern Danubian area.[144]

The territory of Moesia province in the late La Tène period was anything but a united cultural entity: it contained important Celtic communities, who had direct connections with Pannonian and Western commercial and cultural routes. After 279 BC, the Celtic invasions changed radically the cultural and political environment of the area between the Danube and Sava rivers, reducing the influence and power of the Dardani.[145] In the mid-3rd century BC, the Dardani already had military and diplomatic connections with the Romans, especially during the consulship of Publius Sulpicius Rufus.[146] The formation of the new Roman protectorates of Macedonia and Illyria represent an important moment for the political shift, which changed the kingdom of Dardania and initiated the dominant Scordisci period along the Sava River after 141 BC.[147]

Most of the archaeological evidence on the Scordici comes from funerary contexts, which helps us to reconstruct especially their economic and military connectivities. These provide valuable new information that can be added to the already known sources from ancient literature.[148] Yet from the rich material evidence from the 2nd–1st centuries BC for the Scordisci, there are very few that can be connected with space sacralisation or religious communication. Ritual depositions in rivers (in particular the Sava) seem to have been a Celtic tradition attested in this area, especially in connection with the military power elite.[149] This represents a local specificity of the area between the Drava and Sava rivers in south Pannonia and the later Moesia Superior.[150] The warrior elite, who created the strongest visual and material markers in both the worlds of the living and the dead, appropriated their divine agency in the form of so-called 'war gods' – military divinities that were known only through indirect offerings and the material tools used in their worship. A unique case study for such a sacralised space, where the pre-Roman local military elite was probably in repetitive and long-term communication with the war gods, was identified and excavated in 2008–2009 in Osijek. The deposition of a significant quantity of 'weapons, horse gear, wagon pieces, fragments of bronze vessels, as well as human and animal bones have been interpreted as traces of ritual activities of the Scordisci warriors'.[151] The folded and bent weapons represent a universal, Celtic and even pre-historic ritual. Indeed, their concentration in one particular place might indicate their intentional use as material tools in space sacralisation as a form of unique or repetitive religious communication.

Similar contexts and material finds have also been identified in aquatic contexts along the Sava River, as well as in streams and lakes, although this phenomenon was documented especially in southern Pannonia: the closest analogy for the Scordisci territory was attested in Morović.[152] However, their context and use are uncertain: without a proper sub-aquatic archaeological investigation it is impossible to reconstruct the ritual or motivation of the users. Using militaria as *ex-votos* in space sacralisation is more obvious in the case of the hoard discovered at Veliki Vetren, where numerous weapons were identified.[153]

An interesting and intriguing problem in the Romanian and Serbian historiography is the cultural and religious interferences that occurred between the Scordisci and the Dacians. In the relationship of these warrior groups and their elite, similar social structures and regional power identities played a significant role.[154] Instead of ethnicities – a notion that needs to be abandoned forever in pre-modern social history and contemporary archaeological narratives[155] – these objects served as strong social and political markers, whereby warrior identities and hierarchies were reflected in religious art and, probably, also in religious communication. Religious interconnectivity between the Scordisci and the Dacians can thus be traced only through iconographic analysis of the archaeological material, especially those with anthropomorphic and zoomorphic representations.[156] These figurative representations show warrior-like personalities (mostly male, rarely female, figures) with protecting birds and a strong aspect of duality in zoomorphic features: two birds, two horses, two snakes, and featuring a central figure.[157]

This material evidence of the Scordisci and Dacian warrior elite (especially the silver jewellery) has the same topographic distribution as the major commercial routes in the southern Danubian region. Moreover, the distribution of these silver objects,[158] the figurative, possibly, votive material[159] and the commercial routes in the southern Danubian region[160] reflect the same regional distribution in the confluence of the Sava and Danube rivers. This macro-space between the confluence of the Sava and Danube rivers, the valley of the Morava River and the communication routes between the Carpathians and the Balkan mountains represents a sub-unit within the Danubian provinces. It also represents the interconnectivity between the Celtic, Thracian (including Dacian), Hellenistic and Roman worlds since the 2nd century BC. This is well reflected in the iconographic bricolage of the Getae, Dacians and Scordisci, which are often interpreted now as a form of cultural appropriation that is evident in Celtic, Thracian and Hellenistic art.[161] Despite the iconographic interpretations, which tried to identify war gods, celestial gods, ethnic genii and protector gods of different tribes or Hellenistic-Thracian ruler cults in the figurative representations of these objects in this macro-region, without literary sources, the pantheon of the Scordisci and the Dacians remains silent.

A totally different historical and cultural context was established in the Western Pontic shore of the Black Sea and in the area south of the Danube and north of the Balkan mountains – territory that later was known as Moesia Inferior. The so-called Pentapolis, the Greek colonies founded in the 7th/6th centuries BC, represented the most important economic and cultural hubs of the entire region.[162] Their economic roots and interconnectivities in the Black Sea and Mediterranean area, but also with the Thracian and Carpathian regions, are well documented.[163] The religious landscape of the Greek colonies is known almost exclusively from epigraphic material, focusing especially on the Hellenistic cult of the so-called 'Thracian Riders' (*Domna et Domnus*) and the hero cults,[164] the cults of Dionysus-Bacchus,[165] Aphrodite[166] and Magna Mater, the latter of which became very popular in the Greek colonies after the 3rd century BC.[167] In a few cases, sacralised spaces from Classical Greek and Hellenistic periods were attested in this area: the temple of Theos Megas from Histria,[168] several attested or presumed sacralised spaces dedicated to Aphrodite,[169] and other sites that have been interpreted as sacralised spaces in macro- or meso-spaces, mostly in urban environments.[170] The sanctuary of the Pontic Mother of Gods in Dionysopolis (Balchik) is the best-documented case study for religious and spatial continuities, therefore it will be presented later (cat. no. V.4).[171]

The materiality of sacralised spaces along the western shore of the Black Sea reflects what the economic (numismatic and ceramic) material also shows: an intense cultural interconnectivity was established between the Greek colonies of the Black Sea and Aegean Sea and also with the Thracian kingdom.[172] Both the economic routes and the major spaces of religious communication in these urban centres showed a continuous use until late antiquity or even beyond. The region enters in 'Roman history' and in direct political, diplomatic and military connection with Rome after the campaign of G. Scribonius Curio and M. Licinius Lucullus in 75–72 BC and the campaign of M. Licinius Crassus against the Bastarnae in 29/27 BC. A Latin *foedera* contract between the Greek poleis of Kallatis and Rome already existed in the 1st century BC, however its date and historical context are still under debate.[173]

More problematic is the situation in the late Hellenistic/Late Iron Age archaeology of the territory between the Danube and the Balkan mountains in the 1st century BC–1st century AD. This area was part of the so-called Odrysian kingdom, a federation of Gaetae and Thracian tribes with several important rulers and political centres. The fate, history and especially the geographic territory of this kingdom in its late period is part of a historiographic debate that marks the Thracian revival of Bulgarian metahistorical narratives.[174] The history, population and material evidence of this area from the 1st century BC until the 1st century AD is a problematic issue: the archaeological material is extremely laconic and reflects a ruralised society with poor material connectivity with the Dacian, Scordiscian and Celtic environments in Oltenia and the historical territory of the Banat,[175] and almost no interaction with the Greek colonies in the 1st century BC.[176] Literary sources on the interaction between the Triballi and the other tribes along the two banks of the Danube (Moesi, Getae, Dacians) between 44 BC and 86 AD reflect a constant interaction and mobility in the region. The archaeological material of religious communication, however, is almost completely missing in this region prior to the formation of the Roman province of Moesia and Moesia Inferior.

Reinventing religious traditions in Roman context

The Danubian area fell within the sphere of interest for Rome in the 3rd century BC, when there were several military campaigns in the region.[177] D. Dzino ingeniously proved that the territorial expansion of Republican Rome was not only a political, social and economic necessity, but also often an emotional, hazardous consequence of several events.[178] With the territorial expansion of Rome came several legal and ideological issues, too, which went on to reform the administrative system of Rome as well as radically changing their spatial and cultural notion of Barbaricum, giving birth to the complex notion of *provinciae* and the 'Roman world' (*orbis*).[179] A concentric view of the Roman world centring Rome as an axis mundi, the semi-peripheral areas known as provinces and the Limes (*fines, limites* of the 'Roman world') and the edges of known, geographical world inhabited by ethnographically generalised 'Barbarians'[180] marked not only the Roman historiography, where the Danubian area had a secondary importance, but also the later, modern historiography, where the 'provincial Roman archaeology' institutionalised the dichotomy of Rome and its provinces, with a specific place for the Danubian area.[181]

Periods of transition: appropriations, resistance and historical vacuums in the new provinces

The integration of this region into the Roman world was slow and employed various local strategies. It began in the Adriatic area in the 3rd–2nd centuries BC,[182] followed by the Lower Danubian area (the later Moesiae provinces) in the 2nd century BC and the Alpine region after 113 BC. In these early periods, the region and its extremely heterogeneous populations came in direct contact with the Romans, mostly through military conflicts and diplomacy. This, however, presumes a commercial and economic relationship, which is indeed visible in the materiality of the pre-Roman kingdoms, tribes and local populations, especially in the 2nd–1st centuries BC.[183] However, the Roman presence can already be attested in pre-Roman sacralised places and religious communication before this area had become de facto Roman provinces: numerous indigenous sacralised spaces used Roman or Greco-Roman altars and sacrifices, alongside Roman bronze vessels, pottery, terracotta figurines and bronze or marble statues.[184] Thus pre-Roman religious communication was already 'Roman' in its materiality in the 1st century BC in most of the later Danubian provinces and beyond.[185]

So, the formation of 'provincial culture'[186] before the advent of administrative and legal provinciality (*lex provinciae, in formam provinciae redacta*[187]) was present in most of the Danubian provinces. However, this glocal phenomenon of Roman material ecology was not unified and equally homogenously strong in every region.[188] The construction of later ethnic identities of Raetians, Noricans, Illyrians, Pannonians or Dacians was not just the cultural imagining of Roman historiography, but rather an ongoing process that occurred before the conquest of these regions and was expressed through the material 'Roman-ness' of these groups.

The Roman material mobilities shaped not only the group identities of the indigenous inhabitants of the Danubian provinces, but also their religious communication. This can be attested in numerous case studies, especially from the centres and major religious 'capitals' of the indigenous groups, which created – intentionally or not – 'Roman' religious strategies even before the conquest. These reforms contributed to the cultural transition in the formation of a new provincial society and their religious communication. Older approaches argued that the indigenous religious landscape (the divine agents – gods, the sacralised spaces; sanctuaries; the main human actors – priests and the elite; and the material tools used in this communication) was reinterpreted by the newcomers through a complex system of religious syncretism and the *interpretatio Romana*.[189] This approach draws a strict line between 'indigenous' and 'Roman', stressing the dichotomy of religious continuities and discontinuities as arguments and important features of the older historical narrative on Romanisation.[190]

Lately, this view has been contested by the approach of reinvented religious traditions, *interpretatio indigena*,[191] and the concept of local religious appropriation,[192] which focus on the complex interactions between old and new religious knowledge and the major actors and cultural factors of transformations and visual or narrative shifts.[193] In this context, the religious landscapes of the Danubian provinces need to be reinterpreted not through the old approach of *interpretatio Romana*[194] but as a complex interaction of human, material and divine agents of religious communication.[195] In the following, I will present some notable case studies of indigenous religious appropriations and reinvented religious traditions from Roman contexts.

Raetia and the Alpine region underwent a sudden, but less well known transformation, in comparison with Noricum, for example.[196] What the historiography usually terms the 'annexation' or occupation of the Alpine region (the formation of the later province Raetia et Vindelicia)[197] occurred during a short assault, often called a blitzkrieg, by Emperor Tiberus and his son Drusus Julius Caesar on 1 August 15 BC,[198] after which the entire region entered a period of 'calm occupation of the Romans', as Strabo termed it 30 years later.[199] However, in fact this process was not as fast as the literary sources suggest: archaeological evidence shows there was instead a slow process of provincialisation, which represents the major difference between the process being *in formam provinciae redacta de iure* and *de facto*.[200] K. Strobel agrees, arguing that this process was not a single event, but a long process that began with the military campaign between 44–16 BC.[201] The Tropaeum Alpium from 7 or 6 BC also shows that the provincialisation process took several years.[202] From the period of Augustus (before 14 AD), the military presence was scarce, which suggests that the military defence system was just temporary and was not established until the death of the first emperor. This is supported by the fact that the fort of Friedberg-Rederzhausen[203] and the legionary fortress of Augsburg-Oberhausen[204] were the only military settlements in this period, and the Danubian Limes were established only in the period of 14–68 AD.[205] This is further supported by the date of the establishment of the Via Claudia, which reached the Danubian area only in 46–47 AD.[206] Furthermore, the transitional period between 15 BC and 41 AD is well documented through the honorary inscriptions of the first *praefectus Raetis, Vindolicis*,[207] which was followed by the *procurator Augusti et pro legato* after Q. Caecilius Cisiacus Septicius Pica Caecilianus.[208]

In fact, the military and administrative transition and provincialisation took more than half a century and the social history of this period is one of the major questions of Raetian history. What happened to the indigenous, pre-Roman population? Can we talk about spatial and functional continuities in pre-Roman sacralised spaces? How was religious appropriation manifested in the 1st century

AD? These major questions have been answered in radically different ways by German historiography. A minimalist approach argues that there are no or very few certain traces of settlement, place or population continuities.[209] Although most of the later settlement system of Raetia used non-Latin, indigenous (Celtic or Raetian) toponyms,[210] there is no proof of an early Roman *civitates* system in Raetia.[211] Indeed, C. Sommer even questioned the Roman phases of some of the well-known and systematically excavated *Brandopferplätze*, such as the one in Forggensee, that had been until now considered as places where the indigenous religious communication continued for a period after 15 BC.[212] Others emphasise the strong presence of the indigenous population after 15 BC through the materiality of the so-called Heimstetten group, which can be attested in the first half of the 1st century (30–60 AD).[213]

The burial customs of this short-lived and geographically limited group show a very interesting cultural appropriation: while some researchers interpreted this group as members of a 'local resistance'[214] or took their material culture to be a sign of '*nativismus*' ('nativeness'),[215] the materiality of their burials shows a strong influence of Roman material mobility and an incorporated habitus of Roman material culture. However, this Roman materiality coexists in tombs containing some indigenous material elements and where there is evidence of a new type of cattle breeding, which probably offered a new type of living in this area.[216]

The early Roman period also shows archaeological evidence for the reappropriation or continuous use of some well-known *Brandopferplätze*: some of them show a long hiatus, sometimes 100–200 years, in use followed by a short renaissance in the early Roman period (Schlossberg, Burgen, Garschinger-Heide).[217] Others were in constant use since La Tène (Karres, Forggensee), while some exceptional cases show a continuous use, from the Hallstatt period (Campi Neri, Mechel).[218] Exceptional case studies are the sacralised spaces that were found in Spielleitenköpfl and Pillerhöhe, which were used continuously from the Late Bronze Age until late antiquity.[219] Burgstall was used in the Late Bronze Age and early Hallstatt period, and was then reopened after a hiatus of a few centuries after the Roman conquest and was used once more until late antiquity.[220]

The case study of the *Brandopferplatz* in Döttenbichl, near Oberammengau, shows several important particularities of religious reappropriation during early Roman times. The complex sanctuary was established in a narrow valley, between two important peaks (Schaffelberg and Kofel) on a major road.[221] This topographic position is a very common feature of these open-air sacralised spaces – a fact that is one of the major arguments for why these places were continuously reinterpreted and resacralised even after a hiatus lasting a few centuries. The 380 metal objects discovered at the large, open-air sacralised space (1.44 ha)[222] represents mostly early Roman militaria, some of which – such as the famous catapult arrowhead bearing the stamp of the Legio XIX – must have had an impressive history in the period between 15 BC and 9 AD.[223]

The presence of Roman bronze material such as this in many similar sacralised spaces in the Alpine area[224] opened the question of so-called '*nativismus*' in Raetia: why were so many *Brandopferplätze* still in use in Roman times and why were sacralised spaces reused or 'reactivated' after a long historical hiatus? The literature offers numerous possible answers: the minimalist approach argued that the chronology of these sites is problematic and not always acceptable,[225] while others argued and interpreted this as being due to cultural and political conflict between the centre (the Roman provincial administration and army) and the periphery (the local indigenous population).[226]

The case study of the Veldidena (Innsbruck, Wilten) is a good example of the problematic issue of 'continuity' at these pre-Roman types of sacralised space. The discovery of bronze and other metal objects (mostly brooches dated from the Augustan period[227]) together with burnt osteological material in the south-west part of the Roman settlement meant that the site was interpreted as being a *Brandopferplatz* from the Roman period.[228] Several brooches identified in this context were of the same type as those discovered in the tombs of the so-called Heimstetten group.[229] Based on these arguments – mostly from the material evidence and typologies – the reappropriation of pre-Roman sacralised spaces after 15 BC and the appearance of new ones, as the one from Veldidena were interpreted as proof of 'nativeness', a cultural movement of resistance of the pre-Roman society against the expansion of Rome. This historical discourse, however, is a metahistory of modern scholars adopting a postcolonial approach.[230]

In fact, the archaeological evidence is very heterogeneous both in the Heimstetten group and the early Roman sacralised spaces attributed to the indigenous population. Their geographic distribution and chronological specificities show great variety. Many of the reopened *Brandopferplätze* contained Roman material from before the conquest and reveal a continuous Roman material toolkit that persisted for two to three centuries. This might suggest that these sacralised spaces were reappropriated and reopened not necessarily or not only as local identity markers in the changing political, administrative and demographic landscape, but especially as a consequence of all three. Human mobilities, the more intense use of Roman materiality and the intensification of the Via Claudia as a cultural channel between south and north probably contributed to the apparition of a new age of *Brandopferplätze* in the early Roman period.[231]

The curious case of Noricum: reinventing local religion

The transformation of the kingdom of Noricum into a Roman province was almost a voiceless event in literary sources: the slow transition is scarcely mentioned as one of the major glocal events of the Alpine area, which was annexed in 16–15 BC.[232] The transitional period at the end of the Augustan age and the early Julio-Claudian dynasty is still a problematic era in the social history of Noricum (Fig. 2.4).[233] The Austrian literature focusing on this period emphasised two major features: 1) the continuous use of the Celtic theonyms (the so-called *interpreatio romana, indentificatio Romana vel indigena*[234]) or, recently, the *interpretatio indigena* and the functional and spatial continuities/discontinuities of sacralised spaces.[235] The literary sources mentioning the Celtic 'national pantheon' of Noricum – recently named as '*Noricae*'[236] (Tertullian on Belenus[237] but also the problematic case study of Isis Noreia[238]) – and the rich epigraphic evidence of pre-Roman theonyms used abundantly after the Roman conquest[239] suggest an ongoing and complex process of religious appropriation, expressed especially through epigraphic and visual transformations and innovations of the divine agency.

The works of M. Hainzmann made paradigmatic contributions to the linguistic analysis of the theonyms, however these studies do not focus on the agency role of altars and the social history of votive inscriptions.[240] Although the epigraphic habit was present in the kingdom of Noricum even before the Roman conquest, creating and exposing divine names as one of the major tools in space sacralisation is a typically Roman 'product' and habit. The rich variety of Celtic theonyms in Noricum – some of them preserved in Latinised form (Alovnae, Nutrices, Aquo)[241] – shows the emergence of a new provincial society,[242] in which not only did the local elite try to establish their place in the new social order, but also the newcomers, who appropriated local religious knowledge: similar to other Celtic provinces, Norican 'religion' was reinvented after 15 BC.[243]

The Roman emporion of Magdalensberg was a successful experiment for decades before the Norican kingdom was finally transformed into a Roman province: attractive and successful strategies of space sacralisation (Roman temple types, altars, urbanisation) created the precedent for local religious appropriations, whereby the indigenous religious traditions and knowledge (divine agents, sacralised spaces) were slowly transformed into a reinvented, Roman-Norican religious communication. The formative and cohesive nature of religion as a power that makes sense of the human and divine world[244] is reflected in the integration of pre-Roman religious traditions and knowledge in the new provincial society. A successful integration of local, pre-Roman religious knowledge into the universal facets of Roman religious communication also reflects the intensive collaboration of the newcomers and the local elite, who made the transitional period in Noricum anecdotally peaceful. Noricum was thus a truly glocal province, one in which the central and the universal (the global Rome) was present in the form of Roman altars, Latin inscriptions, Roman temples and a new economic elite, using and reinventing local religious knowledge as a strategy for maintaining social, political and cultural balance.

The newcomers used and created new divine agents and invented new theonyms, which reflected not only their personal beliefs, but also the fact that individual religious choice had a very strong social and political message for the local elite and the 'viewers' of the altars in public spaces. An example is the middle-sized altar in Hohenstein that was erected by Chrysanthus, a *servus* and Imperial slave of Cypaerus, which was dedicated to Noreia and probably stood in the sanctuary of the divinity

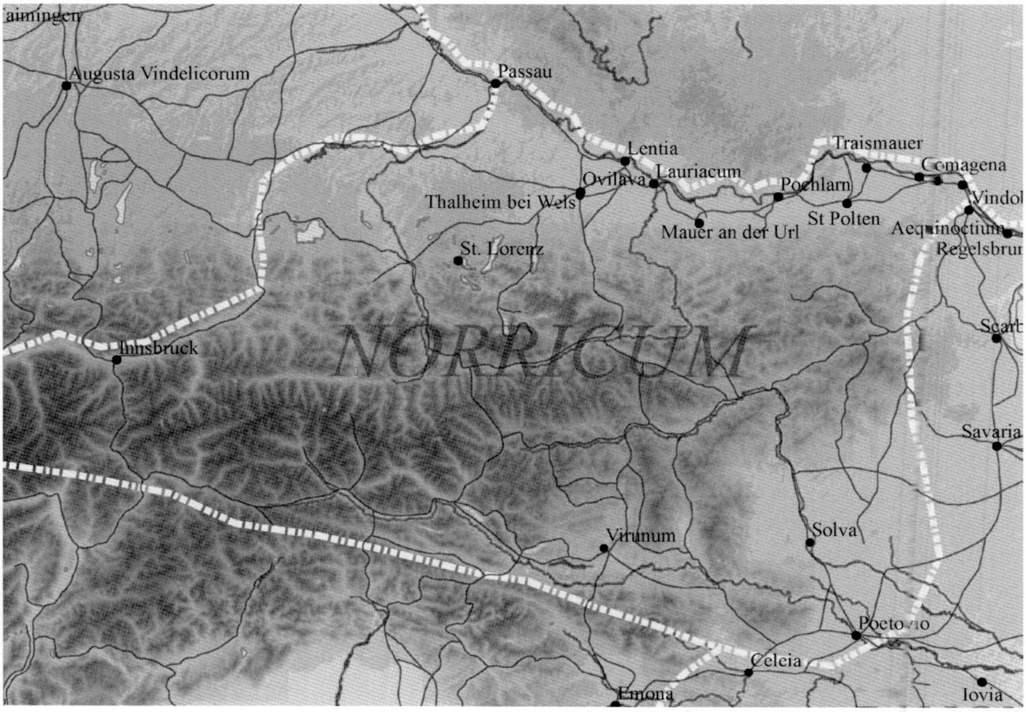

Fig. 2.4 Map of Roman Noricum showing the settlements discussed in the Chapter 2. (Source: Țentea 2011, 229, pl. 1 with the special permission of the author)

or in a public space in front of it (Fig. 2.5).[245] How this process happened is hard to reconstruct, and would require a detailed analysis of the economic and social fusion and interconnectivity between the newcomers and the local population.[246] However the older literature stressed a very important and demographically significant presence of Italic merchants in the newly founded province of Noricum and their impact in creating a new religious landscape and tools of religious communication at each spatial level.[247]

Recently, though, this thesis has become hard to maintain with strong arguments and it is now questioned both by epigraphists and archaeologists.[248] The significant number of Celtic divine names used in religious communication after the conquest suggests not only an indirect appropriation, but also the use and reuse of a religious knowledge, which necessitates the presence of the local elite. The case of Isis Noreia, as a personification of the province, or a 'syncretic goddess' as it is often called in the literature, shows this complex process of creating religious strategies, which contributed to the formation of a global, Roman Noricum with strong local religious identities. This religious glocalisation is also well attested in strategies of space sacralisation.

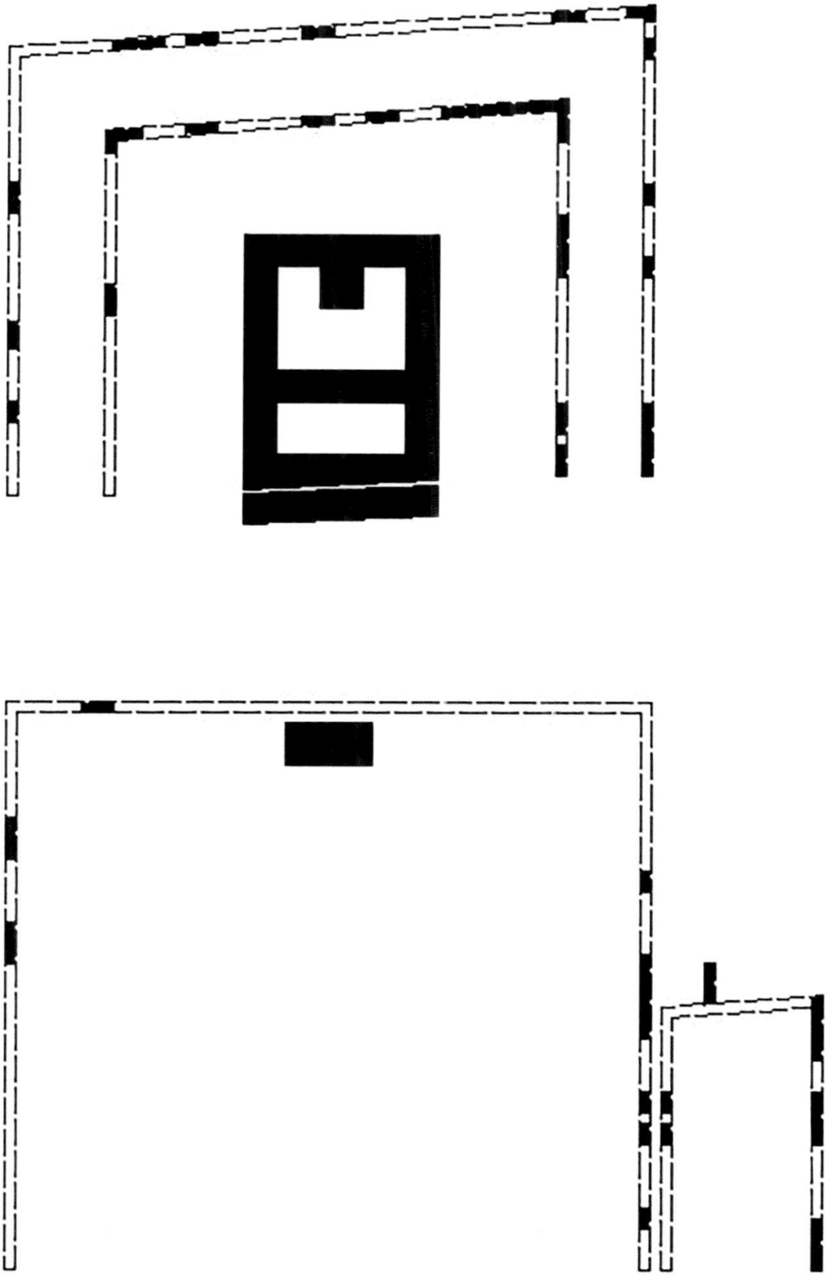

Fig. 2.5 Plan of the Noreia sanctuary in Hchenstein. (Source: Áron Hegedűs and the author after Trunk 1991, 193, Fig. 136)

There are numerous versions of space continuities and reinvented religious traditions in Noricum. The motivation for retaining or reactivating a sacralised space is always very specific and needs to be examined in each case individually and contextually. In most cases, the sacralised space was used continuously between the 1st century BC and the 1st century AD. Many of these sanctuaries were situated in important, key settlements on the major economic and trading roads of the Alpine region. Their visibility to travellers and local inhabitants thus ensured the continuous use of the sacralised space. Furthermore, by transforming these sites into Roman temples with Roman altars, Latin inscriptions and Roman sacrificial performances, the religious landscapes of these key settlements were the most visible landmarks of the new political and administrative order established after 15 BC.

Case studies from rural or remote unpopulated areas of the Norican kingdom serve as rare cases for religious appropriation and probably the best case studies for place continuities. The case study of the so-called Glockner Route between Aquileia and Linz-Freinberg (Lentia), for instance, shows several important stations that were used continuously, and that were almost unaffected by the political and administrative changes that occurred after 15 BC.[249] Elsewhere, evidence from the passage sanctuary in Hochtor shows that it was already in use in the 2nd century BC and – other than perhaps a short intermezzo – that it functioned continuously during the early periods of the Principate (cat. no. II.15).[250] The figurative *ex-votos* found there reflect both a long-term use of the sacralised space and the strong influence of the North-Italic artistic workshops and religious traditions of sacrificial visuality.[251]

In such natural environments and mountain passages, permanent human agency is not a strong maintenance strategy of space sacralisation. The geographical position, the problems of accessibility and the remoteness of the place reduced the visibility of the sanctuary, but also served as an exotic element in the successful maintenance of the sacralised space.[252] The sanctuary at Hochtor thus represents a sacralised place where spatiality and accessibility play the key role, together with liminoid temporality, as most of the visitors would have been temporary worshippers and movers in space. Being accessible to just a few people or even just for individual religious communication, the Hochtor sanctuary is one of the few case studies for religious individualisation, even though the *longue durée* existence of the sanctuary and its traditional geographic position served to create a universalised divine agent and tradition (the so-called Hochtor-Hercules types).

Remote rural religiosity or even individual choices can also be attested in the ceramic finds at Mautern an der Donau (*vicus Favianis*).[253] The pottery masks discovered in a pit there show a great variety in iconography, and consist of mostly zoomorphic and anthropomorphic figures. The Cheshire-style zoomorphic masks, which have small holes on them marking the eyes and the mouths of the wearers, represent a rare type of object in Celtic traditions.[254] The exact functionality of these is problematic, especially in the context of Mautern an der Donau.[255] The analogies discovered in London, Cologne, Worms, Trier, Wiesbaden and numerous other settlements suggest a religious purpose[256] or else one associated with theatres and their attendant religious processions.[257] The pig-headed mask from Mautern an der Donau can also be related to indigenous, Celtic traditions.[258] However, the archaeological context of the discovery does not provide sufficient data on pre-Roman activity in Favianis, where the earliest phases of the buildings are attested in the Flavian period.[259]

Transforming the architectural landscape and giving a Roman facade to local religious traditions (*indentificatio Romana vel indigena*) was a practice that was promoted and maintained especially by the *magistri pagi*, a less well-known category of the early rural settlement system of Noricum.[260] A well-documented case study for this sort of politically dominated space sacralisation is the Roman sanctuary of Burgstall in St Margarethen in Lavanttal (cat. no. II.3 – Fig. 2.6). The sanctuary was dedicated to Latobius Maromogius and was probably under the control of the *magistri pagi*, as one of the inscriptions suggests.[261] In this case of space sacralisation, the divine agent (Latobius) is a Celtic, local divinity who has been appropriated and reinvented as Mars Latobius or Latobius, a Latinised version of the original divine name. In the process of space sacralisation, the theonym and also the visual and physical representation of the divine agent have been translated into the cultural language of the Romans: fragments of a classical Roman statue representing probably Mars Latobicus were discovered there in 1927.[262] Not only was the image of the god translated to the familiar visual language of the newcomers, but also the architectural features of the sacralised space: the sanctuary of Latobius – although it seems to have also existed in the 1st century BC[263] – in the Roman period had classical and universalised architectural features, with several analogies from other Roman provinces and a complex architectural environment comprising several buildings.[264]

The most important and critical period in the transformation of these sacralised spaces is the first part, the consolidation. How was the religious knowledge transferred and appropriated? Who were the major players and how long did it take to adopt a new strategy in religious communication, using old, divine names and spaces, but with new forms and material tools? These questions unfortunately remain mostly unanswered; however, the chronologically dated sources suggest that this process took a few decades, and occurred at some point between 20 BC and 10 AD.[265]

At Frauenberg, a late La Tène sacralised space was attested, although it seems that the use of this ended in the Augustan period before the conquest of Noricum.[266] The finds from the late 1st century BC indicate that the hill was in continuous use even after the Celtic sacralised space had been abandoned.[257] Timber structures suggest a late La Tène settlement or extensive constructions, with uncertain functionality. The sacralised space had at least three major phases (cat. no. II.12). The first phase consisted of a small altar area with an older, so-called 'indigenous' sanctuary. The second phase monumentalised the old building with a large stone temenos. The third phase transformed the older altar area into a podium temple (Fig. 2.7).[268] Since the discovery of the sanctuary in the 1950s, the complex sacralised space has been attributed to Isis Noreia, although recent excavations have revealed numerous

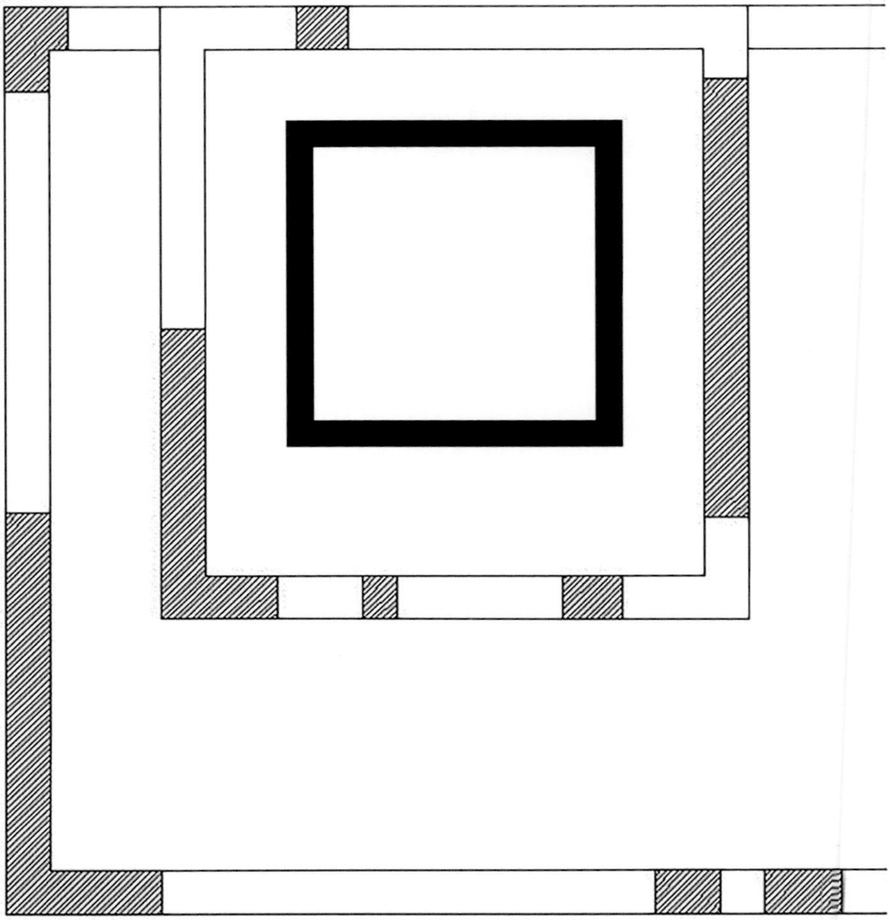

Fig. 2.6 Plan of the sanctuary in Burgstall in St Margarethen in Levanttal. (Source: author after Groh-Sedlmeyer 2007, 31, abb. 1)

statuary ex-votos representing mother divinities[269] that are also known from Poetovio.[270] The cult of the Nutrices was very popular in Poetovio (cat. nos III.63–64), but it seems that it was not only a local success, but that it was also transported to the *ager* (land) of Flavia Solva (Maribor and, possibly, also Frauenberg).[271] The monumentalised sanctuary on the Frauenberg seems once again to be more like a reinvented sacralised space, where the new Roman elite together with certain aristocratic groups of the indigenous populations created a successful new sanctuary. In addition, the podium temple reflects the same architectural atmosphere as is found in Magdalensberg or Burgstall: richly decorated architraves and monumental elements of the building have been preserved, which give a glimpse of the new Imperial aspect of the sanctuary.[272] The relationship with the Celtic, pre-Roman sanctuary and the later Claudian-Flavian constructions is still under debate.[273]

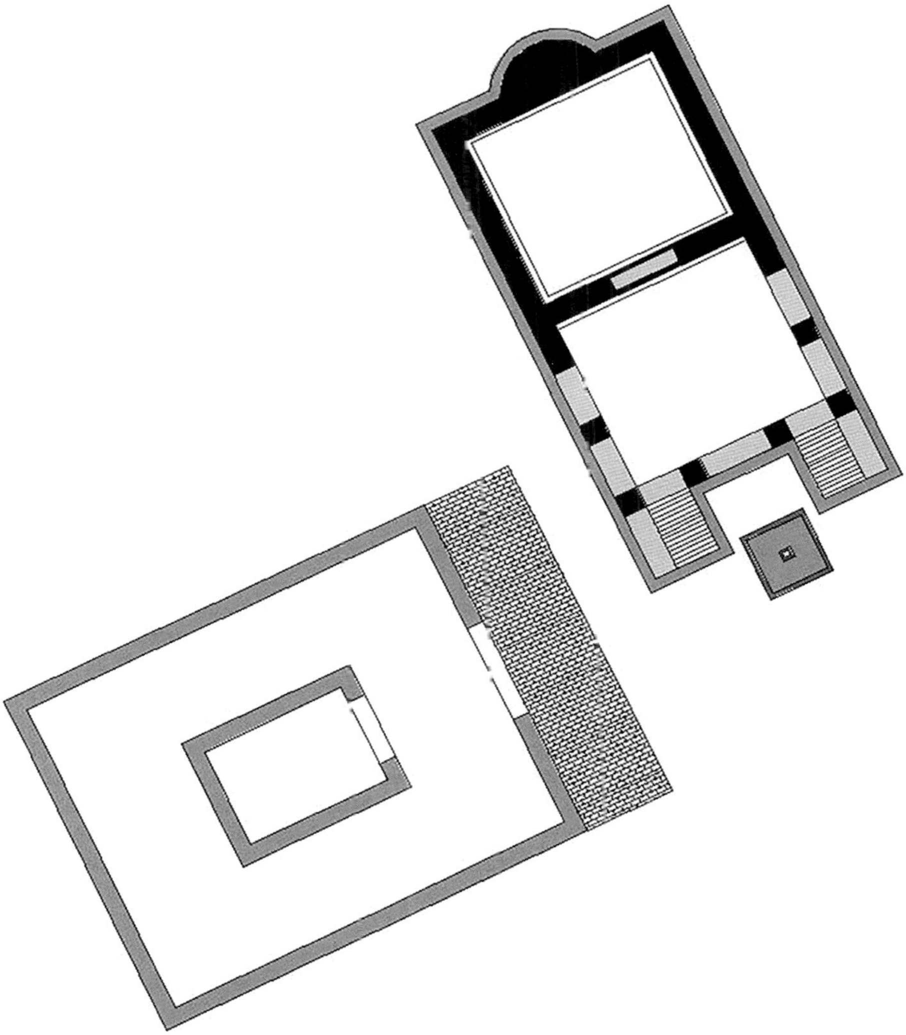

Fig. 2.7 Plan of the sanctuary in Frauenberg. (Source: Áron Hegedűs and the author after Schrettle 2016, 189, Fig. 5)

An important case study for the argument that pre-Roman cult activities continued in Roman times was attested on the border of Pannonia and Noricum associated with the *territorium* of Celeia. In the hamlet of Sava near Podkraj, opposite Klembas and close to the right bank of the Savus River, 10 altars were identified, containing prehistoric material and Roman bricks.[274] Adsalluta and Savus were local, regional Tauriscan divinities attested in numerous local communities and associated with safe travel on rivers. Recently, the local cult of Adsalluta was also associated with the Magna Mater cult, indicating the potential for local appropriation between the water divinity and the goddess of female principle.[275] However, the excavated archaeological material shows an exclusively Roman religious appropriation of various divine agents in visual and epigraphic narratives (for example, in the same area, there is a unique visual narrative representing Apollo in the context of the Magna Mater and Attis cults).[276] The association of Magna Mater with a previous, possibly pre-Roman spring cult must have occurred in a later period, probably in the 2nd century AD, and according to some, it continued even in early Christian and Medieval traditions (the custom of the so-called 'pinewood marriage' in Dalmatia).[277]

In the previous two case studies, pre-Roman religious traditions were reinvented in non-urban contexts by the economic and commercial elite of the new Roman administration, in possible collaboration with the local elite. The case study of Celeia shows a similar phenomenon, but in an urban context, which gives another important spatial factor as well as new strategies of space sacralisation (cat. nos II. 6–9).[278] From the four sacralised spaces attested *extra muros* (Fig. 2.8), only three had pre-Roman, possibly late La Tène archaeological evidence (mostly pottery[279]). The argument of the excavators was that the architectural features and the early datation (before Tiberius) of the material suggest a pre-Roman use of the sanctuaries and imply that the structures were later monumentalised and used continuously after the foundation of the Roman town.[280]

The sanctuaries were positioned on the road alongside the river leading to the later city of Celeia – a route that represents one of the strategic focal points of the pre-Roman Norican kingdom, as an important commercial and communication channel. Therefore, the space sacralisation here also represents a landmark in the natural and economic landscape and an opportunity for the local elite to establish an intensive communication with human (social) and divine agents (gods). Although their position after the late Julio-Claudian period became marginal (*extra muros*) and was overshadowed by the new sacral public space – the forum and the capitol of the town (cat. no. II.5)[281] – the sanctuaries on the bank of the river functioned even after the Roman administration had created new public spaces for religious communication, opening a much wider range of architectural and figurative strategies. The geographic locality and the age of the sanctuaries as an important mnemotic factor in space sacralisation aided the maintenance of these sacralised places, even providing the possibility for architectural monumentalisation in later periods.

Identifying pre- and early Roman religion in Pannonia: a short overview

The transformation of the southern Danubian area (the province of Illyricum) represents a highly debated topic in historiography (Fig. 2.9). Although the Roman Empire had a two-century long military and economic history in this region, the provincial administration was established only in the last decade of the reign of Augustus (13 BC–6 AD).[282] The great Pannonian rebellion of 13–12 BC was one of the starting points in the long administrative history of the later province of Pannonia, although the area of Siscia had already been subdued in the period of 35–33 BC.[283] The political and cultural testimony of Augustus, the Monumentum Ancyranum (*Res Gestae*

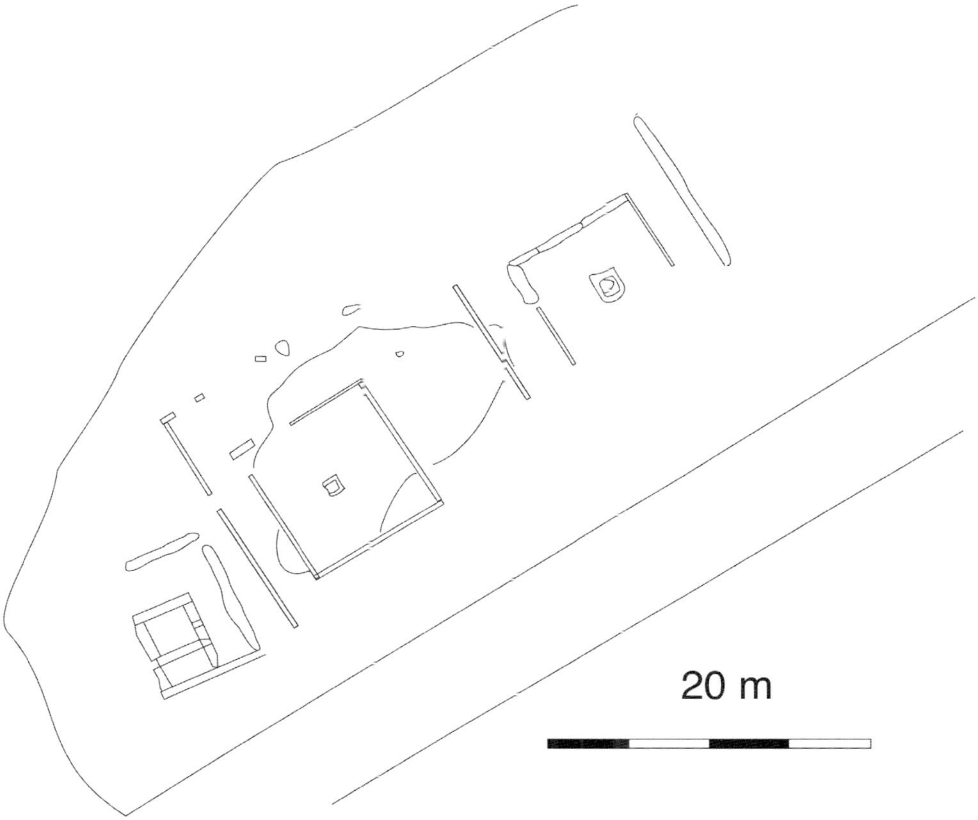

Fig. 2.8 Plan of the sanctuaries in Celeia. (Source: Áron Hegedűs and the author after Krempus et al. *2007, 41, abb. 3)*

Divi Augusti) mentions that the Pannonian area (which is not exactly delimited in the text) was annexed to the province of Illyricum (*protulique fines Illyrici ad ripam fluminis Danuvi*).[284] More precisely, this short passage mentions only the strategic importance of the Danube as a natural border of the Roman Empire and the limits (*fines*) of the Roman world, the Augustean *orbis*. The Danube here appears not only as a symbol of the new administrative and political doctrine of Augustus after the '*bello Variano*',[285] establishing the limits of the Empire on the natural borders of the north, but also as a *longue durée* plan for Roman administrative transformation. The historiography discussed the details of the establishment of Pannonia as a separate province: some authors indicated that Pannonia had already been created in the age of Tiberius, under the name of Illyricum Superior,[286] while others argued for a much later, Flavian creation of a province called Pannonia.[287]

The transformation of the pre-Roman religious landscape, in terms of its human, divine and material agents in Pannonia, began right after the intensification of the

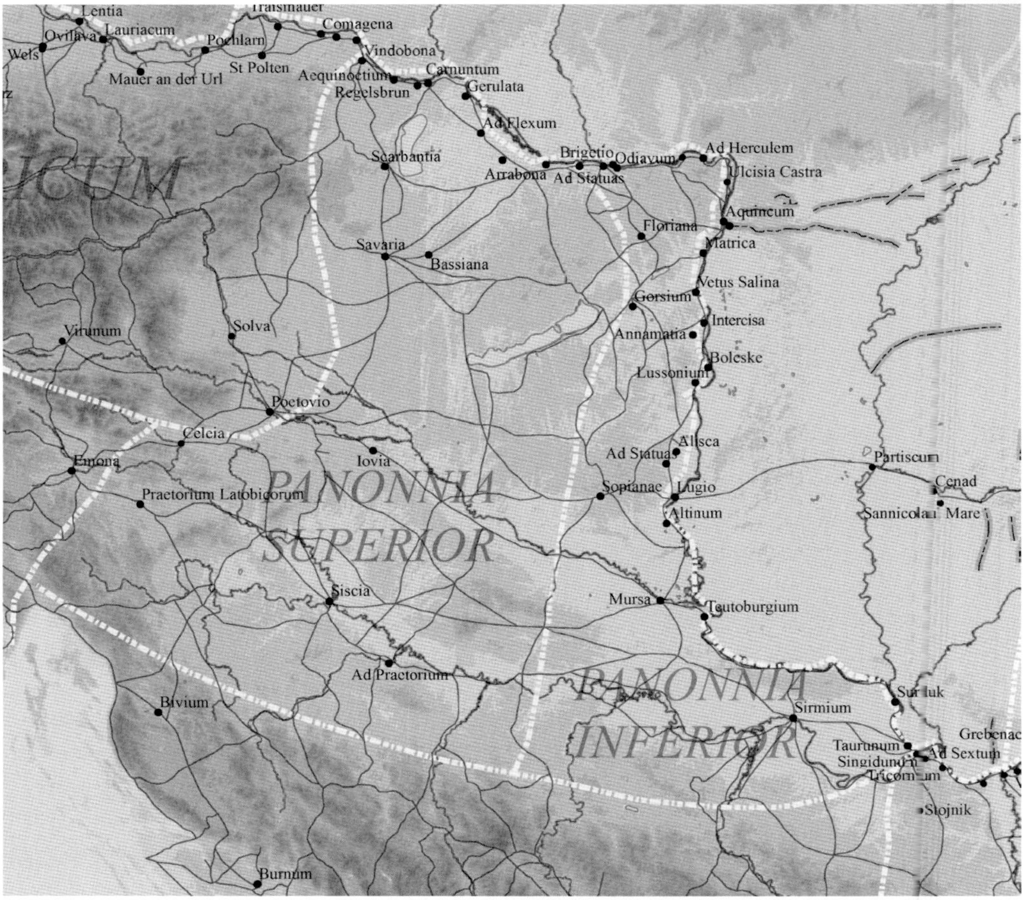

Fig. 2.9 Map of Roman Pannonia showing the settlements discussed in the Chapter 2. (Source: Ţentea 2011, 229, pl. 1 with the special permission of the author)

military dislocations in the area during the Julio-Claudian period (14–68 AD).[288] The transformation was slow, not only in terms of the building of Roman administration, military infrastructure and population mobilities, but also in religious changes.[289] In contrast with Noricum, where Roman religious communication was present for at least a generation before the final transformation of the area into a province, or in Roman Dacia, where the transformation of the former kingdom of the Dacians was fast and aggressive,[290] Pannonia (north of the Drava) was created slowly, carefully and seemingly without a clear strategy. The only certainty in the process was the Augustean doctrine of the Limes, which needed to be fixed and preserved on the Danube.

The earliest sources for religious appropriation and transformations are attested in the urban environment, especially in the area of the Amber Road, which shows a more intense Roman presence in the first half of the 1st century AD. The mobility of the army on the road between Emona, Poetovio and Carnuntum – and all the major settlements along the road (especially Savaria and Scrabantia) – established the first direct contact with the indigenous population.

The earliest case in which Roman material agency was used as an agent in space sacralisation happened in the period of Tiberius at the territory of the *oppidum* Iulium Scarbantia (modern-day Sopron).[291] Most of the earliest datable votive inscriptions from Pannonia are from here, too, although the first sacralised spaces (the Capitolium, for example) were probably built only after the Flavian period (cat. no. III.80, Fig. 2.10).[292] The foundation of the city of Savaria by the veterans of the XV Apollinaris legion represents an important moment in the changes of the religious landscape: the foundation rite (*etrusca ritu*), the *pomerium*,[293] the city wall and especially the building of a provincial altar (*ara Augusti provinciae Pannoniae*)[294] opened a strong, architecturally defined macro-space of religious communication with unusual aspects for the indigenous population in the former territory of the *civitas* Boiorum and beyond.[295] Although the *territorium* Savariense represents the best-documented case study for the indigenous rural settlements (*vici, civitates*),[296] from the Julio-Claudian period onwards, the archaeologically attested indigenous civil settlements offer no

Fig. 2.10 Capitoline triad in Scarbantia, Pannonia. (Photo: Bolodár Zoltán, with the permission of Museum of Sopron, Hungary)

evidence of religious communication.[297] The early interaction and social cohesion between the indigenous population and the newcomers are attested especially in the new Roman materialities (terra sigillata, Roman militaria, new pottery forms) and settlement changes. The early transformations can be attested for example in the indigenous cemetery of Nagytétény, where among the pre-Roman tombs there were a few Roman veterans buried in the first half of the 1st century AD and in the early years of the Flavian period.[298]

The transformation of the indigenous society is well attested, especially in the funerary inscriptions and their evolution from the early 1st century AD until the mid-2nd century AD. Pre-Roman societies didn't have the epigraphic habit, nor did they use iconographic representations on tombs.[299] In the 1st century AD, the Celtic population (especially from the northern part of the later Pannonia Inferior, the territory of the Azali and the Eravisci[300]) changed their habitat from hill settlements to the nearby first Roman forts on the bank of the Danube. In this way, their power elite lost its cohesion and political or military influence; therefore, a new strategy was necessary to establish the first contact with the Roman power. This changed not only their settlement and living form, but also the materiality of their spiritual and religious communication: the tombs of the indigenous population from the 1st century AD are inscribed with a single name (*nomen*), representing mostly indigenous, Celtic names. Some particular case studies, such as the Celtic tombs and names in Páty in the *territorium* Aquicenses, show that the epigraphic habit, as exemplified by the use of new architectural and material tools in religious communication (in this case, between the dead persons and the living), became very popular and spread fast in the Flavian period.[301]

However, although the local Celtic elite seems to have easily adapted its religious language, some elements remained unchanged. A particular case study for a glocal religious appropriation is the presence of astral symbols on the funerary stelae of the Azali tribe.[302] The group was transferred from southern Pannonia to the northern area by Tiberius, and some individuals of the tribe (with the names Aturo, Anbo, Ciliunus and Teitia) seem to have also had a connection with Hispania, especially in the Flavian period following the dislocation of the VII Gemina legion.[303] The presence of numerous tombstones with specific iconography attested only with indigenous inhabitants of the province suggests that they rapidly adapted to the new materialities of religious communication and social habitus and readily adopted a new visual language of self-expression and cultural identity.[304] The formation of the indigenous *civitas peregrina* represents the most efficient type of cultural appropriation: the local, indigenous elite was represented by the *principes*[305] and they created the political and social foundation of the religious transformations and reinventions that occurred after the 1st century AD. At least 25 indigenous civitates are known to have been from Pannonia, although their number was certainly much higher.[306]

The case study of the *civitas* Eraviscorum shows that the indigenous settlement – or the memory of it – existed long after the Roman military settlement had been transformed into a *municipium* and the *civitas* had become part of its *territorium*.[307] The invention of Jupiter Teutanus as an appropriated divine agent of the indigenous population represents an important step in the emergence of a local elite, which went on to consciously transform its principal god so it could be integrated into the social and political network of the new administration and the Roman world.[308] The inscriptions that attest the cult in Aquincum date from the late 2nd and 3rd centuries AD and indicate the successful 'Romanness' of this reinvented god of the Eravisci.

István Tóth suggested that the celestial gods and major divine agencies of the pre-Roman communities were worshipped at the same time, following a common religious calendar, as a collective Celtic heritage of the *civitas* Boiorum at the Pfaffenberg (Jupiter Karnuntinus) and the *civitas* Eraviscorum (Jupiter Teutanus) at the Gellérthegy.[309] Identified by him as a 'national holiday' of the pre-Roman communities that was celebrated on both Mons Sacer, the sacred hills of the Boii and Eravisci, 11 June appears on a late inscription from 237 AD in Gellérthegy dedicated to Jupiter Teutanus. The same date was associated with an inscription from the Pfaffenberg sanctuary from 159 AD and 297 AD.[310] Yet this theory of Tóth's seems to be anachronistic and without any solid proof, especially as an example of common religious heritage between the Pfaffenberg community and that of Gellérthegy.[311] That's not to say the existence of a pre-Roman, common religious calendar is impossible: in many Celtic traditions, religious calendars and iconographic representations survived the Roman administration, and were reinvented and appropriated as a new tool and temporal agent in religious communication.[312]

Controlling the indigenous population and their religious dialogue with the old gods in new shapes required successful strategies, religious power elite and central sacralised spaces: the Pfaffenberg sanctuary was just such a place. The sacred area was established on a hill (cat. no. III.50) located north-east of the legionary fortress in the territory *extra leugam*, which means that the sacralised area on the hill were not under the legal authority of the *legatus legionis*.[313] Instead, during the Roman period, it was under the control of the so-called *magistri montis*, as the priestly officials of the *c(ives) R(omani) cons(istentes) Ca[rn(unti)] intra leug(am)*.[314] All the epigraphic[315] and the statuary material suggest[316] that the sanctuary was used only after the Roman conquest and the establishment of the legionary fort in the second half of the 1st century AD. The earliest inscription is dedicated to Victoria by the Legio XV Apollinaris, which suggest a military foundation of the site.[317] This might suggest an analogy with the early, probably Trajanic inscriptions from Sarmizegetusa Regia and the *Hațeg* mountains dedicated to Apollo and Victoria in Roman Dacia right after the conquest.[318] Although numerous earlier literature sources tried to identify a pre-Roman, Celtic sacralised space on the hill, the archaeological evidence shows no traces of continuous religious communication such as we can observe in some cases in Raetia or Noricum.

The monumentalisation of the landscape – which was also a strong visual message for the Barbaricum and the indigenous settlements in the *territorium* of the fortress – was probably begun by Lucius Aelius Caesar, who was often stationed in Carnuntum in his capacity as a governor of the two Pannoniae and also in 137 AD.[319] The heir of the emperor played a crucial role in the spread of the hero cult of Antinoos (Antinous), lover and divinised favourite of Emperor Hadrian in the Danubian provinces.[320] This is attested in the Pfaffenberg and also in Sočanica (Moesia Superior).[321] If the construction of the small amphitheatre and the first buildings (temple 1) of the sacralised space on the Pfaffenberg are related,[322] this could indicate that the official cult of the new Roman hero was celebrated with occasional games.[323]

The Pfaffenberg temples and complex sacralised space reflect a society in transformation, one in which the political elite used monumentalisation for establishing their own position in a macro-political, Imperial connectivity (the fidelity of Lucius Aelius Caesar), and the local elite – among whom in the early period there were probably indigenous individuals too – embraced the new sacralised spaces as new strategies in religious communication and political *cursus honorum*. The emergence of an oriental type of Imperial cult is reflected not only by the presence of the cult of Antinoos, but also by an inscription from the amphitheatre area dedicated to Jupiter Optimus Maximus Dolichenus from the same period – one of the earliest attestations of the cult in the Danubian provinces.[324] Although it is debatable whether or not the local indigenous population was involved in this sacralised space, the materiality of religious communication of the three temples and the entire hill reflects an oriental (Roman) provincial visuality of religion[325] and some Germanic influences, especially in the famous Jupiter columns present on the hill.[326]

István Tóth rightly recognised that the iconographic representation of Jupiter Teutanus and Jupiter Karnuntinus are similar, which suggests an interesting association with the celestial and aquatic aspects of the gods: the trident on the head of the divinity is a unique representation from the two former Celtic settlements, which might indicate a visual appropriation of the water (Danube) and the celestial (hills, mountains) aspects of the supreme god.[327] In this case, the two divinities attested on the Pfaffenberg and the Gellérthegy indicate a pre-Roman divinity that had been reinvented and reappropriated in the new context of Roman public religion and an Imperial cult. Following the hypothesis of Michael Sage, however, the cult of the Jupiter on the Pfaffenberg is related to one of the divinations of Emperor Hadrian from June 129 AD, which he experienced in Anatolia on Mount Casius[328] and that he associated with Jupiter (Zeus) Kasios.[329] This event – together with the cult of Antinoos and the activity of Lucius Aelius Caesar in Carnuntum – gives a much more interesting context for the sacralised space on the Pfaffenberg, where memorialisation of Imperial divination and religious individualisation, and oriental and Germanic religious traditions seem to be united in a very intriguing form of communication.

Rural, civilian *vici* and *pagi* also represent an important environment for much slower and individualised religious transformations.[330] A well-attested and -documented transformation in the rural environment comes from Budaörs, one of the *vici* from the *territorium pagi Herculius*,[331] an Eraviscan Celtic environment.[332] The late La Tène ceramic material shows the existence of a small, Celtic settlement (with an estimated 70 inhabitants),[333] which went on to be transformed radically in the following two centuries. The presence of the so-called 'Dacian cup' among the usual pottery might represent an intense economic relationship with the Dacians that was already in existence in the pre-Roman period and that probably continued even afterwards.[334] The topography and rich architectural landscape of the *vicus* shows at least two major monumentalisation phases: in the 2nd century AD and during the period of Septimius Severus.[335] The small rural settlement was radically changed in the early phase of transition alone. More than 200 architectural structures were attested in the village, three times more than in the pre-Roman phase. The publishers of the settlement monograph presented very concisely the possible 'sanctuaries' of the settlement,[336] although the only evidence for space sacralisation is the altars dedicated to Jupiter, Hercules and Terra Mater.[337]

Ottományi Katalin presumed that the presence of these altars proves the existence of public sanctuaries dedicated to the above-mentioned divinities, however the few case studies from rural environments where altars have been identified in situ reflects not macro-spaces of religious communication but mezzo-spaces of small groups or micro-spaces of individuals. The altars date to the late 2nd and 3rd centuries AD, therefore there is no evidence of pre-Roman religious activity. The cult of Terra Mater and Hercules were associated, though, with a pre-Roman, indigenous divine agency that was subsequently reinvented and appropriated, especially after the 2nd century AD, in Celtic settlements of Pannonia.[338]

The cult of Silvanus has since the work of Domaszewski been considered the most important local, indigenous divine agency of Pannonia and was reappropriated in numerous forms during the Principate.[339] Silvanus is the second most popular divinity of the two provinces of Pannoniae after Jupiter (Fig. A16 in the Appendices), with more than 330 votive inscriptions attested to him in Pannonia Inferior and Superior.[340] I. Tóth proved in his detailed study that the iconographic variations of Silvanus in Pannonia cannot be divided into the two major categories established by the previous studies: the epigraphic denomination and the iconographic attributes of Silvanus Domesticus and Silvanus Silvestris are often confused and used simultaneously, and we cannot clearly distinguish the two forms of Silvanus – a fact that led Tóth correctly to the conclusion that these variations between the divine names and visual narratives do not necessarily reflect two different divine agents but are instead vivid examples of religious individualisation and appropriation, especially in primary, micro-spaces of sacralisation.[341]

Older literature associated the Illyrian cult of Vidasus with the cult of Silvanus, which was also present in Pannonia as one of the numerous divine agents behind the conventional Roman epithet.[342] It is not inconceivable that there was indigenous religious knowledge behind these forms of Silvanus, but the new visual strategies used by the worshippers and the variety of the divine names indicates a strong religious appropriation, where the previous religious knowledge and tradition probably remained only in the form of a personal experience and the new forms of expression were already associated with a 'Roman' type of religious practice.[343]

The indigenous, pre-Roman aspects of Silvanus can however be attested in the *magnus* epithet of the god and the dedications dated 11 June, which we have discussed above in the context of Jupiter Karnuntinus and Teutanus. A large altar (86 cm high) was dedicated to Silvanus Magnus by Claudius Maximus on 11 June 237 AD – the same day that an altar was dedicated to Jupiter Teutanus on the Gellérthegy.[344] A fragmentarily preserved altar from Savaria mentions the *Dii Augurales* (Silvanus, Apollo, Mercurius and Belenus).[345] Géza Alföldy associated this inscription with local oracular traditions (Pannonian *augures*).[346] I. Tóth, by contrast, associated the oracular aspects of Silvanus with pre-Roman traditions from the Alpine and sub-Alpine regions (hilltop oracular sanctuaries) but without solid archaeological arguments.[347] Oracular traditions were also associated with Faunus in archaic and Republican traditions.[348] If we accept the hypothesis of Wissowa (followed also by Dorcey) – that Faunus is the official, public divine agent of the same divinity that was worshipped in mezzo- and micro-spaces of sacralisation dedicated to the various forms of Silvanus – it seems plausible that the great onomastic variety of the divinity represents not only pre-Roman traditions in transformation but also a contrast between archaic Roman and later traditions.

Fig. 2.11 Relief of Silvanus in Aquincum. (Source: Lupa 10482, photo of Ortolf Harl, with the special permission of the directorate of Aquincum Museum, Budapest)

The confusion and religious memory distortion of Varro and Augustinus himself on the nature of the god Silvanus shows a great range of religious appropriations in mezzo- and micro-spaces, where religious individualisation was very flexible and produced numerous forms and strategies in naming and using the divine agency in local contexts.[349] The research study of Silvanus in the Danubian provinces therefore shows the struggle of a scholarship familiarised with monotheistic traditions to recreate a metahistory of ancient religious traditions and a 'pantheon' that perhaps never existed: to create order in the religious fluidity of polytheism, especially present in mezzo- and micro-spaces, where Roman law was less severe in religious practice and experience (Fig. 2.11) than it was in public or macro-spaces. This fact also makes it difficult to identify the sacralised spaces dedicated to Silvanus in urban and especially rural contexts (cat. nos III.45, III.60, III.65, V.3, V.8, VI.42, VI.48).[350]

Inscriptions mentioning the major rivers using their pre-Roman, indigenous names are present in a Roman provincial context in Pannonia (especially inscriptions dedicated to Danuvius, Dravus, Savus and Agaunus),[351] however these cults seem to be Roman inventions and traditions, at least in terms of their materiality, without any traces of pre-Roman activities (based on Latin votive inscriptions, altars in Roman administrative landscape and ports).[352]

Spring cults and healing sanctuaries were also interpreted in older literature as vivid examples of religious continuities from pre-Roman times.[353] The archaeological evidence from the few well-attested cases of spring cults (cat. nos I.33, II.45, III.15–28, V.11) show no traces of pre-Roman, late La Tène activity. In the earliest phases, the epigraphic material and the monumentalisation of the sites indicate the radical transformation of the natural environment in Aquae Iasae, which was the most important provincial pilgrimage site and bath centre,[354] but a similar, regional spring cult centre can also be presumed to have existed near Tata/Neszmély.[355]

Pre-Roman divinities, such as Aecorna, were transferred and reappropriated as tools of cultural identity and imagined communities formed in urban diasporas, for example the Emonian community living in Savaria.[356] The Nutrices are also considered to be among the most prominent local divinities of Pannonia. Their presence is attested especially in Poetovio, where more than 40 figurative monuments have been connected with the various forms of religious communication with this divine agency.[357] Marjeta Šašel-Kos presumed at least three sacralised spaces where this cult was attested in Poetovio (cat. nos III.63–64). The origin of the three divinities is uncertain: it has often been interpreted as a Celtic religious tradition that was reappropriated during the period of the Roman administration, gaining a classical iconographic programme and visual narrative that echoes the iconography of the Celtic Matres or even the pre-Roman Italic fertility cults of Mater Matuta (Fig. 2.12).[358] The original stories, which were certainly essential in the creation and maintenance of these popular local cults, are unknown: the range of expansion of these local appropriations is limited to the administrative unit of the province (the furthermost example of the Nutrices was discovered in Parndorf, near Carnuntum).[359]

In some cases – such as in Parndorf – the material evidence suggests an individualised religious communication in a micro-space. The size of the miniature altar (24 cm in height) suggests a personal ex-voto or a domestic shrine in this case. Šašel Kos presumed that the few examples of the Nutrices outside of Poetovio might indicate a Poetovian diaspora within the limits of the province. In this case, the cult of the Nutrices was related not only to their original divine agency as fertility gods but also to a cultural and topographic identity. A particular case study – attested only on a hapax inscription – came from a funerary inventory: a ceramic vessel discovered in a tomb from the western cemetery of Poetovio (probably 2nd century AD) bears

Fig. 2.12 Relief of the Nutrices in Poetovio, Ptuj. (Source: Lupa 8763, photo of Ortolf Harl, with the special permission of the Pokrajinski muzej Ptuj – Ormoz)

graffiti in a unique, probably Celtic-Etruscan writing or a local form of the Venetic language.[360] The inscription mentions the name of Brogdos, identified as a god of borders and limits. The object proved that Celtic groups or individuals certainly used their religious traditions even in the 2nd–3rd centuries AD.[361]

András Mócsy rightly observed in the 1990s that one of the specificities of Roman Pannonia is the lack of indigenous, pre-Roman divinities in the epigraphic, iconographic and archaeological material, in strong contrast with the well-documented Celtic provinces (Gallia, Britannia and Germania).[362] However, the lack of material evidence for pre-Roman divine agency does not reflect the erroneous presumption of the total disappearance of pre-Roman religious landscape, but rather a quick and unusually successful process of the *interpretatio Romana* or 'Romanisation' of gods.[363] This process was neither imposed as a political agenda, nor was it likely controlled by religious entrepreneurs. Instead, as the few case studies presented above demonstrate, it was a silent, but long-term, transformation and appropriation in the indigenous communities.

The Dacian paradox: traces of pre-Roman religion in Dacia[364]

In most of the Roman provinces conquered by Rome, sacralised spaces show a continuity in use in Roman times, suggesting that the indigenous population and local groups were left to create and maintain their own Roman culture as they wanted.[365] In order to discuss 'continuity' of a sanctuary and sacralised space, however, some terminological clarification is necessary.[366] Recent discourses emphasise the existence of *longue durée* interaction and continuous transformation of both natural and cultural landscapes from prehistoric times until now, which dissolve the old problem of ethnic or cultural continuities.

One needs to distinguish the continuous existence (maintenance) of the site as sacralised space in two different political or administrative units, or epochs, and the continuity of use of the spaces.[367] The first refers only to the maintenance of a topographic unit or the continuity of sacralisation itself, while the second also presumes the continuity of communities, the memory of the sacred, and the practice of similar rituals and divinities. As Eleanor Ghey's study highlighted through the examples from Roman Gaul, even the first category – the continuous use of a place in two different epochs – is problematic to prove through archaeological methods and data, especially via architectural features.[368] Each case, however, requires human agency to maintain the site as a sacralised one and keep alive a religious narrative, *i.e.* the memory of the sacred. In most cases, then, the indigenous population played the most important role in the continuity of use of pre-Roman sacralised spaces.[369]

Before the Roman conquest, the territory of the later province was covered with sanctuaries and sacralised spaces, more than 50 of them being known so far from the pre-Roman period.[370] Many of these sites, such as the sanctuaries from Sarmizegetusa Regia, the capital of the Dacian kingdom, had already existed for centuries, and were also known from Roman literary sources.[371] The interpretation of the so-called 'sacred area' from Sarmizegetusa Regia was, however, recently questioned and contested, reflecting the problematic state of the archaeology of religion in Romania and, generally, in the Late Iron Age in Central-Eastern Europe.[372]

The main problem, however, is the lack of written sources,[373] with very little being known about the divinities and religious narratives of the Dacians even before the conquest of the region.[374] Until now, archaeology could not prove any kind of religious activity (identical or even different from that attested in Dacian times) in the known Dacian cult sites after 106 AD.[375] Not only was the cult site abandoned as an architectural entity, but, apparently, cultic activity also stopped at the 50 sites known from before the conquest.[376] Similarly, studies of the so-called '*interpretatio*

Dacica' through epigraphic sources failed to prove with certainty the continuity and survival of Dacian divinities in Roman society.[377]

While in other provinces the research on continuity focuses on the limits and alternatives of religious and cultural appropriation and acculturation in a much more local and smaller unit than a province,[378] the case of the Dacians seems to be more complicated.[379] Defining Dacian 'ethnicity' or 'cultural identity' is already a problem: the variety of tribes named in literary sources and associated later with artificially constructed 'Geto-Dacian society' shows that in the age of Decebalus, numerous different ethnic and even political military groups existed in the region.[380] Their religiosity, material culture and 'identity' probably therefore show a correspondingly great variety, as similar case studies have proved for Gaul.[381]

Based on the sporadic literary sources regarding the conquest and the fate of the Dacians, various historiographic traditions (especially the Austro-Hungarian and German literature) emphasised the almost complete 'extermination' of the indigenous population – a theory that is no longer accepted.[382] Recently, the epigraphic and archaeological evidence seems to have slightly changed this aspect. The presence of Dacian pottery and material produced within the Roman settlements,[383] the growing volume of epigraphic evidence on indigenous individuals,[384] and the possible existence of autonomous *vici* near the auxiliary forts[385] seem to prove that in the rural environment, the Dacians remained a distinct presence, if not a significant element of the society.[386] A detailed analysis and comparison with other similar societies in which the indigenous population is invisible in the onomastics needs to be carried out by future research.[387]

To understand the 'Dacian paradox' and its total absence from the archaeological and epigraphic evidence in sacralised spaces, it is essential to highlight some particular aspects of the Dacian religion before the conquest itself. The divinities and mythological figures appear mostly in the material evidence of the higher elite of the Dacian society, such as expensive helmets, militaria, fibulae or silver vessels.[388] Similarly, a monumentalised and public architecture as sacralised space can be attested in very few cases,[389] which suggests that the greatest part of the society, even before the conquest, experienced Dacian religion in a much more private, domestic way with an ephemeral materiality and less visible agency.[390] This could be exemplified by the appropriation of the indigenous religion of the Americans facing the first generation of Christian (Spanish) conquest:[391] the materiality of their religious life consisted mostly of wooden houses, private practices and ephemeral objects, such as wooden totems, textiles and clay figurines, whereas the new power marked the landscape consciously with monumentalised architectural forms. The attitude of the Dacians towards the 'Roman way' of religious experience seems to have been ignored by the remaining Dacians in the province.[392] The epigraphic habit and practice of marking the landscape with inscribed stones or engraved stone monuments – a specificity for the high and middle classes of Roman society – doesn't exist before the conquest and required a certain social and economic status.

Another important factor, which can explain the 'Dacian paradox', is the possible existence of human sacrifices among the Dacian warrior elite.[393] Both factors were totally incompatible with Roman society. Human sacrifice, although practised by Romans until mid-Republican times as the ultimate solution in desperate times,[394] was later associated with the Carthaginians and the Gauls, the traditional arch-enemies of Rome, and used against them as a political discourse of 'otherness' and 'barbarism'.[395] Similarly, the incompatible nature of ancient Jewish monotheism with the Roman law and the Imperial cult was often criticised using the Canaanite tradition of human sacrifices.[396]

The stereotypical nature of the warrior elite of the Dacians represented on Trajan's Column and emphasised by the literary sources seems to contribute to a self-decapitation of their society: an important part of the elite died in the two wars, while numerous others would follow their king in death. Due to these factors and characteristics of the Dacian society, instead of 'competition or interaction between two cultures [...] that supplanted earlier Roman cultures just as much as it did the earlier cultures of indigenous peoples',[397] the case of Dacia seems to be an anomaly for the new definitions of Romanisation.[398]

All of these factors could have shaped the attitude of the Romans towards the religions of the Dacians. It seems obvious that something different happened there compared to most of the provinces: there are no traces of Dacian elite in Roman times, no indigenous divinities, no continuity of practice, or, at least, architectural use of most of the sanctuaries and sacralised spaces that have thus far been attested. Another relevant argument is the research history in Romania, which has ignored until now the archaeology of montane areas, where pre-Roman settlements might have survived in rural contexts, as the case study of Moesia Inferior might indicate.[399]

A case study that shows the conscious transformation of the indigenous natural world and religious milieu of the Dacians was found in the Sub Cununi and Piatra points of Grădiștea Muncelui. In the early 19th century, two important votive altars were discovered in the area, where a possible Roman fort was also identified and dated to after the first Dacian war:

> *A[p]ollin(i) / Aug(usto) L(ucius) Ae/m[i]l(ius) Car[us] / [leg(atus)] Aug(usti) / pr(o) pr(aetore) / [II] I Da[c(iarum)]*[400]
> *Victoriae / Aug(ustae) pro sa/lute Imp(eratoris) / Antonini / Aug(usti) M(arcus) Sta/tius Pris/cus legatus / eius pr(o) pr(aetore)*[401]

While Gábor Téglás presumed that the presence of the altars was related to iron production and saw a continuity in the use of the sacralised natural environment,[402] later studies presumed the existence of a memorial place (*tropaeum*) for the victory over the Dacians here.[403] The two altars dedicated by two governors of the provinces, M. Statius Priscus and K. Aemilius Carus, were commemorating the victory of the Romans in the most sacred place of the Dacians. It is uncertain whether the place where the altars were erected was a sanctuary or a triumphal monument dedicated to Trajan, but the presence of Victoria Augusta and Apollo Augustus shows clearly the Imperial authority, which consciously transformed a Dacian symbolic place into a sacred memory of the Roman victory.

The presence of two altars 50 and 70 years after Trajan's victory thus demonstrates the successful maintenance of the sanctuary or memorial place in Grădiștea Muncelui, which transformed and consciously eliminated the indigenous presence and cultural memory of the Dacians. This only occurred, however, in a place that was already essential for the Roman power elite after the first war of Trajan in AD 102.[404] Similar acts of transformation and religious propaganda cannot be attested in rural or domestic environments in the Trajanic province of Dacia. Possible Dacian divinities and communities were attested, though, south of the Danube, where some votive inscriptions were dedicated to Heros Isasemes, Theos Itiosaros, Theos Kaprenos and Hero Itiosla and were associated with the Dacians.[405]

Reinvented religious traditions and new appropriations: the case of Moesia Superior and Inferior

The integration of the territories south of the Danube and north of the Balkan mountains began in 29–27 BC with the campaign of M. Licinius Crassus and ended in 86 AD when the province of Moesia was divided into two different political entities, Moesia Superior and Moesia Inferior.[406] In the Julio-Claudian period, the Danube had already become a militarised area of the Empire. There are 11 inscriptions dated possibly in the period between 27 BC and 68 AD, most of them from the period of Claudius.[407] Some of the funerary or military inscriptions related to the fortress of the V Macedonica legion in Oescus were dated to the Claudian or post-Claudian period (44–65 AD), which suggests that the Danube was already being strongly controlled by Roman power in the 1st century AD.[408] From this period onwards, the religious landscape of Moesia and later, the two separate provincial entities, was transformed slowly.

Three major areas need to be interpreted separately because of their different cultural, ethnic and historical structure: 1) the former territory of the Dardani and Scordisci; 2) the territory of the Thracians and Getae; and 3) the Pontic cities. Religious appropriation and the invention of new forms of religious strategies, visual narratives and traditions had different mechanisms in these three cultural sub-units within the artificially created provincial limits. Religious traditions and their transformation are dependent especially on the mobility and interconnectivity of small groups: new religious forms (visual and textual innovations) appear in particular in urban environments, where the interconnectivity of the locals and newcomers are much more intense.[409]

The literature focusing on the autochthonous gods of Moesia Superior and Moesia Inferior tried to identify the *interpretatio Romana* in every unusual Latin or Greek epithet and associated the indigenous nature of a god with the hapax or unique reliefs and epigraphic attestations or unusual religious rituals.[410] The major methodological problem with the identification of the pre-Roman divinities in Roman Moesia is like that of the other provinces: the Latin text was ordered and carved by Roman citizens, *libertii* or, rarely, slaves, whose ethnic identity and *origo* is often hard to establish. The Latin epithet of the god is rarely a cultural/ethnic or geographic marker in these cases. In the absence of any knowledge of the gods or the pre-Roman pantheon of the Dardani, Scordisci, Dacians and Thracian groups in the two Moesiae, the identification of their gods in the Roman period is problematic.

An example is the difficult case of trying to identify the nature of Jupiter Optimus Maximus Paternus in Moesia Superior.[411] The divinity appears in various contexts, and is associated with both civilian urban and military personnel. The heterogenous nature of the inscriptions dedicated to this god (or gods?) makes it hard to identify whether this newly established textual form and new visuality of erecting an altar with an inscription – a certainly Roman way of establishing a dialogue with the divine agent in the 2nd century AD in this region – has something pre-Roman in its essence. The unique epithets and names of the gods from Naissus and the region of the Dardani (Andin(us), Dea Dardania, Zbeltiurdud, Deus Attonipal, Silvanus, Dracco and Draccena, Atta Sacra and Deus Mund[412]) were associated with ethnicity. Divine names are often interpreted as ethnic/cultural markers; however, the statistics show that in most cases, new textual constructions and strategies of naming the gods were in fact marking spatial aspects: the origin of the worshipper or the home of the divinity.

The case of Jupiter Paternus shows how a name of a possibly pre-Roman god was recreated in the new political and social context of a Roman province. Jupiter Paternus appears in one inscription as Paternus Aepilofius (!),[413] which has been interpreted as a Latinised version of Zeus Paternos.[414] Some authors identified this divinity with a Dardanian or Thracian indigenous god,[415] while others, such as Péter Kovács, argue that the epithet of *paternus* comes from the *dii patrii* of the cohort Maurorum and the African military groups established in the Danubian provinces.[416] In both cases, the *paternus* is an appropriation: in the first case, it is a linguistic reappropriation of the Greek-speaking Thracian-Dardanian communities, where local hilltop gods and celestial divinities (the Baals and Zeuses of the southern Danubian region) became Jupiters – paternal gods – reflecting an intimate relationship with the pre-Roman religious landscapes and traditions.[417] In the second hypothesis, the *paternus* epithet is a cultural appropriation that comes not from within the Thracian community, but from outside it. The great number of uses of the epithet *paternus* in the inscriptions of Moesia Superior – associated with Jupiter Dolichenus,[418] Sabazios,[419] Genius Daciarum[420] and as a separate divine entity[421] – reflects that it is wrong to associate this epithet with just one god or a single ethnic community: it is probably a local, regional appropriation of the divine agency, which might have a pre-Roman root, or else a central, paternal figure in the Dardani-Thracian pantheon that was transferred to almost all of the major divine agents addressed in religious communication by locals as well as newcomers.

The various forms of the Heros cult and the so-called 'Thracian Riders' (*Domna et Domnus*) cult also offer fascinating case studies of religious appropriations and reinvented traditions. In this case, there are few modifications in religious communication after the Roman conquest: the Hellenistic traditions had already changed the strategies of communication between human and divine. Epigraphic habits, public temples in macro-spaces and portable, small material tools were already part of the space sacralisation in the former kingdom of Thracia. Funerary art and the hero cults were also well known from the pre-Roman period in the territory of late Moesia Inferior.[422] The religious landscape and its constitutive elements (the materiality of religion used in space sacralisation, the visual and textual narratives, the architectural forms of sacralised spaces) had a well-established tradition in the later territory of Moesia Inferior. The long-lasting coexistence and appropriation of Thracian and Hellenistic art in this region created numerous visual programmes and bricolages, which changed only in small details after the political transformations and major population mobilities of the 1st century AD.

The best example for this is the so-called cult of the 'Thracian Riders' (*Domna et Domnus*), a contemporary notion marking a large variety of hero cults in the Thracian region (Moesia Inferior and Thrace).[423] The origin of these cults and the common religious and visual features have been analysed numerous times in the last century. Recent trends claim that the 'Thracian Riders' is not even a single cult, but a cultural phenomenon that united the Greek-Hellenistic cult of Bacchus-Orpheus, the Thracian royal funerary cult and the visual language and material tools of the Greek and Scythian art.[424] The rich variety of the inscriptions associated with the 'Thracian Riders' reflects two major aspects missed by older literature and historiography: the regionality and locality of these cults; and their individual aspect in many cases, whereby the worshipper associated the cult with the locality (*origo*), regional traditions and their individual religious choices. Such a case was well documented and presented by Dragana Grbić through the inscriptions dedicated to Deus Totovitio and Diana Totobisia, a regional cult attested in Singidunum, Naissus, Diana and Viminacium.[425]

The individual choices involved in the maintenance and transformation of pre-Roman divinities are more significant than had previously been emphasised. Divinities such as Ata,[426] Casebonus,[427] Dea Dardanica,[428] Deus Mundtritus[429] and Deus Zbelsurdos[430] were traditionally interpreted as 'indigenous' cults of the Thracians, Moesi, Dardani and Scordisci. Without literary and archaeological sources on the pre-Roman religious landscape, we cannot reconstruct the major steps of transformation of the divine agency, but the language of the inscriptions (mostly Latin, partially Greek in Moesia Inferior), the new name construction of the divinities (often artificially created, such as Dea Dardanica) and the new visual narrative (iconographic programme, as cultural bricolage) associated with these 'indigenous' divinities reflects the appropriation of a local elite or emerging Roman social strata (in particular, the military, as the rising lower/middle class of the Roman social pyramid[431]). The onomastic appropriations can be attested also in the cult of the recently identified Dinithia and the Heros Hephaistos from Zaldapa/Telerig (cat. no. V.26).[432]

Therefore, these new divine constructions were not only reinvented religious traditions and not necessarily continuations of a pre-Roman religious landscape, but they also reflected an Imperial ideology, whereby the new provincial society and its newly forming elite were eager to became 'Roman' while also wishing to preserve their local identity. This glocalisation of religious communication is well reflected by the phenomena of the 'Thracian Riders', the case of Dea Dardanica or the various Genii of the provinces (Genius Daciarum, for example).[433]

For a long time, the so-called 'Danubian Riders' (*Domna et Domnus*) cult was also considered to be direct evidence of the *interpretatio Romana* and the reappropriation of indigenous pre-Roman divinities.[434] The notion itself is a modern construction, as has been demonstrated numerous times, most recently by Ádám Szabó and Richard Gordon.[435] A large proportion of the materiality of religious communication labelled as belonging to the 'Danubian Riders' (*Domna et Domnus*) cult consists of small, portable objects with a rich variety and a well-established, programmatic iconography, which indicates a 'story line' or central 'myth' as one of the key strategies for success of small-group religions of the Principate.[436] The narrative itself is hard to reconstruct, but the detailed analysis of its elements and major features partially reflects a pre-Roman visual heritage and the reappropriation of the iconographic programme of the Roman Mithras cult, Sabazios cult, and Greek and Thracian traditions as well.[437]

This visual narrative, thanks to the presence of religious bricolage, was also identified in the case of the Roman cult of Mithras,[438] which seems to have been in close relationship with the cult(s) of the 'Danubian Riders' (*Domna et Domnus*) (Fig. 2.13).[439] Most of the material evidence related to this religious phenomenon has no archaeological context, although the material is concentrated in the area of Sirmium, Viminacium and Sucidava – the border of Moesia Superior-Dacia-Moesia Inferior.[440] For the few cases in which the archaeological context is known, the evidence mostly reflects a domestic and funeral milieu.[441] In a recently identified case (Quadrata), the small portable object representing the female divinity with her acolytes bears the inscription '*Domino*' (*Dominus*).[442]

Ádám Szabó argued that the case study of Quadrata is proof that the 'Danubian Riders' (*Domna et Domnus*) cult is related to all the inscriptions that carry the *Domna et Domnus* or *Domina et Dominus* formulae, especially in the Danubian area, identifying the central female divinity with the anonymous *Domna* or *Domina* and the male counterpart (possibly an Illyrian or indigenous solar deity) with *Domnus* or *Dominus*.[443] Based on a certain iconographic type, Szabó – following István Tóth's work and theory on the same topic – argued, that the central divine figure of the 'Danubian Riders' (*Domna et Domnus*) cult is not the female goddess, as was thought for a long time, but in fact a solar divinity.[444] According to Tóth's hypothesis, the cult of an indigenous

Fig. 2.13 Lead votive plaque representing the so-called 'Danubian Riders'. (Photo: Manfred Clauss, EDCS-44200062). Open access

solar divinity consitutes the basis of the cult of Mithras and the 'Danubian Riders' (*Domna et Domnus*) as well.[445]

Some of the small plaques and stone reliefs of the cult indeed reflect a well-established iconographic hierarchy of the imagined divine spaces and agents:[446] the upper register – where the *Dominus* inscription appears on the Quadrata plaque – is dominated by the figure of a solar male divinity (interpreted by Tóth as an indigenous Illyrian Sol Invictus).[447] The secondary register is inhabited by the female figure and the two riders (probably the Dioscuri).[448] This might indeed prove that the central figures of this cult – if we can talk here about 'a cult' and not a complex glocal tradition, as Richard Gordon suggested[449] – were not the Riders, but the major solar divinity. Moreover, the iconographic complexity and variations of these plaques indicated several appropriated visual narratives, which had been changed and shaped probably by the owner and the workshop, too.[450]

The discovery of the temple of *Dii Maiores Domnus et Domna*[451] in the *extra muros* sacred area of Colonia Sarmizegetusa (cat. no. VI.37)[452] prompted two major questions: 1) can this sanctuary be related to the famous portable plaques and the few reliefs dedicated to the 'Danubian Riders' (*Domna et Domnus*); and 2) is this divine pair identical to the mysterious *Dii Magni* of Gorsium?[453] Recently, Manfred Heinzmann and Florian Matei-Popescu argued that the *Dii Magni* and *Dii Maiores* formulae always referred to Asclepius and Hygeia,[454] whereas Gabrielle Kremer argued that in the case of the sanctuary in Sarmizegetusa, the *Dii Maiores* refers to Liber and Libera.[455] In addition to the modern myth of the 'Danubian Riders' (*Domna et Domnus*), Timea Varga accepted the hypothesis of I. Tóth and Á. Szabó and associated the cult of Domna and Domnus with small, terracotta figures representing a seated couple.[456] Following indirectly the ideas of Tóth, S. Hijmans argued recently that the cult of Mithras was 'the Roman', global version of a religious practice and communication strategy between human and divine agents, while the 'Danubian Riders' (*Domna et Domnus*) cult can be interpreted as a 'local', popular religious manifestation or ramification of the Mithraic cult.[457]

The common points between the theories of Tóth, Szabó and Hijmans are the iconographic similarities and the interconnected visual language of the two cults. It is unquestionable that numerous elements, divinities or figures are present in both categories of material. The epigraphic evidence of the *Domna et Domnus* couple is indeed concentrated especially in the Danubian area, which might suggest the regional origin or affinity of this cult. This regionality of the epigraphic evidence (if we accept that all the *Domna et Domnus* and *Dii Maiores* inscriptions are related to the same divine couple) also overlaps with the regionality of the lead plaques discovered predominantly in Dacia, Moesia Superior, Moesia Inferior and Pannonia. The hypothetical arguments are strong, but the archaeology is weak: there is only a single documented context in which a portable plaque was found with the inscription of *Domna et Domnus* in a sacralised space. This case of Winden am See presented by Gabrielle Kremer shows a small, sacralised space (meso-space) in a rural environment, near a Roman villa, where the lead plaque with the inscription of *Domna et Domnus* was discovered together with other material tools used in space sacralisation: an altar for Jupiter Optimus Maximus, a dedication for the nymphs, Liber, Libera, a Genius and a cult vessel depicting a snake.[458]

This archaeological context is strikingly similar to the one from the Liber Pater shrine in Apulum,[459] which also contained a votive plaque with the mysterious – and misinterpreted – reading of IDR III.5, 371, read by R. Gordon as '*comes tibi so(m)*'.[460] If Gordon's reading is correct, the cases of Apulum and Winden am See represent two analogies where the small lead pieces of the 'Danubian Riders' (*Domna et Domnus*) were found in meso-spaces dedicated to a *collegium* of Liber Pater.[461] A possible case study might be also attested in the 1980s in Carnuntum.[462] It seems to be a pattern that these small, portable objects were present in numerous contexts (funerary, Bacchium) and were produced in various forms and typologies in the major political, military and commercial centres of the Danubian provinces, such as Carnuntum and Sirmium.[463] The struggle to identify the divine agency behind the mystery of the *Dominus et Domina* (*Domna et Domnus*) inscriptions represents more a historiographic struggle and speaks less of the complex polytheistic interconnectivities (a divine *synnaoi theoi*) between divine agency combined in meso-spaces and also in the visual and textual narratives. The few inscribed plaques bearing the inscription of '*comes tibi som*' also indicates the memorialisation of a pilgrimage, possibly to one of the major religious centres of the cult of *Domna et Domnus* (or Liber and Libera).

***

The aim of this chapter was to present a short selection of pre-Roman religious case studies from the Danubian provinces, focusing especially on neglected aspects in historiography, such as the impact of commercial routes and macro-spaces before the Roman conquest in the creation, maintenance and transformation of sacralised spaces, visual narratives (iconographies) and religious entrepreneurs.[464] The case studies in Raetia, Noricum, Pannoniae, Dacia and Moesiae represents a large variety of often contradictory examples of religious appropriations, but are vivid examples for reinvented religious traditions, where Roman imperialism, individual choices of the new, emerging elite and influential religious entrepreneurs also played a crucial role in transforming and therefore saving the pre-Roman religious traditions, especially in Celtic and Hellenistic environments.

Notes

1 Strabo, 7.5.1 τὰ Ἰλλυρικά; App. Ill. 1, 6; Pliny, NH 3.139 *nunc totum uno nomine Illyricum vocatur generatim* ('now, the whole is called with one name – Illyricum'): Dzino 2010, 3.
2 See Chapter 1 on the history of the notion.
3 See the methodological approach of the book in Chapter 1.
4 The region also shows numerous similarities in climatic and geographic terms. See: Miklós 2010.
5 Frei-Stolba 1984; Frei-Stolba 1991; Woolf 2011.
6 Maurus Servius Honoratus, Commentary on the Georgics of Vergil 2.95; Dalby 2000, 90.
7 Bezeczky 1998.
8 Livy V.33.11. For a complete analysis of the literary sources and the topographic aspects, see: Marzatico 2019.
9 Pliny, *Natural History* III.24. On the origins of the Etruscans, see also: Posth *et al.* 2021.
10 CIL V 7817; Šašel 1972.

11 AÉ 1973, 323; AÉ 1999, 0995; AÉ 2002, 899; AÉ 2005, 958.
12 For a detailed attempt to map these groups, see: Strobel 2009, 444, ab.1. after R. v. Uslar.
13 Schmidts 2005.
14 Dietz 2004. See also: Rapin 2021.
15 Idem, 18 list no. 5; Roymans-Derks 2009, 244. See also: Steinacher 2019.
16 Marchesini 2013, 74–78.
17 Tomedi 2017, 193–194.
18 Marchesini-Roncador 2015.
19 Marchesini-Roncador 2016, 268–270.
20 Trixl *et al.* 2017.
21 Idem, 277–178.
22 Rieckhof-Pauli 1985, 15–17.
23 Grabherr 2006.
24 Staudt 2010.
25 Marzatico 2019, 78, Fig. 8.
26 Idem, 75–77 and 79, Fig. 9.
27 Metzner-Nebelsick *et al.* 2017; Trixl *et al.* 2017.
28 On the problem of the notion, see: Unruh 2000; Gleirscher 2002; Marzatico 2014, 315; Ballmer 2017; Oberrauch 2019.
29 Trixl *et al.* 2017.
30 Marzatico 2019, 77, Fig. 7.
31 Idem, Fig. 6.
32 Gleirscher 2002, 218–263, Ballmer 2017, 75.
33 Marzatico 2014, 316, Fig. 4.
34 Ballmer 2017, 74–75.
35 Marzatico 2014, 316, Fig. 4.
36 Fontijn 2002. See also: Fontijn 2007.
37 The ingenious study of Ballmer omits the anthropological analogies and examples of transhumant animal trade and mountain mobilities from historical times (18–19th centuries) and the oral transition of knowledge of agricultural socieities. Ballmer 2017. For a detailed analysis of agricultural and botanical knowledge transfer in this area, see: Grabherr 2009.
38 Ballmer 2017, 84–85.
39 See next subchapter on Pannoniae.
40 Ballmer 2017, 86.
41 Arnold 2014, 25.
42 Tecchiati 2018, 214–215.
43 For recent research on Alpine sacrificial places, see: Putzer 2011.
44 Heiss 2010.
45 Glerischer 2002, 176.
46 For another example for fibula dedication, see: Marchesini-Roncador 2015, 50.
47 Hye 2013.
48 Marchesini-Roncador 2015, 21–22.
49 Marchesini 2012.
50 Marzatico 2012, 327.
51 Wendling 2013, 464.
52 http://www.oppida.org/page.php?lg=fr&rub=00&id_oppidum=77. Last accessed: 25.08.2020.
53 Wendling 2013, 467–468.
54 Boutsikas 2020, 5–6. For Sarmizegetusa Regia, see: Stănescu 2014; Oprea-Oprea 2015.
55 Wendling 2013, 468.

56 Idem, 482. There are no traces of space sacralisation and functional or spatial continuities after 15 BC: Sommer 2008, 214. See also: Trixl *et al.* 2017.
57 Alföldy 1974. See also: Woolf 2004, 423.
58 Alföldy 1974, XXI.
59 Alföldy 1966, Alföldy 1974, 15. See also: Eichner *et al.* 1994, 138.
60 Idem, 18, Fig. 1.
61 Idem, 26–27.
62 A similar process happened much later with the Dacian tribes, who were united under the rule of a central tribe of Burebista. See the next pages on Dacia.
63 Idem, 43–44.
64 Urban 2006, 94; Artner 2007, 17. See also: Gleirscher 2005.
65 Artner 2007, 26. For an analogy, see: Gleirscher 2015, 138.
66 Alföldy 1974, 17 and 34.
67 Eiter-Reiter 2011, 70–71; Gleirscher 2015, 142.
68 Tiefengraber-Tiefengraber 2019, 105.
69 CIL III 14366: *Iovenat / Aug(usto) / Attia Ing(e) / nua v(otum) s(olvit)*
70 Kohler-Schneider *et al.* 2015.
71 Idem, 536.
72 Opreanu 2015; Opreanu 2019.
73 Alföldy 1974, 44–45. See especially: Strobel 2012; Handy 2016; Nagy 2016, 160.
74 For the enormous literature on the city, see: Gostenčik-Schindler 2019.
75 For more on the so-called 'Noreia question' of the Austrian historiography, see: Strobel 2003; Strobel 2012, 26–27.
76 Glaser 2004, 91.
77 Alföldy 1974, 45.
78 Bezeczky 1998, 225; Gostenčik 2018.
79 Alföldy 1974, 43.
80 Gallego Franco 1997; Gostenčik 2018, 26–27.
81 Alföldy 1974, 44–45 especially footnotes nos 33 and 34; Gleirscher 2007, 114; Gleirscher 2015, 196–197. See also: Dolenz 2009.
82 Gostenčik 2018, 23. Alföldy cites Egger, who suggested that the Magdalensberg *emporium* was founded after 88 BC when the Roman trading settlement from Delos was destroyed: Alföldy 1974, 41–45, footnote no. 37.
83 Bezeczky 1998.
84 Gregoratti 2015.
85 Dolenz 2011, 91, Fig. 2.
86 Dolenz-Strobel 2009, 4; Dolenz 2011, 90–91.
87 Dolenz 2007, cat. no. 52.
88 Dolenz 2011, 95.
89 Sedlmayer 2009, 232–235.
90 Glaser 2002; Dolenz-Strobel 2009, 4.
91 The exact location and the building hosting the statue is unknown.
92 Glaser 2002, 90, abb.1.
93 CIL III 4815/ AÉ 2000, 1152: *A(ulus) Poblicius D(ecimi) l(ibertus) Antioc(hus) / Ti(berius) Barbius Q(uinti) P(ubli) l(ibertus) Tiber(---) // M(arcus) Gallicinus Vindili f(ilius) L(ucius) Barb(ius) L(uci) l(ibertus) Philotaerus pr(ocurator) Craxsantus(!) Barbi P(ubli) s(ervus)*
94 Glaser 2002, 96–97.
95 Alföldy 1974, 46.
96 Zajac 1979, 60–61; Gostenčik 2018, 18.

97 Handy 2019, 59–60.
98 Dolenz 2011, 93, footnote no. 9.
99 Hofeneder 2010.
100 On the 'national gods' of the provinces, see: McMullen 1975.
101 On the notion of architectural landscape and atmosphere, see: Pallasmaa 2014; Maschek 2016.
102 Dolenz 2011, 95.
103 Alföldy 1974, 52.
104 Mócsy 1974a, 65.
105 For the most important works on the political (factual) and military history of the region, see: Mócsy 1974b; Mócsy-Fitz 1990; Dzino 2010; Kovács 2014; Szabó-Borhy 2015.
106 Szabó 2005.
107 For most detailed summary of the major linguistic changes in the region from the Celtic invasion until the Roman rule, see: Mócsy 1974a, 7–32. See also: Burns 2003, 194–200.
108 Idem, 65. A slightly different ethnic map: Šašel Kos 2013, 173 Fig. 3. See also the regionalisation of István Tóth: Tóth 2015, 19–20.
109 Dzino 2010. See also: Šašel Kos 2012.
110 Mócsy 1974a, 72.
111 For the major political changes of the region between 268 BC and 15 AD, see: Szabó 1990.
112 For the importance of long-distance economic mobilities, see: Woolf 2013.
113 Tóth 2015, 21, Fig. 1.
114 Mócsy 1974a, 14–19.
115 Tóth 2015, 22–23. See also: Holzer 2008, 405.
116 Melhard 1900; Thomas 1963; Tóth 2015, 23. For similar Luna decorations, see also the splendid funerary monument of a Norican woman from Lendorf-Klagenfurt: Lupa 851.
117 Melhard 1900, 386–388.
118 Thomas 1963, 75.
119 Petres 1976; Burns 2003, 195–200.
120 For analogies, see: Sireix *et al.* 2002.
121 Szabó 1963. For analogy, see: Tóth 2015, 34.
122 Rendic-Miocevic – Segvic 1998.
123 See the following subchapter on reinventing religious traditions.
124 Šašel Kos 1998.
125 Tóth 2015, 22–26.
126 Nagy 2016.
127 Tóth 2015, 33, Fig. 11.
128 Fitz 1998, 53; Szabó 2005, 100–101.
129 Haynes 2014; Szabó 2018b, 85.
130 Szabó 2005, 100. See also: Ardagna *et al.* 2004. Literary sources: Diod. Sic., xxxiv. 13; Strabo, iv. 4; Orosius, v. 16; Schol. on Lucan, Usener's ed. 32.
131 For analogies from pre-Roman Dacian case studies, see: Sîrbu-Dăvîncă 2020.
132 Petres 1972.
133 Szabó 2005, 100–101.
134 Horváth 2019.
135 Idem, 121.
136 Maumené 2016.
137 Ilon *et al.* 2001.
138 Fischl 1999, 133.
139 Webster 2015.
140 Fitz 1998, 53; Tóth 2015, 38–39.

141 Maráz 2007, 36.
142 Szabó 2005, 94–95. The altar discovered at the Tabán (Rezeda street 14.) is the only link between the cult of Teutanus and the metahistorical 'sanctuary' on the Gellérthegy (CIL III 10418). See also the following subchapter and the continuities of indigenous traditions in Pannonia.
143 Alaj 2019.
144 For an example for such intercultural and material appropriation, see: Egri-Rustoiu 2010.
145 Mócsy 1974b, 11.
146 Burton 2017, 28–30.
147 Mócsy 1974b, 12. For more on the Scordisci as a metahistorical notion and cultural 'reinvention', see: Mihajlovic 2019.
148 For Scordiscian cultural changes and conviviality, see: Egri-Rustoiu 2008. On mostly funerary rites and rituals and their cultural appropriations in Late Iron Age Balkans, see: Bereczki 2012. See also: Potrebica-Dizdar 2014.
149 Idem, 138. See also: Mihailevic-Dizdar 2007.
150 Dizdar-Radman-Livaja 2015.
151 Idem, 211. See also: Filipović 2010, 41. The author mentions: 'After excavation of the Roman strata and structures, numerous prehistoric finds were recorded, which are ascribed to a southern peripheral part of the settlement, the centre of which was on an elevation alongside the Drava. In research at the site of the Education Faculty the digs of numerous pits and dug outs were recorded, but the most important discovery was in the south east part of the excavations where the remains of an oval pit were found with finds of weaponry and human and animal bones. The remains of a ditch were picked out, containing fills with numerous finds of parts of weapons and riding equipment of the La Tene culture, while in somewhat smaller numbers there are parts of clothing, fragments of bronze vessels, parts of wheels and coins. Fragments of ceramic vessels were also found. The finds of weapons, equestrian gear and parts of wheels can be concluded not to have belonged to the ordinary part of the inventory of the Scordisci settlement. This was part of the settlement that had a special function. Very probably, these are finds that can be ascribed to the remains of a holy place or some other cult site the central part of which was in the immediate vicinity of the surface excavated, most likely on the eastern side. Because of the finds collected, the explored part of the settlement can be dated to the period of middle and late La Tene, that is, to the 2nd and 1st centuries BC'. A more detailed account of the sanctuary was published in: Dizdar-Filipović 2020.
152 Drnić 2014, 211.
153 Stojić 2003.
154 Rustoiu 2018, 29.
155 Florea 2020, 32–33. See also: Jones 1997.
156 Spânu 2013, 13.
157 Idem, 14, Fig. 1.
158 Popović 2011, 180, Fig. 3.
159 Spânu 2013, 13, Fig. 1.
160 Rustoiu-Egri 2014, 133, Fig. 8.
161 Kaul 2011.
162 A short summary of the region and its material heritage is in: Avram *et al.* 2004, 924–973.
163 Glodariu 1976; Ruscu 2004; Conovici 2006; Tsetskhladze 2015. See also: Preiser-Kapeller-Daim 2016.
164 Coja 1974.
165 Pippidi 1959.
166 Brîndușa 2019.
167 Alexandrescu-Vianu 1980. See also: Avram *et al.* 2004, 933–934.
168 Mârgineanu-Cârstoiu 1989; Rabadjiev 2017.

169 Brîndușa 2019, 131–158.
170 Domăneanțu 1993.
171 Lazarenko *et al.* 2013.
172 Porozhanov 2017.
173 ISM I.1. See also: Avram 1999; Buis 2014, 169.
174 Delev 2018.
175 Stoyanov 2000–2001, 219. The author claims, that 'after the collapse of the capital at Sboryanovo (= Helis?), the political and economic centre of the Getae returned to its previous locality in the region of Borovo. The concentration of coin imitations in the lower basin of Rousenski Lom in the 2nd-1st centuries BC have led D. Ivanov to suggest that the centre of political and economic life in the area was then based somewhere in the Pirgovo-Rousse-Nikolovo territory'.
176 Ruscu 2013, 15.
177 Dzino 2010 has the best synthesis on the expansion of Rome and the relationship of the empire with this area of Europe.
178 Idem, 19–20.
179 Talbert 2012.
180 Woolf 2011.
181 Mócsy 1974a, XIX. See also: Woolf 2004.
182 Dzino 2010, 44–80.
183 Rustoiu-Babes 2018; Metzner-Nebelsick 2018.
184 Woolf 2015, 473–474.
185 See the famous case of Bibracte and the Roman architectural influence in Gallia before the Roman conquest: Reddé *et al.* 2011.
186 Woolf 1995.
187 Diaz-Fernandéz 2021, 46–47.
188 On material ecology of the Roman Empire see: Woolf 2017.
189 The most detailed summary of this approach: Nemeti 2019, 31–73.
190 On the problem of continuties and discontinuities, see: Ghey 2007; King 2007; Szabó 2018b, 143.
191 Haeussler 2012.
192 Raja-Rüpke 2015, 16–18.
193 Busch-Versluys 2015.
194 Ardevan 2015.
195 See the methodological approach in the Introduction.
196 The literary sources are various, rich but repetitive and the details of the campaign of Drusus and Tiberius in 15 BC are still unknown: Von Schnurbein 1985, 17–18.
197 The Alpenfeldzug in German literature. For a complete bibliographic summary for the problem, see: Strobel 2009, 437–438.
198 Dietz 2004, 9.
199 Von Schnurbein 1985, 18. See also: Strobel 2009, 468–470.
200 Vell. 2.39.2: *at Ti. Caesar quam certam Hispanis parendi confessionem extorserat parens Illyriis Delmatisque extorsit. Raetiam autem et Vindelicos ac Noricos Pannoniamque et Scordiscos nou- as imperio nostro subiunxit prouincias. ut has armis, ita auctoritate Cappadociam populo Romano fecit stipendiariam* The notion of '*subiunxit*' doesn't mean necessarily a complete administrative reform but rather a successful military conquest or control of the region: Strobel 2009, 476.
201 Idem, 439–441.
202 Sommer 2008, 209.
203 Farkas 2015, 17.
204 Idem, 13. See also: Dietz 2004, 16.

205 Farkas 2015, 196–200. Compare also with the map of the earliest Roman cemeteries: Grünewald 2018, 164, abb.1.
206 Strobel 2009, 474.
207 Idem, 482–483.
208 CIL V 3936: *Q(uinto) Caicilio / Cisiaco Septicio / Picai(!) Caiciliano(!) / procur(atori) Augustor(um) et / pro leg(ato) provinciai(!) / Raitiai(!) et Vindelic(iai)(!) / et Vallis Poenin(ai!) auguri / flamini divi Aug(usti) et Romai(!) / C(aius) Ligurius L(uci) f(ilius) Vol(tinia) Asper / |(centurio) coh(ortis) I c(ivium) R(omanorum) ingenuor(um)*
209 Sommer 2008, 212–213.
210 Idem, 214, footnote no. 46.
211 Ditz 2004, 9.
212 Idem, 212. See also: Zanier 1999.
213 Trixl *et al.* 2017.
214 Schmidts 2005.
215 Zanier 1999, 147–149; Gleirscher 2001, 469; Sommer 2008, 212.
216 Trixl *et al.* 2017.
217 A complete analysis of the Roman-era *Brandopferplätze*: Gleirscher 2002, 197, abb.3.
218 Arnold 2014, 28, Fig. 1.2.
219 Idem, 26. See also: Tschurtschenthaler 2010.
220 Niederwanger 2002.
221 Zanier 2016, 46. See also: Haupt 2016, 400.
222 Zanier 2016, 47.
223 Keppie 2000, 161–166.
224 Gleirscher 2002, 197, abb.3.
225 Sommer 2008.
226 Schimdts 2005.
227 Höck *et al.* 1997; Gugl 2001, 315.
228 Gleirscher 2002, 227–228.
229 Höck *et al.* 1997, 174.
230 See also: Versluys 2014; Busch-Versluys 2015.
231 Gleirscher 2002, 197.
232 Alföldy 1974, 52.
233 Handy 2016.
234 Stempel-Hainzmann 2020, 18–19.
235 Ciglenecki 2016.
236 Stempel-Hainzmann 2020, 92.
237 Rives 2001, 430.
238 Stempel-Hainzmann 2020, 499–504. See also: Polleres 2007.
239 Stempel-Hainzmann 2020, 89–94.
240 On epigraphy and Roman religion, see: Scheid 2012; Busch-Schäfer 2014; Rives 2015.
241 Stempel-Hainzmann 2020, 92.
242 Alföldy 1974, 70–76.
243 On the 're-invention' of Celtic religion in a Roman province, the work of G. Woolf is still paradigmatic: Woolf 1998, 219.
244 Ibidem.
245 CIL III 4808: *Nor(eiae) / Chrysanthus / Cypaeri / Ti(berii) Claudi(i) Caes(aris) / Aug(usti) / ser(vi) vic(arius) / v(otum) s(olvit)* See also: Dolenz 2007, 87–88.
246 For the complex and problematic notion of Romanisation in Noricum see: Zimmermann 2017; Hainzmann 2019.

247 Scherrer 2002.
248 Hainzmann 2019, 245.
249 Harl *et al.* 2014, 37, Fig. 20.
250 The chronology of the site is problematic: there are only a few cases found on the site of brooches from 120 BC and 20 AD, while the figurative monuments reflect predominantly Augustan and early Julio-Claudian finds: Idem 54–60 and 73.
251 Idem, 58–59.
252 See also: Scheid 2015b.
253 Kenner 1950.
254 Harding 2007, 54 and 126. See also: Tóth 2015, 35.
255 On the settlement, see: Groh-Sedlmeyer 2012.
256 Marsh 1979, 265.
257 Pfahl 1999, 24–25.
258 Meier 2004, 78. See also: Szabó 2005, 103.
259 Groh-Sedlmeyer 2012, 494.
260 Alföldy 1974, 102. The author omits the inscription from Burgstall. See also: Linderski 2016.
261 *Maromogio / pag(i) mag(istri) / v(otum) s(olverunt) l(ibentes) m(erito)* See: Groh-Sedlmeyer 2007; Stempel-Hainzman 2020, 873.
262 CSIR Virunum 20; Lupa 13356.
263 Groh-Sedlmeyer 2011, 26–27.
264 Groh-Sedlmeyer 2007, 32 and Groh-Sedlmeyer 2011, 38.
265 Idem, 36–37.
266 Groh-Sedlmeyer 2007, 36; Schrettle 2019, 297.
267 Idem, 263–265, especially abb. 176.
268 Idem, 271, abb. 179.
269 Idem, 272–275. Lupa 30208.
270 Šašel Kos 2016.
271 Idem, 168–169.
272 Lupa 5949.
273 Schrettle 2019, 272.
274 Šašel Kos 1998, 19.
275 Šašel Kos 2010a.
276 Idem, 247.
277 Idem, 253.
278 See also: Chapter 3 on urban religion and citification.
279 Krempuš *et al.* 2007, 40, abb. 2.
280 Lazar 2011, 26.
281 Idem, 28, Fig. 2.
282 Mócsy 1974a, 37–42.
283 Kovács 2008, 237.
284 Idem, 238.
285 CIL XIII 8648.
286 CIL III 1741. Kovács 2008, 240.
287 Šašel-Kos 2010b, 130 as a response for Kovács 2008.
288 For a comprehensive analysis of the military history and its archaeology of this period, see: Mráv 2010.
289 Šašel-Kos 2010b, 130 cites the words of Ronald Syme on the fluidity and calm nature of transforming Pannonia into a separate province in four to five decades in the 1st century AD.
290 See the previous subchapter.

291 Kovács 2002; Gömöri 2003, 82; Kovács 2013, 132.
292 AÉ 1969–70, 541: *Cereri / M(arcus) Valerius / v(otum) s(olvit) l(ibens) m(erito)*; CIL III 4235: *Iovi O(ptimo) M(aximo) sacrum / Sex(tus) Proculeius L(uci) f(ilius) / Lem(onia) Rufus vet(eranus) leg(ionis) XV / posu{u}it*
293 Koortboijan 2020. See also: Kovács 2010a.
294 Tóth 2001; Szabó 2006, 233–236.
295 Scherrer 2003.
296 Gabler 1995; Biró 2017.
297 Idem, 34, abb. 11.
298 Mráv 2010, 91.
299 Ottományi 2007, 254.
300 Topál 2000, 198.
301 Mráv 2007.
302 The most detailed analysis of the topic still remains: Nagy 1941. See also: Tóth 2015, 36–37.
303 Topál 2000, 197.
304 See for example the tombstones from Kékkút: lupa 724, 3413, 3410. Kovács 2017, 67.
305 Mócsy 1974a, 71.
306 Kovács 2013, 133–136.
307 Kovács 1999.
308 On the cult of Teutanus, see: Póczy 1999.
309 Tóth 2015, 97–99.
310 AÉ 2000, 1186: *[I(ovi)] O(ptimo) M(aximo) / [pro salute] / Im[p(eratoris) Caes(aris) T(iti) Aeli[i] / An[ton] ini Aug(usti) [Pii] / et M(arci) [A]urel(i) Ca[es(aris)] / c(ives) R(omani) cons(istentes) Ca[rn(unti)] / intra leug(am) / C(aius) Pompon(ius) Saturn[i]n[us] / C(aius) S[at]urnin(ius) Candi[dus?] / P(ublius) [---]I Vale[---] / [-] An[n(ius)? Pl]acidus / [mag]istri mont[i]s / [Qui]ntillo et [Prisco c]o(n)s(ulibus)* AÉ 1982, 0783: *I(ovi) O(ptimo) M(aximo) K(arnuntino) / [p]ro salute dd(ominorum) nn(ostrorum) / [Di]ocle[tiani et] / M[aximiani Aug(ustorum)] et / C[onstanti et Max]i/m[iani ---] / [------ // Dederunt [d(edicaverunt)] III [Idus] / I[u]nias d[d(ominis) nn(ostris)] / [Ma]ximi/[ano Au]g(usto) V e[t Maxi]/[mi]ano n[ob(ilissimo)] / [Ca]es(are) II c[o(n)s(ulibus)]*
311 For the critique of Tóth, see: Nagy 2016; Szabó 2018b.
312 On the Coligny calendar, see: Rankin 1987, 282; Swift 2002.
313 Piso 1991, 140.
314 Idem, 137, Dészpa 2017, 138.
315 Piso 2003a.
316 Kremer 2004.
317 The earliest inscription is from the Julio-Claudian period. AÉ 2003, 1381: *Victoriae / [s]a[c]rum / [- Val]erius / [---] Fabia / [--- l]eg(ionis) XV / [Apol(linaris) ------*
318 Opreanu 2000.
319 Vita Hadr. 23, 11; Vita Ael. 3, 2. See also: Šašel Kos 2009, 182.
320 Idem. On the cult of Antinoos, see: Vout 2005; Jones 2010, 74–84. On the military history of the region in 135–140 AD, see: Mócsy 1974b; Juhász 2019, 45–46. For a representation of an Egyptianised emperor or Antinoos, see: lupa 13687.
321 Piso 2003a, 19–20, cat. no. 4.
322 The inscriptions show the same chronological period: Jobst 2003, 11–12.
323 Hervás 2020.
324 Dészpa 2017, 137. AÉ 1936, 132 = CCID 217: *Pro sal(ute) Imp(eratoris) C/aes(aris) Tra(iani) Hadr(iani) Aug(usti) / p(atris) p(atriae) porta(m) et muru(m) per / pedes lon(gum) C altu(m) p(edes) VI / iuvent(us) colen(s) Iove(m) Doli/chen(um) inpe(n)sa sua fec(it)*
325 Jobst *et al.* 2018.

326 Kremer 2004. See also: Woolf 2001.
327 Tóth 2015, 104–105. See also: Cook 1925, 786
328 HA *Vita Had.* 14.3. See also: Sage 1987, 161; Collar 2020a.
329 See also: Jobst 1978.
330 Biró 2017.
331 Mráv-Ottományi 2005.
332 Ottományi 2012.
333 Idem, 293.
334 Visy 1995; Szabó 2014.
335 Ottományi 2012, 299–302.
336 Idem, 97.
337 Mráv-Ottományi 2005. See also: Sanader 1996.
338 Mráv-Ottományi 2005, 75. See also: Mráv 2017, 103–104.
339 Domaszewski 1909; Tóth 2015, 81 with a complete bibliography of the topic. See also: Dészpa 2012, 95–136; Perinić 2016, 9–10.
340 Tóth 2015, 81.
341 Idem, 86–87.
342 Mayer 1942.
343 On Vidasus, see also: Cambi 2013, 84.
344 AÉ 1937, 208: *[Silv]ano Mag(no) // Cl(audius) Maximi/nus pro sal(ute) / Cl(audii) Probini / fili(i) quod voverat / v(otum) s(olvit) l(ibens) m(erito) / III Idus Iuni(as) / Perpetuo / et Corneli/ano co(n)s(ulibus)* See also: Tóth 2015, 87.
345 AÉ 1961, 0002: *Dii Augura/libus ite/m Silvano / et [Ap]olli/ni et Mercu/[rio] it(em) Be[l(eno) / Augu] sto / [---?* See also: Dészpa 2012, 157–162.
346 Alföldy 1960.
347 Tóth 2015, 90.
348 Dorcey 1992, 39.
349 Idem, 35–38. On the notion of memory distortion in religion and art, see: Dészpa 2012, 255.
350 Idem, 274–276.
351 Rendic-Miocevic–Segvic 1998, 9; Mráv 2017, 102–103.
352 CIL III 3416: *Danuvio / Defluenti / Haterius Ca/l(l)inicus vo(tum?) / [---]V[---] / [------*; CIL III 10395: *Danuvio / sacrum / [V]etulenus / [A]proni[a]nus / leg(atus) leg(ionis) [II] / [ad]i(utricis) p(iae) [f(idelis)] / [------*. See also as an analogy, the inscriptions from Stepperg (Lupa 6872): *I(ovi) o(ptimo) m(aximo) / Nept(uno) / Dan(uvio) / Toppo fe(cit)* and Risstissen (CIL III 5863): *In h(onorem) d(omus) d(ivinae) / I(ovi) o(ptimo) m(aximo) et Danu/vio ex vot/o Primanus / Secundi v(otum) s(olvit) l(aetus) l(ibens) / Muciano et Fabi[iano co(n)s(ulibus)]*
353 Rendic-Miocevic–Segvic 1998, 8–9.
354 Szabó 2020e.
355 Mráv 2017, 102.
356 AÉ 1934, 68: *Aecornae / Aug(ustae) sac(rum) / Emonienses / qui / consistunt / finibus / Savar(iae) / v(otum) s(olverunt) l(ibentes) m(erito)* See also: Šašel Kos 1998, 18.
357 Šašel Kos 2016.
358 Mantzilas 2018.
359 AÉ 2006, 1075: *Nutr[icib(us)]*
360 Egri 2007, 42.
361 Eichner *et al.* 1994.
362 Mócsy 1990, 256.
363 Ibidem.
364 See also: Szabó 2018b, 141–145.

365 King 2007, 17; Gleirscher 2015.
366 On the notion, see also: Busch-Versluys 2015, 7–19.
367 For an important contribution on this, see: Ghey 2007, 22–23.
368 Idem, 21.
369 Jackson 2007, 48.
370 Sîrbu 1993; 1994, 39–59; Sîrbu-Florea 1997, 39–41; Pescaru 2005; Sîrbu 2007, 183–211. Some of the buildings interpreted as sanctuaries were recently reanalysed: Opreanu 2015. See also the important studies in Sîrbu-Peţan 2020.
371 Mateescu 2012; Peţan 2015. See also: Sîrbu-Florea 1997, 39–41.
372 Opreanu 2016. See also: Sîrbu-Peţan 2020.
373 On the historiographic problem of Zalmolxis and related divinities, see: Dana 2011.
374 Spănu 2013, 13–22.
375 An interesting case study is the great circular sanctuary and solar disk of Sarmizegetusa Regia, on which possible traces of burning or fire remains were attested as dating to Roman times. The nature of the activity that caused this anomaly is impossible to determine: Mateescu 2012. See also: IDR III/3, 267–274.
376 Varga 2019.
377 Florea 2013.
378 Haeussler 2007, 99 and especially Tóth 2015. On his book and on the regionality in Pannonian religion, see: Szabó 2018a.
379 Known as the 'Dacian paradox': Nemeti 2013b, 138. See also: Visy 2015.
380 Oltean 2007, 46.
381 Haeussler 2012.
382 Köpeczy 1986, 46–48. See also: Ruscu 2003; Nemeti 2013b, 145; Ibarra 2014, 167. For the latest detailed synthesis on the problem of the Dacians in the Roman Empire, see: Dana 2019.
383 Bolindeţ-Cociş 2006, 557; Bolindeţ 2014, 249, for the extremely interesting case study of Soporu de Cămpie. See also: Glodariu 1983 (for Slimnic). For a more careful and critical opinion on the archaeological material regarding the Dacian presence in the Roman period: Rustoiu 2002, 139–141. See also: Gudea 2008, 79 for the case study of Stupini.
384 Dana-Zăgreanu 2013, 145–159.
385 Nemeti 2014, 79–100.
386 Dana 2013, 177–201; Ibarra 2014. An old-fashioned and nationalistic view: Protase 2010.
387 Wells 2015; Busch 2015.
388 Sîrbu-Florea 1997; Spănu 2013.
389 Sîrbu-Florea 1997, 39–41.
390 It is also plausible that religion consisted only of large rituals, without monumentalisation in architecture.
391 Owen 2011.
392 The monumentalised form of sanctuaries attested in pre-Roman times at a few centres of the Dacian tribes, such as Sarmizegetusa Regia, was much more a landmark of the power of the ruling tribe, following Hellenic architecture and technique. For most of the population, these structures were deemed simply odd and unusual, 'non-Dacian'.
393 On possible human sacrifices in Dacian society, see: Babes 1988, 3–32. See also: Rabadjiev 2015, 450.
394 Várhelyi 2007, 277–304; Berthelot 2007, 154, fn. 14; Várhelyi 2011.
395 Grottanelli 1999, 41–59; Berthelot 2007, 152. Reid 1912, citing Cicero, *Foteius*, 31, where the same *topos* is used against the Gaul elites. See also: Várhelyi 2011, 126, fn. 7.
396 Várhelyi 2011, 154–156.
397 Woolf 1997, 341. See also: Versluys 2014, 7–8.

398 Woolf 2014.
399 Matei-Popescu 2017.
400 IDR III/3, 275. See also: Diaconescu 1997; Opreanu 2000; Oltean 2007: 54; Opreanu 2015.
401 IDR III/3, 276; Opreanu 2015; Lupa 19484–1.
402 Téglás 1902, 146.
403 Opreanu 2000, 162 citing the idea of M. Macrea and C. Daicoviciu. See also: Lăscoiu 2013, 373–379.
404 Oltean-Hanson 2017.
405 Dana 2013.
406 The well-documented but still-problematic chronology between these two dates was discussed in: Mirković 2008, 249–259.
407 AÉ 1967, 0425; AÉ 1967, 0426; AÉ 1957, 0286; AÉ 1957, 0298; AÉ 1944, 0070; AÉ 1977, 0742; AÉ 1927, 0051; AÉ 1910, 0176; CIL 03, 01698; AÉ 2001, 1731.
408 Boyanov 2008.
409 See Chapter 3 on urban religion.
410 Dorcey 1988; Gavrilović 2010, 69; Vucović-Bogdanović-Jovović 2015, 699.
411 See the list of divinities in Moesia Superior in the Appendices and Fig. 61: CIL III, 6303 (p 1454); CIL III, 08148 = IMS-I, 9; IMS-01, 00010; IMS-I, 11; IMS-I, 13; IMS-I, 21; IMS-I, 102; AÉ 1913, 176; CIL III, 14565; AÉ 1979, 521; IMS-IV, 20 = AÉ 1934, 207; IMS-IV, 22 = AÉ 1979, 522; IMS-IV, 23 = AÉ 1979, 523; AÉ 2013, 1324; AÉ 1995, 1311; ILJug II, 572 = AÉ 1971, 427; EDCS-11201467.
412 Ferri 2011.
413 AÉ 1901, 0016 = CIL 03, 14565 = IMS 4, 021: *I(ovi) O(ptimo) M(aximo) Pa/terno Ae/pilofio(!) / Sanc(---) Oriens / Cor(nelius) Mide P(ublius) / Ael(ius) Cocaius / vet(erani) leg(ionis) VII Cl(audiae) Sev(erianae) / ex voto posu(erunt) / Maximo et Aeli/ano co(n)s(ulibus)* See also: Kovács 2000, 243.
414 Cook 1925, 948. Vasile Pârvan wrongly identified this divinity with Zalmolxis: Pârvan 1928, 163.
415 Idem,
416 Kovács 2000, 246. Thracians were also recruted in the Danubian provinces for the Mauretanian troops, therefore the interconnectivity between the Mauretanian and Thracian groups might be worthy of complex analysis: Speidel 1977; Farkas 2011.
417 Alföldy 1957, 214–215.
418 AÉ 1981, 0739 = CCID 126.
419 AÉ 1966, 0338 = ILJug 1283.
420 ILJug 0469.
421 IMS 1, 021.
422 Teichner-Drăgan 2016, 98–99.
423 The best summary of the historiographic and terminological issues related to the cult was given by Boteva 2011.
424 Idem, 86, footnotes 17 and 18.
425 Grbić 2013. See also: IMS-04, 00119; AÉ 2003, 01531 = AÉ 2013, 01318; IMS-02, 00016; IMS-02, 00221; IMS-02, 00309; CIL 03, 08147; IMS-01, 00078.
426 ILJug-02, 00576 = AÉ 1972, 00535.
427 CIL 03, 08256.
428 AÉ 2011, 01113 = AÉ 2012, +01258; IMS-04, 00104 = AÉ 1952, 00192.
429 AÉ 1968, 00452.
430 CIL 03, 14550 = IMS-06, 00214; CIL 03, 08191 = IMS-06, 00018.
431 Alföldy 2011, 196.
432 Dana *et al.* 2017; Nikolova 2020, 172.
433 On the relationship between Dea Dardanica and Roman imperialism, see: Mihajlović 2016.

434 The bibliography focusing on this cult is extremely rich. For the latest catalogues of the finds, see: Tudor 1976; Ertl 1996. For the full bibliography on iconographic analysis, see: Nemeti 2015 and Szabó 2017b, 61, footnote no. 3.
435 Gordon 2017, 287; Szabó 2017b, 12–26.
436 On the Mithras myth as a recently re-evaluated story: Nagy 2012. Ádám Szabó argued that the lost mythologem must be focusing on the creation of the world: Szabó 2017b, 73.
437 Idem, 27–54. See also: Hijmans 2016, 95–96. For more on the visual bricolage of the Sabazios cult, see an ambitious, although not completely acceptable theory in: Georgiev 2021.
438 Faraone 2013.
439 Hijmans 2016, 95.
440 Szabó 2017b, 103.
441 Idem, 101–126.
442 Gordon 2017, 287 wrongly states that the inscription comes from Carnuntum and not Quadrata, probably confusing it with the one from Winden am See (Kremer 2019, 276) or with the bronze *thymiaterion* from Carnuntum: AÉ 1992, 1429. See also: AÉ 2006, 1052 and Szabó 2017b, 27–42, especially 41–42.
443 Idem. See also: Tóth 2015, 182–191. Both István Tóth and Ádám Szabó claimed that the relief from Poetovio representing a solar divinity is related to the so-called 'Danubian Riders' (*Domnus et Domna*) cult, however their argument in this regard is limited exclusively to the iconographic similarities: Idem, 184–189.
444 Szabó 2017b, 55–58.
445 Tóth 2003.
446 Tóth 2015, 184, Fig. 116; Hijmans 2016, 97, Fig. 5.13.b.; Szabó 2017b, 57, Fig. 1.
447 Tóth 2015, 182–191. He has argued since the 1970s that the cult of Mithras originated in Poetovio or somewhere in Illyricum following the work of Beskow: Beskow 1980.
448 Szabó 2017b, 67.
449 Gordon 2017, 286–287: 'set of religious ideas and practices'.
450 Nemeti 2015.
451 AÉ 2010, 1383 = EDCS-59500075.
452 Fiedler-Höpken 2010.
453 Alföldy 1997.
454 Hainzmann 2017; Matei-Popescu 2021.
455 Kremer 2019.
456 Varga 2019.
457 Hijmans 2016, 98.
458 Kremer 2019, 279.
459 Haynes 2014. See also: Szabó 2018b, 78–92.
460 Clauss 2006; Gordon 2017, 287, footnote no. 36.
461 Kremer 2019.
462 Idem, 282.
463 Gordon 2017, 288.
464 For a recent synthesis, see also: Pazmany 2019, especially 94–100.

3

Lived religion and its macro-spaces in the Danubian provinces

Religion beyond provinces: large-scale mobilities

The Roman Empire was most often viewed as a system of urban networks and provincial administrative units. The largest administrative unit of the Empire was the province, whose limits were established as a result of a long and often difficult process of militarisation, based on geographic, economic and militaristic concerns and rationalities. Publishing the *lex provinciae*, and founding the capital of the province (the Ara Augusti and the first provincial forum) were the first legal aspects once an established territory had become legally integrated into the Roman Empire.[1] Roman religious communication, however, was only partially defined and influenced by the establishment of these provincial limits. For this reason, 'provincial religion' as it was known for a long time in the literature, can no longer be a valid category and methodological approach.[2] This is because provincial limits do not affect the mobility of the military, the small-group religions and the individuals who played such a crucial role in establishing new sacralised spaces, especially meso- and micro-spaces. By contrast, macro-spaces in public, mostly urban and military environments were more dependent of the provincial, administrative construction and institutionalisation of the political environment.

Provincial religion and the limitation of Roman religious communication within the provincial limits and borders in older historiography was based especially on the locality and unique attestation of certain divine instantiations and the rather artificial dichotomy of 'Imperial' (central) and 'provincial' (peripheral). The category of the 'Imperial' in this context comes from the art historian traditions, where material production of the Roman Empire is distinguished in these two traditional categories.[3] This also influenced Roman religious studies and the materiality of Roman religion, especially in provincial archaeology, where objects were interpreted for a long time as local products of micro-spaces, thereby marginalising the glocal aspects and the mobility of objects and their owners.[4]

Divine and human agency of religious communication is especially formed and shaped by individuals and small groups in micro- and meso-spaces. This is attested by the fact that most of the material evidence of Roman religion comes from these two categories. For this reason, recent archaeological studies are focusing on these two spatial categories as ideal case studies, through the lens of glocalisation. However, macro-spaces and large spatial clusters were also active agents, especially in the *longue durée* mobilities of material and human agency of religion, but also in religious knowledge production. In the following, I will focus on some of the most important clusters and macro-spaces in the Danubian provinces or those that created an interconnectivity within this macro-unit of the Roman Empire and had a long-lasting, attestable impact in space sacralisation and Roman religious communication.[5]

Publicum portorii Illyrici*: the economic macro-unit*

The Roman Empire was not only a complex network of urban and rural settlements connected by cultural and military boundariess and mobilities, but also a complex economic and financial system. The major economic units of the Principate were the *publicii* and the *vectigalii*, the customs system of the Roman Empire.[6] The macro-units of this system (*Quadragesima Galliarum, Quattuor publica Africae, Quadragesima portuum Asiae et la Quadragesima Bithyniae*)[7] formed a dynamic network of hierarchically and professionally connected individuals and groups. This was known as the 'staff of the customs system', in which slaves, freedmen and citizens participated in the maintenance of the financial system of these macro-units, and also, but due to their intense mobility, contributed to the religious networks of the Empire.[8]

One of the major macro-units of the customs system was the *publicum portorii Illyrici*, which was also known after the Hadrianic period as *publicum portorii Illyrici et ripae Thraciae*.[9] Since the end of the 19th century, the literature has analysed this financial and economic sub-unit of the Empire numerous times,[10] focusing especially on the *villici* and the mobility of the freedmen within the *publicum*.[11] One author, Siegfried de Laet, identified 68 *stationes* of the *publicum portorii Illyrici*, however his list has since been contested and reinterpreted several times.[12] He also identified several major routes within the customs system that connected the Po area and Aquileia with the Alpine provinces of Raetia and Noricum and the Danubian area in Pannoniae, Moesiae and Daciae.[13]

The customs system played an essential role in the mobility of objects and connected the major economic hubs of the Roman Empire, concentrating especially in Aquileia and in the major legionary centres, such as Poetovio, Carnuntum, Aquincum, Apulum, Viminacium and Novae.[14] The mobility of this economic network can be best attested through the case study of the *conductores publici Illyrici* and the *vilici* of the *publicum*, but also through the interconnectivity of the local, provincial elite, who often surpassed their provincial limits, having supra-provincial functions (and snappy job titles), such as the *procurator publici portorii vectigalis Illyrici per Moesiam Inferiorem et Dacias Tres* or the *procurator publici portorii vectigalis Illyrici per Raetiam et Noricum et Dalmatiam et utramque Pannoniam et Moesiam Superiorem*.[15]

High functionaries and their staff represented the major mobility force of the Roman Empire, maintaining the economic and political connection of the urban network. In many cases, these functionaries played a key role not only in the customs system, but also in mining and the political administration of the provinces.[16] Most of the inscriptions dedicated by the staff of the *publicum* reveal the divine legitimacy of their political fidelity for the Empire, which is evidenced through dedications for IOM and the Genius of the *publicum*. The case study of Porolissum, where a small, sacralised space dedicated to the Genius of the customs system and Jupiter was created, is one of the best-documented case studies for the political, economic and religious devotion united in the divine figure of the *Genius portorii Illyrici* (cat. no. VI.25b).[17]

The key role of the *publicum portorii Illyrici* and its staff in the spread of the cult of Mithras is well known due to the articles written by Per Beskow and István Tóth.[18] These highlighted the importance of the Danube as the main commercial and cultural route in the mobility of the staff of the *portorium*. From the epigraphic sources, the leading personnel (*vilici, conscriptores, arcarii*) and their slaves or freedmen connected with the *portorium* are now known from 10 settlements in Dacia.[19] In particular, the so-called second generation of the *portorium*'s staff – Quintus Sabinius Veranus, Titus Iulius Saturninus and Caius Antonius Rufus[20] – are attested in the province.

Fig. 3.1 Genius of the publicum portorii Illyrici *in Apulum. (Source: Lupa 12238, photo of Ortolf Harl, with the special permission of the National Museum of Union Alba Iulia)*

Even if we don't have any Mithraic inscriptions by them, their direct link with the Poetovian community suggests their important role in establishing a direct connectivity between Pannonia and Dacia. The presence of Titus Julius Saturninus in Apulum proves the existence of a bureau of the *portorium* and a direct link with Poetovio.[21] His monumental statue base (121 cm) is unique, mostly because of its iconographic features. The lateral sides of the large monument are adorned with the bust of Mercurius and an enigmatic divine figure, probably the Genius of the *publicum* (Fig. 3.1).[22] The figurative representation of a supra-provincial macro-space on a local religious tool – in this case a statue base[23] – shows that macro-spaces were integrated forms of religious spatiality and had a conscious visual representation reflecting not only a spatial, geographic area, but also the economic (Mercurius), cultural and ideological unity (Genius) of the *portorium*.

The most interesting link between the social network of traders and the Mithras worshippers in Apulum is the personnel of the *salinae* and the role of this institution in the spread of the cult.[24] The geographical position of Apulum made the city not only an important strategic point between Porolissum and Ulpia Traiana Sarmizegetusa, but also a commercial centre.[25] The presence of the Mureş River also contributed to the importance of the city, being an significant station of the gold and salt commerce route.[26] There is no direct evidence for the existence of an office of the *salinae* in Apulum.[27] However, there are many indirect ones that may suggest the presence of this institution in the city. First, the continuous use of the Roman salt mines and the existence of a salt bureau in Medieval and modern Gyulafehérvár (Alba Iulia)[28] could imply an indirect continuity of this institution in this area. A more eloquent argument is the strong links of the *conductores salinarum* with Apulum.[29] From the four known *conductores*, three appear in Apulum.[30] The name of Caius Iulius Valentinus appears on three votive inscriptions: one dedicated to Sol Invictus,[31] in Homoródszentpál (Sânpaul); one to IOM Dolichenus,[32] in Tibiscum (as *flamen municipii*); and the other in Apulum, where he is attested as the first *IIIIvir* and the patron of the *collegium fabrum* in the newly founded Municipium Septimium Apulense.[33] However, his activity, according to the latest interpretations, is not related to the cult of Mithras.[34] His role in the spread of the solar cults is obvious. Publius Aelius Strenuus[35] is known from two inscriptions. One is a statue base from Apulum erected by Rufinus, his *libertus.* He was also the patron of the *collegium nautarum,* which might suggest that he fulfilled the title of *conductor pascui, salinarum et commerciorum* in Apulum.[36]

Without doubt, the most interesting figure associated with the salt trade and the local Mithraic community is Publius Aelius Marus (or Marius).[37] An inscription erected by his *libertus*, Publius Aelius Euphorus, was discovered in Micia, an important commercial and customs centre of the province.[38] His *libertus* is known from another inscription found in the same settlement, where he erected an altar in the newly reconstructed sanctuary of the Invincible God.[39] Another inscription, possibly from Tibiscum,[40] was erected by Hermadio, *libertus* of Turranius Dius,[41] and is dedicated to Mithras. Hermadio was considered by István Tóth to be a 'prophet' of the cult in Dacia. However, since the text doesn't mention the function of Publius Aelius Marius, some scholars don't accept the identification of the two persons from Micia and Tibiscum.[42]

The next inscription was discovered in 1911 at Bilak (Domneşti), another important centre for salt mining.[43] The text of the inscription has been interpreted many times, in different ways,[44] but it is certain that the person – Aelius Marus, *conductor salinarum et pascui et flamen coloniae* – is the same one who appears in Micia and Tibiscum. The first part of his title – *conductor salinarum et pascui* – matches the one that appears on the inscription from Micia. His *flamonium* was related either to Napoca[45] or to Ulpia Traiana Sarmizegetusa.[46] It is very possible that it was a *flamen* of Colonia Aurelia Apulensis, where a salt trade office probably existed. His sacerdotal title also appears on an inscription discovered in 2008 (cat. no. VI.7)[47] and his name was also attested on an inscription from Porolissum.[48]

The three chief *conductores* who appear in Apulum and their widespread personnel – Marcus Turranius Dius, the local conductor from Tibiscum, the actores Hermadio, Ursio, Iulius Omucio, Aelius Atticus and Publius Aelius Euphorus – had a very strong commercial and familial relationship and a direct link with Poetovio, the main centre of the Mithraic cult in the *publicum portorii Illyrici*. They monopolised the local salt mining trade and also held an important spiritual role in the province, representing the newly and rapidly emerged 'business class' of the province, as a consequence of the Roman consumer revolution in Dacia.[49] The inscriptions of the *conductores* in Apulum are not direct evidence for the existence of a *salinarum*, nor even for the headquarters of the salt trade of the province, but it is certain that these persons played a key role in the spread of the cult. This has changed our view on the Roman cult of Mithras, which was viewed for a long time as a 'military' cult of the province.[50]

The role of the *publicum portorii Illyirici* as a macro-space in the communication between small-group religions of the Danubian provinces can also be attested in several textual and visual choices and strategies in this region of the Empire: as Beskow and Tóth argued in the 1980s and later, the Mithraic inscriptions dedicated to the Fons Perennis and Transitus Dei, the avatars of Mithras, represent clear evidence for interconnectivity between the Mithraic groups of Poetovio, Savaria, Aquincum and Apulum.[51] Certain iconographic features, such as the representation of Cautes on bucrania or Sol on complex reliefs with seven sunbeams, seem to have travelled through the *publicum* or else its major social agents (army, commercial staff).[52]

Archaeological objects and ideas could also travel great distances via commercial routes or circumstances that are hard to reconstruct, but certainly required the macro-structures and infrastructure of the Roman Empire. The small, round reliefs used in the cult of the so-called 'Danubian Riders' (*Domna et Domnus*) and the cult of Mithras in the Danubian provinces seems to be a unique, local visual appropriation, although in a few cases we can find particular examples in other provinces, too (Hawarte, Londinium Mithraeum). Similar connections were attested with the Londinium Mithraeum shrine and the Liber Pater one in Apulum: in both cases, Cambodunum 306 type was used in deliberate destructions within the sacralised space.[53]

Religious knowledge production in a local context was therefore almost instantly transformed into transferable information and ideas, which travelled through various social groups, helped by the necessary macro-spaces and supra-provincial units of the Roman Empire, creating a glocal religious appropriation in the Danubian provinces and beyond.

The Roman officium *and the network of the* beneficiarii

The Danubian provinces were also interconnected by administrative macro-networks. Besides the intense mobility of the army, which represents the most important framework of social and human mobility in this area of the Roman Empire due to the major dislocations during three major historical phases (those of Trajan, Marcus Aurelius and Septimius Severus),[54] an important group who created a strong network within the Danubian provinces was the *officium Imperiali*. The administrative staff of the *officium*, the Imperial 'security' network and auxiliary staff of the governor represent a dynamic group attested in most of the Danubian provinces.[55] The exact role and political, administrative, juridical and economic duties of the *beneficiarii* have been debated numerous times and the matter still provokes intense scholarly discussion.[56] Yet since the first publications, the cohesive power of the *stationes* and the *beneficiarii* in the communication routes of the Roman Empire and in the Imperial cult and public religious communication has been consistently emphasised.[57] Their religious choice shows a rather uniform nature, similar to the individual choices of the *conductores* of the *publicum portorii Illyrici*.

The *stationes* of the *beneficiarii* from the Danubian provinces are well attested, several of them offering a wide range of materiality of religion in the creation and maintenance of space sacralisation, which served as religious and ideological network hubs of the official, administrative staff of the Empire. The most impressive case studies were identified in Praetorium Latobicorum (18 altars),[58] Celeia (27 altars)[59] and Sirmium (84 altars: cat. no. III.83).[60] The large quantity of altars dedicated predominantly to Jupiter Optimus Maximus represents the continuity the administrative function of the *beneficiarii*, who dedicated these altars as material evidence of Imperial fidelity and served as an active, religious agent in the sacralised open space visible for the visitors and the next generations of *beneficiarii*. That these altars stood in a large, unusual density in a relatively small space demonstrates the annual change-over of the *beneficiarii*[61] and the memorialisation of their administrative function and fidelity for the Roman power elite (Fig. 3.2). The altar here is therefore not only a tool in religious communication, but serves especially as a political manifestation.[62] This was not new. 'Hoarding' altars as ex-votos and material tools in social and religious communication was an archaic method that had already been attested in the Roman Republican period, as the case study of Satricum shows.[63] Both the monumentality of the altars and the epigraphic text as visual narrative had the same impact on the visitors: they reflected the continuity, power and unity of the Roman Empire.

The *statio* of the *beneficiarii* were intensive and dense sacralised spaces, where political communication was harmoniously and organically united with the divine protection of the space. Similarly, when it came to the large macro-spaces of the urban environments, the altars of the *statio* were spaces of religious memorialisation and political performances, although their visibility and accessibility was much more limited than that of the macro-spaces of an urban forum or public temple.

Fig. 3.2 Altars discovered in the sanctuary of the beneficiarii station in Sirmium. (Source: after Mirković 2008 with the permission of Nadežda Gavrilović Vitas)

These altars and the dynamic mobility of the *beneficiarii* thus represented a supra-provincial cohesion between religion and politics. Their network and mobility need to be analysed in more detail: recent studies have focused especially on their local impact in the daily life of a province,[64] however their mobility shows that the *stationes* of the governors' *beneficiarii* represent one of the most important supra-provincial networks of the Roman Empire, as Alfred von Domaszewski proved in 1902.[65]

Danube catchment (Summuntorium-Troesmis)

The Danube is the second-longest river in contemporary Europe, but it was the longest and most important fluvial route of the Roman world.[66] It flows 2,850 km from the border of Germania Superior and Raetia to the Black Sea and the coasts of Moesia Inferior, crossing at least seven Roman provinces. The catchment of the Danube, however, represents an even more important hidrographic-ecologic and cultural unit within the Roman Empire and goes beyond the administrative limits of it: the Danube River Basin and its catchment includes the Isar, Inn, Salzash, Mura, Morava, Drava, Dru, Sava, Ipel, Va, Tisza, Una, Drina, Mureș/Maros, Someș/Szamos, Olt, Argeș and Siret/Szeret and Prut rivers.[67] The 801,000 km^2 catchment of the Danube, of which around 660,000 km^2 and 6 million inhabitants were within the borders of the *limes*[68], accounts for almost 15 per cent of the territory of the Roman Empire.

This large area represented not only an important ecological region of the Roman Empire – essential for agriculture, flora and the fauna and, indirectly, for the primary food supply of the local population[69] – but also a supra-provincial macro-region in terms of civilian and military communication, defence and transportation.[70] The Danube provided a link between the major military and urban settlements of the entire northern fluvial limes (Ripa). Indeed, most of the military centres (in particular, the legionary fortresses) were situated on the river, which offered direct communication between the major military forces of the Roman Empire, creating a fast and safe mobility between the legionary centres. Travelling from Carnuntum to Novae entailed a 38-day-long journey, although fluvial mobility was very much dependent on the season and topography or the regional specificities of the Danubian area.[71] The Danube, when it was navigable, thus served as the major commercial and military route between Pannoniae and Moesia Superior, as well as between Moesia Superior and Inferior and the southern part of Dacia.[72] Medieval and pre-modern sources confirm that the Danube was also navigable from east to west.[73]

We presume that all the major military settlements (auxiliary and legionary forts and fortresses) on the Danube had a port on the riverside, however few of these are well documented archaeologically.[74] Claudiu Munteanu in his work focusing on transportation and navigation on the Danube in the Roman Empire enlists 69 possible Roman ports (civilian and military, stations of the *classis*) in seven Roman provinces.[75]

The catchment of the Danube and the interconnectivity of the major rivers of the provinces also had an impact on the transfer of religious ideas, materialities and human agency, but we can find few cases where divine agencies were also defined and shaped by the hydrological aspects of these provinces. The most obvious evidence is the personifications of the rivers, which is attested in epigraphic sources.[76] The Danube, Drava and Sava rivers are particularly well attested, which might suggest a local, Pannonian or Celtic, pre-Roman tradition.[77] The divine pair of Savus and Adsalluta in Noricum[78] and the cult of Acheloos in Celeia[79] are examples of the important role of rivers and their impact on cultural transfer in this region. The possible sanctuary of Hrastnik dedicated to river divinities and the one in Aquincum[80] dedicated to Danuvius are superficially documented, although the concentration of multiple altars on the banks of the river might suggest a sacralised space dedicated specially for river personifications.[81]

What we do know is that the Danube played a crucial role in economic and cultural transfer between the Pontic cities and the Danubian provinces: archaeological material (especially amphorae, terra sigillata,[82] lamps, food supplies and luxury goods[83]) suggest a constant interconnectivity along the Danube.[84]

The presence of the *nautae* and *navicularii* in the Danubian region[85] and the possible attestation of a *collegium nautarum* in Apulum[86] demonstrate the commercial role of the inner rivers within the Danube catchment. The Marisia (Mureș-Maros) was particularly important because it served as the major commercial and communication route between Dacia and the Barbaricum east to Pannonia.[87] The river also played a crucial role in the salt trade and the mobility of the *conductores salinarum/pascui et salinarum* responsible for the salt mining and the Imperial estates.[88]

A particularly interesting and unique relief was found in 1943 in the south-west corner of the legionary fortress of the XIII Geminae legion. The small object represents a beautifully carved and half-naked central figure (the Genius) with cornocupia, a fire sacrifice, *libatio* and a ship in the left corner, probably with a *nauta* (Fig. 3.3). The context of the discovery is uncertain. However, the topography of the find suggests that it was from the area of the Municipium Septimium Apulense, which was limited and separated from the hill of the legionary fort and the palace of the governors (*praetorium consularis*) with a backwater of the Ampoita River.[89] This indicates that the relief was probably part of a construction or small sacralised space related to this river, which communicated with the Marisia in the south.[90]

A monumental, colourful relief representing an aquatic monster or divinity was also discovered in the territory of Apulum, however the context of the find is uncertain.[91] This represents a strong visual message, which indicates a building or environment related to a port or a sacralised space dedicated to aquatic divinities.

The cult of Neptunus is also well attested in the Danubian provinces.[92] A particular case study was attested in Viminacium, where Neptunus and Magna Mater shared the same sacralised space.[93] The inscription was dedicated by Caius Valerius Vibanus, a *nautarum quinquennalis* who donated 2,000 *sestertii* to the reconstruction of the temple of Neptunus along with a *signum* (probably a statue) of Magna Mater.[94] The association of Magna Mater and Neptunus is rarely attested, but it reflects the philosophical tradition attested in Lucretius, where the contrast between earth and water is reflected by the divine agencies of Magna Mater and Neptunus.[95] The case of Viminacium is particularly interesting because the members of the *collegium nautarum* are also attested in the cult of Mithras.[96]

Fig. 3.3 Relief of a Genius nautarum *in Apulum. (Source: Lupa 19332-3, photo of Ortolf Harl with the special permission of the National Museum of Union Alba Iulia)*

Pilgrimage routes[97]

Identifying ancient pilgrimage through the evidence of archaeology is no easier than defining this notion for Greco-Roman realities. Despite the decade-long research on ancient pilgrimage, for many scholars this notion is just an anachronism, a contemporary phenomenon forced on ancient realities.[98] Recent approaches and studies seem to prove that religiously inspired, long-distance mobilities of and visits to sanctuaries and sacralised spaces were widespread in the ancient Mediterranean region and produced specific architectural and material evidence, although the evidence is not always clear and it can be hard to understand the motivation behind a 'religiously motivated voyage'.[99]

Based on the definition of Thierry Luginbühl and Jaś Elsner, ancient Greco-Roman pilgrimage can be defined as a long- (extra-provincial) or short- (intra-provincial) distanced and religiously motivated voyage, although the motivation and aim of the voyage can be very different: healing, consulting an oracle, participating in religious festivals and processions, making or observing sacrifices, or simply feeling the sensorial presence of a divinity.[100] In the case of a religious pilgrimage, the displacement itself is an important agent in religious communication and the spiritual path of the voyager: it defines the difference between religious tourism, for which the road itself is just a tool, and pilgrimage, for which the displacement is part of the religious ritual and transformation. The archaeological evidence of the latter is, however, extremely sporadic, especially in the Danubian provinces, as the following examples will show.

The contribution of M. Grünewald showed that this phenomenon was common not only in the Greek part of the Empire, but also in the Celtic and Germanic regions north to the Alps – a symbolic border of cultural and historiographic limits.[101] His examples focused mostly on long-distance mobilities of people visiting famous mineral and thermal baths, which reflects the plurality and complexity of the notion of ancient pilgrimage as Luginbühl's typology had already proved. Visiting a thermal bath was motivated mostly by medical or leisure issues; the presence of the divine agency was a secondary motivation.[102] By contrast, in the case of oracular sanctuaries and mystery cult sites, the presence of a specific divine agent was crucial. This range of motivations for religious voyages (pilgrimages) was also reflected by Williamson, who also highlighted in his 2005 article the slight differences between religious 'tourism' and 'pilgrimage' in antiquity.[103]

In the Danubian provinces, short- and long-distance pilgrimages were identified in very few places. This is mainly explained by the contemporary state of research, which has focused mostly on military types of mobilities, although the role of the sanctuaries in these long-distance mobilities was highlighted in some recent works.[104] Grünewald based his study on identifying ancient pilgrimage sites mostly on epigraphic and cartographic sources, which were rarely supported by the archaeological evidence, such as the so called 'hostels' near the thermal baths. A similar approach can be made for the region discussed in this book.

In the case of the Danubian provinces, spa vignettes on the Tabula Peutingeriana were also present, however in most of the cases, it is impossible to associate them with major sanctuaries in the vicinity.[105] The great concentration of the spa vignettes in Dalmatia is not surprising, due to the geographic specificities of the province and the large number of aquatic Illyrian divinities – many of which were transported to other provinces, such as in Dacia after 106 AD.[106] None of the six spa resorts can be associated, however, with long-distance pilgrimages, although, with the exception of Stanecli,[107] all of them were situated on major Imperial roads, connecting Aquileia and Rome with the Danubian provinces, which does presume long-distance mobilities.[108]

The population from Dalmatia, by contrast, is known to have participated intensively in various religious pilgrimages. The presence of the cult of Artemis Ephesia in Salona suggests a strong link with the Mother sanctuary of the divinity or at least the presence of a diaspora from Asia Minor.[109] The spa centres and bath complexes of Moesia Superior, meanwhile, are less researched and there are only two cases where possible traces of religious pilgrimage have been attested (Fig. 3.4). An interesting case is the one at Mediana, the hoard found in a villa in 1972, which contained a group of statues made of marble and porphyry.[110] Most of the statues show the figures of Asclepius, Hygeia, Telesphorus and Heracles.[111] The bronze railing decorated with busts of Asclepius and Luna was yet another argument for the researchers to assume the existence of a small temple at the site, probably consecrated to the group of Iatric deities.

The connection of such deities with baths and water facilities was not unique. A similar link was attested at Osmakovo and Krupac near Pirot in south-east Serbia, although these sites were documented in just a single line of an article in 1966.[112] The lack of the epigraphic material doesn't allow us to suppose an intra-provincial pilgrimage site here. The studies of András Mócsy and Zoltán Kádár also highlighted the important healing sanctuary of Paracin in Moesia Superior, where a syncretism between Asclepius and the so-called 'Thracian Riders' (*Domna et Domnus*) cult was attested – a great example of local religious appropriation.[113] Incubation was often associated with hero cults, which gives a whole new perspective to the popularity of the cults of the 'Thracian Riders' and the 'Danubian Riders' (*Domna et Domnus*) in the Danubian provinces, which were often discovered in the vicinity of Asclepieia.[114]

Much better known is the situation in the provinces of Pannonia, where the presence of intra-provincial and even extra-provincial pilgrimages can be attested. The main religious centres of the province since the early Claudian and later Flavian period were established along the Amber Road, which created an important economic, military and cultural connectivity between Rome and the Barbaricum. This connectivity can be traced back to the Bronze Age, and the Pannonian road system followed the same commercial routes attested in the pre-Roman era.[115] The presence of early militaria and rich military graves with specific Italic equipment suggest the intense mobilities of the military in this area.[116] Poetovio was one of the key points on this road. As an important centre of the *publicum portorii Illyrici*, the city became

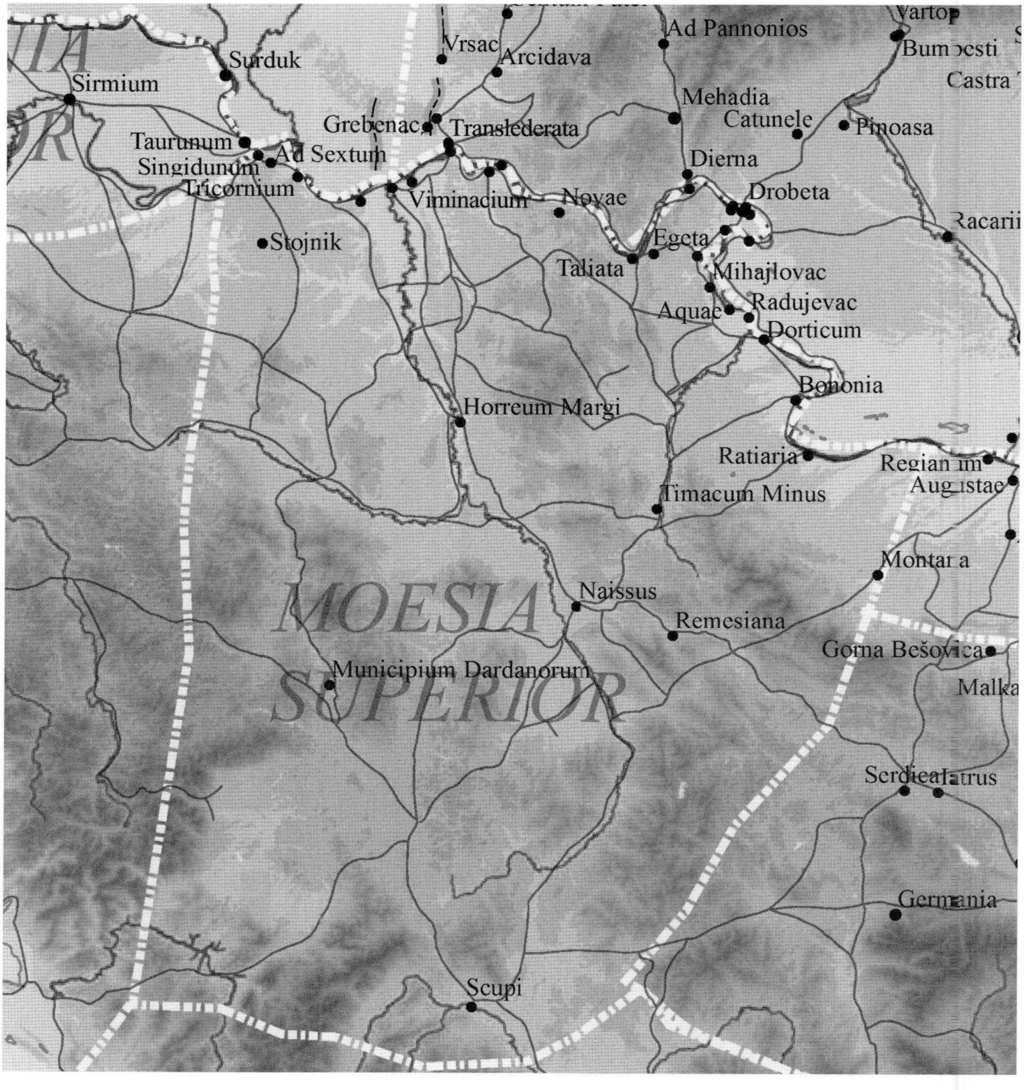

Fig. 3.4 Map of Roman Moesia Superior. (Source: Țentea 2011, 229, pl. 1. with the special permission of the author)

in the Trajanic period one of the most important religious centres of Pannonia. Although the archaeological material suggests the presence of an Asclepeion, it has not yet been excavated.[117]

Another relevant example of a pilgrimage site is the Iseum of Savaria (Fig. 3.5). The sanctuary was established in the 1st century AD and had an almost four-century-long existence (cat. no. III.75). The archaeological material – especially the recently published terra sigillata finds,[118] but also other vessels – and the epigraphic material

Fig. 3.5 The Iseum of Savaria. (Source: author)

suggest an intense economic relationship with Aquileia and northern Italia, as well as with Scrabantia and Aquincum.[119] Recently, it was suggested that the sanctuary functioned as a regional centre of the Isiac cults in Pannonia and even Dacia.[120] The Iseum also produced special lamps bearing Isiac iconography, which suggests the presence of religious souvenirs.[121] Based on the materiality of the sanctuary alone, however, we cannot determine for sure whether the sanctuary was a regional or an extra-provincial centre of pilgrimage. Healing and incubation were also recurrent aspects of numerous Iseia in the Roman Empire, but there is no certain evidence for medical care in the Iseum of Savaria.[122]

An interesting case was found in Kékkút, Hungary, also on the Amber Road, where Iulia Martia, a woman from a Germanic province, dedicated an altar to the nymphs, although its archaeological context has not yet been clarified.[123] The presence of small thermal springs on the crossroads and along the main commercial and military roads created short-term sacralised spaces, which served as temporary third spaces for the visitors and travellers. The presence of such small roadside shrines do not represent pilgrimage sites but they nevertheless had the same effect on the worshippers, whose religious and corporeal health while en route were assured by their presence.

One of the most important pilgrimage sites of Pannonia was at Varaždinske Toplice, the ancient Aquae Iasae (cat. no. III.3–5).[124] The thermal springs were already being used in the 1st century AD as the most important healing site of the Iasi tribe (known also as the 'spa people') and had existed for 400 years by the Constantinian age. The complex follows the typical structure and topography of the thermal baths, surrounded by sacralised spaces, baths, a basilica, roads and fountains with a well-established functionality and adorned with decorative language. All the elements – the functionality of buildings, the visual language and the power of the ex-votos – served the successful maintenance of the site.

Numerous high-rank officers, *beneficiarii* and the staff of the *publicum* visited the site, while some of the pilgrims, such as Lucius Claudius Moderatus from Savaria, visited regularly.[125] The architectural atmosphere of the sacralised space was shaped and transformed into a religious third space by the heavy financial investments of some notable visitors.[126] These people, who hailed from Savaria or Poetovio, used this pilgrimage not only for their own religious experience but also for a social and economic communication.

By the 4th century AD, the three nymphs of the Iasi had become associated not only with the *Dii Consentes* (Minerva, Juno, Apollo), but also with Isis and Serapis. The presence of the iconography of Apollo-Sol and several inscriptions associated with Serapis and the nymphs suggest that the sanctuary also functioned as an oracle site in the 3rd century AD.[127] This could have been intensified after the so-called 'temple visits' of Emperor Caracalla from 212–217 AD, when he visited numerous oracle sites throughout the Empire. The site was also visited by Emperor Constantine.[128]

The unhealthy and threatened body of the emperor as a malfunctioning third space of the Empire itself had a direct effect on the materiality of religious communication in the Danubian provinces. Sanctuaries – especially healing sites – were decorated with ex-votos dedicated to his health. The popularity of Apollo Grannus in the Danubian provinces also increased significantly in this period. What's more, the beautiful representation of Asclepius, Telesphorus and Hygeia at Aquae Iasae was dedicated to the health of Caracalla. Such important pilgrims served as agents in ancient and modern space sacralisation, creating and recreating religious traditions.[129] Aquae Iasae had a renaissance in the end of the 19th century after another Imperial visit – this time by Franz Joseph – and it is still in use as a tourist attraction, as well as being used by the local religious groups to attract pilgrims to their churches.

Aquincum and Carnuntum, two of the most important military and urban settlements of Pannonia Inferior and Pannonia Superior, had employed medical staff for the Roman legions (*valetudinarium*), however there were no Asclepeia attested archaeologically.[130]

In Roman Dacia, most of the healing sites and sanctuaries were formed in Roman times (106–271 AD), without any certain pre-Roman history.[131] From the six known healing sites, the only one with a probable use during pre-Roman period is the healing complex of Germisara (Cigmău, Romania). This suggestion was based exclusively on onomastic studies; no stratigraphic or other archaeological data prove this hypothesis (cat. no. VI.17).[132] In the first Roman phase of the sanctuary, the cavity containing a hot lake was probably used as a natural bath, where religious communication with the divine agency was established by ritual purification, as one of the recently published inscriptions suggest.[133] More than 600 coins, a statue of Diana and at least 11 gold plaques were found as votive offerings in the lake (Fig. 3.6).[134] The site is a great example of how the natural environment – the cavity and the springs – could be systematically transformed and integrated into a complex sanctuary, serving as a religious third space for the provincial visitors, some of whom, such as Marcus Statius Priscus, were attested no fewer than three times in inscriptions.[135]

Another site in Roman Dacia that became a provincial pilgrimage site was found in Aqua Herculis – Ad Mediam (Băile Herculane, Herkulesfürdő). Here, the hot springs and cavities were transformed into an entire road network of sacralised spaces dedicated to Hercules, Aesculapius, Hygeia, Genius Loci and the local spirits of the waters (*Dii et Numini Aquarum*). The importance of the site is well reflected by the official diplomatic delegation and dedications led by Marcus Sedatius Severianus[136] and by the miraculous healing of Iunia Cyrilla.[137] Both case studies served as important religious agents in the long-term maintenance of the pilgrimage site and the successful existence of the sanctuaries as a religious third space. The Roman site had a renaissance after the 18th century when it was discovered, written about, and recreated as one of the most important bath and leisure attractions of the Balkans during the age of the Austro-Hungarian Empire (1867–1918).[138]

Fig. 3.6 The Roman spring and sanctuary of Germisara. (Source: after Szabó 2018b, photo of Aurora Pețan with the special permission of the author)

The Asclepeion of Sarmizegetusa (cat. no. VI.35) is well documented archaeologically and represents one of the main healing shrines of the province.[139] It served not only as a local sacralised space *extra muros* of the capital city of Dacia, but also became a regional, provincial centre of religious pilgrimage. The site was also in direct communication with the major Roman road that ran outside the city and connected with the northern part of Dacia. Its position allowed complex processions and interactions with the Ara Augusti and the amphitheatre of Colonia Sarmizegetusa.[140] The statuary programme and architectural features of the sanctuary complex of Aesculapius and Hygeia reflect a strong influence from Asia Minor, especially Pergamon.[141]

A similar healing site is also presumed in Apulum, in the north-east part of the Colonia Aurelia Apulensis, near Tauşor Lake. Although the site was never excavated and researched systematically, the rich epigraphic material and the numerous statuary and figurative monuments from that area show not only the existence of an important healing shrine and complex sanctuary, but also a sacralised space used by the local elite to show off their wealth, especially members of the *ordo decurionum*.[142] In the case of Apulum, numerous alternative options were present on the so-called 'religious marketplace' of the conurbation: the cult of Glykon, a Dolichenum and an intensive presence of the cult of Serapis and Isis in the fort, the palace of the governor, and also in the civil environment. This rich variety of healing shrines and religious strategies in divine communication was thus a fertile atmosphere for religious third spaces and imaginary spaces, such as the sick human body in communication with the divine world.[143]

Further macro-spaces and long-distance mobilities

Religious groups and individuals were also connected in numerous other ways: the Amber Road (between Aquileia and Carnuntum)[144] represented one of the cardinal communication routes of the region, creating a permanent and intense economic and cultural connectivity between Italy, Noricum and Pannonia, but also with the Barbaricum.[145] Senatorial families and the Italic elite were actively involved in large-scale trading mobilities especially in pottery material.[146] The Taurisci elite from Emona seem to have been intensively involved in the formation of the first Roman settlements and the transformation of the demographic and cultural landscape of the newly formed province of Pannonia since the age of Augustus and Tiberius.[147] The cult of Aecorna (Aequorna) was interpreted as a religious transfer from the Aquileia-Emona region to the *territorium* of Savaria.[148]

Another important and highly frequented road that connected the capital of the Empire with Dalmatia – Moesia Superior and Roman Dacia – traversed the Balkans (Porolissum-Ratiaria-Naissus-Lissus-Rome or Sarmizegetusa-Sirmium-Salona-Rome).[149] This road represented one of the principal communication routes of the Roman army between Moesia Superior and Dacia, but it was also important in a diplomatic sense since it connected the capital of the Empire and the lower Danubian provinces. A particularly interesting inscription dedicated to the aquatic divinities (*Dii et Numini Aquarum*) discovered at Ad Herculis (Băile Herculane/Herkulesfürdő) mentions the successful diplomatic journey of Decimus Terentius Scaurianus, a former governor of Roman Dacia who became consul in Rome, accompanied by five *legati.*[150] The journey from Colonia Sarmizegetusa (or Apulum) to Rome took at least 33–35 days to complete and would involve using either the Sarmizegetusa-Drobeta-Naissus-Rome road or, more plausibly, going through Singidunum and Salona. In both cases, the route crossed several foggy, woody and dangerous mountain areas, such as the valley of the Cerna River. This region seems to have been particularly dangerous, especially for dignitaries and magistrates – a fact that is attested by three inscriptions mentioning Roman citizens being attacked and killed by *latrones.*[151] Similar cases might be also expected in the territory of Moesia Superior.[152]

Maritime routes also played a significant role in the extra-provincial networks and connectivity of religious groups in the Danubian provinces. The maritime routes that connected the Pontic area of the western coast of the Black Sea with Italy and the Mediterranean world (Tomis-Byzantium-Alexandria Troas-Corinthus-Messena-Ostia) was a crucial channel for small-group religions, especially those from Asia Minor and the Greek-speaking members of the former Hellenstic world. Anna Collar proved in her paradigmatic work on religious networks that small-group religions are formed around charismatic religious leaders and a central core group whose mobility will define the dynamics of a cult and its geographic spread.[153] Small-group religions – such as the cult of Theos Hypsistos in Dacia and Asia Minor,[154] the Dolichenian groups of Dacia, Moesia Inferior[155] and Thracia,[156] and the movement of Alexander of Abonoteichus and the cult of Glycon in Asia Minor,

Moesia Inferior and Dacia[157] – used both of the roads between Dacia and Thracia, but also the maritime routes between the western coast of the Black Sea and the Aegean Sea. Mobilities between Syria and Asia Minor and the Danubian provinces are well attested by small-group religions, especially in urban environments, although their mode of transport was not exclusively civilian, especially in the case of the Syrian-Palmyrian groups.[158]

The Danubian provinces also had few exotic connectivities with the most far-flung regions of the Roman Empire: the military dislocations between Mauretania and the Danubian provinces during the period of Antoninus Pius and Marcus Aurelius created an intense connectivity between North Africa and this region (cat. no. VI.21).[159] The significant number of dedications to Dea Caelestis and Saturnus in the region is one of the consequences of these long-distance mobilities[160] and, later, the intense political connectivity of Numidia with Pannonia and Dacia.[161] Rare, long-distance connections also existed between Aegyptus and the Danubian provinces: in a few cases, onomastic sources[162] and material evidence from Isiac contexts suggest direct Egyptian or Eastern origins.

New spaces: cities and forts

The Roman Empire changed radically the cultural landscape of continental Europe and the Mediterranean.[163] The large number of urban settlements and the first professional, long-lasting army in constant extra-provincial mobility created a demographic network, which represents a radically new macro-space and transformative agent in religious communication. Roman urbanity was long identified as one of the key factors in the expansion of the Roman *orbis*, which the literature termed 'Romanisation'. Roman urbanism is now a booming research field that focuses on the impact of urban settlements on the macro-economy of the Roman Empire,[164] landscape and trading networks.[165] Urbanism as a transformative agent cannot, however, be analysed without historic contextualisation. The Roman Empire during the Principate, especially at the end of the 1st century AD, united several macro-regions in Europe, North Africa and the Hellenistic world with radically different demographic and settlement patterns: while the Hellenistic world (including the multi-millennial traditions of urbanity in Egypt and the Near East) had a strong urban tradition with well-established institutions and urban trading and cultural networks,[166] the Celtic world had a different settlement pattern, known as the *oppida* system.[167] In both cases, the established commercial and cultural routes and networks played a crucial role in the later development and transformation of these regions within the Roman Empire and had a direct impact on religious communication, too.[168] Urbanism in the territory of the Roman Empire during the Principate did not begin everywhere with the Roman administration, but urbanity did stop within the limits of the Empire in most of the European region, which was in intense contact with a few commercial and urban settlements in Hellenistic Central Asia and the Mesopotamian world.[169]

Urbanity in Roman times was a complex notion and had numerous particularities and glocal aspects. One of these is the legal state of urbanism: the two legal categories (*municipium* and *colonia*) radically restructured the urban society of Roman settlements, and had a strong impact on their economic-financial status, religious communication and space sacralisation, too.[170] Roman urbanity is therefore a deeply legal aspect and condition. However, Roman urbanisation also had both a global and glocal impact on reshaping the macro-economic routes and the financial system of the Roman Empire, especially after the great territorial expansions in the 1st and 2nd centuries AD.[171]

Recently, the formation of urban systems and settlement networks was reinterpreted through the lens of a new space theory in the project conducted by Luuk de Ligt and his team.[172] Their project aimed to go beyond the micro-historical and focused approach on individual cities and urban centres and highlighted the importance of regionality, glocality and the immense interconnectivity of urban centres and their social, political, economic and cultural patterns. The project produced numerous important contributions focusing on the western part of the Roman Empire and – for the first time in recent years for a prestigious international project – also on the Danubian provinces.[173] Damjan Donev's approach used a complex and in many ways problematic spatial theory and a new taxonomy of urban systems and settlements, highlighting the importance of old (autohtonity, military vs civilian) and new (regionality, agricultural terrains, *territoria*, the notion of small *municipia*) criteria in the interpretation of urbanity.[174]

Urbanity in the Danubian provinces cannot be understood either locally, in traditional provincial units, or in this artificial and historiographic entity.[175] The area of our study unites the most diverse urbanities of the Roman Empire: it englobes the periphery of the proto-urban type of *oppida* system in the Celtic world (especially in Raetia, Noricum and Pannonia),[176] the Hellenistic urban traditions found on the shore of the Black Sea and the newly formed urban systems (*colonia deducta*) formed during the Principate, especially as a consequence of the military mobilities and dislocations that were particularly prevalent up to the age of Trajan.[177] In some rare cases, these three major types of urbanities in the Danubian region overlapped and coexisted. For instance, the Celtic *oppida* system and Hellenistic urbanism, as well as Roman urban structures, can be observed in Sarmizegetusa Regia, the former capital of the Dacian kingdom,[178] as well as in the Hellenistic-Roman emporion on Magdalensberg and perhaps in pre-Roman Sirmium, although the archaeological data from the latter is extremely limited.[179]

Donev's work proved that the evolution of the urban systems in the Danubian provinces had a radically different history in the Adriatic and the Thracian-Hellenistic environment, whereas in Pannonia, Moesia Superior and Dacia, urbanisation was almost exclusively a Roman phenomenon: urban centres in these provinces were strictly dependent on the presence of the Roman army, especially the legionary troops. The largest and most important conurbations of the region were those that were formed on the territory of the *canabae* and civil settlements near legionary forts: Vindobona, Carnuntum, Aquincum, Brigetio, Poetovio, Singidunum, Novae, Durostorum, Apulum, Potaissa and Troesmis. In a few cases, Roman urban systems were formed around civilian settlements that had sprung up because of the expanding Roman administration and new political entities. The most significant centres of this kind were Savaria, Scrabantia, Sirmium and Colonia Sarmizegetusa. Following the idea of András Mócsy on the evolution of urban centres in the Danubian provinces, Donev goes further, highlighting the regionality of urban systems and the role of the so-called small *municipia*, or middle-sized towns, as well as large and urban-like *vici* that again seem to be a consequence of the large number of auxiliary troops in this region.[180]

During the Principate, from the Julio-Claudian period, but especially in the 2nd–3rd centuries AD, the settlement systems of the Danubian provinces changed radically, creating a complex and highly interconnected network of urban centres especially along the Danube and the major commercial routes. In less than a century, more than 60 settlements gained the title of *municipia* and *coloniae*, although the number of urban-type settlements was much higher (Fig. A3 in the Appendices).[181]

Despite this impressive transformation of the settlement system and the architectural landscape, the Danubian provinces remained a 'busy periphery' of the Roman Empire: the density and demography of urban settlements as well as the presence of the *collegia* and professional associations were much lower in this macro-region than in any other area of the Empire, the estimated population of the 60–70 urban settlements being less than half a million.[182] While the urban settlements of Roman Dacia existed for less than two centuries, most of the Danubian urban systems had a four- or five-century-long history.[183] The Greek colonies in Moesia Inferior represent an exceptional 10–12-century-long urbanity in this macro-region.

A specific aspect of the urban system is the double cities that were formed near the legionary fortresses, where a civilian and a military urban centre coexisted side by side, albeit usually in two different legal and geographic entities. Despite the long, repeated and demographically unquestionably peripheral aspect of the Danubian provinces, the historical timing of their urbanisation (1–2nd centuries AD) created a very dynamic and multicultural urban network, which played a crucial role in Roman religious communication and the shaping of religious visual narratives and media.

Citification as religious agent

Institutionalised religion and urbanisation were for a long time treated strictly together, a habit that was later the basis of the 'polis-religion' concept developed by Fustel de Coulanges and many others.[184] Case studies analysing Roman religion in an urban context in the 19th and 20th centuries focused especially on the local aspect of religious communication, in many cases limiting their research to the quantitative approach, enlisting the local archaeological material without contextual interpretation. Urbanity in these works was limited and defined as an administrative and legal unit, in very few cases going beyond this conventional definition. By contrast, case studies on Palmyra, Ostia or Pompeii[185] had already opened a new approach, concentrating not only on the topography of the materiality of religion, but on specific facets of religious communication, such as sacralised spaces and their transformation, religious specialists and their careers, or the inventory of the domestic and public spaces. Yet few studies tried to offer a complex methodology, where urban atmosphere and urbanity is a living agent in religious communication. The work of Angelo Brelich on the religious life of Aquincum can be considered as such a rare paradigmatic work, although its historiographical impact was extremely limited due to its inaccessibility outside Hungary.[186] Another important contribution was the theoretical model of Hubert Cancik, who offered a complex space taxonomy with his sacred landscape notion,[187] although urbanity was not introduced in his model.

Urban religion goes far beyond the infrastructural, legal and institutional factors. Citification – the formation of religious communication by urbanity[188] – examines the agency role of the city (urban landscape) in a much broader, complex dimension. Urban religion was recently also reinterpreted from the perspective of the conceptual space (spatial turn) and globalisation.[189] In my model of urban religion (Fig. 3.7), urbanity as a living agent in religious communication has eight major factors: demography (population size), multiculturality (population composition),[190] economic variety (financial possibilities), interconnectivity (human and material mobilities), building density (complex architectural atmosphere), high level of visibility and accessibility (or the chance for the opposite, invisibility), legal and administrative control (priests, magistrates) and historicity (time and continuity). These factors are not exclusively urban products and specificities, but their coexistence represents a typical urban environment. Due to the architectural complexity, material and human interconnectivity and the financial possibilities, the city defines religion as a spatial practice.[191] It creates the opportunity for greater visibility for small-group religions and provides greater chances for religious survival, mimicry and the maintenance of a religious group.[192] A Roman city – like the Roman army as an imagined space, and the Roman fortresses as legal boundaries – represents the transition between macro-spaces and meso-spaces in religious communication. Cities unite a large diversity of human agency and religious meso-spaces, which creates a fertile environment for a broader range of visual, textual and spatial appropriations, too. Density, therefore, is the essential factor of urban religion: the focalisation of demographic, material, divine, administrative, infrastructural, architectural, financial and knowledge concentration in urban environments gives a unique opportunity and serves as fertile ground for the diversification and constant transformation of religious communication and space sacralisation.

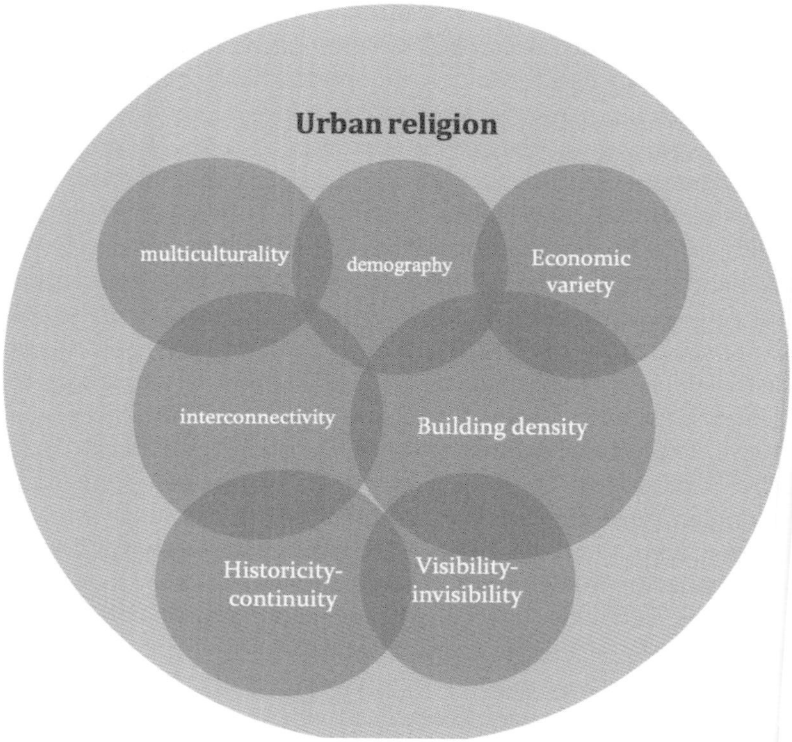

Fig. 3.7 Urbanity and citification in religious communication. (Source: author)

The most visible heritage of Roman religious communication – the votive epigraphic and figurative material – was produced mostly in the urban settlements of the Danubian provinces (68 per cent of the epigraphic material).[193] In these transitional spaces, such as the cities, which are part of the larger, spatial clusters and macro-spaces of the Empire, small-group religions and meso-spaces flourished in the age of the Principate. Not only were urban spaces and their specific factors shaping religion, but by creating long-lasting sacralised spaces, religion was also maintaining urbanity. This reciprocal idea was recently debated in prehistorical works, focusing especially on the very origins of religion and urbanity.[194]

Roman urban centres produced several large-scale, public spaces dedicated exclusively to religious communication. One of them was the Ara Augusti, a large square with a central altar dedicated to the Imperial cult and the council of the province. Similar monumental sacralised spaces were attested in Cambodunum[195] and presumed in Sarmizegetusa and Savaria.[196] Recently, a similar monumental square was proposed by Ádám Szabó in the area of the civilian town of Aquincum.[197] The centrality and political-economic role of cities were also reflected in the density of the sacred area, a special zone of the urban landscape that was agglomerated with numerous sacralised spaces. Such urban environments were identified archaeologically in Cambodunum in the Area Sacra, where 20 small or middle-sized buildings dedicated probably for religious communication were discovered in Sarmizegetusa, where the Area Sacra had a similar density of urban constructions.[198] These monumental areas in the urban environments marked not only the major religious events in the public space, but also the evolution of the urban planning and settlement history.

I will now focus on case studies of urban religions, analysing the eight conditions listed above and the formative factors of religion in the cities of the Danubian provinces.

Religion and urbanity: case studies

Four types of urban evolution can be identified in the Danubian provinces: 1) urban systems formed in the vicinity of a legionary fortress (civilian towns or *canabae*, which went on to later gain a municipal status); 2) cities formed in the vicinity of a military *vicus* (near the auxiliary forts); 3) autochthonous (pre-Roman) settlements (*civitates*) transformed into Roman cities (including the Greek colonies); and 4) the few attested cases of *colonia deducta*, Roman towns formed by the veterans.[199] The formation of these urban centres also defined the religious density and the major aspect of urban religion in these settlements; therefore, they need a particular focus and individual analysis as macro-spaces in religious communication.

From all the macro-regions of the Roman Empire, the Danubian provinces were the richest in urban centres formed in the vicinity of a legionary fortress.[200] These macro-spaces (the cities and the fortresses) represent one of the key elements in the history of Roman religion in this macro-region of the Empire. They produced a significant quantity (41 per cent) of Roman materiality of religion (2,385 votive inscriptions from the total of 5,724 found in seven provinces),[201] but more importantly, they represent most of the sacralised spaces attested in this region. The impact of the legionary troops, the stability and historicity of a legionary fortress and the intense human mobility (*dislocatio*) of the legionary vexillations created a unique network of religious interconnectivity.[202]

In most cases, the urban topography of the legionary conurbations has been poorly researched, however modern non-destructive methods have now opened a new chapter in the study of urban topography in Brigetio, Troesmis and Novae.[203] Yet the ancient topography and historical geography of these settlements are not comparable with Rome,[204] Ostia,[205] Pompeii[206] and the Roman cities of North Africa and the Near East,[207] where urban religion can be researched through the innovative methodology of high-definition archaeology, which focuses on material and human mobility, the impact of the natural environment, geology, hydrography, stratigraphic and material culture analysis, database cataloguing and related analysis – all of which are methods from the natural sciences and place the architectural atmosphere in historical perspective.[208] Of the urban centres of the Danubian provinces, only two have been documented in such detail and can therefore serve as case studies of urban religion near legionary fortresses: Carnuntum and Aquincum.[209]

The importance of these regional centres is well reflected by the quantity of the epigraphic material concentrated there: more than 615 votive inscriptions and more than 160 figurative, anepigraphic monuments were attested in Carnuntum[210] and 577 in Aquincum.[211] The density of Roman material religion in these two conurbations (two civilian settlements, two fortresses, two *canabae* and their *territoria,* which includes the pre-Roman settlements) is comparable only to the large urban centres of the Near East and Rome (Fig. 3.8).[212] The two urban systems show numerous similarities not only in their political and military history, but also in the religious landscape and 'pantheon' of the divine agency attested there.[213] This can be explained by numerous factors: both conurbations were formed in the vicinity of important Celtic settlements and were in close cultural interconnectivity even before the Roman conquest.[214] Although the hypothesis of István Tóth on the so-called '*Fasti Pannonici*', the festival of Pannonia, might not be entirely plausible, the close association of Jupiter Karnuntinus[215] and Jupiter Teutanus[216] remains a valid point. Both settlements experienced relative stability in terms of military dislocations and mobility since the Trajanic period, which meant that the multicultural aspect of the population was mostly civilian and commercial. Both settlements were composed of multiple distinctive macro-spaces, divided not only by a significant (2.2 km or 1 *leuga*[217]) physical distance between the legionary fortresses and the surrounding *canabae* and their civilian settlements, but also by their legal status, which had an almost identical chronological path.[218] Both Carnuntum and Aquincum were also situated in a similar geographic and hydrographic environment, one in which the pre-Roman hilltop settlement and the Danube played an important role in commercial and religious communication.[219]

In the case of Aquincum, the hills of Buda in the western part of the Roman conurbation represented a natural defensive line, while the Danube was the major communication channel between all the settlements along the Ripa Pannonica and even beyond, connecting the major legionary centres of Pannonia Superior, Pannonia Inferior, Moesia Superior and Moesia Inferior. The urban macro-space of Aquincum was a linear one: it begins in the south on the Gellérthegy and its surroundings, where the possible Eraviscan *oppidum* was identified on the top of the hill.[220] Unfortunately, except for two votive inscriptions, no sacralised spaces have been discovered in the Gellérthegy-Tabán or the five other Eraviscan sites that have been identified on the contemporary territory of Budapest, therefore a spatial continuity between the pre-Roman sacralised spaces and the newly established legionary fortress and its conurbation cannot be established.[221]

Some 5 km north from the Celtic settlement, the military core of the Roman macro-space was formed at the end of the 1st century AD,[222] and went on to shape the entire region of the Eravisci for the following three centuries. The legionary fortress and the small fort of the *alae*[223] represent probably the very first macro-spaces of the new, Roman presence, which changed not only the natural environment, but also created

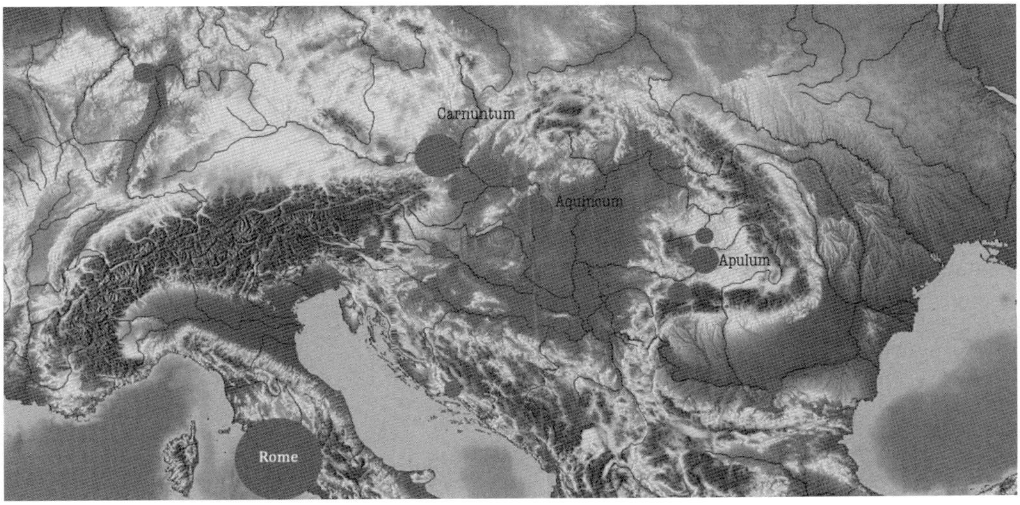

Fig. 3.8 Geographic distribution and density of votive inscriptions in urban centres of the Danubian provinces. (Source: author)

new sacralised spaces, now featuring new forms of religious materiality, media and architectural atmosphere. Following the same major road, which connected the large territory of the Erasvici in a linear line along the Danube, around 2.2 km north of the legionary camp, we find the civilian settlement, which later became a Hadrianic *municipium* and a *colonia* after the faithful participation of the II Adiutrix legion in Septimius Severus's campaign.[224] The civilian settlement probably began its existence after 106 AD when the II Adiutrix legion replaced the X Gemina legion, which left few epigraphic traces in the city. However, it is unclear whether there were any sacralised spaces before the Trajanic period.[225]

During the Hadrianic period, Aquincum began its urbanisation, changing radically the architectural atmosphere and creating the major macro-spaces that went on to serve as public spheres of religious communication in the following four decades until the Marcomannic Wars (117–160 AD).[226] The major urban structures and macro-spaces that were formed in this period were: the palace of the governors, with several altars and a Fortuna statue identified in different compartments;[227] the Capitolium; the forum of the civilian town (cat. no. III.6), which has also been interpreted as a place for the Imperial cult;[228] the two amphitheatres (the military and the civilian), both with a small Nemeseion;[229] and several other sacralised spaces in the same northern area of the civilian town, in the continuation of the forum (Fig. 3.9). While the palace of the governors represents a unique case study for a macro-space hosting the invisibility of religious communication and a transition between accessibility and inaccessibility in religious dialogue between human and divine agency,[230] the macro-spaces of the civilian settlement are typical forms for openness.

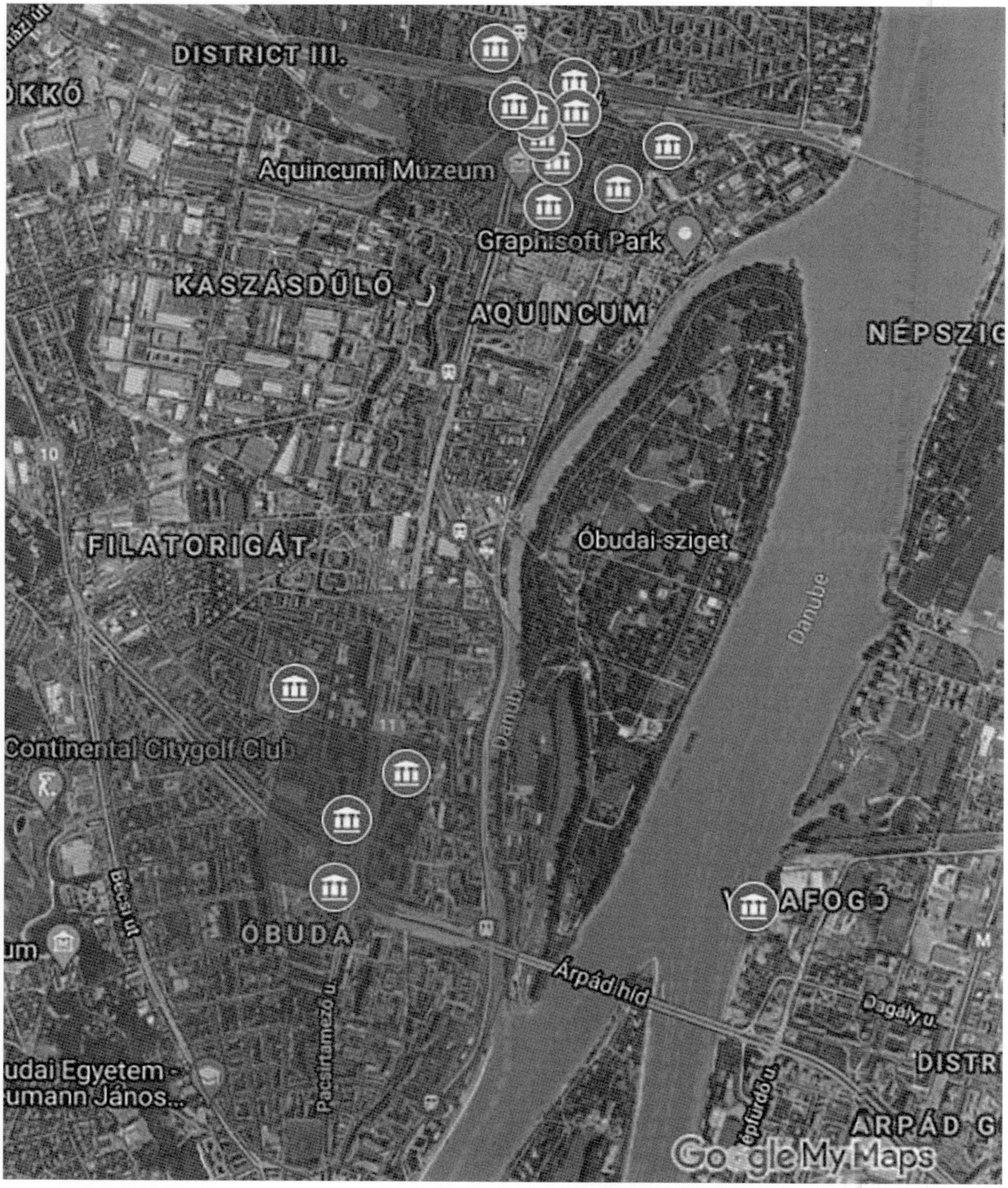

Fig. 3.9 Urban plan of Aquincum with the most important sacralised spaces attested. (Source: author from the DAS map)

The close proximity of the civilian amphitheatre and the forum with this northern area of the town suggests that these often large public buildings played an important role in the formation of the urban skeleton and were in close interconnectivity with each other. The numerous monumental building inscriptions from the amphitheatre region indicate that these public spaces were used intensively by the local elite for self-expression, as well as in the political and social competition that already featured in religious communication in 162 AD and especially after the rebuilding of the Nemeseion in 214 AD.[231]

The case study of the *Mithraea* from Aquincum shows the well-documented topographic centralisation and dynamics from the periphery towards the centre of the city: while the first *Mithraeum* to be attested was located in the periphery of the city, the later ones were much closer to the core of the urban macro-spaces (cat. no. III.10–14, Fig. 3.10).[232]

The macro-spaces of religious communication had a second, monumentalised phase after 194 AD, when the city was transformed into a *colonia* and its legal status changed after 212 AD.[233] These central spaces defined not only the religious communication and the major public festivals, their processions and their spaces, but also the topographic evolution of the city: the position of the forum and the civilian amphitheatre represented the Area Sacra of Aquincum, a well-defined earthly *templum*, a sacralised landscape separated from the domestic area of the city. However, here, we cannot observe such a strict delimitation as was observable in the case of Colonia Sarmizegetusa in Roman Dacia, for example, where the Area Sacra and its several public temples was in an *extra muros* area.[234]

The connectivity of the religious macro-spaces in Aquincum and the major urban centres of the Danubian provinces can be observed especially in the case of the healing divinities and springs or water cults: this essential natural element represented not only a necessary feature of the landscape in the Asclepeia,[235] but also in the basic urban infrastructure in every Roman city. The starting point of the aqueduct in Aquincum was a large, sacralised space with 14 springs and its own shrine. An altar and two monumentalised buildings were also part of this complex sacralised space, which was dedicated for the nymphs, Asclepius and Hygeia, Silvanus and Jupiter (cat. no. III.15–28).[236]

Based on the epigraphic material and literary sources on Floralia, Klára Póczy presumed that this sacred area was in direct connection with the civilian amphitheatre on yearly occasions and public festivals, when during the Floralia festival, religious processions travelled from the spring complex to the amphitheatre and possibly to the forum of the city. A similar topographic feature can be observed in Colonia Sarmizegetusa, where the Asclepeion is in close proximity to the amphitheatre and the Ara Augusti of the province (cat. no. VI.35).[237] A similar situation can be attested in Brigetio[238] and also in Apulum,[239] where springs outside the city (*extra muros*) were sacralised spaces that had been transformed, monumentalised and integrated in the essential infrastructure of the city. These macro-structures (amphitheatres, fora, aqueducts and the sacralised spaces) possessed strong interconnectivity. Numerous important epigraphic and statuary finds have been identified in these short-lived macro-spaces of religious communication in Aquincum, but nevertheless the density of religious materiality there is hard to reconstruct because a large part of the finds were found in the legionary fortress, meso-spaces and domestic micro-spaces.

Fig. 3.10 The so-called 'Symphorus Mithraeum' in Aquincum. (Photo: author)

Carnuntum evokes in many senses the macro-spaces and religious topography of Aquincum, although its rich archaeological heritage and post-Roman history preserved an unusual quantity of religious materiality: 615 votive inscriptions,[240] which represents the largest amount of material evidence of religious communication from all the Danubian urban centres and even beyond, there being no similar mass production of religious materiality either in the Germanic provinces or in Italy. The central role of Carnuntum as a major conurbation and the largest glocalised metropolis of Rome north to the Alps is also reflected by its rich connectivity: its sanctuary dedicated to the Qadriviae and Jupiter Heliopolitanus, but also the cult of Antinoos[241] and the Egyptionised material radiated from Carnuntum, as a central place in the religious sphere of the Danubian provinces.[242] The centrality of the Danube and the position of Carnuntum between the Alpine region, the Adriatic and the Carpathian Basin also provided an advantage. In addition, Carnuntum was the focal point and central hub for the Amber Road, which connected the Roman Empire with the Barbaricum between Aquileia and the Germanic world.[243]

The geographic and strategic position of Carnuntum on the crossroads of the above-mentioned macro-spaces of the Roman Empire also shaped the major facets of religious communication. In common with the major legionary centres of the Danubian provinces (especially Aquincum and Apulum), Carnuntum united all the major macro-spaces of urban religion, which means that it provides the best documented case study for a detailed, high-resolution archaeology and lived religion in the urban context. The urban system (almost 270 Ha)[244] of Carnuntum consists of a 8.5 km-long linear system of macro-spaces that formed and evolved between the 1st century AD and the late 4th–5th centuries AD. The major elements are the pre-Roman sacralised spaces of the Pfaffenberg,[245] the legionary fortress,[246] the palace of the governors,[247] the *canabae* and the civilian settlement. These units housed several of their own macro-spaces, which played a crucial role in space sacralisation and maintaining long-term religious communication.

Each of the macro-spaces within these units shows a different density of religious materiality. Most of the epigraphic and figurative material used as tools in religious dialogue was discovered in the territory of the *canabae* (184 objects), the legionary fortress (124 objects) and the civilian settlement (111 objects).[248] This shows again that the materiality of religion in urban systems was omnipresent, and also demonstrates a very complex embedded aspect of religion, where spaces of religion – both legal and functional – were overlapping and interconnected. Macro-, meso- and micro-spaces of religion were united in these urban units, especially in the civilian town, where all three categories were represented. Although the legal state of such places could be radically different,[249] their spatial co-existence is well attested in Aquincum, Carnuntum, Virunum and Cambodunum, where extensive parts of the domestic spaces were systematically excavated and researched.

The major characteristics of urbanity and urban religion I listed at the beginning of this chapter can be exemplified with a well-documented case study from Carnuntum.

Jupiter Heliopolitanus from Baalbek became one of the universal gods of the Roman Empire, a production of and religious bricolage that exemplifies the best case studies of Roman religious appropriations and glocality: the local Baal of Baalbek was transformed into a new divinity, which on one hand evoked the local Anatolian-Syrian divinities and their stereotypic features (akin to the numerous Aphroditae and military gods of the region), but on the other, already featured some minor decorative elements (heads of the Olympian gods, Roman floral and geometric motives) on his armour that gave him a Hellenistic and later, Roman, Imperial aspect.[250]

This process of transforming local celestial divinities (Baals, Zeuses) from Syria, Anatolia and North Africa was a consequence of religious appropriation and universalisation of divine agents.[251] Jupiter Heliopolitanus is a typical case study for global divinities in an Imperial context: not only did the visual narrative of the god radically change and adopt new, recognisable and universal aspects that represent the exoticism of the East ('orientalised gods'[252]) and the military rigidity of Imperial power, but even the theonym of the god reflected some aspects of urban religion. Heliopolis was one of the important urban centres of Hellenistic and Roman Syria, therefore the toponym in the name of the god is much more than just a geographic reference and exotic, attractive element in religious appropriation. Jupiter Heliopolitanus is a cultural construct, a product of urbanity and urban religion in the East, which went on to conquer the entire Roman Empire like the even more successful Jupiter Dolichenus, Jupiter Hierapolitanus or the Baal of Edessa.

Jupiter Heliopolitanus arrived in Carnuntum in the early 2nd century AD, probably after the oriental campaign and special divination of the god in the age of Trajan, the major restructuring of the Danubian provinces and the intensive military dislocations in 106 AD.[253] His monumental temple in Baalbek,[254] his visual attractiveness and exoticism, and his military and global aspects are products of urban religion, which would be imitated in Carnuntum and Micia (cat. no. III.41. See also VI.20).[255] His sanctuary here underwent multiple phases (at least three major periods), but the most important one was the reconstruction of the sanctuary during the reign of Septimius Severus.[256] The large-sized sanctuary complex was intentionally destroyed and rebuilt a few years later with a lavish decoration and visual programme inside the sanctuary, including numerous wall paintings, which evoke not only the monumental temple of Baalbek, but also the floral decorations of some of the statues of Heliopolitanus. T

he sanctuary of Heliopolitanus was a reproduction of the grand urban design of Baalbek in a no-less impressive monumentality in Carnuntum (90 × 100 m), creating an orientalised, complex sanctuary.[257] Urbanity in religion (or urban religion) played a significant role in creating, maintaining or redesigning such massive architectural projects and investments. This is emphasised even more by the elegantly elaborate Imperial statue of Septimius Severus or one of his successors whose Imperial armour was decorated with the figure of Jupiter Heliopolitanus, who became not only the protector of the emperor, but by this new visual narrative also an official, global and universal god of the Roman Empire (Fig. 3.11).[258] Thus the city of Baalbek and Carnuntum not only shared a common divinity in Jupiter

Fig. 3.11 Representation of an emperor (probably Septimius Severus) with Jupiter Heliopolitanus. (Source: Lupa 11574, photo of Ortolf Harl with the special permission of Archäologisches Museum Carnuntum)

Heliopolitanus, but both urban centres were directly linked to Septimius Severus, who contributed to the reconstruction of the central sanctuary of Jupiter in Baalbek and in 194 AD donated the title of *colonia* to Carnuntum (Colonia Septimia Aurelia Antoniniana Karnuntum).

Moreover, Carnuntum and Septimius Severus were further closely related because he was a resident of the city from 191 to 193 AD as governor of Pannonia Superior, when he was elected as emperor by the XIV Gemina legion.[259] His statue decorated by Jupiter Heliopolitanus therefore had both a political and a religious meaning, which united two far-away urban centres of the Roman Empire and reflects a personal attachment of the army, the urban community and the emperor. Such concentrations of power, religious density and spatial rearrangement were possible only in urban centres in the Roman Empire, which makes these conurbations special case studies in which micro-, meso- and macro-spaces were overlapping each other.

Space sacralisation inside and outside the forts

The Danubian provinces were and are considered par excellence 'military provinces':[260] the large number of auxiliary and legionary units stationed there from the time of Augustus until the end of the Principate, and the quantity of *militaria*, as materiality of the Roman army,[261] provide a strong argument for this historiographic claim. The material evidence of Roman religion related to the Roman army in this area is also significant, yet featured in few systematic studies until recently. That said, the number of individual case studies and local approaches is endless.[262] It is not the task of this chapter to present in depth the various case studies of Roman religious communication that occurred inside or outside the Roman forts in the Danubian provinces, but rather to focus on few methodological aspects, defining the Roman fort as a dynamic and active macro-space and transformative agent in Roman religious communication.

For a long time in historiography, the *religio militum* (religion of the soldiers) and *religio castrensis* (the religion within the fort) were notions with legal, spatial and ritual aspects that were often interpreted using a contrasting and comparative approach.[263] The Roman fort was viewed as a separate entity, divided from the civilian world by strong physical walls and religious, but also legal, borders and boundaries.[264] These liminal, *templum*-like features of the forts also appear in literary sources. However, the archaeological reality shows that borders and boundaries were in fact hard to maintain in such macro-spaces and complex societies as the Roman army, and were easily permeable. In effect, the Roman fort as a macro-space in religious communication was inseparable from the military *vici* and *canabae* and the civilian settlements. There have been past attempts to establish a comparative approach of the religion of the civilian society and the *religio militum*,[265] but their results didn't show a radically different result: the 'pantheon' of the soldiers was almost identical with the divine agencies evoked in a civilian context, with a predominant presence of Jupiter Optimus Maximus and the *Dii Consentes*.

Thanks to the paradigmatic work of C. Heidenreich, the notion of *religio castrensis* can also be reinterpreted: his study proved that within the legionary forts, Roman religious communication was much more diverse and heterogeneous than was previously thought. Not only was the spatial distribution and topography of the material evidence much more varied, but the divine agencies and the range of religious experiences were too. The same paradigmatic shift is emerging in the study of the Roman army as a community:[266] the religiosity of the solider, acting as an individual or as part of his troop, also needs a more detailed, contextual analysis focusing on forms of religious individualisation and local appropriation. The use of this method in relation to the Roman army and its members was missing from the paradigmatic works of Jörg Rüpke in the past.[267] This can be explained by the predominantly urban nature of the literary and archaeological sources used as analogies in the recent works: the macro-spaces of religion are interpreted as par excellence urban ones. Military spaces – such as the fort and their *vici* or *canabae* – are rarely used as analogies, although the legal state, the topography and the architectural atmosphere of the forts represents a heterogenous space between urban and rural, where the conflicting categories of 'urban' and 'rural' are united in a complex macro-space with a specific legal status.

The fort as a religious macro-space is, however, a very heterogenous notion with a great variety of architectural and spatial arrangements. The smallest units were the temporary or marching camps. There are a few cases of well-excavated camps of this kind in the Danubian provinces, the most well-known being in the territory of Brigetio and Carnuntum,[268] and in the Hațeg mountains.[269] These cases – mostly because of their short-lived existence and temporality – don't provide significant data about the religious communication of the soldiers or space sacralisation in these environments. In some instances, though, unusual finds suggest that these camps – which always represent a moment of tension, crisis or intensification of military action[270] – did produce a materiality of religion. Such a case was recently presumed in a place called 'Sub Cununi' in the Hațeg mountains, in the valley of Grădiștii, on the road that connected the two major Dacian, and later Roman, forts and temporary camps in Costești-Cetățuia and Sarmizegetusa Regia.[271] This place was interpreted for a long time as a tropaion, built after the Dacian wars,[272] however recent finds suggest that the large, rectangular buildings identified in the 19th century might be part of a military *vicus* or a large public building that was visited regularly and repeatedly by the governors of the Roman province of Dacia long after the conquest of the region.

The Hațeg mountains are very rich in small, temporary camps and marching camps, but there were probably also structures dedicated to religious communication, such as the one in Sub Cununi suggests. These were strictly related to the memorialisation of war and the Roman army, even if their sacralisation might have occured much later. Here, the natural landscape itself was used as a tool in space sacralisation: the memory and third space of the Dacian past was consciously used to create and maintain the sacralised spaces.

Another important and much better researched category is the auxiliary forts and their military *vici*.[273] In many cases among the great number of these macro-spaces, space sacralisation was superficially preserved and identified. From the few cases where the sacralised spaces of the auxiliary fort and their environment are well attested, I will present the case study of Micia (today Vețel/Vecel village, Romania).[274]

The ancient settlement complex of Micia lay on the western edge of the Limes Dacicus, formed in a crucial place on the bank of the River Mureș (Marisia),[275] connecting the inner part of the province with the Barbaricum.[276] The western limits of the province are still under debate, however according to the recent *Limesforschung* of the Romanian Limes Commission, the western frontier of Dacia ended with the Ampelum-Apulum-Cigmău and Micia line, following the course of the Mureș River.[277] Micia was not only an important auxiliary fort, hosting the Ala I Hispanorum Campagonum,[278] Cohors II Flavia Commagenorum and Numerus Maurorum Miciensium,[279] but also serving as an important commercial and administrative hub in the intra- and extra-provincial networks between Pannonia, Barbaricum and Dacia.[280]

The fort of Micia was a very large one, which made it a dominant architectural feature in the macro-space on the bank of the Mureș River: the position of the fort also defined the evolution of the rest of the buildings. In every so-called military conurbation or urban system, the building of the fort represents a central element, and is the most important, defining feature in landscape and space sacralisation. The very existence of human agency in religious communication in such settlements is dependent on the fort and their military purpose. After these forts were abandoned and ceased being used asa military centres, that religious communication also faded.[281]

The fort defines the sacralised spaces, too: the delimitation of the fort (the very foundation of an auxiliary or legionary fort) is a religious act. By creating a new 'templum' in space, the fort also represents legal territoriality and liminality. Everything that is inside the fort and in the *intra leugam* area is subject to military law, while the civilian settlements and their human agency were subject to a different legal state.

This complex multi-spatiality (in both legal and religious terms) can be attested in Micia, too. Here, the fort is surrounded by numerous sacralised spaces, especially in the eastern and southern parts, although materiality of religion was discovered over a very large territory.[282] From the total of 180 inscriptions, 89 are votive monuments, which represents almost 50 per cent of all Roman material heritage. The large quantity of stone and epigraphic monuments produced in less than 150 years in Micia can be compared only with the middle-sized urban settlements of the Danubian provinces.[283] Numerous other figurative monuments are known, especially a rich material of gemstones and small bronze statuettes representing Egyptian divinities.[284] The quantity of gems discovered in Micia might indicate the presence of a workshop there.

The territory of the fort was surrounded by two archaeologically excavated sacralised spaces (meso-spaces of small-group religions) built by the group of the Maurii for the paternal gods, and another one for Jupiter Heliopolitanus – a meso-space that represents a rarity in the Danubian provinces and reflects a close connectivity with Baalbek and Carnuntum (cat. no. VI.20-21).[285] Two other sacralised spaces – an Iseum and a Mithraeum – are known from epigraphic evidence,[286] and five others are presumed to exist based on the abundant materiality of religion.[28]

The macro-spaces of religious communication in the *pagus* Miciensis are hard to reconstruct, however the currently known topography of the settlement suggests that the close proximity of the Iseum to the bank of the river, the small amphitheatre, the sacralised spaces dedicated to Nemesis and the Ara Miciensis mean that it could belong to a religious macro-space in the north-eastern part of the settlement. Similar to most of the auxiliary forts, the one in Micia is also surrounded by meso-spaces of small-group religions, which fragmented the *pagus* and the *vicus*.[288] Although the identified sacralised spaces in Micia were far from being monumental and there are no traces of large-scale monumentalisation in architectural forms, these buildings were not only integrated in the urbanised skeleton of the growing settlement, but they also created the major hubs around the fort, contributing to the maintenance of the spatial, cultural and social coherence. The sanctuary of Jupiter Heliopolitanus and the Templum Dii Patrii Maurorum represent essential, cultural features and ethnic expressions or appropriations of the soldiers from Northern Africa and the Levant (Asia Minor and Syria).[289] The altar dedicated to Mercurius by M. Antonius Sabinianus, a princeps of the army or of the African community of the Maurii, on the territory of the *pagus* shows the interconnectivity of the military, civilian and religious identities, and the role of these macro-spaces in constant interaction.[290] The presence of the Mithraeum – known only from epigraphic sources – suggests that this group from the *publicum portorii Illyrici* was also a strong economic hub, essential for the existence of Micia as a military, strategic and commercial centre on the western edge of the province.[291]

The case study of Micia is a great example of military macro-spaces being interconnected with an expanding urban system of middle-sized settlements, densely populated with sacralised spaces. The religious material from the fort and the sacralised spaces outside of it evolved together and they are inseparable tools and actors in a religious communication that defines the history of these semi-urban macro-spaces, named by D. Donev as middle-sized urban systems.[292]

Legionary fortresses represent the most important military centres of the Roman Empire. Besides their defensive and strategic roles in macro-spaces, such as provinces or even extra-provincial routes and regions, legionary fortresses were also important factors in urbanisation and religious appropriation.[293] The Danubian area was the richest in legionary fortresses in the entire Roman Empire: one-third of the 106 fortresses (35 settlements) were located in these seven provinces in an unusual concentration, with less than 100 km separating them (Fig. 3.12).[294] The network and intense connectivity of legionary fortresses signified the most enduring and constant force of human and material mobility.[295] In addition, these military centres and their *canabae* represent the largest hubs and concentrations of materiality of religious communication: in most of the cases, at least a quarter of the entire epigraphic material of a province is concentrated in one or several legionary centres.[296] Yet, although there are almost 30 legionary fortresses attested archaeologically in the Danubian area, few of them offer a systematic and complex

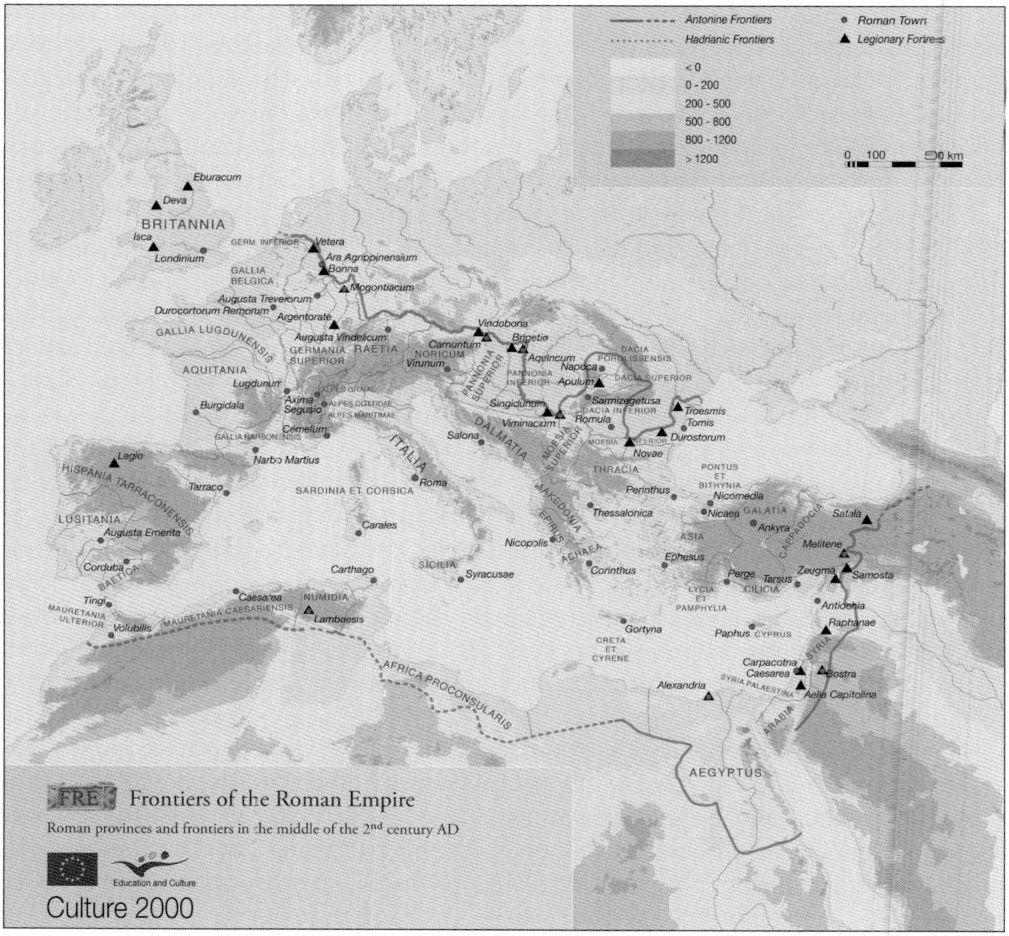

Fig. 3.12 Frontiers of the Roman Empire depicting the legionary fortresses. (Source: https://www.univie.ac.at/limes). Open access

view on the inner structures and space sacralisation inside and outside the fortresses. The best-documented case studies are the legionary fortresses of Carnuntum,[297] Potaissa[298] and Novae.[299]

For a long time, historiography considered only a single building dedicated to religious communication within a fort and legionary fortress, the *aedes signorum* in the *principia* (cat. nos I.1, 2, 3, 4, 5, 32, 34, 36, 39, 41, 42, 45, 47, 48, 49, 50, 52, 53, 54, II. 1, 4, 18, 22, 46, III.1, 2, 32, 57, 58, 85, 87, IV.2, V.12, 23, VI.5, 9, 10, 11, 12, 13, 14, 16, 18, 19, 22, 26, 29, 30, 32, 49, 51 and 54).[300] This small, usually rectangular building was dedicated to the military insignia, especially the eagle, the genii of the legion and the symbols of Imperial power and the cult of emperors.[301] The visibility, accessibility and religious density of this small sacralised space is still a matter of debate in the literature; in many cases, the building was attested only superficially and without any materiality of religion.[302] Other cases, such as the *aedes signorum* in Apulum, can be reconstructed only indirectly, through the rich epigraphic material discovered in the surrounding area of the *principia*.[303] The paradigmatic study of C. Heidenreich showed that religious communication produced a great variety of spaces within the legal limits of the legionary fortresses.[304] The case study of the legionary fortress of Carnuntum clearly demonstrates that a large concentration of material tools of religion was used *intra muros castra legionis*:[305] 186 votive objects were identified in 74 different places within the fortress.[306]

Another well-documented case study is the legionary fortress of Novae in Moesia Inferior. One of the largest military centres of the Danubian provinces, the fortress functioned from the late 1st century AD (around 72 AD) until the early 5th century AD, and produced significant material evidence of religious communication inside and outside the fort. In all, 114 votive inscriptions are known from Novae,[307] although only a few of these have an exact provenance.[308] Many of the 258 inscriptions from the territory of the legionary fortress were found in a secondary position, rebuilt in the 3rd or 4th–5th centuries AD, and few of them are votive inscriptions.[309] The most significant ones are those that were found *in situ*.[310] The inscriptions found in the area of the *principia* and the inner structure of the fortress evokes the Capitoline triad: Jupiter, Mars and Urbs Roma. All these divine agents were associated with the military identity and Imperial power, reflecting the fidelity of the army and the supreme, divine protection. The epigraphic material used in space sacralisation in this macro-space usually reflects a communal religious act: the collective participation and dedication of the entire legion is named in the inscriptions. In this sense, *religio castrensis* indeed has some unique particularities: a strong religious collective identity manifested in numerous, though not necessarily repetitive, collective events.[311]

The most interesting case study from the legionary fortress in Novae is the *valetudinarium* (cat. no. V.15).[312] Known as the 'hospital of the legion', the monumental building dominated an entire quarter of the fortress. The large scale of the *valetudinarium* represents a significant factor in the spatial organisation of the fortress and shows its importance in the life of the army. From the few well-documented case studies of *valetudinaria*[313] there are only two excavated case studies in the Danubian provinces: in Carnuntum[314] and Novae. The inner structure of the two buildings is very similar, however the *valetudinarium* in Novae had a more organised and rectangular shape, with a central sacralised space in the inner courtyard of the building complex.[315] This raised several questions about its functionality and chronology, although most of the authors argued that it was used for religious communication, dedicated to the healing divinities of Asclepius and Hygeia.[316]

The archaeological material discovered *in situ* (one statue base and five altars)[317] is a good example of collective and individual religious communication, controlled spatial and material agency, and religious competition. The altars and statue bases dedicated to Asclepius and Hygeia were erected by prominent members of the legion (*legatii, tesserarii, centurioni, medici*),[318] but also as a collective military dedication of the I Italica legion.[319] The altar dedicated by the legion held a central position within the inner court, in front of the sacralised space. The preserved statue bases mention the weight of the silver statues dedicated by the *legati*: C. Mansuanius Severus dedicated in the name of the legion a silver statue representing Asclepius weighing 1.774 kg, while M. Clodius Laetus dedicated a silver statue to Hygeia that weighed 1.54 kg.[320] The two *legati* mentioned the weights of the statues in order not only to identify the divinity and the importance of their own religious and financial investment, but also to establish a tradition of competitiveness and continuity in public space sacralisation and memorialisation.[321] The silver statues represent the bodies of the gods, and the material of the statues here plays an important role in the successful space sacralisation and creating the 'house of the god'.[322]

Such financial aspects of religious communication in public macro-spaces are not rare.[323] It was normal for the local military or civilian elite to express their financial prosperity and to maintain the sacralised space with exquisite visual tools, which served as important agents in sacralised spaces. These included the Asclepeion within the *valetudinarium*, the most important water springs and pilgrimage sites[324] in the area of a forum or *principia*[325] or in sacralised spaces with a macro-regional impact, such as the one in Virunum (Hohenstein).[326]

The macro-spaces of the legionary fortresses produced a large number of material tools used in religious communication, having an important role in maintaining the sacralised spaces within and outside the walls of the military building and contributing to the social and moral cohesion of the Roman army. The legal boundaries played an important role in establishing and maintaining religious dialogue in military contexts, but the case studies in Novae also show the possibilities of religious individualisation in macro-spaces. Visibility, accessibility and religious investment, as strategies for social competition and cohesion, were key factors in macro-spaces such as the forts, fortresses, fora, complex sanctuaries and other large-sized macro-spaces in both urban and military contexts.

Controlling and designing religion

Communication with the gods – termed recently 'not-quite-tangible counterparts'[327] – is an investment. It requires a divination, a strong, life-changing and lived experience with the divine agency. In addition, in most cases, the creation and maintenance of this dialogue between human and divine agency needs special spaces, tools, and repetitive and unique actions to enable successful communication and to create religious traditions and memorialisation of the sacralised space.[328] One of the most important tools for this purpose is religious media (especially visual narratives: reliefs, figurative monuments) and religious control and monopolisation.

Figurative media (reliefs, votive objects, public statues, statuettes, figurative architectural elements) use the cognitive power of religious communication: the visual narratives are universally accessible, translatable tools that use cognitive strategies to establish a visual narrative that will transfer the religious message necessary for communication between human and divine agencies.[329] However, the communicative agency and short- or long-lasting effect of visuality in sacralised spaces always depends on the viewer or beholder who is entering the space or interacting with the object. This co-dependency of the materiality of religion and the visual narratives creates an unprecedented number of views and messages, possible interpretations and appropriations.[330] The recent discourse on religious images opened a much wider range of possible interpretations and the art historical, descriptive approach of the modern viewer is challenged and questioned.[331] Visual narratives are produced and intensively used in a living space, therefore their aestheticscape[332] has a cognitive, neuropsychological role in creating and maintaining religious communication.

Beyond this, though, visual narratives need stories, too: the contents and religious knowledge are as important as the visual representation itself. The interpretation and appropriation of these together – knowledge and visuality – gives in each case the individual viewer the potential to translate the message based on his or her own view.[333] Religious visuality for the local authorities also serves as a tool of political and social competitiveness and memorialisation of their status. Increasing and constantly changing the material density of a sacralised space represents an essential strategy of the local political and religious elite to maintain a social order, or in some rare cases, to establish a new space for social or economic representation.

Religious media in macro-spaces

The agency role of images and their constructive power in space sacralisation is a universal human strategy of mediation and communication. David Morgan argued, that 'images are experienced by many viewers as commanding a presence'.[334] Modern scholarship has discussed endlessly the problematic issues of terminology (how to name the body of the gods and their various forms of visual representations) and functionality (the role of objects or agency of divine representations).[335] While some of the material agency used in religious communication indeed had a much stronger association and appropriation with the divine power, categorising objects through their functionality and religious intensity is highly problematic, as P. Stewart convincingly proved in his paradigmatic work on Roman art and figurative representations.[336] What can we define as 'religious media'? Without proposing here a definition, I will focus on some well-documented case studies, where figurative monuments of divine figures are concentrated in a large number or are of exquisite quality in public macro-spaces. These images of gods in such macro-spaces have their own power and commanding presence, although the aim of the maker and the appropriation of the viewer might not always be aligned.

The forum of a Roman city represents the most important macro-space. It was a central space designed and created to convey a strong visual narrative and propaganda,[337] for social, political and religious memorialisation, and to serve as urban *lieux de mémoires.* Although it was not the first urban space designed as a place of centrality (see also the agora of the Greek cities or the central sanctuaries of Celtic settlements), the Roman forum represented the essence of Imperial macro-space, where the density and power of the images were consciously intensified. Based on their form, Roman fora can be divided into four types: (1) long and narrow: Assisi, Pompeii, Tarragona; (2) Vitruvian: Conimbriga, Timgad, Severan Forum at Leptis Magna; (3) nearly square: Paris, Thuburbo Maius; and (4) square: Doclea, Nicopolis at Istrum.[338]

Among the cities of the Danubian provinces, the most well-preserved Roman fora were attested in Brigantium, Virunum, Solva, Teurnia, Colonia Sarmizegetusa, Oescus and Nicopolis ad Istrum.[339] The fora of Carnuntum and Aquincum were also researched, and their plans can be reconstructed mostly based on geophysical evidence.[340] The forum of Scarbantia was partially revealed, along with an important section of the Capitolium.[341]

The forum of Virunum has been systematically excavated and researched since the late 19th and early 20th centuries (Fig. 3.13).[342] The centre of Virunum is a long-type forum that was built in the middle of the 1st century AD, probably under Claudius.[343] It is located in the north-eastern part of the city[344] and has a long rectangular shape with a large *temenos* closed in the north by the walls of the temple and in the south by the basilica and its square, bounded by several small annexes.[345] The rectangular temple (24.6 × 34.6 m) was divided into several small compartments, however it is unclear whether Egger's detailed plan also reflects the different phases of the building.[346] As is the case for many large-sized, public sacralised places in urban macro-spaces, including fora, this building is also extremely problematic when it comes to identifying the functionality of the small compartments, their role in public festivals and religious communication and, especially, the identification of the divine agency. Traditionally, this building was associated with Jupiter and the Capitoline triad, and was thus considered as the Capitolium of Virunum. However, the identification of the provincial Capitolia was recently questioned.[347] The inner structure of the building contains small rectangular compartments, only one (marked 'A' by Egger) of which is sufficiently large for complex religious rituals or statuary dedications (around 10 × 15 m), although it might have served as a pronaos.[348] The archaeological material of the sacralised place didn't produce enough material to identify the divine agency, though a possible head of Minerva was associated with the place.[349]

In contrast with the central building of the forum in Brigantium, where the sacralised space had a much larger inner cella,[350] the one at Virunum had an unusual inner structure that reflects several phases of reconstruction or a reuse of the building. Although it is not certain that this building was indeed a Capitolium, the inner intimacy of the place has something in common with other Capitolia in terms of the contrast of the inside and outside spaces: while the inner spaces of the Capitolium were preserved for exceptional events and human agency, the outside (the forum and the additional buildings nearby) reflected a much higher visibility, accessibility and human density.[351]

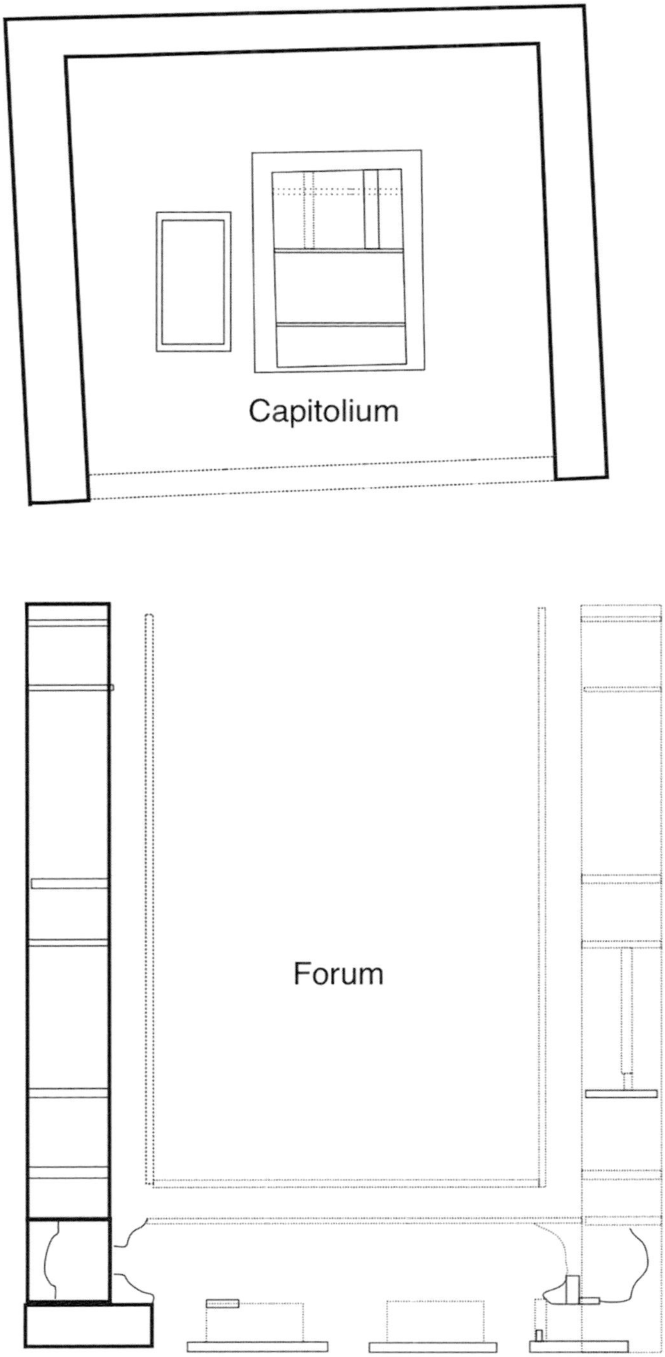

Fig. 3.13 The plan of the forum in Virunum. (Source: author)

A much better-documented case study for space sacralisation in a forum is the Trajanic Forum Vetus of Sarmizegetusa (Fig. 3.14).[352] This has a radically different form from the ones in Virunum and Brigantium, which can be explained in particular by the architectural fashion during the age of Trajan, which produced numerous major macro-spaces and fora in urban environments.[353] The fora of Tarraco, Tamugadi, Ulpia Traiana (Xanten) and Sarmizegetusa show not only a chronological and contextual similarity, but also an architectural one, however in all of the cases there are significant local appropriations in the architectural atmosphere. The first forum of Sarmizegetusa was a wooden-stone construction built in the period of 109–130 AD, after a vexillation of the IV Flavia Felix legion had abandoned the site.[354] From this phase, the forum contains a few elements that indicate religious communication occurred in this site: the Area Sacra of the city was built outside the walls (*extra muros*), although its Trajanic phase is poorly documented.[355]

The forum was built in the southern part of the monumentalised macellum of the city, a structure that was commonly built in the central area of Trajanic and Severan cities as well.[356] The second phase of the Forum Vetus represents the monumentalisation of the building complex during the period of Hadrian. Two nymphaea were built near the entrance of the forum with beautifully elaborated statues representing Neptunus and the nymphs (cat. no. VI.33).[357] Interestingly, water went on to play a significant role in the rebuilding of the Forum Vetus and the macellum in the age of Hadrian and Antoninus Pius. The two separate nymphaea in front of the forum were related to the piscinae of the macellum, separating the forum from both sides with a channel.[358] This infrastructure served two possible functions: 1) it enabled the circulation of water between the macellum and the nymphaea and 2) it created a physical border between the forum and the rest of the city. This border, however, was not just a pragmatic water channel: it represents the centrality of the space and its special meaning in urban settings. Similar visual programmes can be attested in Gorsium and Aquae Iasae, too.[359]

Centrality is an important urban element: it attracts attention, it represents the starting point of urban development (the presence of the groma in the vicinity of the forum) and it creates and shapes the major public events.[360] Centrality is also present in the major square of the early Trajanic forum, where a monument dedicated to the emperor was erected.[361] This monumental statue (with a base measuring 5.6 × 5.6 m) was unfortunately not preserved, but archaeologists excavating the area suggested a triumphal monument (a smaller-sized tropaion) representing military spoila or perhaps the emperor himself.[362] Imperial power is represented in the initial forum in a clear and visually powerful, minimalist way: the central triumphal monument and the large building inscriptions dedicated to Trajan reflect the elegant structure and centrality of Trajan's forum in Rome.[363]

During the reign of Antoninus Pius, the central area of the city was radically changed with the creation of a second central space, a Vitruvian forum with a Capitolium and a large square marked by two cryptoporticuses.[364] The Capitolium

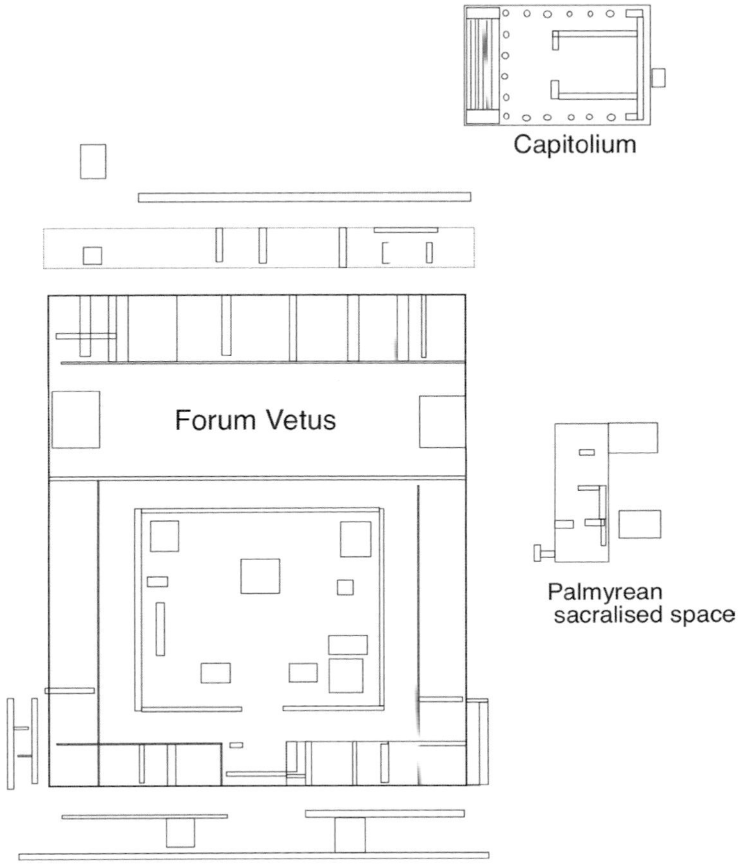

Fig. 3.14 The plan of the forum in Sarmizegetusa. (Source: author after Piso 2017b)

of the Forum Novum was a classical podium temple with a large inner cella dedicated to the Capitoline triad.[365] While the new forum became the most important macro-space for religious communication within the city walls, the Forum Vetus at the end of the 2nd century and in the early 3rd century AD was transformed into a space of memorialisation, agglomerated with honorary statues and inscriptions dedicated to the emperors,[366] governors and local political elite.[367] The switch in role and functionality of the two fora – from central, religious and commemorative spaces into honorary and self-representative spaces of political memorialisation – is also reflected in the buildings and annexes next to the Forum Vetus. An assembly house of a small religious group from Palmyra was established next to the Trajanic forum, which indicates that the topography of space sacralisation changed radically in the 3rd century AD, especially in the age of Septimius Severus and Caracalla.[368]

The architectural atmosphere of the provincial fora intentionally recreated the motifs and quality of materiality of the macro-spaces of the Imperial capital: architraves decorated with lavish visual tropes imitating the architecture of Imperial building programmes of Rome, Pergamon or other major urban centres can be found in Oescus,[369] Sarmizegetusa,[370] Ratiaria,[371] Tomis,[372] Savaria[373] and many other cities where urban macro-spaces (fora, governors' palaces, Capitolia, public baths) have been attested.[374]

In contrast with the forum of Sarmizegetusa, where religious communication was limited to the later Capitolium and a few meso-spaces and annexes of the Forum Novum (such as the assembly house of the *collegium fabrum*[375]), the forum of Oescus reflects a radically different ceremonial space, where there is materiality of divine agency dominates: the forum contained three large sacralised buildings dedicated to Jupiter, Juno, Minerva and Fortuna (cat. no. V.16-18, Fig. 3.15).[376]

The religious nature of visual narratives is not always obvious and there have been numerous cases in antiquity in which the interaction between human and divine agencies has been hard to establish. There was certainly a hierarchy of objects and spaces in religious communication, where besides the density of religious experiences and materiality of religion, memorialisation of religious performances played a significant role.[377] Where this density of religious experience and memory of performances are lacking, the visual narratives and media (public statues in macro-spaces, for example) play a less important role in religious communication. Such places were the public baths, palaces, amphitheatres and public sports complexes in urban centres. The rich statuary material (20 statues of exceptional quality) discovered between 1785 and 1906 in Virunum in the so-called '*Bäderbezirk*' west of the forum[378] represents probably a late antique reassembled inventory of statues from the macro-spaces of Virunum (probably also derived from the forum or private buildings).[379] Although the *in situ* nature of the statues was recently questioned, the artistic elaboration and similar style of the statues indicates a common origin and space. Similar statuary inventories can be identified in the late antique phase of the Walbrook Mithraeum in Londinium and in Tomis, where the most exquisite statues of the Roman city were collected in a spolia.[380]

Architectural atmosphere in the case of public sacralised spaces (*templa*)[381] also played a very important part in maintaining the sacralised space and became a direct religious agency via its visual narrative: reliefs in the tympanum, pediment and frieze of the buildings were communicating with the viewers and visitors.[382] The case study of the Iseum in Savaria – one of the best-preserved Isiac sacralised spaces in the Danubian provinces (cat. no. III.75)[383] – clearly demonstrates that the figurative decoration of the exterior of the temple had a very strong role in establishing the exoticism and attractiveness of the sacralised space. The representation of Isis sitting on the Sothis dog,[384] a priest (or the divinity) of Anubis,[385] and classical Greco-Roman iconographies representing Mars and Fortuna[386] had a strong agency function in creating the visual

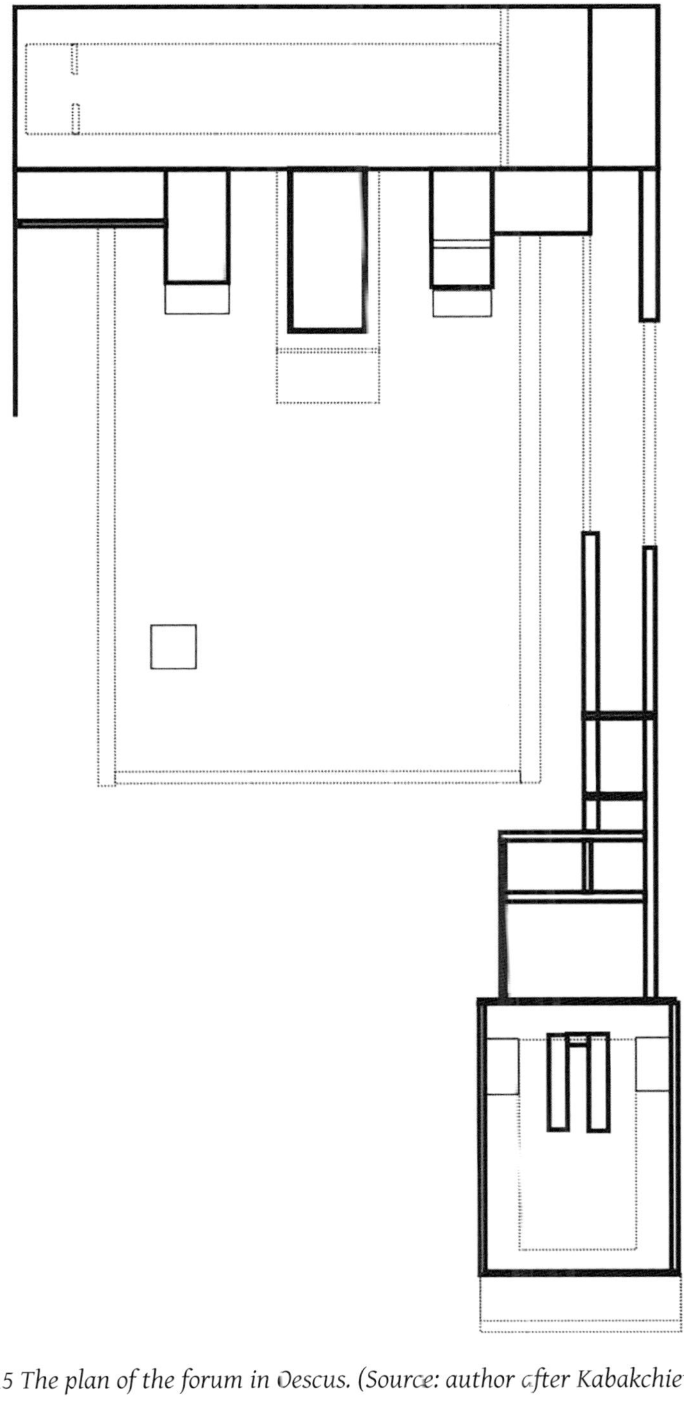

Fig. 3.15 The plan of the forum in Oescus. (Source: author after Kabakchieva 2014)

Fig. 3.16 Isis-Sothis relief in the Iseum of Savaria. (Source: with special permission of the Museum of Savaria)

language of Egyptianism, as one of the tools in space sacralisation associated with the Iseum (Fig. 3.16).[387]

The Iseum of Savaria had several classical 'Roman' elements adopted from Italic and early Imperial traditions, such as the monumentalised building inscription and the classical Vitruvian architectural elements and building decorations, but the strongest visual message for the visitors and viewers was represented by the exotic, Egyptianised elements. These faced the main road of Savaria, communicating directly with the macro-spaces in an urban context. In contrast with the sacralised spaces of small-group religions, where the external aspects and architecture of the building had a marginal, secondary role, the Iseum of Savaria thus combined the monumentality and classical visual canon of the Roman, Vitruvian architecture, playing consciously with the exotic visualities representing Egyptian divinities and scenes known not only by the initiated, but also indirectly identified as 'exotic' elements by the non-initiated groups.

Accumulating titles and beyond: religious knowledge and its specialists

The maintenance of sacralised spaces and religious communication between divine and human agency was dependent on numerous factors, but a significant role was played by the priesthood and religious specialists, who often controlled religious knowledge and introduced authority and contributed to the constant innovation and appropriation of religions and groups.[388] Although they didn't have full control and monopolisation on religion, their impact in religious communication in macro-spaces was nevertheless dominant.[389] Termed 'experts and providers',[390] priests also possessed a special legal status and public, political role in religious communication, especially in macro-spaces, such as urban environments. The categorisation and identification of 'priests', however, is problematic: while some scholars used a united category for religious providers, others used this notion only for official, collegial priesthoods that had an additional political role in urban and provincial administration.[391]

The Danubian provinces are very rich in the epigraphic evidence left by priests (400 inscriptions),[392] although there are only few iconographic representations of religious specialists and their auxiliary staff, and many of them are difficult to interpret. For example, the representation of Anubis or an Anubis priest on the relief in Savaria is still under debate.[393] There are at least two representations of Palmyrian priests from Belgrade, although the exact origin of these is unknown (they are certainly productions of Palmyrian workshops).[394] There are two almost identical bronze plates from Pannonia representing a sacrificial scene, in which a *victimarius* and a *popa* are present.[395] Similar scenes of sacrifices and the auxiliary staff of priests (*victimarii, popae*) and *vici magistri* are represented on several altars that have been discovered in the Danubian provinces.[396] A particular case study represents a lavishly decorated sarcophagus from Tomis, which probably represents the *instrumenta sacra* of a *sacerdos* (probably related to Magna Mater, Jupiter Dolichenus or other small-group religions)[397] and the beautifully carved funerary monument of Marcus Antonius Marcianus, a *pater nomimus* of Hecate from Tomis, without any particular sacerdotal attributes.[398]

Based on the large amount of epigraphic material left by the priests and religious specialists in the Danubian provinces, Ádám Szabó established the most comprehensive catalogue of Roman priests (collegial administrative titles, such as *antistes, augur, flamen, pontifex, haruspex, sacerdos*) for the provinces of Pannonia, Dacia and Noricum.[399] The case studies analysed in depth in Dacia, for example, show the important role of some influential priests in creating and maintaining macro-spaces of religious communication and the marketisation of public religion, especially in urban environments.[400]

From the province of Moesia Inferior, there are 70 preserved inscriptions related to the main priesthoods of the province.[401] The majority of the inscriptions were dedicated in Latin. However, a significant number (11 inscriptions) are in Greek, due to the dual aspect of urbanisation of Moesia Inferior (which had Greek and Roman foundations and cultural traditions of urbanity). The number of *sacerdotes* is surprisingly high, especially those related to Magna Mater, Jupiter Dolichenus and Liber Pater.[402]

The mobility of the religious specialists is attested not only within the province, but also in some exceptional cases with large extra-provincial connectivity, too. Official priesthood represented an important step in the *cursus honorum* and their public activity shaped the macro-spaces of urban settlements. A case study that demonstrates the intense connectivity between the Danubian provinces can be read in the detailed *cursus honorum* of Titus Iulius Capito (Fig. 3.17):[403]

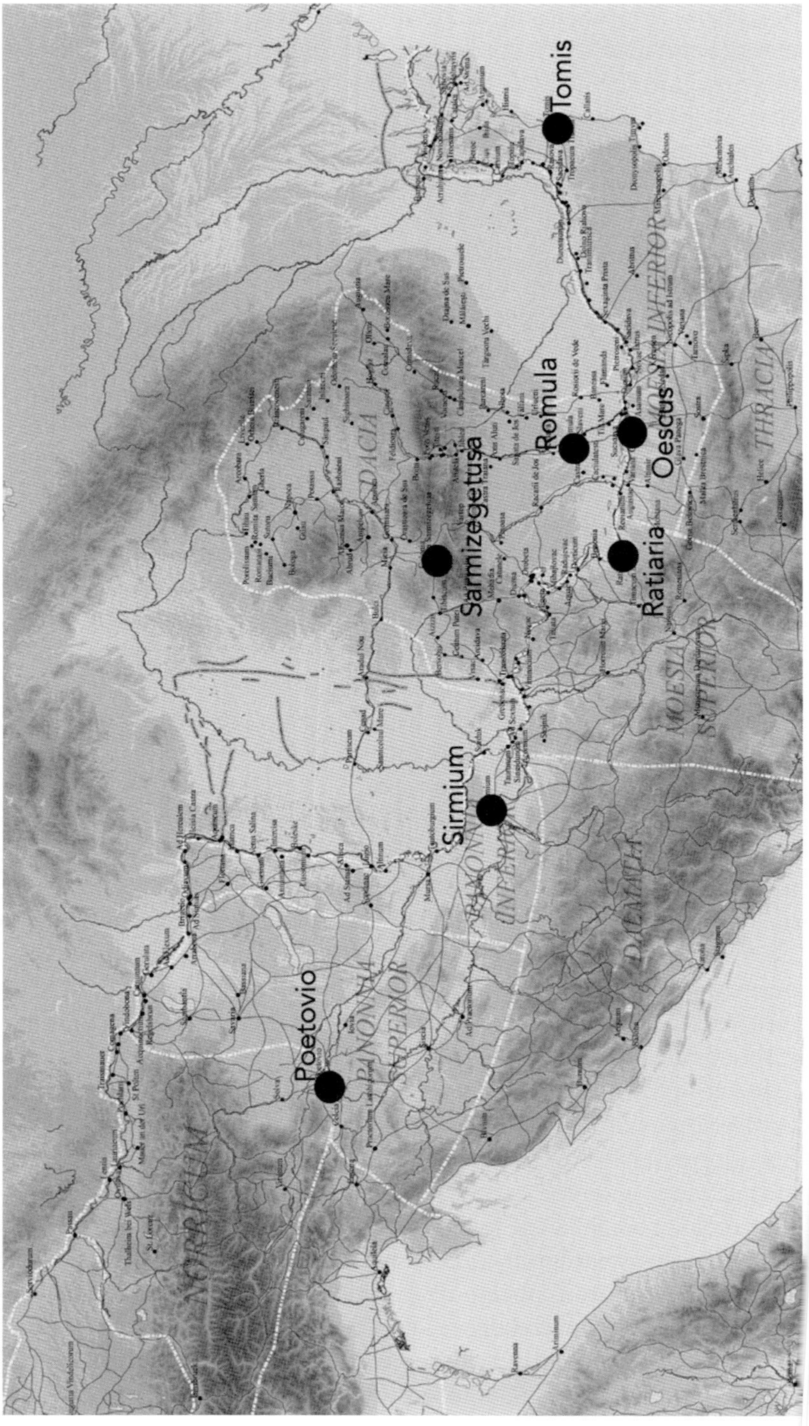

Fig. 3.17 Itinerary of Titus Iulius Capito in the Danubian provinces. (Source: author after Țentea 2011)

> *T(ito) Iul(io) Capitoni c(onductori) p(ublici) portorii) Illyric(i) / [e]t R(ipae) T(hraciae) omni(bus) honorib(us) ab ord(ine) / [co]l(oniae) Fl(aviae) Sirmiatium honorato et / [s]ententiae dicundae item sacerdotalib(us) / ab ordine col(oniae) Ulp(iae) Oesc(ensium) et statua(m) aere col(lato) / decretis iam pridem ab eodem ordine / ornamentis IIviral(ibus) item decuriona/lib(us) ornamentis honorato ab ordinib(us) / coloniar(um) Ulpiae Poetovionensis / ex Pannonia superiore Ulp(iae) Ratiar(iae) / ex Moesia superiore Traianae Sarmi/zegethusensium ex Dacia superiore / item IIviralib(us) ab ordine municipi(i) / Romulensium buleutae civitatis / Ponticae Tomitanorum patrono / Aug(ustalium) col(oniae) Ulp(iae) Oesc(ensium) / ordo col(oniae) Ulp(iae) Oesc(ensium) statuam aer(e) / collato cum ornamentis sacer/dotalib(us) ex decreto et ornament(is) / IIviral(ibus) iam pridem honorato / ob eius erga se merita honore / contentus impendium remisit / l(ocus) d(atus) d(ecreto) d(ecurionum)*

His *cursus honorum* probably began in Poetovio or Sirmium.[404] His life was strictly limited to the *publicum portorii Illyrici*, where he had several important functions in the second half of the 2nd century AD. Capito was one of the numerous *conductores* from the *publicum* who played an important role in the religious life of the Danubian provinces: they had an enduring impact on the financial and religious institutions of the major urban and customs centres.[405] Their role can be attested in the formation and maintenance of small-group religions, especially in the case of Mithraic groups.[406] Accumulating public titles and administrative, political and religious functions represented a well-attested strategy among the priesthood acting in macro-spaces (urban centres, public temples and festivals).[407] Titus Iulius Capito held several of the honorific titles in the major urban settlements of the Danubian provinces between 168 and 180 AD: he was *omnibus honoribus functus* and had the *sentetia dicunda* in Sirmium; *sacerdos* in Oescus, where he also gained a public statue; *decurio* and *duumvir* in Poetovio, Ratiaria and Sarmizegetusa; and member of the *bulé* in Tomis. He was also a *patronus* of the Augustali in Oescus, which is probably why he was offered a statue in the forum of the city. His carrier shows how priesthood was just one of numerous titles and public duties, which served not only the continuity of sacralised spaces and religious communication in urban macro-spaces, but also established a strong network between cities within and outside the provinces.

***

This chapter aimed to present the particularities of macro-spaces: large, open, public spaces with numerous layers and space hierarchies, such as extra-provincial units (routes, customs systems, rivers, mountains), provinces and their sub-units, and large urban systems and their spaces. Religious communication in macro-spaces possessed special features: accessibility, density, legal aspects and the canonisation of architectural rules were much more intense here than they are in the examples of the next chapter, where space is transformed into an introverted and much more intensively lived, individualised experience.

Notes

1 Freeman 1998, 32–33.
2 See also: Cancik-Rüpke 1997 and Woolf 2004 for the limits and possibilities of going beyond the provincialisation in Roman Studies.
3 Stewart 2008 on the issue of imperial vs provincial.
4 For a new perspective of Roman objects and their production, see: Van Oyen-Pitts 2017.
5 For a general and briliant approach on large-scale religious mobility in the Roman Empire, see: Price 2012.
6 On the difference of the two notions (*publicum* and *vectigalia*), see: Carlsen 1995, 49 citing especially the works of Peter Ørsted.
7 See the major groups in Laet 1949.
8 For a general introduction on the history of the Roman publicum, see: Kritzinger 2015.
9 Opriș-Rațiu 2016, 90.
10 Nesselhauf 1939; Dobó 1940; Laet 1949, 175–240; Gerov 1980; Ørsted 1985 as the most important synthesis on this region.
11 Bîrliba 2007.
12 For Roman Dacia, see: Piso *et al.* 2016. For Moesia Inferior, see: Opriș-Rațiu 2016; Sarnowski 2017.
13 Laet 1949, 178–219.
14 Zaccaria 1985 for the main epigraphic sources attesting the elite from Aquileia.
15 Alföldy 1974, 164; Hirt 2010, 240.
16 See also: the case of Lucius Aelius Ianuarius (CIL II 4135 = ILS 1365): *[L(ucio)] Ael(io) Ianuario / [v(iro) p(erfectissimo) p]roc(uratori) hereditat[i]/[um] proc(uratori) Hosdroe[n(ae)](!) / Syriae Coeles / [proc(uratori)] vect(igalis) Illyric[or(um)] / [proc(uratori)] prov(inciae) Hispa[n(iae)] / [cite]rioris Tarrac(onensis) / [prae]sidi prov(inciae) Ting[it(anae)] / [praes]idi prov(inciae) Mau[r]etaniae)] / [Caes(ariensis) ---] / [------*
17 AÉ 1988, 0978 = ILD 678*: I(ovi) O(ptimo) M(aximo) / pro salute Imp(eratoris) M(arci) / Aurel(i) Antonini / Aug(usti) [[[et Commod]i]] / [[[Caes(aris)]]] et Genio p(ublici) p(ortorii) / vectigalis Illyr(ici) / procurante Pompe/io Longo proc(uratore) / Aug(usti) Felix eius vil(icus)*; AÉ 1988, 0977 = ILD 677: *Pro salute / et victoria / Imp(eratoris) Caes(aris) [[M(arci)]] / [[Aur(eli) Antonini]] / [[Commodi P(ii) F(elicis)]] / Aug(usti) n(ostri) restitu/tori(s) commerc(iorum) / et Genio p(ublici) p(ortorii) Illy/rici Cl(audius) Xenophon / proc(urator) Aug(usti) n(ostri) per / Marcion(em) et Pol(lionem) vil(icos)*. See also: Piso *et al.* 2016.
18 Tóth 1977, 385–392; Tóth 2015, 171–182.
19 Gudea 1996; Protase 2010, 207–208; Piso 2013a, 277–285. See also: Egri *et al.* 2018.
20 AÉ 1998, 01074; IDR III/5, 702; Piso-Moga 1998, 105: *[G]enio p(ublici) p(ortorii) / [et] T(iti) Iul(ii) Sa/[t]urnini / conduc(toris) / p(ublici) Illyr(ici) / Maximianus / [se]r(vus) vilic(us) ex privatis) / [pr]o s[al(ute) s]ua [suorumq(ue)]. Q. Sabinius Veranus* (AÉ 1986, 571, CIMRM 1491, 1533) served together with Titus Iulius Saturninus (IDR III/1, 35, CIL III 1568, IDR I/XXIV, AÉ 1934, 107, AÉ 1928, 153) and C. Antonius Rufus (CIL V 820, Dessau 4244–4245, CIL III 5122, AÉ 2001, 1576, CIL III 13283, CIL III 5117, CIL III 14354, CIL III 1568, CIL III 10605) before the Marcomannic Wars (Dobó 1940, 155; Laet 1949, 238, 386). Their slaves constituted an important Mithraic community of the I Mithraeum in Poetovio (CIMRM 1490, 1493, 1501, 1846): Zaccaria 2010, 68.
21 Dobó 1940, 168–169; Piso-Moga 1998, 105–108.
22 See also: Lupa 12238.
23 Unfortunately, the statue itself is missing. It can represent the Genius or Jupiter, too.
24 For the institution in Dacia: Wollmann 1996, 240–249; Balla 2000, 136–140; Piso 2007, 179–182; Benea 2007, 41–46.
25 For the *negotiatores provinciae Apulensis* (CIL III 1068, 7761), see: Husar 2002, 337–338.
26 Timoc 2006, 213–218.

27 The idea was raised by Doinea Benea in her recent article. However, her 'proof' that the presence of a *salariarius* in Apulum has a direct connection with the salt trade office is inacceptable. Benea 2013, 120. For the *salariarius,* see: Méa 2012, 207–21; Deac 2013, 313–314; Szabó 2014b, 533–544.

28 The first Mithraic discovery in Apulum was made by a *salis ponderum* (weight master), Franciscus Kaftal: Szabó 2013, 53.

29 On the notion and its problematic attributes, see: Egri *et al.* 2018, 270.

30 Piso 2007, 182.

31 IDR III/4, 248: *Soli Inv/icto/pro/salute<m>C(ai)Iuli Valen/tini c(onductoris) sallinar(um)/Iulius Omucio/ libertus actor posuit.* I.I. Russu and Vermaseren (CIMRM 2011) interpreted the inscription as Mithraic. Garbó Garcia doesn't accept this: Carbó-Garcia 2010, 608.

32 IDR III/1, 139. See also: Szabó 2007, 94–95. It is not sure if the person from Tibiscum is the same with that from Homoródszentpál or Apulum as Doinea Benea affirms: Benea 2007, 43.

33 IDR III/5, 204. About Caius Iulius Valentinus, see: Balla 2000, 139–140, Piso 2007, 182.

34 Carbó-Garcia 2010, 608–609.

35 III/5, 443, Szabó 2004, no. 5b. About the person, see: Balla 2000, 136–140; Piso 2007, 182; Benea 2007, 44; Szabó 2007, 38–40; OPEL IV 96.

36 The *collegium nautarum* was present in Apulum: Ardevan 1998, 306–307. Szabó Ádám affirms, however, that the seat of the *conductor salinarum, pascui et commerciorum* was in Sarmizegetusa: Szabó 2007, 40. He is the only one from the four *conductores* who had this title, which might suggest an internal reform of the institution after 212 AD: Piso 2013b, 194.

37 For more on his activity as an important Mithraic member in Apulum, see also: Egri *et al.* 2018.

38 IDR III/3, 119. His name appears in the genitive case as *P(ubl.) Ael(i) Mari.* With 12 analogies from all over the Empire (mostly from Celtic areas), it could easily could be read as 'Marius' (OPEL III, 59; Balla 2000, 138; Piso 2007, 182 note 13.) and not as 'Marus': Benea 2007, 43; Szabó 2007, 31.

39 IDR III/3, 49. Garcia doesn't accept the Mithraic nature of this inscription (Garcia 2010b, 601), however there are some analogies in Dacia, where Mithras appears as Deus Invictus: IDR III/5, 720; Haynes 2005, 44. See also: Vermaseren 1960, 422–423.

40 IDR III/1, 145. I. I. Russu cited Ackner, who affirmed that the inscription was found in the garden of a house at Caranşebeş.

41 Probably the same person as Marcus Turranius Dius from Tibiscum: IDR III/1, 141. The Turranius *gentilicium* appears on five other inscriptions in Dacia (CIMRM 1993=IDR III/5, 285, IDR III/2, 445=AÉ 2005, 1299, IDR III/2, 400, IDR III/2, 556, Bărbulescu 2012, 10). See also: Ardevan 2005, 200–201; Săsărman 2013, 201. According to István Tóth, Turranius Marcellinus from Apulum and this person from Tibiscum were strongly related and played an important role in the spread of the cult in Dacia and in Apulum: Tóth 1992, 153–160.

42 Benea identifies the two persons: Benea 2007, 43.

43 Christescu 1929, 50; Moga 2006, 54.

44 AÉ 1930, 10; AÉ 1967, 388; Ardevan 1992, 47–53; Balla 2000, 137; Piso 2007, 181; ILD 804; Szabó 2007, 30–31; Benea 2007, 43; Benea 2013, 121. A possible new reading: *[I(ovi)] O(ptimo) M(aximo) ⌜et⌝/T(errae) M(atri) / [p]ro s⌜alut⌝(e) Ael(i) /Mari fl(amen) col(oniae) / ⌜co⌝nduc(toris) pas(cui) / ⌜et⌝ salina(rum) At/ticus ag(ens) eius? /v(otum) s(olvit) l(ibens) m(erito)*

45 Balla 2000, 139.

46 Szabó 2007, 31.

47 Details about the discovery: Ota 2012,46, 94–95; Szabó 2013b, 56–57; Rustoiu *et al.* 2014, 17; Egri *et al.* 2018; McCarty *et al.* 2020.

48 Dana-Zăgreanu 2013, 28–29.

49 Egri 2007, 103–111.

50 Gordon 2009, 413–414.

51 Tóth 2015, 173–175; McCarty *et al.* 2019, 309, Fig. 10.

52 Szabó 2015.
53 Haynes 2014. See also: Szabó 2018b, 80–86.
54 There is no synthesis on the complete movement of the military units in the seven Danubian provinces between Raetia and Moesia Inferior. See also: Matei-Popescu 2010; Lőrincz 2011; Țentea 2012; Farkas 2015.
55 The inscriptions dedicated by the *beneficiarii* before 1986 were collected in: Schallmeyer *et al.* 1990. See also: Mirković 1991; Dise 1997; Nelis-Clément 2000.
56 Mirković 1991, 255; Nelis-Clément 2000, 211–268. See also: Blumell 2008.
57 Nelis-Clément 1994, Nelis-Clément 2000, 14–15.
58 Dise 1996, 287, footnote no. 4 mentioned only 17 altars. See also: Nelis-Clément 2000, 184.
59 Dise 1997.
60 Mirković 1991.
61 There are few cases of *iterata* or *tertia statio*: idem, 253.
62 See also: the sub-chapter on the religious monopolisation in macro-spaces.
63 Moser 2019, 109–120.
64 Cupcea 2012.
65 Domaszewski 1902. For a glocal case study of Celeia, see: Dise 1996.
66 Olson-Krug 2020.
67 Liska 2015, 3–4, Fig. 1.
68 Grüll 2017, 124 after Walter Scheidel.
69 For the historical-natural reconstruction of the Danube catchment in antiquity, see: Miklós-Neppel 2010. For the food supply and the Danube and the domestication of the common carp (*Cyprinus carpio*), see also: Grüll 2017, 206.
70 Drăgan 2020, 195–199. For the role of the Danube in the grand military strategies and dislocations of the Roman army, see: Breeze 2015 with previous bibliography.
71 Orbis Stanford Geospatial Network Model of the Roman Empire.
72 Ilić *et al.* 2011.
73 Somervell 1926; Blăgoi 2018.
74 For the case study of Aquae, see: Petrović 2018. For Dunakeszi port, see: Mráv 2017.
75 Munteanu 2015, 132–152.
76 CIL 03, 11894; CIL 03, 05863 (p 2328, 50); AÉ 2012, 01054; CIL 03, 03416 = CIL 03, 10379; CIL 03, 10395 = TitAq-01, 00045; CIL 03, 10263.
77 See Chapter 2. See also: Munteanu 2015, 248–252.
78 CIL 03, 11685 = ILLPRON 01784; CIL 03, 05134 = CIL 03, 11680; CIL 03, 05135 = ILLPRON 01938; CIL 03, 05136 (p 1828, 2328, 26) = ILLPRON 01939; CIL 03, 05138 = ILLPRON 01941; CIL 03, 11684 = ILLPRON 01859; AIJ 00255 = RICeleia 00249; ILLPRON 01874 = AÉ 1938, 00151; CIL III 3896; 4009; AÉ 1938, 151–152.
79 Mussini 1998; Munteanu 2015, 175.
80 Mráv 2017, 102.
81 Šašel Kos 1994.
82 Zhuravlev 2008.
83 Munteanu 2015, 60–92 with a comprehensive list of economic connectivities and supplies between the Danubian provinces. See also: Nemeth 2007.
84 Bounegru 2002.
85 Munteanu 2015, 20–46 with the complete bibliography on the personnel of river navigation and transport. For the difference between the *navicularii* and *nautae*, see also: Drinkwater 1983, 127.
86 CIL III, 1209 = IDR III/5, 443: *P(ublio) Ael(io) P(ubli) fil(io) Pap(iria) / Strenuo eq(uo) / p(ublico) sacerd(oti) arae / Aug(usti) auguri et / IIviral(i) col(oniae) / Sarm(izegetusae) augur(i) / col(oniae) Apul(ensis) dec(urioni) / col(oniae) Drob(etensis) pat/ron(o) collegior(um) / fabr(um) cento/nar(iorum)*

et naut/ar(um) conduc(tori) pas/cui salinar(um) / et comme-/cior(um) Rufinus / eius. The literature associated the collegium with the Maros-Portus and the southern part of Colonia Aurelia Apulensis: Barbuta-Ciobanu 2000; Mihăilescu-Praporgescu 2011, 92; Munteanu 2015, 148–149.

87 Nemeth 2007.
88 Bîrliba 2016.
89 Szabó 2018b, 70.
90 The possibility has not been excluded, however, that the relief was found in a secondary position and originally was in the southern part of the Colonia Aurelia Apulensis.
91 Berciu-Băluță 1974 mentions that the relief was found in a secondary position in 1963, built in the wall of a house on Republicii 46 Street (Regimentul V Vănători today) in the central area of the Colonia Aurelia Apulensis.
92 CIL III, 10248; CIL III, 10248; CIL III, 03486; CIL III, 10430 = TitAq-I, 196; TitAq-II, 942 = AÉ 1937, 203; CIL III, 10219; CIL III, 05866; CIL III, 5197; CIL III, 5137; CIL III, 00259. See also: Alföldy 2011; Mráv 2015–2016, 182; Mráv 2017, 102.
93 IMS-II,61 = CCCA-6, 380 = AÉ 1905, 153 = AÉ 1907, +40 = AÉ 2012, +1249: *Pro salute Aug(usti) / C(aius) Val(erius) Vi/bianus / nautar(um) / q(uin)q(uennalis) sig(num) Ma/tris deum et / ad restitu/tionem tem/pli Neptuni / s(estertium) II(milia) n(ummum) d(onum) d(edit).* See in detail: Gavrilović Vitas 2021, 37.
94 The contrast between the aquatic and earthly divinities also appears as reappropriation in the work of Cellini: Arneth 1859, 104.
95 Sellar 1863, 275.
96 Gavrilović-Vitas 2020, 37.
97 See also: Szabó 2020e.
98 See Elsner 2017, 265–74, footnote no. 7 with all a bibliography on critical approaches on ancient pilgrimage.
99 I found very convincing the typology and approach of Luginbühl 2015, 52 Table 3.4 and the critical approach and terminology of Elsner 2017.
100 Luginbühl 2015, 54; Elsner 2017, 266.
101 Grünewald 2017, 130–151.
102 Fagan 2002. See also: Țentea 2015, 13–21.
103 Williamson 2005, 219–253.
104 Nemeth 2007.
105 Fodorean 2012, 211–221. See also: the case of Thracia and Aqua Calidae: Avramova 2019.
106 Piso 2004, 271–307; Nemeti 2010, 109–133.
107 Petrovic 2013, 265, especially footnote nos 973 and 975 with further bibliography.
108 Zaccaria 2010, 53–78; Gregoratti 2013, 133–153.
109 Szabó *et al.* 2016, 231–243.
110 Jankovic 2012, 34.
111 Renberg 2017, 684.
112 Petrovic 1966, 250.
113 Kádár 1981, 78.
114 Renberg 2017, 107. See also: Gordon 2017, 277–316.
115 Burghardt 1979.
116 Mráv 2013a, 49–100 with a complete bibliography on the economic and political role of the Amber Road in Pannonia.
117 Jerala 2011, 75–87.
118 Gabler 2015, 247–266.
119 Sosztarits *et al.* 2013.
120 Deac 2013.

121 Sosztarits *et al.* 2013, 195–206.
122 Renberg 2017, 344–346.
123 CIL III 4133. See: Kádár 1981, 66. Mommsen mentioned in 1873 that the altar came from the hot spring and thermal bath of Kékkút, however all the previous sources between 1823 and 1873 stated that the altar was found in a secondary position: László 1980, 73–76.
124 Kádár 1981, 65–66 with older bibliography. See also: Kusan *et al.* 2015, 40–49.
125 AÉ 1978, 468.
126 AÉ 1985, 714. In this case, Flavius Hermadion's donation represents a significant financial investment, which reflects his and his family's attachment to the site.
127 Kusan *et al.* 2015, 95–96.
128 CIL III 4121.
129 Busch-Versluys 2015, 7–18.
130 Van der Ploeg 2018, 184–185. See also: Kremer 2012, 27–28.
131 On the religion of the Dacians in the province, see: Varga 2019 and Chapter 2. On the healing sites, see also: Fodorean 2012, 211–221.
132 Ardevan-Cociş 2014. See also: Piso 2017a, 47–68.
133 Piso 2017, 48–50.
134 Szabó 2018b, 148–154.
135 Rusu 1991, 653–656.
136 CIL III 1562.
137 CIL III 1561.
138 Benea-Lalescu 1998, 267–301.
139 Schäfer 2007, 64–75.
140 Boda 2015, 281–304.
141 Szabó 2018b, 68–70.
142 Ibidem, 70–78.
143 Petridou 2016, 434–449.
144 Teichner 2013, especially 54, Fig. 4 which shows the scale of Roman material mobility on the Amber Road.
145 Gregoratti 2013. See also: Chapter 2 on Raetia and Noricum in pre-Roman and Roman times.
146 Schneider-Daszkiewicz 2011; Gabler 2014.
147 Mráv 2010–2013; Teichner 2013, 55.
148 Idem, 55–56, Fig. 5 (AÉ 1934, 68 Fig. 1 = RIU I 135).
149 Filipović-Petrović 2007; Fodorean 2016, 124.
150 CIL III 1562 = IDR III/1, 56. See also: Piso 1993, 45: *Dis et Numinib(us) / Aquarum / Ulp(ius) Secundinus / Marius Valens / Pomponius Haemus / Iul(ius) Carus Val(erius) Valens / legati Romam ad / consulatum Seve/riani c(larissimi) v(iri) missi incolu/mes reversi ex voto / E A*
151 AÉ 1960, 0339 = AÉ 2007, 1205 = CIL III, 1579: *D(is) M(anibus) / L(ucio) Iul(io) L(uci) fil(io) Sergia / Basso dec(urioni) mun(icipii) / Drobetae quaes/tori interfecto a / latronib(us) vix(it) an(nos) / XXXX Iuli(i) Iulianus / et Bassus patri / piissimo / et Iul(ius) Valerianus / frater mortem / eius exsecutus / f(aciendum) c(uraverunt).* AÉ 1960, 0339 = AÉ 2007, 1205 = CIL III, 1559: *D(is) [M(anibus)] / P(ublio) Aeli[o] / [Ari]or[to] / [IIIIvir(o) an(nuali) m(unicipii)] / D(robetae) interfec[t(o)] / a latronibus / vix(it) an(nos) L Ulp(ia) / Digna con(iugi) / pientissimo / et P(ublius) Ael(ius) fil(ius) et P(ublii) / Ael(ii) Val(ens) e[t A]u/[dar]us n(epotes) b(ene) [m(erenti)] p(osuerunt);* CIL III, 01585 = CIL III, 8021: *[------] / I(?) A(?)C(?)[---] / interfecta a latro(nibus) / et vindicata / Ulcudius Baedari / et Sutta Epicadi / p(arentes) p(ientissimae) fil(iae) tit(ulum) p(osuerunt) / D(is) I(nferis) M(anibus) Ulcudius / B(ae)dari v(i)xi(t) an(nos) L.* See also: Petraccia 2007; Bîrliba *et al.* 2010.
152 Hirt 2010, 194; Gavrilovic-Vitas-Grasar 2020.
153 Collar 2013. See also: Woolf 2016.

154 Nemeti 2005, 270–279; Nemeti 2019, 286–296; Collar 2013, 224–286, see also: pages 242 and 272.
155 For a Dacian and Moesian connection, see also: I. L. Bulg 279 and De Blois 2019.
156 Idem, 79–145; Szabó 2018b, 130–140. See also: Chapter 4.
157 Szabó 2020f. See also: Chapter 4.
158 On the Syrian units of the Danubian provinces, see: Țentea 2012.
159 Farkas 2011; Farkas 2014. See also: the Roman settlement of Sidi Kacem/Sidi Qacem/Aquae Dacicae (AÉ 1946, 37). For the commercial relationship and the African material, see: Alexandrescu *et al.* 2016, 207–208.
160 Nemeti 2019, 109–137.
161 Birley 1950, especially 64 and 68. See also: Watkins 2002 based on Piso 1993 and the *cursus honorum* of the governors of Dacia during the reign of Septimius Severus.
162 Deac 2017.
163 Woolf 2012.
164 Wilson-Flohr 2016, 23–55.
165 De Ligt-Bintliff 2020.
166 On urbanity in the Hellenistic world, see also: Woolf 2020, 209–247.
167 Fernández-Götz 2020.
168 On the role of the *oppida* system on religion, see: Fernandéz-Götz 2014.
169 Pines-Biran-Rüpke 2021. See also: Hanson 2016.
170 On the legal aspects of Roman urbanity, see: Johnston 1999, 61–66 on legal aspects of urban property and its social-economic impact.
171 Monteix 2020.
172 De Ligt-Bintliff 2020, 1–34.
173 Donev 2019.
174 Donev 2020.
175 See Introduction and the historiography of the notion on the Danubian provinces.
176 Fernandez-Götz 2020, 35–66, especially Fig. 2.1.
177 Šašel-Kos 2014; Matei-Popescu 2014; Piso 2014 on the case studies of Poetovio, Tropaion Traiani and Colonia Sarmizegetusa.
178 Florea 2011.
179 Jeremić 2016, 303 enrols only few, sporadic finds from the pre-Roman phase of Sirmium and the pre-Roman history.
180 For a comprehensive map of the urban systems: Donev 2019, 75, map. III.2. and 119, map. IV.1. See also: Hanson 2016.
181 For an almost comprehensive list of urban settlements in the Danubian provinces: Piso 2003b. See also: the list of settlements in Donev 2019, 322–379.
182 Hanson *et al.* 2017, 4, Figs 1 and 8, Fig. 4. Despite this peripheral aspect, the Roman urban systems and road network went on to play a crucial role in the formation of the medieval urban settlement system in Central-Eastern Europe. The urban density surpassed this level in Transylvania, for example, only in the 18–19th century. On the role of the major Roman roads and their medieval survival, see: Szilágyi 2014 for Pannonia and Gáll *et al.* 2017, 127–140.
183 Most of the urban settlements in the Danubian provinces experienced long-term depopulation and ruralisation in the 4–5th centuries AD, some of them undergoing a relatively short and fast transition (Savaria, Sirmium, Singidunum).
184 Woolf 1997. For a historiographic overview of the study of Roman religion in the cities, see: Szabó 2019a.
185 Dirven 1999; Kaizer 2002; Rieger 2004; Andringa 2009.

186 Following the phenomenological current of the 1930s, the work of Angelo Brelich on the religious life of Aquincum set the bar to a new level in research. The author notes in the introduction that he wishes to 'resurrect' the living religion of the ancient man. He brilliantly recognises the geological, geographical and meteorological factors that greatly influence religious life. In his chapters written about polytheism and the pantheon of Aquincum, one can espy the influences of Wissowa, Kerényi and Walter F. Otto, although the author gives an individual interpretation of the problematic notion of *interpretatio Romana*. The advantage of his study is that he knew how to apply the methods of the era and his own ideas, and did not forget about the archaeological evidence, or the epigraphic, onomastic and iconographic sources. The studies of Tibor Nagy and Géza Alföldy are merely historical, archaeological and epigraphic addendums to Brelich's work. See: Brelich 1938; Nagy 1942; Alföldy 1963.
187 Cancik 1986.
188 Urciuoli 2019. For a similar notion (urbanology and central place theory) but without a detailed theoretical approach, see: Duling 1999, 158–159.
189 Rüpke 2020, 5–6.
190 See also: the notion of heteropolitanisation: Gentile *et al.* 2012, 291–293.
191 Rüpke 2019b.
192 See the next subchapter on small-group religions.
193 See also: the conclusions of this book and Fig. 54 in the Appendices.
194 Urciuoli 2019 citing Hodder 2018.
195 Wamser 2004, 97.
196 Szabó 2018c.
197 Szabó 2019b, 496, Figs 1–2.
198 For the topography of Cambodunum, see: Weber 2000, 73. For the topography of Sarmizegetusa, see: Boda 2015, 288, Fig. 7.
199 Mócsy 1974b, 135–166. Colonia Sarmizegetusa as *colonia deducta* was contested numerous times in the recent historiography. On the formation of the city, see: Piso 2017b.
200 See also: Bishop 2013, 16, Fig. 2.
201 After the EDH Database (April 2021). See also: Fig. A4 in the Appendices.
202 Fischer 2012, 21, abb. 6 for the lists of the Roman legions and their mobility during the Principate. For the case study of Raetia, see: Farkas 2015. Similar, recently established, and detailed analysis of military dislocations are missing from the literature. For Moesia Inferior, see: Matei-Popescu 2010. For Roman Dacia, see: Piso 2000.
203 For Brigetio, see: Bartus-Borhy 2014. For Troesmis, see: Alexandrescu *et al.* 2016. For Novae, see: Sarnowski *et al.* 2016. See also: the Digital Atlas of Sanctuaries in the Danubian provinces: *danubianreligion.com*. Last accessed: 10.05.2021.
204 Arnold 2020.
205 Rieger 2004; Stöger 2011.
206 Andringa 2009. See also: Flohr 2020.
207 Raja 2015.
208 Raja-Sindbæk 2018, 13–17. See also: Selheimer 2020 and Pitts 2020 on Romanisation 2.0 and high-definition archaeology.
209 A similarly rich urban system was attested in Apulum. For a detailed analysis of urban religion in Apulum, see: Szabó 2018b, 101–127.
210 After the EDH Database (April 2021). See Kremer 2012, 325. The number of small plaques dedicated to the so-called 'Danubian Riders' (*Domna et Domnus*) discovered in Carnuntum is uncertain, although recently it was estimated at hundreds of objects: Kremer 2019, 282–283.
211 After the EDH Database (April 2021). The first volume of the *Tituli Aquincenses* presents 468 votive inscriptions from the *territorium* of Aquincum.

212 1315 votive inscriptions were identified in Rome on the EDR Database (April 2021).
213 There is no comprehensive analysis on Roman religion in Aquincum. From the rich bibliography produced on Roman religion in local context, the most important one is the above-mentioned study of A. Brelich and the following studies of T. Nagy, G. Alföldy and P. Zsidi: Brelich 1938; Nagy 1942; Alföldy 1963; Zsidi 2011. See also: *Tituli Aquincenses* I. for the votive inscriptions by Á. Szabó and P. Kovács. For a comprehensive analysis of the material evidence of Roman religion and the local pantheon attested in Carnuntum, see: Kremer 2012. For the Pfaffenberg sanctuary, see: Piso 2003a. The two cities are often used for a comparative approach: Groh *et al.* 2014; Grammer 2015.
214 Tóth 2015, 97–113. See also: Chapter 2.
215 AÉ 1991, 1314 = AÉ 1995, 1262 = AÉ 2003, 1381; AÉ 1982, 783 = AÉ 2003, 1381; AÉ 2003, 1393 = AÉ 2004, 93; AÉ 2003, 1394 = AÉ 2004, 93; AÉ 2003, 1395 = AÉ 2004, 93; EDCS-22400105; EDCS-22400108; AÉ 1982, 785a = AÉ 2003, 1381; EDCS-22400109; EDCS-22400110; AÉ 1982, 785c = AÉ 2003, 1381; EDCS-22500277; EDCS-22500278; EDCS-22500279; EDCS-22500280; EDCS-22500281; EDCS-22500282; EDCS-22500284; EDCS-22400106; EDCS-22400107; EDCS-22500283; EDCS-22500285; EDCS-22500286; EDCS-22500287; EDCS-22500288; EDCS-22500289; EDCS-22500290; EDCS-22500291; EDCS-22500292; EDCS-22500293; EDCS-22500294; EDCS-22500295; EDCS-22500296; EDCS-22500298; EDCS-22500299; AÉ 2003, 1400. See also: Piso 2003a; Kremer 2004.
216 The cult is well attested in Pannonia Inferior and known only from few exceptional epigraphic sources outside the province: AÉ 2003, 01408; AÉ 2003, 01409; AÉ 2003, 01410; AÉ 2003, 01411; AÉ 2003, 01412; AÉ 2003, 01414 = AÉ 2006, 01096; AÉ 2003, 01415 = AÉ 2014, +01037; AÉ 2003, 01416 = AÉ 2006, 01097; AÉ 2003, 01417; AÉ 2003, 01418; AÉ 2003, 01419; AÉ 2003, 01421; AÉ 2003, 01422; AÉ 2003, 01423; AÉ 2003, 01424 = AÉ 2005, 01241; AÉ 2003, 01426; AÉ 2003, 01427; AÉ 2003, 01428; AÉ 2003, 01429; AÉ 2003, 01430; AÉ 2003, 01431 = AÉ 2005, 01242; AÉ 2003, 01432; AÉ 2003, 01434; AÉ 2003, 01435; AÉ 2003, 01436; AÉ 2003, 01437; AÉ 1991, 01324 = AÉ 2003, 01413; TitAq-01, 00166 = AÉ 1965, 00349; CIL 03, 10418 = TitAq-01, 00165.
217 Doneus *et al.* 2013, 172–190.
218 Mráv 2013b, 208–211.
219 Zsidi 2003, 43–46.
220 Póczy 2003, 75–77. See also: Chapter 1.
221 Idem, 78.
222 Németh 2003, 87.
223 AÉ 1939, 0263 = AÉ 1986, 0590 = *Tituli Aquincenses* 0001: *[Imp(eratori) Caesari Vespasiano Aug(usto) pontif(ici) maxim(o)] / [trib(unicia) pot(estate) III imp(eratori) X p(atri) p(atriae) co(n)s(uli) IIII desig(nato) V censori] / T(ito) Caesar[i Vespasiano imp(eratori) IIII pont]if(ici) [co(n)s(uli) II desig(nato) III] / Caesar[i Aug(usti) f(ilio) Domitiano co(n)s(uli) II p]rincip(i) [iuv]en[t(utis)] / C(aio) Calp[etano Rantio Quirinale] Val(erio) Festo leg(ato) / ala [prima Tungrorum] Frontoniana / L(ucio) M[---]ore praefecto*
224 Mráv 2013b, 209–210.
225 CIL 03, 10479 = *Tituli Aquincenses* I. 0429: *------] / [------] / Ius[t]us trib(unus) / mil(itum) leg(ionis) X g(eminae) / v(otum) s(olvit) l(ibens) m(erito).* See also: Alföldy 1963, 48.
226 The impact of the Marcomannic Wars on the religious life of Aquincum is hard to estimate, although it appears in numerous publications as a literary topos: Alföldy 1963, 51. The author clearly divides the chronology of the epigraphic sources into two major categories: before and after the Marcomannic Wars.
227 Vasáros-Havas 2019.
228 Zsidi 2011, 161–162; Grammer 2015, 43.
229 Wittenberg 2014, 50–52. For analogies, see: Kremer 2012, 337–341; Szabó 2018b, 43–45.
230 See also: Schäfer 2014 and Szabó 2018b, 53–56.

231 AÉ 1976, 0541 = CIL 03, 10439 = *Tituli Aquincenses* I. 267: *Pro salute d(omini) n(ostri) / Imp(eratoris) M(arci) Aurel(i) An/tonini Aug(usti) / Aureli(i) Florus et M/ercator IIvir(i) q(uin)q(uennales) / c[o (oniae)] Aq(uincensium) temp{u}lum / [Ne]mesis vetustate / [con]lapsum restituer(unt) / [Mess(alla)] et Sabi(no) co(n)s(ulibus) VIII K(alendas) Iul(ias) / [---] Aur(elio) Suro sala(riario);* CIL 03, 10440 = *Tituli Aquincenses* I, 026: *Deae Dianae Nemesi Aug(ustae) / honoribus et fa(v)oribus / G(aio) Iul(io) Victorin<o> eq(uo) p(ublico) aedili(cio) / IIvirali et T(ito) Fl(avio) Luciano / q(uaestoricio) IIvirali pontificibus / q(uin) q(uennalibus) col(oniae) Aq(uincensium) / Pupili(us) Hyliatianus(!) / antesstis(!) numini eius / deae posuit V Kal(endas) Iulias // Aemiliano // et Basso co(n)s(ulibus);* CIL 03, 03485 = *Tituli Aquincenses* I, 0286: *Deae Nemesi Aug(ustae) // pro salute / Aureliae Aude/ntiae filiae / suae et pro sua / incolum(itate) Aurel(ius) / Audentius c(urator) r(ei) p(ublicae) / Aqui(ncensium) e sacer(dotalibus) pro/vinci(ae) libenti ani/mo suscepta // [vot]a conplevit*

232 Zsidi 2011. See also: the topography of the sanctuaries in the Digital Atlas of Sanctuaries in the Danubian provinces: *www.danubiareligion.com*.

233 After the hypothesis of Ádám Szabó: Szabó 2020g.

234 Boda 2015. See also: Schäfer 2007.

235 Marcus Vitruvius Pollio, *de Architectura* 1.2.7.: *Naturalis autem decor sic erit si primum omnibus templis saluberrimae regiones aquarumque fontes in his locis idonei eligentur in quibus fana constituantur, deinde maxime Aesculapio, Saluti et eorum deorum, quorum plurimi medicinis aegri curari videntur. Cum enim ex pestilenti in salubrem locum corpora aegra translata fuerint et e fontibus salubribus aquarum usus subminis trabuntur, celerius convalescent. Ita efficietur uti ex natura loci maiores auctasque cum dignitate divinitas excipiat opiniones.* See also: Festus, *De verborem significatione* 110.

236 Póczy 1998, 33–34.

237 Szabó 2004; Boda 2015; Szabó 2018c.

238 Póczy 1980, 16–17.

239 Szabó 2004; Szabó 2018b, 68–75.

240 After the EDH Database. The EDCS enlists 836 votive inscriptions, including the Imperial dedications and instrumenta inscriptions. G. Kremer mentions 772 stone monuments (epigraphic and figurative) from the conurbation of Carnuntum: Kremer 2012, 325.

241 Kremer 2015.

242 Tomorad 2018, 82.

243 Mráv 2010–2013, 55.

244 Doneus-Scharrer 1999.

245 See Chapter 2.

246 Gugl-Kastler 2007 for older excavations.

247 Doneus *et al.* 2013, 85–100.

248 Kremer 2012, 325.

249 On the various legal states of the religious spaces in public space (*locus publicus*), see: Szabó 2020g.

250 Nemeti 2019, 254–257.

251 Woolf 2018–2019.

252 On this complex and highly debated notion, see: Alvar 2008; Bricault *et al.* 2015.

253 On Trajan and Jupiter Heliopolitanus, see: Macrobius, *Saturnalia* 1.23.14.

254 Paturel 2019, 194–246.

255 CIL III, 01353: *I(ovi) O(ptimo) M(aximo) / Heliopolitan(o) / Q(uintus) Licinius Ma/crinus (centurio) / leg(ionis) IIII F(laviae) f(elicis) / v(otum) s(olvit) l(ibens) m(erito)*

256 Steigberer-Tober 2013.

257 On the notion of complex sanctuary, see: Raja 2015.

258 On the official, Imperial propaganda of the temple on coins, see: Butcher 2019.

259 Sage 2020, 44.
260 Baker 2004; Coulston 2004. The notion appears in numerous other studies, too, almost as a disciplinary topos, a repetitive metahistorical notion.
261 Bishop-Coulston 2006, 17–18, almost half of the settlements from the 268 sites are in the Danubian provinces.
262 Szabó 2003; Popescu 2004; Ştefănescu-Oniţiu 2009. See also: Speidel 1978.
263 I have discussed this issue in detail here: Szabó 2018b, 20–22.
264 Heidenreich 2013, 224–226.
265 Popescu 2004; Ştefănescu-Oniţiu 2009.
266 Haynes 1999.
267 Religion and the Roman army are presented neither in Raja-Rüpke 2015 nor in Rüpke 2018. See also: Scheuermann 2013.
268 Szabó *et al.* 2020.
269 Oltean-Fonte 2020.
270 On war and religion, see still the best summary: Rüpke 1990.
271 Oltean 2019, 120–121. See also: Oltean 2007, 76, Peţan 2015, 157.
272 Opreanu 2000. See also: Szabó 2018b, 145.
273 For the comprehensive study of auxiliary forts and their *vici*, see: Gudea 1997; Gudea 2001; Visy 2003; Flynt 2005; Gudea 2005; Marcu 2009; Farkas 2015; Gudea 2013, See also: the Römische Limes in Österreich series: https://verlag.oeaw.ac.at/kategorie_80.ahtml. Last accessed: 15.05.2021.
274 For another case study for a military vicus and religion, see: Nemeti 2010.
275 On the geographic and hydrographic features of the area, see: Negula *et al.* 2020, 18.
276 The settlement and the fort were for a long time interpreted as an important auxiliary fort on the bank of the Mures River, although it was not on the margin of the province, which extended as far as the River Tisza (the presumed Parthiscus). This old topographic position and metahistorical map of Roman Dacia is contested today.
277 See also: the map of Roman Dacia in: Marcu *et al.* 2017, 20 and Petculescu-Mitar 2018, 96.
278 See also: the *Ala I Bosporanorum*: Idem, 95.
279 Marcu 2009, 144.
280 Gabler 2011, 44 and 48.
281 There are execeptional cases, however, when some parts of the fort are reused as sacralised spaces, such as the case of the House of Laticlavii in Aquincum, the Dolichenum from Vindolanda or a possible mithraeum from Pojejena. All of these cases are from the late 3rd century AD.
282 Deac-Simion forthcoming.
283 See Fig. 54 in the Appendices.
284 Ţeposu-Marinescu 1964; Cristea 2015.
285 Alicu 2004 for the sanctuaries of Micia.
286 Szabó 2015 (2020), 313–314 for a detailed bibliographic list on the topic.
287 Idem, 322.
288 There is an ongoing debate in Romanian literature on the dual nature (*pagus et vicus*) of the settlement around the auxiliary fort. See especially: Floca 1968.
289 Nemeti 2019, 132–137. See also: Price 2012, 4–5.
290 CIL III, 1306 = IDR III/3, 110: *Deo Mercuri/o Marcus Anto/nius Sabini/anus princeps / v(otum) s(olvit) l(ibens) m(erito).* See also: Onofrei 2007, 276.
291 Szabó 2015.
292 Donev 2019, 375.
293 Heidenreich 2013, 1–33.

294 Bishop 2013, 3, Fig. 2. Many of the 35 legionary fortresses were functional only during the Dominate (late 3rd and 4th century AD), after 285 AD – a time period that is not the subject of our study.
295 Żyromski 2008; Roselaar 2016, 148.
296 Kremer 2012, 325–326. See also: Appendices.
297 Gugl *et al.* 2017.
298 Bărbulescu 2020.
299 Tomas 2018, 751; Zakrzewski 2020.
300 Petrikovits 1975, 75–78. The old thesis of A. von Domaszewski was contested by H. von Petrikovits.
301 Hidenreich 2013, 40–50.
302 Marcu 2005.
303 Szabó 2018b, 24–30.
304 Heidenreich 2013.
305 Kremer 2012, 328, fig.Fig. 12.
306 Idem, 325.
307 Based on the EDH Database. In the EDCS, there are 116 inscriptions in the *tituli sacri* category.
308 For the case study of the Jupiter dedications, see: Sarnowski 2015.
309 Based on the EDH Database. Most notably, the inscription dedicated to the eagle of the legion, the *signum*. AÉ 1982, 0849: *Signum originis / pro salute dominorum nn[[[n(ostrorum)]]] Immpp(eratorum) / Severi et Antonini Augg(ustorum) [[[et P(ubli) Septimi]]] / [[[Getae nob(ilissimi) Caesaris]]] et Iuliae Augustae / matris Augusti [[[et Caes(aris)]]] et kastrorum / M(arcus) Aurelius M(arci) f(ilius) Aelia / Paulinus Ovilavis p(rimus) p(ilus) / leg(ionis) I Ital(icae) Aquilae d(ono) d(edit) // Felicissi[mis tem]/poribus dd[d(ominorum) nnn(ostrorum)] / Imp(eratore) Anton[ino Aug(usto)] / ter [[et Geta Caes(are)]] / iterum co(n)s(ulibus) I[d(ibus)] / Mais dedi[cante] / Iul(io) Faustin[iano] / co(n) s(ulari) et Val(erio) Q[---]/tiano le[g(ato) leg(ionis)]*
310 AÉ 1975, 0755; AÉ 1985, 0735; AÉ 1988, 0984; AÉ 1972, 0526; AÉ 1989, 0634; AÉ 1990, 0863; AÉ 1994, 1520; ILBulg 322; AÉ 1998, 1130; AÉ 1998, 1131; AÉ 1998, 1132; AÉ 1998, 1134; AÉ 2015, 1215; AÉ 2015, 1216; AÉ 2015, 1217; Possibly also: AÉ 1966, 0347; AÉ 1966, 0346; AÉ 1991, 1370.
311 On the problem of military *fasti* and collective festivals in a military context, see: Reeves 2005.
312 For a complete bibliography of the building, see: Dyczek-Kolendo 2010, 36.
313 Petrikovits 1975, 98–102.
314 Kremer 2012, 350–351.
315 Dyczek-Kolendo 2010, 36, Fig. 1.
316 Künzl 2005. For a radically different view, see: Baker 2004.
317 Dyczek-Kolendo 2010, 39, Fig. 6.
318 Idem, cat. nos 1–6.
319 AÉ 1998, 1130: *Aescula/pio sacrum / leg(io) I Ital(ica)*
320 Dyczek-Kolendo 2010, 39. AÉ 1998, 1131: *[A]esculapium / ex donis arg(enteum) / p(ondo) V unc(iis) V / C(aius) Mansuanius / Severus leg(atus) Aug(usti) f(aciendum) c(uravit)* and ILNovae C07: *Hygiam / ex donis arg(enteam) / p(ondo) IIII unc(iis) VII[---] / M(arcus) Clodius / Laetus leg(atus) / Aug(usti) f(aciendum) c(uravit)*
321 Moser 2014, 13–14.
322 On the silver body of the gods, see: Nemeti 2012, 146; Estienne 2015, 385.
323 For a comprehensive study of the economic aspect of Roman religious dedications in public spaces, see: Duncan-Jones 1965.
324 At Aquae Iasae: AÉ 1985, 0714=AÉ 2013, 1207: *Nymphis / Iasis / Fl(avius) Herm/adion cir(citor) / vec(tigalis) Illy(rici) et / Ul(pia) Piste ei(us?) / cum Avito / et Suriaco / f(iliis) phialam / arg(enteam) p(ondo) II d(onum) d(ederunt)*

325 In Viminacium, CIL III, 06308: *[In honorem] / Imp(eratoris) Caes(aris) Aug(usti) / C(aius) Memm[ius?] Cyri[a]/cus [Au]g(ustalis) IIvira[libus] / [orna]m[e]n[ti]s [---] ab or[dine] / [--- e]t ab or[dine ---] in se con/latum statuam / arg(enteam) ex p(ondo) lib(ris) XL / [------]*
326 CIL III, 4806: *Noreiae / Aug(ustae) sacr(um) / Q(uintus) Fabius / Modestus / domo Roma / dec(urio) al(ae) I Aug(ustae) / Thracum / phialam / argent(eam) p(ondo) II (quadrantem) / embl(ema) Noreiae / aurea / uncias duas / d(onum) d(edit)*
327 Rüpke 2018, 36 on 'not indubitably plausible actors': Idem, 103. See also: Rüpke 2021, 43.
328 See also: the methodological introduction of the book.
329 On the cognitive aspect of religious media, see: Johannsen-Kirsch 2020.
330 Elsner 2013, 167–168.
331 Bremmer 2013; Estienne 2015.
332 Luchesi 2020, 207–218.
333 Elsner 2007, 11–12.
334 Morgan 2018, 44.
335 From the rich literature, see: Mylonopoulos 2010; Kiernan 2020, 4–24.
336 Stewart 2003.
337 Frakes 2013.
338 Idem, 251.
339 For a less comprehensive list, see: Quinn-Wilson 2013, 170.
340 Groh *et al.* 2014. For Carnuntum, see also: Neubauer *et al.* 2002.
341 Gömöri 1990, 406.
342 For research history, see: Harl 1989, 521–523; Luschin 2003, 149.
343 Alföldy 1974, 89.
344 Trunk 1991, 237, abb. 177.
345 Alföldy 1974, 89.
346 Trunk 1991, 238–239.
347 Luschin 2003, 158–159; Quinn-Wilson 2013, 149.
348 See the plan in Trunk 1991, 238, abb. 178.
349 Idem, 239.
350 Kandler 1992.
351 On performance and lived religious experience associated with Capitolia, see: Patzelt 2020.
352 For the monographic synthesis of the forum, see: Piso 2006.
353 Meneghini 2014; Le Bohec 2014; Schalles 2014.
354 Diaconescu 2010, 11.
355 Schäfer 2007, 17–25.
356 Cristilli 2015.
357 Lupa 15341, 15342. See also: Diaconescu 2010, 53.
358 Idem, 12.
359 Boda 2015, 289. See also: Fishwick 2000.
360 On centrality in urban planning, see: Davies 1957.
361 Piso 2014, 258.
362 Diaconescu 2010, 79.
363 Piso 2014, 265–269.
364 Idem, 260.
365 Piso *et al.* 2012.
366 Floca 1965.
367 Diaconescu 2010, 80–87. His reconstructions are often based on small fragments and need to be considered hypothetical in many cases, especially on the possible bronze statues of the Forum Vetus.

368 Țentea-Olteanu 2020.
369 Kabakchieva 2014, 190, Fig. 10.
370 Diaconescu 2010, 55–56. See also: Bota-Diaconescu 2003.
371 Dimitrov 2015, 577–576.
372 Toma 2004.
373 Lupa 9782, 7977, 8025.
374 In the database of Ortolf Harl there are five architraves from Raetia, 69 from Noricum, 13 from Pannonia Inferior, 19 in Pannonia Superior and 16 from Moesia Inferior. The numbers did not reflect the real number of architectural monuments.
375 Diaconescu 2010, 66–67.
376 Kabakchieva 2014, 187, Fig. 7.
377 On memory and religion, see: Orlin 2007, 84–85.
378 Scherrer 2007, 52.
379 One of the annexes were interpreted in the older literature as a a *schola* or *curia* of a Bacchic small religious group, however this interpretation was based only on the mosaic discovered in one of the rooms: Nash-Williams 1950, 170.
380 Kristensen 2013; Alexandrescu 2016.
381 On the legal aspects of public temples, see: Szabó 2017c.
382 Maschek 2016.
383 Sosztarits *et al.* 2013.
384 Lupa 8007.
385 Gasparini 2021, 40.
386 The side representations of Lupa 8007 and 8009.
387 Gasparini-Gordon 2018, 578–587.
388 For a new approach on Roman priesthood, see: Rüpke-Santangelo 2017; Rüpke 2018, 296–326.
389 Rüpke-Santangelo 2017, 16–17 claims that priests never monopolised religious communication.
390 Rüpke 2018, 296.
391 See the definition of Ádám Szabó: Szabó 2006, 4–5.
392 According to the the Clauss-Slaby Database, there were the following numbers of inscriptions: Raetia 13, Noricum 31, Pannonia Inferior 59, Pannonia Superior 73, Moesia Inferior 70, Moesia Superior 37 and Dacia 117.
393 Lupa 9762. For a better analogy of an Anubis priest, see a case study from Venetia: Lupa 19782.
394 Gavrilović-Vitas 2020, 174–177.
395 Gyurka-Szebenyi 2016, 115.
396 Lupa 951, 4859, 4874, 6049, 6196, 6231, 21914.
397 Covacef 2011, 221. See also: lupa 15365 and Van Haeperen 2021 on the cista of Magna Mater, however she did not cite the sarcophagus.
398 Lupa 21263. See also: Bărbulescu-Câteia 2007. A possibly funerary representation of a *sella curulis* and a *lictor* with a *scriba* was associated with a *flamen*: Lupa 1177 = Schäfer 1989, 352.
399 Szabó 2006; Szabó 2007; Szabó 2010.
400 For the case study of Caius Iulius Valens from Apulum, see: Szabó 2018b, 64–66.
401 *Haruspex*: Marcus (CIL III 14214), Claudius Aelius Optimus (AÉ 1957, 295); *Sacerdos*: Flavius Petronianus (AÉ 2015, 1238), Antinius Marinus (AÉ 2015, 1239), Aurelius Flavius Aquila (AÉ 2015, 1241, EDCS-59400151), Marcus Ulpius Antipater (CIL III 773 = CIL III 6170), Tiberius Vitales (CIL III 7506), Iulianus Tauri (IlgBulg 440), Aurelius Marinus Romanus (CCID 62), Elas Bit (AÉ 1912, 190), Ruf[us et(?)] / [3]A[3] [---] (AÉ 2014, 1149), Mama Dada (CIL III 7559), Castor et Licinius (CCID 77), Aurelius Antiochianus (CCID 76), Aelius Seucus et Polydeuces Masculinus et Gaius et Lucius Decimus (CCID 64), Aelius Flavus et Marinus (AÉ 1998, 1143), Iulius Alexander et Germanus Baronas (AÉ 1998, 1144), Ulpius Claudianus (EDCS-77700191), Polydeuces Theophilus

et Lucius Kapito et Flavius Reginus (CCID 60), Lucius Oppius Maximus et Lucius Oppius Ianuarius (AÉ 1995, 1362 and CCCA 385), Verus (AÉ 2006, 1205), Publius Aelius Epitynchanus (AÉ 2012, 1270), Valerius Villanus (AÉ 1974, 570), Titus Iulius Capito (CIL III 753=7429), Luginus Dometi et Aquila Barsemon et Flavius Damas (CCID 61), Lucius Petronius Sentius (CIL III 12428); *Augur:* Lucius Publicius Viator (CIL III 6200), Festus (CIL III 7509), Caius Arrius Quintianus (CIL III 7560); *Flamen*: Caius Valerius Longinianus (CIL III 6235), Marcus Titius (CIL III 14211); *Pontifex*: Marcus Ulpius Marcianus (CIL III 7504), Caius Valerius Plautianus (AÉ 1957, 00294); *Archymista*: Ulpius Dionysios (CIL III 6150); *Pater*: Marcus Antonius Marcianus (AÉ 2007, 1231), Celso (AÉ 1973, 479), ISM II 83 and 160; *archidendrophorus*: C(aius) Antonius Eutyches (CIL III 763); *Sodales*: Lucius Anninus (CIL III 6154); *Archibucolus*: Herculanus Chresti (IlgBulg 219); *Dendrophoris et dumopiretis*: CCCA 385.

402 See also: Chapter 4 on small-group religions and their sacralised spaces.

403 CIL III 753=CIL III 7429=AÉ 2010, 1388. For the complete bibliography, see also: Agócs 2017, 248–249.

404 His name was mentioned also in CIL III, 751 (p 992); CIL III, 6126; CIL III, 5121 (p 2198); CIL III, 6124. Agócs 2017, 248.

405 Dobó 1940.

406 Beskow 1980; Szabó 2015.

407 Szabó 1999; Szabó 2018b, 58–64.

4

Space sacralisation in meso-spaces

The previous chapter focused on the macro-spaces of religious communication. As was stated in the methodological introduction, macro-spaces can vary from extra-provincial routes and continental networks to major public spaces, and may be established in urban and military contexts. Accessibility, visibility and the density of religious tools (objects, human agency, spatial dimensions) are the common features of macro-spaces.

Religious communication between human and divine agency also created numerous meso-spaces, where all the above-mentioned factors are reduced: the number of individuals participating in such spaces is less than 100 (usually 10–30), therefore their accessibility is limited. This limitation is often controlled by religious specialists and legal tools (*lex sacra*, *collegia* rules, *sacramentum*), but also the physical dimensions and liminality of the sacralised space.[1] In these conditions, where space is reduced and the human and material agency has its own dimensional limitations, the external features (architectural, environmental) of these sacralised spaces plays a secondary or marginal role in religious communication. What is more important – and makes the meso-spaces very popular – is the introverted aspect of spatial religion.

The inner design, structure and constantly changing inventory of these spaces reflects much more the individual religious choices and creates an ideal space for religious appropriations and individualisations. Individuals – such as the founders of religious ideas, groups or essential tools (texts, visual narratives) – as well as group identities create a much greater possibility for religious dialogue and connectivity in meso-spaces. In these relatively small but well-connected spaces we can identify and analyse much more easily the individual; the inner hierarchies and their dynamic changes; the mechanisms of religious grouping and networking; the religious experiences, divinations and visual and textual narratives used in religious communication; and the various forms of appropriations.

This chapter will focus on meso-spaces by examining these major factors, alongside asking some crucial questions. Where were these spaces predominantly formed? Why were there so many of them during the Principate in the Danubian provinces? Through particular and well-documented case studies, I will also analyse the 'biographies' and lived ancient religion within these meso-spaces.

Using this spatial and qualitative notion of religious dimensions (meso-space[2]), my aim is to break the traditional categories that identified these spaces with a certain divinity or human agency (Mithraeum, Dolichenum, Bacchium, Iseum, Serapeum, Phrygianum, etc.). For a long time, these spaces were associated with a cultural-religious orientalism, modern historiography claiming their oriental (Eastern) origins.[3] Others highlighted the mystery aspect of these cults and the associated spaces and groups; however, it has always been problematic to find material sources for the scant literary evidence.[4] Recently, these religious groups have been analysed in the context of group formation,[5] mobility[6] and cognitive features.[7] Small-group religions – often called elective cults[8] – were interpreted mostly from the perspective of their human or divine agency, but rarely from a holistic approach, in which the participants, the divine power, the materiality of religion, facets of lived religion and the spatial arrangements and investments were all analysed.[9] In the following, I will present some of the major facets of religious communication,[10] starting with the creation and creators of small-group religions and their meso-spaces and moving on to the strategies of maintenance and disappearance of these in the Danubian provinces during the Principate.

Founders and entrepreneurs

Founding a religious group is never an easy task. For a very long time, religious founders and entrepreneurs were analysed exclusively from the perspective of Christian theology, using Jesus as a prototype of religious founders and small-group religions.[11] Recent studies have focused intensively on the mechanisms and complex phases of founding, creating, maintaining and disappearing religious groups through innovative methodologies, such as networks studies[12] or modern epidemiology.[13]

To understand the life cycle of a small-group religion and its growth and evolution in the religious market, it is important to present a general model for the process itself (Fig. 4.1). The evolution of small-group religions is very similar to and inseparable from the process of space sacralisation itself, as presented in the theoretical introduction. Small-group religions usually have a founder or a founding group. In the case of a single and documented founder, the crucial moment is the lifetime and the first years following the death of this personality. In most cases, new religious movements and their religious entrepreneurs fail within the lifetime of the founder. If the founder is a so-called charismatic religious leader,[14] he or she[15] will need to enhance the religion with some essential features in order to achieve a successful strategy and religious communication. The personality and cognitive aspects of the founder are therefore essential: the detailed presentation of Alexander of Abonoteichus by Lucian (his attractive physical appearance, gestures, voice and interactions with his friends and the urban crowds) represents the prototype of a charismatic religious entrepreneur.[16] However, his case is not comparable with the successful founders, prophets and charismatic leaders of Abrahamic religions in the Near East or Asia.[17]

Ann Taves analysed in detail the paths and evolution of contemporary religious founders or leaders and their personal, cognitive and physical transformation, and the qualities that served as direct and active agency in creating a new religious group.[18] Taves argues that a successful founder needs a revelatory religious event (a divination, an epiphany, a direct contact with the divine agency), which will represent not only the single, transformative event of his personality and existential-cognitive body, but also the source and basis of the narrative (oral, later textual or visual), the central 'story', or as Rodney Stark argued, an impactful cultural capital.[19] The story (cultural capital) will be the essential element that is used to establish the core group of the new religious movement. This phase is usually amical and familial.[20] Taves termed these early individuals and initiates 'key collaborators', who play an important role in helping the founder to expand the core group. In the case of Alexander, the false prophet, we know from literary sources that he had only one key collaborator in the very beginning of his revelatory event.[21]

Convincing the key collaborators represents the first obstacle in the life cycle of a religious group and is a crucial step. To achieve success, the founder and his early followers will need further strategies, possibly multiple revelations (epiphanies) and materialised religious tools.[22] In the case study of Alexander, this materialised religious agent was his snake and later the materialised form of it, which was discovered in Tomis and Apulum (partially preserved). Materialisation of the narrative represents the memorialisation of the epiphany, which can subsequently be reproduced and transferred more easily. The invention of new iconographic features and programmes in antiquity reflects these early phases in the life cycle of a religious group. Unfortunately, in the majority of cases, these early steps are impossible to reconstruct in the archaeologically attested small-group religions of classical antiquity. Very few founding myths have been preserved and in most instances, the founder – or the founding group – is unknown. However, not all small-group religions need a personification of the founder: for the most part, this role is replaced by a central figure of a divinity or mythological figures, or a hero (Orpheus, for example).

In this early phase of the new religious movement, space sacralisation is still a secondary aim: the core group and the founder(s) are creating the first sacralised spaces, especially the space where the first revelation-epiphany occurred. This can be a stone, a cave, a desert, the domestic environment of the founder, a forest or any other natural or even imagined realms.

Another crucial moment in the life cycle of the religious group is the expansion and replication of the core group outside of familial bonds. This phase is called the 'ecology of the cult', which works similarly to epidemiological models and networks.[23] Stark argued that in this phase, the competitive aspects, novelty and attractiveness (exoticism) of the cultural capital of the group has a significant impact.[24] Successful movements that go on to create an extended group and network will also produce a large number of material evidence and will contribute to the appropriation and reinterpretation of the religious knowledge of the founder.[25]

The next obstacle of small-group religions is surviving the founder him or herself: in many cases, the disappearance of the charismatic religious leader represents the fading phase of the group. Almost all the known religious groups from antiquity that have been attested archaeologically in the Danubian provinces are successful small-group religions, which survived their foundation phase and produced several generations of followers and members. The most famous – and the only literary documented exception in the Danubian provinces – is the case of the cult of Glykon, founded by Alexander of Abonoteichus (Fig. 4.2). His newly founded cult in Asia Minor was rapidly transported to Moesia Inferior (Tomis – Fig. 4.3) and Dacia (Apulum), probably by the expanded group and his 'key collaborators', although their network is impossible to reconstruct. The two altars dedicated by Marcus Aurelius Onesas[26] and Marcus Aurelius Theodotus[27] were erected by two possibly related people who came to Apulum from a Greek-speaking area of the Empire. Thanks to the major mobilities of the period between 166 and 168 AD, the dislocation of the V Macedonica legion in Potaissa from Moesia Inferior attracted a significant group of Greek-speaking individuals and established a much more intense economic and cultural connection with the Pontic area.[28] The names of the two dedicants suggest not only the chronology of the monuments – likely erected in the period of Marcus Aurelius (166–180 AD) or early Commodus – but also their possible familial relationship.

Thereafter, the followers of Alexander from Asia Minor spread quickly in Tomis and Apulum, probably in the lifetime of the founder or shortly after. In this phase of religious group formation, space sacralisation becomes essential, and new groups in urban contexts need a permanent space. However, the context of the two altars in Apulum and the exact provenance of the famous statue of Glykon in Tomis is unknown, therefore we don't know whether the divinity had a separate sacralised space or if his worshippers shared a space with other small-group religions – a common phenomenon, especially small-group religions associated with Syrian ethnic groups and local divinities (*theoi synnaoi*).[29] The two altars of Glykon in Apulum were dedicated after a dream divination (*ex iussu/iusso dei*), a religious practice that was monopolised for a long time by the Asclepeia in the Roman world.[30] In the 2nd century AD, however, this monopolisation was contested by emerging new religious groups, such as the core group of Alexander worshipping Glykon or the cult of Jupiter Dolichenus, who was also associated with divine dream divinations.[31] From the few monuments dedicated to Glykon, it seems that the earliest attempts of the group to achieve external replication failed around the period of Commodus and they were never able to reproduce the core group after the death of the founder.

The phase of expansion – when a small-group religion goes beyond the core group and its original settlement (*origo*) – produced ample material evidence and

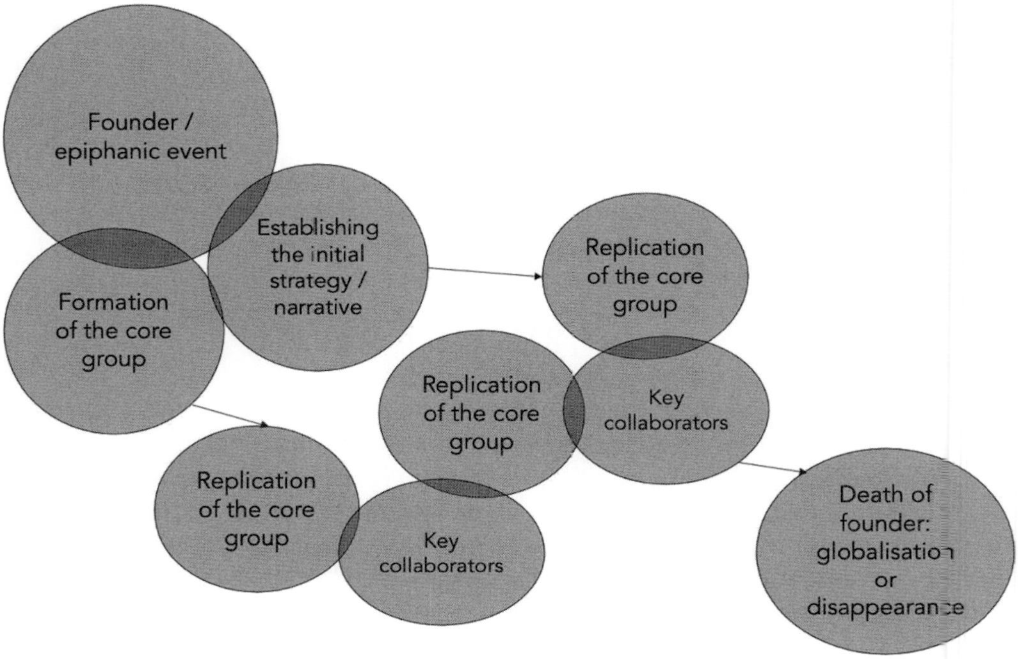

Fig. 4.1 Life cycle of small group religions – a model. (Source: author)

it is during this phase that the religion is also noticed by external and competitive groups. In fact, most of the observable instances in the Roman Empire of small-group religions are observable *only* from this phase, when the core group has developed and replicated in numerous other settlements and external networks. Although the founders are not present at this level and they can hardly control the ecology of expansion, charismatic religious leaders – usually from the core group or on a secondary level – will play a significant role in group replication and the diffusion of the new religious group.[32]

One of the most popular small-group religions that experienced glocal success within the Roman Empire in the 2nd–4th centuries AD is the cult of Roman Mithras.[33] The core group of this cult is unknown: there have been numerous speculations and theories regarding its origin and/or the possible existence of a real or mythical founder.[34] If there were a single founder and a core group, they must have been active in the period of Nero and during the early Flavian era (60–90 AD). After this period, the number of material, literary and iconographic sources is so widespread and canonised in its iconography that it seems obvious that from 90 AD onwards the Mithras group replicated in numerous small groups comprising local followers. The origin of the core group, however, seems to be Rome or one of the large urban centres of the Empire. The iconographic bricolage and appropriation reflected in the earliest statues and reliefs suggest that the founder and the core group consciously used not only Persianism, as an exotic and attractive element in the cult, but also the classical, Hellenstic sacrificial scenes inspired by the representation of Niké-Victoria with the bull.[35] The religious knowledge built into the Mithraic iconography thus reflects a core group with strong connections with the oriental and Hellenistic parts of the Empire.[36]

Fig. 4.2 Altar dedicated to Glykon in Apulum. (Source: Lupa 11284-1, photo by Ortolf Harl with the special permission of the National Museum of Union Alba Iulia)

The cult appeared in the Danubian provinces in the Trajanic period, which represented a dynamic age of human mobilities, due especially to the military projects and offensive politics of Trajan. One of the oldest Mithraic monuments was erected in Novae, although its original setting is unknown.[37] Charagonius Philopalaestrus was one of the earliest *conductores* of the *publicum portorii Illyrici* around 100 AD and is also known from the famous *horothesia* from Histria.[38] As a *conductor*, he played a crucial role in creating the economic networks in the Danubian provinces and in the establishment of the *publicum*.[39] How and where Charagonius Philopalaestrus met the earliest Mithraic groups of the Roman Empire remains one of the intriguing mysteries of the early history of the group, but his activity shows that the administrative staff of the *publicum portorii Illyrici* played a crucial role in the replication of the Mithraic groups in the Danubian provinces.[40]

A particular case study was attested in Poetovio, Pannonia Superior. In the first Mithraeum discovered at the end of the 19th century (cat. no. III.67), rich epigraphic material was attested, in the form of an almost complete inventory of the sanctuary (Fig. 4.4).[41] Two aspects are strikingly unusual in this small-group religion sacralised

Fig. 4.3 Statue of Glykon in Tomis. (Source: Lupa 21360–1, photo by Ortolf Harl with the special permission of the National Museum of History and Archaeology in Constanța)

space: both monuments feature statue bases with the fragmentarily preserved statue still visible on the pedestal.[42] On one of the statues, the figure can be still interpreted as a sitting person, with his right leg stepping in front of his vestment.[43] This iconography can also be identified in some of the representations of the *pater*, the religious leader of Mithraic groups.[44] The interpretation and datation of the two almost identical inscriptions and monuments are problematic: Vermaseren argued that the inscriptions are dedicated to the founder of the Mithraeum, Hyacinthus,[45] and that the statues represent Cautes and Cautopates.[46] The inscriptions were dated between 130 and 170 AD.[47] If the presumption of Vermaseren is correct and Hyacinthus was indeed the founder of the very first Mithraeum of Poetovio, and we accept the Hadrianic date of the monuments, we can presume that Hyacinthus was active in the age of Trajan, like Philopalaestrus of Novae.[48]

Whoever the founder was, there are very few cases in the Roman Empire where a founder of a religious group or sacralised space is commemorated visibly within a sacralised space. One example was attested in Sarmizegetusa, where Sextus Attius Secundus was commemorated by his fellows from the *collegium fabrum*, however the provenance of the monument is unknown.[49] Another is the possibly Mithraic relief that was identified in a tomb in Zámoly (Pannonia Inferior) in 1894, which indicates special treatment of the *pater* even in funereal contexts.[50] Funerary commemoration can also be attested in case of the group in Virunum, where several dead members of the group were commemorated on 26 June 184 AD.[51]

In the 2nd century AD, the replication of the core group was an Imperial-scale success that transformed the cult in less than a generation into a universal religion that was present in every corner of the Roman Empire in the Antonine period.[52] The success of this small-group religion lies in its complex philosophical

Fig. 4.4 Mithraic altar in Poetovio. (Source: Lupa 9330–1, photo by Ortolf Harl with the special permission of Pokrajinski muzej Ptuj – Ormoz Museum)

knowledge, exotic visual narrative and soteriological message, which was unusual and apparently more complex even in the context of other mystery religions and initiation processes.[53] This important step in the ecology of the cult (multiple replication and establishing extra-provincial networks) is clearly reflected in the new books and literary passages dedicated to Mithras that were published in the 2nd century AD. This clearly marks the universalisation of the cult, as a next step in the life cycle of the movement: the treaties of Pallas and Eubulos on Mithras, as well as the works of Porphyr, were created between 130 and 170 AD and contributed to the conscious or unconscious mystification of this religious movement.[54]

Several key collaborators and religious entrepreneurs played a key part in establishing the Imperial network and replication of this small-group religion, especially among the staff of the *publicum* and the Roman army. One example is Marcus Valerius Maximianus, who was attested as an active member of Mithraic groups in Poetovio, Aquincum, Apulum and Lambesis.[55] Another important person who played a crucial role in establishing several well-connected small groups dedicated to Mithras in Pannonia Superior and Dacia were vital in the establishment of local core groups within a single province, such as Publius Aelius Marus (or Marius) in Dacia.[56] Similar central figures can be found in most of the archaeologically attested sacralised spaces of the Danubian provinces, especially if we associate the reconstruction of a building with founders and re-founders of a group (Table 4.1). Several other members played a formative role in maintaining the sacralised space or creating a new one by means of ex-votos or monumental statues and reliefs.

Table 4.1: Reconstructions of Mithraic sanctuaries in Noricum and Pannonia.

Name	*Public or group function*	*Place of discovery*	*Bibliography*
Valerius Venustus	*v(ir) p(erfectissimus) p(raeses) / p(rovinciae) R(aetiae)*	Zwiefalten (Raetia)	CIL III, 05862 = CIMRM 1397 = Lupa 7446.
Aurelius Hermodorus	*v(ir) p(erfectissimus) pr(aeses) / pr(ovinciae) N(orici)*	Virunum, Zollfeld (Noricum)	CIL III 4796 = CIMRM 1431.
Hilarus	*Libertus Augusti tab(ularius) pat(rimonii?) r(egni) N(orici)*	Virunum (Noricum)	CIL III 4800 = CIMRM 1438.
Epictetus	*Ark(arius) Augusti*	Virunum (Noricum)	CIL III 4800 = CIMRM 1438.
Iulius Secundinus	*Pater*	Virunum (Noricum)	AÉ 1994, 01334 = AÉ 1996, 01189 = AÉ 1998, 01016 = AÉ 2016, +00006.
Trebius Zoticus	*Pater*	Virunum (Noricum)	AÉ 1994, 01334 = AÉ 1996, 01189 = AÉ 1998, 01016 = AÉ 2016, +00006.
Caius Caecina Calpurnius	-	Poetovio (Pannonia Superior)	CIL III 14354, 28 = CIMRM 1494–1495.
Aurelius Iustinianus	*Vir perfectissimus dux*	Poetovio (Pannonia Superior)	CIL III 4039 = CIMRM 1614.
Valerius et Valerianus		Stix-Neusiedl (Pannonia Superior)	CIL III 4540 = CIMRM 1661.
Caius [...]		Carnuntum (Pannonia Superior)	CIL III 4420 = CIMRM 1673.
M. Aurelius Frontonianus / M. Aurelius Fronto	*Milites legionis II Adiutricis*	Aquincum (Pannonia Inferior)	CIL III 3383 = CIMRM 1792–1793.

Most of the Mithraic groups identified in the Danubian provinces are attested in an urban context, however several sanctuaries were formed in rural and natural environments, especially on the major roads that connected the strategic military points (Decea Muresului in Dacia, Fertőrákos in Pannonia Superior, on the Amber Road[57]). Similar charismatic religious leaders can also be identified in the case of the Dolichenian, Bacchic, Isiac, Hypsistarian or Jewish groups in the Danubian provinces.[58] This role was performed in particular by the sacerdotal elite, who had an essential task in maintaining the continuity and replication of the group.[59]

These small-group religions survived in the Danubian region until the end of the 3rd/beginning of the 4th centuries AD. In contrast with the older presumptions regarding the deliberate destruction of sanctuaries in the 3rd century AD,[60] recent studies have argued that sacralised spaces of small-group religions faded and disappeared slowly and often with several revivals at the end of the 3rd/beginning of the 4th centuries AD.[61] The crisis of maintenance of such small-group religions can be linked to several factors, but the rise and institutionalisation of Christianity was probably the least important one, especially in the Danubian provinces. The collapse of the urban system and the infrastructural-administrative coherence of provincial society seems to have been a much more important factor.

Religious grouping and networks

The study of the group styles or networks of Roman religion is a booming field. The notion of 'group styles' was used by P. Lichterman, J. Rüpke and his colleagues in a paradigmatic study on religious grouping in antiquity, arguing that groups need to be interpreted as fluid entities of societies.[62] Other important studies contributed to the inter- or even transdisciplinary approach between networks – and religious studies focusing on some examples of the Roman Empire.[63] The identification of nodes, vertices, links and hubs is part of the Central Place Theory and the Actor-Network Theory, too.[64]

Religious networks, however, are more than just the identification of central sites (hubs) that play an important role in the replication of groups and the maintenance of central sacralised spaces. Such places in the Danubian provinces have been identified in all kinds of forms and contexts: sacralised spaces in Magdalensberg, the Mithraea of Poetovio, the Isea of Savaria, the temple of the Nutrices in Poetovio, the sacralised space of Jupiter Heliopolitanus in Carnuntum, the possible centrality of Sirmium and Singidunum in the cult of the so-called 'Danubian Riders' (*Domna et Domnus*). These hubs also had both provincial and extra-provincial links and nodes. They were formed by complex networks and influenced by numerous factors, such as the mobility of the army, the major commercial roads, the economic centrality of their locations, the urban density and demography, and other, specific local factors as well. Other cases, such as the Palmyrian diaspora, the Jewish diaspora or the Hypsistarians from Asia Minor, the Balkans and Dacia represent a more specific network, however their connectivity and the interpretation of the nodes and links between the major hubs in these cases is problematic.[65]

Another issue that has been rarely analysed in religious networks of the Roman Empire is the sociological aspects of the hubs, human agency and the formation of nodes and links. A. Collar argued that in the case of Jupiter Dolichenus, the Roman army and military dislocations played a crucial role in the replication of groups and the formation of new sacralised spaces,[66] such as major hubs and nodes, although these groups were exclusively military. Urban factors were also critical to the maintenance of sacralised spaces and Dolichenian groups in the Danubian provinces. Based on the studies of M. Speidel, A. Collar argued that the soldiers worshipped Dolichenus especially while they were 'abroad' during their military service but that they didn't transport the god back home, which might indicate that there was also an official, ideological aspect of the cult related to the group formation of the military.[67] Indeed, in contrast with the 'locality' of religious communication attested among the soldiers, the priesthood of Dolichenus was almost exclusively Syrian-oriental in origin, and they demonstrated a strict internal hierarchy[68] and a dynamic connectivity and mobility.[69] The impact of this very closed sacerdotal society in the formation and maintenance of sacralised spaces and the transfer of religious knowledge seems to have been greater than it was in other, similar small-group religions. A possible analogy might be the priesthood of Magna Mater and Attis, although their visibility in epigraphic and archaeological material is much less well attested.[70]

A particular case study of Dolichenian networks can be attested between Porolissum and Augusta Traiana (extra-provincial nodes) and Ampelum-Apulum and Doliche. The cult of Jupiter Dolichenus was attested in Porolissum, Roman Dacia by numerous important finds, but their chronology is very problematic: no there was no recorded archaeological context for most of the finds had before 1996 and the ones discovered by N. Gudea and his team were also debated numerous times by I. Piso and others (cat. no. VI.23, Fig. 4.5).[71] From the existing data, we know that the sacralised space dedicated to Jupiter Dolichenus had its peak of activity in the first half of the 3rd century AD, when three *sacerdotes* of the god built a Dolichenum *extra muros* of the Roman auxiliary fort.[72] This group was certainly connected with another Dolichenian group from Augusta Traiana, where Aurelius Sabinus, son of Theophilus, and Aurelius Primus Astius contributed to the rebuilding of a Dolichenum in the period of Septimius Alexander, a few years before the construction of the Dolichenum in Porolissum.[73] Aurelius Sabinus mentions in the Greek inscription his sacerdotal function and his role as a wine merchant between Dacia and Thracia. His colleague was a *decurio* of Porolissum. His name was not attested in the Dolichenian context in Porolissum, however the role of merchants and *negotiatores* in Dolichenian mobility and group formation is attested in other inscriptions.[74]

The *sacerdotes* of Ampelum and Apulum were also connected, possibly by familial bonds and with direct connection to the central sanctuary of the cult from Doliche.[75] This is evidenced in particular by the inscriptions dedicated to Jupiter Dolichenus and the mysterious 'Deus Commagenorum'.[76] The identification of the second divinity on the inscription dedicated by Aurelius Marinus, Adde Barsemei and Oceanus Socratis is an epigraphic mystery: the epithet 'Commagenorum' appears numerous times in Roman Dacia and once in Rome in various forms (Jupiter Optimus Maximus Commagenorum,[77] IOM Commagenorum Aeternus,[78] Jupiter Optimus Maximus Dolichenus Commagenorum,[79] Deus Magnus Commagenorum,[80] Deus Commagenorum[81]). With one exception – the one dedicated by Adde Barsemei and his fellow *sacerdotes* – all the other inscriptions name a single divinity. The inscription of

Ampelum is unique and odd because it clearly separates Jupiter Dolichenus and Deus Commagenorum. Both divinities are named as 'Commagenian' gods – as the case study in Ampelum and Micia show (IOMD Commagenorum) – but the votive column from Ampelum suggests that there were two different divine entities who were probably worshipped as ethnic mountain gods.[82] The question remains: who is the other god of Commagene? A possible answer could be Turmazgades, a divinity who appears on a few inscriptions and reliefs.[83] Originally an Aramaic mountain divinity, Turmazgades was associated with the Ba'al of Doliche (also a mountain god) and replicated as part of a pair divinity in Dura Europos and Dacia, especially by the Roman army.[84] The 'new' Jupiter Turmazgades, known in Ampelum as Deus Commagenorum, is a classical example of a local, ethnic divinity that has been reinvented and appropriated by the new social and religious influences of the Roman Empire during the Principate (Fig. 4.6).

Fig. 4.5 Statue of Jupiter Dolichenus from the Dolichenum of Porolissum. (Source: Lupa 20363, photo by Ortolf Harl, with the special permission of the Museum of Zalău)

The Dolichenian groups from Apulum also show a direct connectivity with the Mother sanctuary of the cult in Doliche: the epigraphic formula of '*ubi ferrum nascitur*' ('where the iron was born') indicates a local religious narrative, transported directly from Anatolia to Moesia Superior and Dacia.[85]

The connectivity of the Mithraic groups and the formation of their Imperial-scale network had a different mechanism. Although key collaborators and individuals of the cult played an important role in replication and space sacralisation, the role of inter-urban group mobilities here seems to be more significant. The living bond and connectivity between these second-generation founders and their groups are reflected in numerous iconographic appropriations, ritual strategies and epigraphic habits: the epigraphic attestation of the Transitus dei inscriptions for example seems to reflect a direct connection between the

Fig. 4.6 Statue of Turmazgades Hero Romula, Dacia. (Source: Lupa 21951, photo by Ortolf Harl with the special permission of the National History Museum of Romania, București)

sanctuaries in the Danubian provinces centred in Poetovio, which produced at least five sacralised spaces dedicated to Mithras.[86] These connections seem to have survived the test of time at least for two or three generations: the third Mithraeum of Poetovio was founded in the vicinity of the first two, reusing many of the monuments established by the military elite of Apulum, who visited Poetovio around 260–268 AD and founded (or re-founded) the third Mithraeum of the city.[87] Networks of Mithraic groups can be attested not only between Pannonia and Dacia, but also within provincial borders: the epigraphic material dedicated to Mithras in Micia and Apulum, too, shows a direct link between the Mithraea founded by the staff of the *publicum portorii Illyrici*.[88]

Between the foundation and the disappearance of a group, the main aim of small-group religions was at a simplistic level to survive and replicate which is very similar to the contagion model of epidemiology and immunology.[89] As a recent study focusing on the network model of the SARS-COV-2 virus shows, contagion (in this case religion) can replicate and spread only if there is an existing and complex network in human society (called a 'starting network').[90] Our case studies prove that the starting networks of religious group style and replication are indeed fluid and dynamic, although some of the basic elements are indispensable: the Roman road system, the major commercial routes, the constant mobility of the army (*dislocatio*) and the existence of central religious hubs. In the first phase of the 'contagion', the very first contacts occur in local and sporadic places, and it is usually based on familial and personal, intimate links. In epidemiology, this early phase takes 10 days and occurs between days 10 and day 20. In religious networks, this phase – as Ann Taves argued – needs much more time, from weeks to many years, until the core group and the key collaborators of the founder(s) have been formed.

Between days 20 and 70, the replication of the virus depends on the mobility and interconnectivity of the core group. In this phase, the role of the so-called 'super spreaders' is essential: they can contribute to a large cohort of new patients. In the case of small-group religions, this second phase seems to occur much faster than the first phase – a significant difference from the epidemiologic model. In the case of Jesus, for example, the age of 'super spreaders' ended within 30 years (68 AD). A similar model can be presumed in the case of the cult of Mithras, too, between 60–90 and 117 AD.

After day 70, the network of the virus almost completely overlaps the starting network. This phase is rarely achieved by small-group religions: there are many provinces in the Roman Empire in which Mithras, Dolichenus, Isis or Magna Mater are rarely attested. At this level, the model of R. Stark and J. North on religious market competition might still have a value: social factors, personal choices, linguistic barriers and cultural identities were important factors in creating and ending nodes and links in the complex networks of small-group religions.[91]

Experiences

Religious experience is a very problematic notion. In the early 20th century, pioneers of religious studies argued that religious experiences are radically different from all other kinds of human experience, stressing that the 'special' nature of these is based on one of the key elements of religious communication, which cannot be identified in other types of activities (*i.e.* the divine agency, often called 'god', 'gods' or 'numinous powers').[92] The 'specialness' of religious experience was interpreted in 1902 as a psychological phenomenon by William James, who opened a radically new approach in religious studies, contributing to the formation of psychology of religion as a sub-discipline as well as a methodological approach.[93]

In the 1970s, Robert D. Margolis and Kirk W. Elifson established a typology of religious experiences: although their approach united several layers and manifestations of experiences – especially from the perspective of human agency – their typology can hardly be interpreted for classical antiquity, for which empirical data is rarely preserved.[94] They identified seven transcendental experiences based on security, an increased feeling of relatedness, a feeling of peace, a noetic quality, and feelings of ecstasy, oneness and out-of-body experience.[95] They also identified several 'vertigo experiences' (music, drugs, loss of control, visions and voices), life-changing experiences and visionary experiences. However, many of their categories overlap and it is not clear what the role and interaction of divine and human agency is in these.

Based on contemporary studies of neuroscience, in 2009 Ann Taves redefined religious experience as 'a subcategory of transitive consciousness' and argued for a more fluid definition of religious 'specialness', which can now be interpreted as also being a scholarly (academic) construct.[96] Given these issues with its definition, studying religious 'experience' is problematic. What seems to be a common denominator in all the definitions and methodologies of the scholarship is the need to prove the 'specialness' of the communication between human and divine agencies.[97]

In antiquity, too, religious experience had no real definition. Experiencing divine power and communicating with the non-human is always dependent on numerous individual and collective factors (human agency factors), but also on cultural-historical factors (cultural system, habitus and knowledge production). Jörg Rüpke argued that: 'lived ancient religion – with its focus on individual appropriation of tradition, personal experiences and responses, the incoherencies of situational interpretation, isolated performances, and local and group-specific styles – depends upon the intellectual as well as the embodied availability of "traditions" and their situational salience'.[98] Experiencing the 'specialness' therefore cannot be separated from the historical, geographical, individual and collective context, where all the three major agencies (human, divine, material) contribute several factors, which together build up the 'specialness' or 'religiousness' of an experience.

This relativity of religious experience can be attested in several literary sources and passages from Roman religion,[99] however when it comes to the archaeological evidence and the materiality of religion, identifying religious experiences becomes more complicated.[100] The most common examples of religious experience from antiquity are manifested by sacrifices, initiations, meals and banquets, purification rituals, and watching or 'experiencing' rituals. These experiences can occur in macro-, meso- and micro-spaces and their impact on the individual and the group is hard to measure, although both ancient and modern authors have tried to establish a hierarchy of religious experiences, based on the intensity, closeness and life-changing nature of the experience. Such direct and impactful experiences are for example the divinations and epiphanies, which need a special focus.

Sacrifice was one of the essential forms of religious experiences.[101] A not necessarily violent (killing animals) act, *sacrificia* had numerous forms, temporal aspects, spaces and actors. The *sacrificium,* as an essential strategy of religious communication in the Mediterranean world and beyond,[102] was a controlled, legally bonded act, charged with easily transmissible, learned religious knowledge. It also presumed the presence of special personnel, vestments, timing (religious calendar – *fasti*), spaces and material tools.[103] Although sacrificial acts can be attested in the Danubian provinces even before the Roman conquest, these became part-public macro-spaces only after the new Roman religious language had been established.

Sacrifices in the Danubian provinces can be attested in three major sources: iconographic, epigraphic, and archaeological (osteology). The first two categories are present especially in public macro-spaces in urban and military contexts: sacrifices of the leading military staff, the urban magistrates and priesthood were publicly performed in open macro-spaces, such as the inner courtyard of the *principia*, the Ara Augusti, the forum of the city or in front of sacralised spaces (*sacrum*) within the city walls. Iconographic representations preserved from the Danubian provinces show in particular the chief military and administrative staff of the cities performing these sacrifices, using the well-known procedures and all the materiality of religion, which are also attested in literary sources.

The case of a famous monumental altar (127 cm high, 76 cm wide) discovered in the 16th century in the fortress of Abusina (Eining) in Raetia represents a typical iconographic programme for open-air, public sacrifices and religious experience, where both the participating individuals and the viewers had a strong, perhaps long-lasting religious experience.[104] Titus Flavius Felix, *praefectus* of the Cohors III Britannorum, is represented in *capite velato*, performing the sacrifice together with his family, a *popa*, a musician and a servant in front of an altar (probably the self-representation of the dedicated altar itself).[105] Such sacrifices in public macro-spaces involving numerous participants were controlled and performative acts, in which the intensity of religious experience and the direct communication with the divine were combined with the strong social, political and economic messages that were prepared consciously by the performers. Sacrificial scenes representing the *vici magistri* from Poetovio[106] and Carnuntum[107] show not only stylistic similarities, but also reflect the ceremonial piety of the sacrifice, in which the performative act, the living message for the viewer, and human agency seem to be much more powerful in combination than merely establishing a lived religious experience with the divine agency.

Sacrifices performed in meso- and micro-spaces (domestic religion, small-group religious spaces) indicate a much more intimate atmosphere, where the number of participants and the controlled aspect of the performance was reduced. The altar dedicated by Barsemis Abbei and his wife, Aurelia Iulia, for Jupiter Optimus Maximus in the vicinity of the fort of Intercisa is particularly interesting because it represents the intimate, individual religious experience of a couple performing a sacrifice:[108] the Syrian *magister* of the Cohors I Hemesenorum milliaria, who was born in Carrhae (Mesopotamia),[109] is represented in front of an oriental type of altar[110] with his wife sitting. The intimate scene is in striking contrast with the public sacrificial performances and serves as a strong example of representative religious individuality.[111] Animal sacrifices also had a strong, cognitive impact and can be considered one of the most powerful religious experiences both for the performer and the viewer: the sensorial effect and impact of such communicational strategies in religion can be measured or studied in contemporary polytheistic societies.[112]

Rites of initiations are considered life-changing religious experiences. Although the cults of Mithras, Isis and Liber Pater were associated with initiations and a strict inner hierarchy of the participants,[113] the material evidence of initiation rituals have rarely been preserved and most of them can only be presumed. In most cases, initiations occurred in meso-spaces and in the presence of a small, intimate group, which made these rituals highly individual and personal experiences. The sacralised spaces dedicated to Mithras in Poetovio are among the few preserved examples that have a rich iconographic and epigraphic heritage.[114] Some of these contain unique or rarely attested iconographic narratives, which might indicate the personal attachment of the worshipper and his personal experience during the dedication of the object in the sacralised geography of the Mithraeum. One of the inscriptions dedicated in

Fig. 4.7 Mithraic inscription, memorialisation of an initiation. (Source: Lupa 9348, photo by Ortolf Harl with the special permission of Pokrajinski muzej Ptuj – Ormoz Museum)

the third Mithraeum mentions a unique epigraphic formula, which indicates that is memorialises an initiated member of the Mithraic group, who 'elevated in the manner of the Sun' (Fig. 4.7).[115] Another inscription that might indicate the memorialisation of a life-changing religious experience (a new grade of initiation) was discovered probably in Colonia Sarmizegetusa in Roman Dacia.[116] P. Aelius Artemidorus, who originated in Macedonia, was *creatus pater*, a person initiated at the highest level of Mithraic grades. Similar experiences of memorialisation of initiations can be attested in several other Mithraic inscriptions in the Danubian provinces, which mention the grades of *pater*[117] and *leo*[118]. The 'death' of the Mithraic members in the famous Virunum album was also interpreted as an epigraphic metaphor of initiations, a life-changing experience in which the non-initiated dies and is reborn as the Sun.[119]

Sensorial effects (multisensoriality, synaesthesia, sensescapes[120]) and cognitive dimensions of small-group religions represent a booming field in the study of religious experiences,[121] even though the material evidence and archaeological memorialisation of such dimensions are rarely attestable, especially in the Danubian provinces, where the majority of the materiality of Roman religion was discovered before the 20th century and relevant details (inner structure of buildings, small finds, inventory and personal belongings of worshippers, *instrumenta sacra* of the priesthood, human-object agency) were not documented. The case of the Iseum from Savaria represents one of the few case studies in which a reproduction and reconstruction of the religious *sensorium* was analysed, based on the comparative analysis of the archaeological and literary evidence on Isiac initiations and rituals.[122]

Divination and epiphany

Divination (dreams, ecstasy, oracular traditions, auguries, prodigies, haruspicy[123]) as a special strategy in Roman religious communication presumed an intensified method of establishing a contact between human and divine agency. Divination creates specia religious third spaces, where time and space dissolve and lose their meaning: during divination, the human agency (dreamer, interpreter, oracle, priest) will dissolve the dimensions of time by communicating with the divine agency in the present, asking questions or receiving messages regarding the future and interpreting or channelling the message with learned religious knowledge from the past.

Cicero argued that divination can occur naturally (dreams, ecstasy) or by using a learned religious technique (auguries, prodigies, oracular and haruspicy interpretations). Although oracular traditions were very popular in the Mediterranean world,[124] the presence of oracular shrines and institutionalised oracular traditions seems to be missing from the Danubian provinces, especially prophecy interpretations. The only cultural transfer of divination that was implemented after the 1st century AD in the Danubian provinces is the *incubatio*, the dream interpretation within the Asclepeia.[125] These healing sanctuaries represent the ultimate form of monopolisation of dream interpretation and religious pilgrimage in the Danubian provinces, where physicians played a crucial role in establishing and maintaining the divinatory religious practices.[126]

Raetia and Noricum show a radically different aspect in this sense: the cult of Asclepius is rarely attested in the Alpine region and the cult of the classical healing divinities in Noricum was replaced with a strong presence of various local nymph, water-cult and Egyptianised divinities (Fig. 4.8).[127] The only significant exception is the large sacralised space (*templum*) of Asclepius from Iuvavum, although the architecture and the materiality of religion discovered in the building do not prove the presence of the *incubatio* as divination technique (cat. no. II.20).[128] The number of inscriptions dedicated to Asclepius and Hygeia (Pannonia Superior: 8; Pannonia Inferior: 11; Moesia Superior: 3; Moesia Inferior: 16; Dacia: 64) shows that the classical healing god was more popular in the lower Danubian area, where significant Greek-speaking communities had been established. The unprecedented number of inscriptions dedicated to Asclepius in Dacia can also be explained by the direct religious and human agency networks that existed between the major cities (Apulum, Sarmizegetusa) and Pergamon or other important centres containing Asclepeia in Asia Minor.[129]

However, the cult of Asclepius and Hygeia was not monopolised by the dream interpreters and healing sanctuaries:[130] sanitation, medical care and the worship of the healing gods are well attested in military,[131] public (baths) and domestic environments, too. The cult of Asclepius was also associated with funeral and soteriological aspects in Thracia and Moesia Inferior, although the religious narrative and details of the central myth of this local appropriation is not yet clear.[132]

Direct encounter with the divine agency through dreams using the incubation method represents one of the most powerful religious experiences, and a 'natural' divination is also often described by literary sources as the most intense strategy to access and experience the body of the gods.[133] During the incubation phase, space itself disappears and an imaginary cognitive third space (the dream) replaces the meso-spaces of the Asclepeia, where the patients are hosted: the sick body of the ancient patient will be transformed for a short period into a living, religious experience. Thus communication with the gods in dreams was deemed an essential strategy and technique for medical, bodily healing, too.[134]

Divination and communication through dreams were not exclusively monopolised by the Asclepeia and the healing gods of Asclepius and Hygeia: numerous other divinities, such as Jupiter Dolichenus, Sabazios, Silvanus, Isis, Mithras, Mercurius and Jupiter Optimus Maximus asked for ex-voto donations in dreams.[135] In particular case studies – such as the ones attested in Rome and Apulum – Jupiter Dolichenus and Asclepius were not in religious competition, but acted in a fruitful symbiosis and collaboration.[136] The cult of Asclepius gained special support from Emperor Caracalla, who visited several sacralised spaces dedicated to the healing divinities in Raetia and Dacia (especially Phoebiana and Tibiscum).[137] His special relationship with Apollo Grannus occurred after his nightmare or hallucinations about his dead brother, although the short literary passages could be later interpretations.[138]

Fig. 4.8 Statue of Asclepius from Iuvavum, Noricum. (Source: with the special permission of Salzburg Museum – Domgrabungsmuseum)

Divination was also recorded in the *Disciplina Etrusca*, although the presence of religious specialists in haruspicy is rarely attested. Two examples we do know of were Claudius Aelius Optimus from Moesia Inferior (probably Oescus), who was *pontifex*, priest of Dea Roma and *haruspex*,[139] and Iulius Salutaris from Phoebianae, Raetia, who was also a *haruspex*.[140] The case study of Lucius Vibius Primus and his family from Virunum, Noricum shows that the role of the haruspicy was hereditary and an exceptional familial tradition that saw religious knowledge being transferred as a cultural heritage.[141] The important role of specialists in divination can be attested in the honorific inscription of Lucius Tuccius Campanus, a *haruspex* who received a smaller than life-size statue in Virunum, donated by the citizens of the settlement.[142] The most impressive information about a *haruspex* from the Danubian provinces can be attested in Dacia, where the rich activity of Caius Iulius Valens was memorialised in at least six inscriptions between 212 and 235 AD.[143] His carrier represents the importance of citification and the urban infrastructure, and administrative and political milieu in building up and maintaining a carrier of a specialist in divination.

Epiphanies represent another large and special aspect of religious experience and have special significance. However, the definition of 'epiphany' is still a problematic terminological and historiographic issue: Georgia Petridou argued in her book that epiphany is a 'manifestation of a deity to an individual or a group of people in sleep or in a waking reality, in a crisis or cult context'.[144] Epiphanies are direct and intense contacts with the divine presence, in which human and divine agency are equally present. In contrast with divinations – which are predominantly focused on the future and require a provider of religious knowledge (specialist, priest, religious entrepreneur) – epiphanies occur in the present and have a much higher level of religious individualisation. The temporal aspect of epiphanies ('now and immediately') intensifies the sensorial and cognitive aspects of religious experiences: miracles, wonder making and direct divine (natural) interventions (lightening, animal behaviour) are rare attestations of divine epiphanies.

One of the most discussed divine interventions (epiphany, *prodigia publica*[145]) occurred during the Marcomannic Wars, when an Egyptian magician or charismatic religious entrepreneur called Arnuphis[146] evoked the so-called 'rain miracle' with the help of Thot.[147] Interpreted by later literary sources as one of the most decisive moments of the wars of Marcus Aurelius, the 'rain miracle' was also chosen as one of the most iconic visual narratives on the column of the emperor in Rome. However, in the Roman religious propaganda, the divine interventions came from Jupiter, the supreme god and ultimate helper of the emperor (Fig. 4.9).[148] In this divine epiphany, the presence of a charismatic religious leader (Arnuphis or the emperor, as *pontifex maximus*[149]) was equally as important as the intervention of a powerful divine agency (Thor or Jupiter). The collective religious experience and long-term impact of the 'rain miracle' legitimized the transformation of the event into a celebrated public miracle (*prodigia publica*).

Places where lightning strike were also considered important *lieux de mémoires* of religious experience. The memorialisation of direct divine *prodigia* and interventions were legally indicated and protected. Two cases of such religious memorialisation – one in Savaria and the other in Apulum[150] – are known in the Danubian provinces, although the cult of Jupiter Fulgurator is attested in several inscriptions.[151]

A particular case study of direct divine epiphany was memorialised on a column dedicated to Jupiter Optimus Maximus in the central area of Colonia Aurelia Apulensis

Fig. 4.9 Representation of the rain miracle at the column of Marcus Aurelius. (Source: Wikicommons) Open access

in Roman Dacia.[152] The medium-sized column (155 × 26 cm) was discovered in 1866, probably in the forum of the Roman civilian town, in the central part of the Marosportus area of Alba Iulia (Gyulafehérvár). Although the exact provenance and archaeological context of the find is unknown, the column was certainly part of a sacralised space, probably a public temple in one of the macro-spaces dedicated to Jupiter in Apulum or (less likely) a building maintained by a small-group religion. Furthermore, several similar columns dedicated to Jupiter or Deus Aeternus were discovered here in the 19th and early 20th centuries.[153] This inscription is unique because it goes beyond the traditional and conventional votive formula: the two dedicants – Aurelius Marinus Bassus and Aurelius Castor,[154] probably with Greek-speaking or oriental origins[155] – observed a direct divine epiphany: the celestial fight of Jupiter. This is depicted by his zoomorphic avatar and messenger, the eagle alongside the symbol of the enemy, destructive power, 'an evil brute', the snake This motif is a very famous Greek[156] and Hellenistic narrative,[157] although similar visual and textual narratives can also be found in the Near East.[158] The victorious eagle as a symbol of Jupiter and the celestial divine agency also appears in military and funerary contexts in the Roman world: the exact story of an eagle fighting with a snake can be identified on a Roman bronze cheek guard discovered at the Dacian site of Sarmizegetusa Regia, the former capital of the Dacian kingdom, probably from the Trajanic period (102–106 AD).[159] In that case, the divine epiphany is an indirect, learned and transmitted cultural knowledge that serves an abstract collective military message of the victorious Roman army, as community,[160] whereas the textual narrative from the Apulum column is a more vivid memorialisation of a direct, personal religious experience of the two persons.

Similar personal epiphanic content and soteriological messages can be attested on funerary monuments representing the fight and victory of the eagle with the snake. For instance, the famous case study of the recently discovered Londinium statue is a remarkable example of a cultural, literary tradition transformed into a visual narrative in various forms and contexts.[161] The unique textual evidence of a directly observed divine epiphany is an interesting combination of religious traditions and spontaneous individual appropriation and observation of the divine agency.[162]

Religious narratives

Divination and epiphany are religious narratives that originated directly from the divine agency with a highly intensified content of religious interconnectivity between the communicative partners (human and divine). In contrast, the material and textual narratives are indirect, human-made tools that serve an important role in the diffusion and maintenance of small-group religions as well as in macro- and micro-spaces of religion. Jörg Rüpke argued that 'narratives changed real or imagined processes, for example genealogies and rituals, into a knowledge that could be retold'.[163] Storytelling – as one of the key elements of religious narratives (oral, visual and textual) – is one of the oldest cognitive methods in human behaviour, which aimed to achieve individual acceptance or group cohesion.[164]

Oral storytelling is the oldest strategy in the maintenance of religious groups, although there is no direct evidence of it from classical antiquity. The existence of oral traditions is, however, mentioned in numerous literary sources and can be presumed from several case studies to have existed even in the Imperial era.[165] Orality of religious narratives evolved very early in visual transformations and languages: the practice of transmitting religious knowledge through images and iconographic programmes (composed, static and centralised linguistic abstracts of a religious tradition) has been present since the Late Paleolithic era.[166] Marking the human body and later creating physical and material bodies of the gods represented the first steps of materialising oral religious traditions. David Morgan argued that in contrast to the product (the iconography, mark or picture), this process is a dynamic human self-production, a creative and social enterprise.[167]

Visual narratives act as a language, which is why such religious communication was adopted so early in human history. The creation of visual narratives, however, requires several important conditions: oral traditions need to be centralised and controlled (collected, organised) by religious specialists or leaders; and the visual narratives need skilful craft, artists and workshops. It is an abstract, indirect and static language: visual narratives show a sequence or a summary of a dynamic and much larger, more complex story. Therefore, visual religious narratives cannot exist without the oral and later, textual, traditions. The problematic issue of the interpretation of ancient visual narratives derives especially from this semantic aspect of figurative language. Just as the ancient Roman people read the figurative and visual narratives with their eyes (*perlegerent oculis*),[168] contemporary archaeologists and historians do the same. The major difference is that our knowledge and access to several aspects of religious communication, the nature of the gods and the interaction of human and divine agency are limited and corrupted, which often leads to metahistorical interpretations.

Controlling oral and visual narratives can thus lead to the textualisation of religion, yet this process is a consequence of administrative and bureaucratic structures in evolved societies.[169] For this reason, oral, visual and textual narratives coexist in few ancient societies: one of the most prominent changes wrought by Roman expansion and the Romanisation of religious communication in the Danubian provinces was the textualisation of religion. Pre-Roman religious communication in most of the Danubian regions was exclusively oral and visual, and lacked a significant tradition of textuality. The only exception was the Pontic area, where Greek textualisation produced a different religious landscape and the coexistence of all three types of narratives.

After the Roman conquest and the boom in Roman epigraphic traditions,[170] however, the three narratives became interconnected and shaped each other.[171] Nevertheless, textual traditions in the Danubian area are limited almost exclusively to the epigraphic sources, administrative and legal inscriptions, member lists, and inscriptions on souvenirs and portable objects. Such visual narratives are vivid proof that Greek and Roman textual traditions (especially mythological and literary sources) were circulating in this region. The interconnectivity of visual and textual narratives was mostly present in funerary and public contexts and rarely in meso-spaces of religious communication. Mythological scenes from Homeric literary traditions are among the most common motifs (Fig. 4.10): the most popular scenes were the judgement of Paris[172] and the adventures of Odysseus,[173] Ajax,[174] Achilles,[175] Perseus,[176] Icarus,[177] Hercules and Alkestis.[178] While only 12 mythological reliefs were preserved in Raetia and Moesia Superior,[179] there are 19 in Moesia Inferior, almost 100 in Noricum, 89 in Pannonia Inferior and 132 in Pannonia Superior. In Dacia, there are very few small finds representing mythological scenes, according to the database of Ortolf Harl.[180]

Scenes from classical Greek and Roman mythology were used especially in macro-spaces (public sacralised spaces, funerary contexts) and domestic micro-spaces and are almost completely missing from meso-spaces established by small-group religions. Meso-spaces were instead populated with visual narratives of new religious movements from the 2nd century BC to the 2nd century AD (Magna Mater, Liber Pater, Isis, Mithras, Dolichenus, Sabazios).[181] In a few instances, the epigraphic evidence suggests that the formation of these visual narratives was also associated

Fig. 4.10 Funerary relief representing Perseus and Andromeda Hero Moosburg, Noricum. (Source: Lupa 1069, photo by Ortolf Harl, Pfarrkriche St Michael und St Georg). Open access

with oral traditions: such a case can be attested in the Dolichenian inscriptions in Apulum, Vetoniana and Novae, which mention probably the only fragment of a possible oral narrative tradition associated with the cult of Jupiter Dolichenus.[182] The exact origin, formation and transmission of this oral tradition later textualised in just a few inscriptions is unknown, however there has been speculation about possible Anatolian origins.[183] Interestingly, most of the inscriptions associated with this unusual narrative fragment come from the Danubian provinces, which could indicate a direct relationship with the Mother sanctuary in Doliche and the mobility of Commagenian soldiers.[184]

Oral and possibly textual narratives might have played a role in the rituals performed both within and outside the sacralised spaces dedicated to Dolichenus, as demonstrated by the famous bronze triangles and the rich Dolichenian inventory from

Mauer an der Url, Noricum (cat. no. II.31).[185] The strict hierarchical composition of the bronze triangles – which were probably used in dynamic processes and performances in, around and outside of the Dolichena – suggest a sophisticated narrative, in which the celestial divinities (Jupiter, Juno, Sol, Luna, Helios), mythical heroes or perhaps constellations (Castor and Pollux) played a crucial role. It is uncertain, however, how this narrative was created and what the transmissible message for the participants and viewers might have been.[186] Based on the hierarchical structure of the priests of Dolichenus, it may be plausible that the central narrative was created in the Dolichena and transmitted very carefully by the priesthood, A similar situation can be attested in the case study of Roman Mithras in the Danubian provinces. The existence of oral and textual traditions is extremely scarce and hard to prove,[187] although a few cases might indicate a transmissible religious narrative in which the Persian elements represent the exotic nature and consciously built strategy of the cult.[188] The rich visual narrative of Mithras seems to have been completed in the early 2nd century AD and as the *signum* of the god in Aquincum[189] and Apulum shows (Fig. 4.11),[190] the early cases reveal a direct connection with the iconographic programmes attested in Italy.

The visual narrative of Mithras in the Danubian provinces was for a long time associated with the Germanic area, too: the 19th- and 20th-century literature argued that the formative role of the Roman army of the frontiers in the creation of a particular visual narrative was expressed especially through the so-called panelled reliefs, which seem to be particularly present in the Danubian provinces.[191] The formation of these large objects and static narratives goes together with the establishment of small-group religions and their central place in the urban environment.[192] The complex panelled reliefs of the Mithraea in Virunum, Sárkeszi, Siscia, Poetovio, Viminacium, Apulum and Sarmizegetusa present numerous scenes and story sequences, and were probably formed at the end of the 1st century AD by the core group and the founder(s) of the cult.[193] The case for this central myth can be argued by the numerous, repetitive moments (predellas) that are represented in most of the Mithras stories depicted on panelled reliefs or statues. They include the dream of Saturnus-Uranus, Mithras Petrogenitus and Mithras in bucolic environments with animals, the bull in its house, the careful appropriation of Mithras and the bull, hunting scenes, Mithras Taurophoros, the central scene of Mithras Tauroctonos, banquet scenes, the transformation of Mithras and the ascension of the divinity with Helios, the eternal world of Saturnus.[194] Despite these common factors, however, these are not universally identical elements, and many scholars have argued that an 'Urbild' – an original, central myth of Mithras – is questionable, although their proofs remain inconclusive.[195]

It is highly plausible that a 'prototype' of the visual narrative never existed, but a well-established, intellectually constructed and centralised oral narrative of Mithras was certainly necessary for the formation of this small-group religion – something that is suggested by the repetitive elements and iconographic constructivism (bricolage) of the panelled reliefs. Using well-known Roman and Greek-Hellenistic iconographic

Fig. 4.11 Mithras Tauroctonos from Apulum. (Source: author, after Szabó 2013)

motifs – such as the killing of the bull by Niké-Victoria or the Perseus-Medusa and Hercules-lion killing scenes – as prototypes,[196] the creation of receptible, translatable and easily transmissible visual narratives turned out to be a successful strategy (Fig. 4.12).

The 'Mithras myth' can be only partially reconstructed, due to the lack of a textualised version of the oral narrative. Nonetheless, the materialisation of the religious storytelling produced several case studies, which show the major steps of religious narrative formation: the intellectual creation of a central myth by the founder

Fig. 4.12 Victoria (Niké) killing the bull, Rome, Villa of Antoninus Pius. (Source: British Museum, cat. no. 1805,0703.4.)

or core group; the transmission and replication of the oral narrative; the transformation of the original story into various visual forms by the so-called 'super spreaders' or religious entrepreneurs; and finally, when the new religious movement had become visible to outsiders, the appearance of textual interpretations, speculations and guides, such as the lost books of Pallas and Eubulos. The small number of the members, the interconnected nature of similar religious groups, and the exclusive nature of the replication and initiations didn't allow the small-group religions to create a centralised and canonised visual and textual narrative. The only exceptions were, of course, Judaism and Christianity, as monotheistic movements of the Roman Empire for which textuality played a fundamental role in the maintenance and replication of the groups.[197]

Appropriations: between centre and periphery

In terms of the creation, replication and diffusion of oral, visual and textual narratives, our best case study and prototype is the Christian myth itself. The core group of the founder and his early followers in the 1st century AD created numerous versions of the oral tradition, without many visual and textual sources. The canonisation and control of the large variety of oral traditions in the mid-2nd century AD also led to the appearance of the textualisation and later, visualisation of the religious story. This phase is the most interesting part in the evolution and lifespan of a small-group religion, when oral traditions of religious narratives are transformed in various types of visual representations. These have several common features, but also a similar number of unique, individualised local appropriations. Jörg Rüpke argued that religious appropriation 'denotes the situational adaptation and deployment of existing practices and techniques, institutions, norms and media to suit contingent individual or group aims and needs'.[198] By 'situational adaptation and deployment', we understand the freedom of the individual members and collective groups to establish new languages of visuality in religious communication. Although religious control is obviously present in small-group religions, especially those that can be associated with rites of initiation, hierarchisation of priesthood, membership restrictions and inner rules adopted from the tradition of Roman *collegia* systems,[199] visual narratives never gained a universal, 'Imperial'-scale control and centralisation, which meant that there were numerous local appropriations and adaptations.

It is unknown how these local variations of visual narratives were established: in most cases, we cannot reconstruct the *chaîne opératoire* of a material tool (relief, statue, statuette) from the workshop up to the dedication and the afterlife of the artefacts. Object biography is a popular method for analysing the creation of the object in a workshop, the role of artists or craftsmen in this process, the transportation of the artefact to the place of the consumer, the use of object in direct religious communication and space sacralisation, and the afterlife of the artefact.[200] Gosden and Marshall argued that all the objects are 'accumulating histories' during their lifetime, which goes much beyond the lifespan of the first generation of creators and users.[201] Most of the objects used in religious communication with the aim of creating and maintaining the central narratives of divine agencies were produced locally, in urban and, rarely, rural workshops. The analysis of 116 marble objects from Carnuntum and 120 objects from Roman Dacia, for instance, show this pattern.[202] In the case of Carnuntum, the marble was transported from Noricum, where several quarries were functioning and served as the major source of material for marble artefacts in Raetia, Noricum and Pannonia Superior.[203] In a few cases, marble objects with Greek and Mediterranean provenance were also attested.[204] In the case of Roman Dacia, there were 36 imported marble objects, mostly from the famous Greek quarries and workshops.[205]

Although modern science can help us to identify the origin of the object itself, the identification of the workshops and artists and the process of making and creating the visual narratives of reliefs and statues are much more difficult to ascertain. Individual choices, group identities, local habits and financial situations are all important players in this process. In many of my previous works focusing on individual objects, such as the Mithraic relief from Dragu, Dacia Porolissensis, I tried to identify the motivations of the customer for ordering a radically new, unusual and appropriated version of

Fig. 4.13 Mithraic relief in Dragu, Dacia Porolissensis. (Source: after Szabó 2012 with the special permission of the National Museum of History of Transylvania, Cluj-Napoca)

the Mithraic tauroctony – a flying figure associated with the well-known scenes of the Mithras myth (Fig. 4.13).[206] In this case, we can observe a personal choice of the worshipper that was probably related to his path within the hierarchy or initiations of the cult. However, the relief found in a rural context is also a good example of the limitations of artistic and financial potential in the periphery of a province.

Such individual choices and artefacts can be found in great number in the Danubian provinces, especially in the case of the cults of Liber Pater or the 'Thracian Riders' (*Domna et Domnus*), in which religious appropriation was used as a strategy within the religious groups, reflecting their ethnic, cultural or financial status and competitiveness. Another relief from the second Mithraeum represents a unique scene probably from a complex panelled relief depicting the Mithras narrative.[207] One of the scenes represent three miniature figures in the form of a cedar tree, a motif that rarely reappeared in large panelled reliefs.[208] This case study shows that oral traditions and religious narratives gained new visual forms in local contexts, which reflects the best case of glocality in Roman religion.[209]

In many instances, local appropriations of visual narratives went beyond the borders of the individual and the spaces of small-group religions. Indeed, we can

Fig. 4.14 Cautes with bucranium in Apulum. (Source: author photo after Szabó 2015b)

trace the replication of local iconographic programmes and narratives. Such a case study can be attested in Apulum, Sarmizegetusa (Dacia) and Boppard (Germania Superior) in the rare representation of Cautes with the bucranium (Fig. 4.14).[210] The unusual iconography of the torchbearer of Mithras standing with the head of a bull was discovered exclusively in Roman Dacia and thousands of kilometres away from this province, in Boppard, Germania Superior.

A more complex process also occurred in the case of the 'Danubian Riders' (*Domna et Domnus*) cult,[211] which can probably be identified as the only original religious invention of the Danubian provinces that gained an extra-provincial, macro-spatial popularity. Similarly to the Mithraic myth and its local appropriations, the small and portable objects representing a large variety of visual narratives of a lost religious story had a central, common core of visual elements (the celestial divinities – Sol, Luna; the central female goddess; the two riders; and many secondary, probably human agencies). These elements were combined in a fascinating complexity of local appropriations and variations. However, the religious knowledge and message of these visual narratives is almost impossible to understand.[212]

The case of these small, portable objects also represents a striking example of religious interconnectivity between small-group religions and coexisting religious knowledge: several iconographic elements (snakes, banquets, *dextrarum iunctio*, animal sacrifices, lion with a krater, leopards) are repeated in the visual narratives of the cults of the 'Danubian Riders' (*Domna et Domnus*), Mithras and Sabazios.[213] This visual overlapping suggests not only a strong connectivity between small-group religions, but also the limitations and possible iconographic tools available for creating new religious narratives and views.

***

If we could walk again in one of the urban centres of the Danubian provinces on an average day, we would find several small or medium-sized buildings, with unusual external aspects, where small-group religions were formed, maintained or failed by a constantly changing, dynamic and interconnected population. Some of the big urban settlements, such as Aquincum, Apulum and Carnuntum, but also medium-sized urban systems, contained several small religious groups whose buildings were stacked with a rich material used in religious communication. These groups were well connected not only in their own meso-spaces through familial, amical or economic bounds, but also on a macro-level, surviving in extra-urban and, sometimes, extra-provincial commercial and religious networks. Small-group religions therefore represent one of the strongest and most complex systems of the Danubian provinces and created a fascinating material, religious heritage that distinguishes this region even on the scale of the Roman Empire.

Notes

1 On the architectural features and evolution of such places, see: Nielsen 2014; Nielsen 2015.
2 See the theoretical approach in the Introduction.
3 On the problematic – and highly debated – notion of oriental cults and orientalism: Versluys 2014; Gordon 2014; Alvar 2017.
4 Belayche-Massa 2020 for a detailed analysis of material and visual representation of mysteries.
5 Rebillard-Rüpke 2015; Lichterman *et al.* 2017.
6 Price 2012; Collar 2013; Woolf 2016.
7 Martin 2014; Panagiotidou-Beck 2017. See also: Gordon 2017, 278 footnote no. 4 and Kloppenborg 2019, 123 footnote no. 3 for recent trends and publications.
8 Price 2012, 2, 7. See also: Steinhauer 2014, 16–17 on terminology.
9 For a new approach, see: Dirven 2015.
10 For a detailed presentation, see: Rüpke 2018, 1–20.
11 One of the most influential books in this sense is the work of A. D. Nock from 1933, one of the earliest case studies in which the complex mechanisms of religious group formation is

contextualised in the dichotomy of the Christian-pagan context. For a comparative approach, see: Nock 1933. See also: Duling 1999; Price 2012, 2.

12 Remus 1996.

13 Kloppenborg 2019, 122–123.

14 On the Weberian notion of charisma and its religious connotations, see: Riesebrodt 1999.

15 There are no female religious founders known from classical antiquity. Their impact in religious life is however significant, especially in the Greek and Hellenistic world: McClure 2019, 117–119.

16 The notion was used by R. Gordon for religious leaders who had a small or insignificant impact in the long term: Gordon 2017. For Alexander, see: Chaniotis 2002.

17 Gray 2016, 1–15.

18 Taves 2016.

19 Stark 1996, 135.

20 Taves 2016, 18–20.

21 Lucian, Alexander, 5–6: 'Among others, he had an admirer who was a quack, one of those who advertise enchantments, miraculous incantations, charms for your love-affairs, "sendings" for your enemies, disclosures of buried treasure, and successions to estates. As this man saw that he was an apt lad, more than ready to assist him in his affairs, and that the boy was quite as much enamoured with his roguery as he with the boy's beauty, he gave him a thorough education and constantly made use of him as helper, servant, and acolyte. He himself was professedly a public physician, but, as Homer says of the wife of Thon, the Egyptian, he knew "Many a drug that was good in a compound, and many a bad one," all of which Alexander inherited and took over. This teacher and admirer of his was a man of Tyana by birth, one of those who had been followers of the notorious Apollonius, and who knew his whole bag of tricks. You see what sort of school the man that I am describing comes from!'. Translated and notes by A. M. Harmon, 1936, Published in Loeb Classical Library, 9 volumes, Greek texts and English translation: Harvard University Press. This extract is transcribed by Roger Pearse, 2001. Open access.

22 Taves 2016, 50–66.

23 Kloppenborg 2019, 122–123.

24 Stark 1996, 136–137.

25 Taves 2016, 66–82.

26 See also: CIL VI 6128 = OPEL III, 113.

27 IDR III/ 5, 85 = CIL III 1021: *Glyconi / M(arcus) Ant(onius) / Onesas / iusso dei / l(ibens) p(osuit);* IDR III/ 5, 86 = CIL III 1022: *Glyco(ni) / M(arcus) Aur(elius) / Theodo/tus ius/so dei p(osuit)*

28 Nedelea 2016.

29 Gawlikowski 1997.

30 For the cult of Asclepius and religious communication in his sacralised spaces in Apulum, see: Szabó 2018b, 68–78.

31 Renberg 2017, 620. See also: the case studies from Mauer an der Url (Locus Felicis), AÉ 1939, 265: *I(ovi) o(ptimo) m(aximo) D(olicheno) Marr(ius) Ursinus veter(anus) ex ius(su) pos(uit) l(aetus) l(ibens) m(erito);* and Apulum, IDR III/5, 220.

32 Such an individual was identified for example in Panóias, Portugal. On the role of G. Calpurnius Rufinus as founder of a new religious group, see: Rüpke 2018, 314–315; Gasparini 2020.

33 From the rich literature on the cult produced in the last decade, see: Gordon 2007; Gordon 2012; Clauss 2012; Faraone 2013; Dirven 2015. See also: Rüpke 2018, 315–317.

34 Chalupa 2016 for a comprehensive analysis of this topic. For a radically different view, see: Mastrocinque 2017.

35 Faraone 2013, 109.

36 Beck 2001.

37 AÉ 1940, 100 = ILGBulg 289 = CIMRM 2268–69 = EDH 020910: *[Invicto] / Deo / Melichrysus / P(ubli) Caragoni / Philopalaestri / [cond(uctoris) publ(ici) por(torii)] / [ripae Thraciae] / [ser(vus) vil(icus) posuit]*

38 AÉ 1919, 10. See also: Gordon 1976, 153; Olteanu-Amon 2008.

39 Bounegru 2007a.

40 Beskow 1980. See also: Tóth 2015, 169–172.

41 CIMRM 1487–1508.

42 CIL III, 14354, 33 = CIMRM 1500=CIMRM 1501: *Primitivos(!) / C(ai) Antoni Rufi / proc(uratoris) Aug(usti) p(ublici) p(ortorii) |(contra)scr(iptor) / in / memoriam / Hyacinthi* and CIL III 14354, 34 = CIMRM 1502: *Primitivos / C(aii) Antoni Rufi / proc(uratoris) Aug(usti) (servus) p(ublici) p(ortorii) c(ontra)scr(iptor) / in / memoriam / Hyacinthi*

43 CIMRM 1501 = Lupa 9330.

44 László *et al.* 2005 II, 33–35. See especially the representation of a possible *pater* from the Mithraeum of Santa Prisca: CIMRM 480.

45 This cognomen is predominantly present in Latin form in Italian provinces (seven cases): OPEL II, 186.

46 CIMRM 1501.

47 Lupa 9330–9331.

48 See also: Tóth 2015, 172–173.

49 AÉ 1978, 0668 = CIL III, 12589 = IDR 3, 2, 385: *In memoriam / [Sex(ti) At]tii Secundi / [patr(oni) col] l(egii) fabr(um) / [------*

50 Tóth 2006.

51 Beck 1998.

52 Woolf 2018–9, 119–120.

53 Bremmer 2014, 125–141.

54 László *et al.* 2005, 107–111.

55 Tóth 2015, 177.

56 Szabó 2015; McCarty *et al.* 2019.

57 On the local importance of the Mithraeum of Fertőrákos and its significance in religious networks, see: Tóth 2007.

58 On the Jewish communities of the Danubian provinces, see: Kovács 2010b, 161–162; Grüll 2016.

59 For the 'council' of Dolichenian priests from Pannonia, see: CCID 200 and Tóth 2015, 157–159.

60 Tóth 1973 on the destruction of the Dolichena in the Danubian provinces.

61 Walsh 2019.

62 Lichterman *et al.* 2017, 4.

63 Most importantly, the works of A. Collar. She used the network models established by Watts especially: Collar 2013. See also: Brughmans *et al.* 2016, 3–21; Woolf 2016.

64 Collar 2013, 19; Woolf 2016, 45.

65 The model of Hebraisation as a network is hard to understand from the nature of primary sources (scant epigraphic material from the Danubian provinces) and the arguments of A. Collar in this chapter seem inconclusive: Collar 2013, 221–224.

66 Idem, 79–145.

67 Idem, 145. A classic example for military group formation, for example the dedication of soldiers and veterans from Carnuntum: AÉ 1983, 767 = AÉ 1982, 0786 = CIL III, 11135 =CCID 232: *[I(ovi) O(ptimo)] M(aximo) / Dolic[h(eno)] / pro sal(ute) / [[[Imp(eratoris) Caes(aris)] C(ai)]] / [[[Iuli] Veri] Max]]/[[[imini P(ii)] F(elicis)]] / [[[Invic(ti) Au]g(usti)]] / [---] / [---] /[--- Ulpi]us / Amandianus / mil(es) leg(ionis) / XIIII g(eminae) / librarius / numeri s(uprascripti) / cus(tos) arm(orum) / [s]ignif[er] / opti[o] / o[cta]v[i] / pr(incipis) pr(ioris) / candidatus / numini / cum U[l]pio / Amando / [ve]t(erano) le[g(ionis)] s(upra) s(criptae) / p[osuit?]*

68 Rüpke 2014, 36–45. A similar priestly hierarchy can be observed in the case of the Thracian god of Sabazios in Thracia: Taceva-Hitova 1983, 185.

69 Idem, 139–140. See also: Tóth 1971, 24; Tóth 2015, 158, CCID 200 especially: *I(ovi) O(ptimo) [M(aximo)] / Dolc(eno) pro / sal(ute) dd(ominorum) nn(ostrorum) / Augg(ustorum) tot(ius) pr(ovinciae) / sacerdote[s]*
70 Roscoe 1996.
71 A summary of the problem can be found in: Szabó 2018b, 132–135.
72 AÉ 2001, 1707 = ILD 683 = AÉ 2006, 1125: *I(ovi) O(ptimo) M(aximo) [D(olicheno)] / pro salute et [incolu]/mitate Imp(eratoris) C(aesaris) M(arci) [Ant(oni)] / Gordiani Pii Fel(icis) Aug(usti) / et coh(ortis) III Camp(estris) M(arcus) Aur(elius) Fla(v)/us IIIIvir m(unicipii) S(eptimi) P(orolissensis) M(arcus) Ant(onius) Maximu[s] / vet(eranus) et dec(urio) o[rnat]us ornam(entis) IIIIvir(alibus) / m(unicipii) s(upra) s(cripti) et Aure(lius) Fla(v)us dec(urio) m(unicipii) vegesi[m]a[r(ius)](!) / sacerdotes dei et coh(ortis) s(upra) s(criptae) [t]emp[l(um) cum] / tabernis (a)ere suo feceru[nt]*
73 CCID 50. See also: Gudea-Tamba 2001, 43–44; Szabó 2007, 61–62, cat. no. D.37.
74 CIL III 7761 = CCID 153 from Apulum: *I(ovi) O(ptimo) M(aximo) D(olicheno) / Aurelii / Alexan/der et Fla/(v)us Suri / negotia/tores ex / voto l(ibentes) p(osuerunt)*
75 Szabó 2018, 163.
76 CIL III, 07835 = CIL III, 01301b = ILS 4299 = IDR 3, 3, 299 = CCID 148: *I(ovi) O(ptimo) M(aximo) D(olicheno) et / deo Com/mageno(rum) / Aurel(ius) / Marinus / et Adde / Barseme/i et Ocea/nus So/cratis sa/cerdotes / v(otum) l(ibentes) p(osuerunt)*
77 IDR III/3, 298.
78 CIL III 7834 = IDR III/3, 298.
79 IDR III/4, 86 = CCID 162. See also: CCID 160.
80 AÉ 1940, 0076 = CCID 376
81 CIL III 7791 = IDR III/5, 223.
82 Blömer 2017, 107.
83 Idem, 111–114; Nemeti 2019, 251–254.
84 Blömer 2017, 108.
85 Schwertheim 1981, 195; Facella 2013; Petrović 2015.
86 Tóth 1977, 386; McCarty *et al.* 2019, 309.
87 CIMRM 1578. See also: Tóth 2015, 178–179.
88 For a detailed analysis, see: Szabó 2015.
89 Woolf 2016, 51–52.
90 Firth *et al.* 2020, 1616–1622, Fig. 1.a.
91 North 1992.
92 Taves 2009, 3–4.
93 On the impact of his work in the study of religious experience, see: Proudfoot 2004.
94 Margolis-Elifson 1979.
95 Idem, 65.
96 Taves 2009, 58. See also: Idem, 177–179.
97 For several other definitions and approaches, see also: Gordon 2020, 23–24.
98 Rüpke 2021, 75.
99 Barchiesi *et al.* 2004.
100 Raja-Rüpke 2015, 13–15.
101 On the notion of *sacrificium*, see: Schultz 2016.
102 Animal, floral, fire, smoke and funerary sacrifices were among the most universal strategies in the communication between divine and human agency: Neusch 1994. Human sacrifice represents an extreme, rare and exceptional form of religious strategy that was always related to intesification of human anxiety and uncertainity: Bremmer 2007, 1–9.
103 For a general synthesis about Roman sacrifice, see: Scheid 2007.

104 CIL III 5935 = Lupa 6231: *[Pro salute dd(ominorum) nn(ostrorum)] // Imp(eratoris) [Caes(aris) M(arci) A]ur(eli) Antonini Pii / [Aug(usti) [[et Imp(eratoris) Caes(aris) P(ubli) Sept(imi) Getae Aug(usti)]]] et Iul[iae] // Aug(ustae) matri(s) Aug[[[g(ustorum)]]] et kast(rorum) I(ovi) O(ptimo) [M(aximo)] / et Iun(oni) Re(ginae) et Miner(vae) sac(rum) Genio / coh(ortis) III Brit(annorum) aram T(itus) Fl(avius) Felix / praef(ectus) ex voto posuit l(ibens) m(erito) / dedicavit Kal(endis) Dec(embribus) / Gentiano et Basso co(n)s(ulibus)*

105 The altar was interpreted for long time as the so-called 'Caracalla altar' of Abusina, associated with the presumed visit of the emperor to Raetia in 213 AD, however the datation and reinterpretation of the text indicates that it was erected in 211 AD and has nothing to do with an Imperial visit: Matijević 2012.

106 Fitz 1998, 75, ct. no. 67 = Lupa 6196. See also: Lupa 4859.

107 Lupa 4874.

108 RIU 1073 = CIL III 10307 = Lupa 6049.

109 Fehér 2008, 102.

110 This oval and elegant shape of altars often also appears in Dura Europos and there is also one in the Museum of Intercisa (verbal confirmation of András Szabó in 2015).

111 On the notion and typology of religious individualisation and individuation, see: Rüpke 2013, 11.

112 Weddle 2013.

113 On mystery cults in Roman times, see: Bremmer 2014.

114 CIMRM 1487–1618. See also: Gojkovič 2018.

115 CIMRM 1581 = Lupa 9348: *ele]vavit in modum Solis / [--- Ca]uti et Cautopati in (h)onor[em]*. See also: Tóth 2015, 173.

116 CIL III 968 = 7728; IDR III/2, 306a; IDR III/4, 30; CIMRM 2008. See also: Nemeti 2012, 148–149.

117 CIMRM 1531, 1598, 2250.

118 CIMRM 1711, 1773.

119 Beck 1998.

120 Grand-Clément 2021.

121 From the rich literature on cognitive approach in ancient religions, see: Czachesz 2015; Geertz 2017.

122 Hódi 2012 as a continuation and reinterpretation of Tóth 2015, 131–146 published originally in 2000. For a detailed analysis of the Bacchic religious experiences from Apulum, see: Szabó 2018b, 78–86.

123 On Cicero's notion on divination, see: Beard 1986; Burkert 2005, 31.

124 Kindt 2015.

125 Renberg 2015.

126 Israelowich 2014. See also: Chapter 3 on macro-spaces and pilgrimages.

127 RICIS-02, 00612/0402 = RICIS-S-02, p 293 = AÉ 1990, 778.

128 See also: CIL III 11758, CIL III 11538, CIL III 4772.

129 On the cult of Asclepius and Hygeia in Dacia, see: Varga 2005; Szabó 2018b, 68–78. On dreams and oracular activities in Dacia, see: Zugravu 2005.

130 On the notion, see: Petridou 2016a.

131 Especially in Aquincum and Novae: Póczy 1998, 33–34; Kolendo-Dyczek 2010.

132 Van der Ploeg 2018, 178–179.

133 On the Neoplatonic views of Proclus on the nature and body of the gods, see Nemeti 2012, 17–18.

134 On the particular case study of Aelius Aristeides and his medical dreams, see: Harrison 2013, 205–206; Petridou 2016b.

135 There are 40 inscriptions from the Danubian provinces that have the *ex visu* formula. For a comprehensive study of the *ex visu-ex iussu* dedications, see: Weber 2005–2006, 55–121.
136 CIL III 1614 = IDR III/5, 220: *I(ovi) O(ptimo) M(aximo) D(olicheno) / ex praecepto / num(inis) Aesculapi / somno monit(us) / Veturius Marci/an(us) ve(teranus) l(egionis) XIII g(eminae) p(ro) s(alute) s(ua) suor(um)q(ue).* See also: Szabó 2008, 97–108; Szabó 2018b, 75.
137 Cassius Dio 78.15.6; *IvEph* 3.802. Van der Ploeg 2018, 131–132. See also: Opreanu 2015.
138 Hofeneder 2013.
139 AÉ 1957, 295.
140 AÉ 1990, 772.
141 AÉ 1999, 1198: *L(ucio) Vibio Primo / [h]aruspici et / [--- F]estae ux[ori] / [et L(ucio) Vibio] Sabi[no et] / [L(ucio) Vibio] Ianuari[o] / [L(ucius) Vibius] Primigenius / [haru]spex fecit*
142 CIL III 4868: *L(ucius) Tuccius / L(ucii) f(ilius) Pol(lia tribu) / Campanus / haruspex et / Sollonia P(ublii) fil(ia) / Sabina / ob meritum rei / public(ae) Virunens(ium) / dederunt*
143 Szabó 2007, 85–89. See also: Szabó 2018, 64–66.
144 Petridou 2016c, 2.
145 Rüpke 1990, 125–127.
146 See also: AÉ 1934, 245.
147 For more on the rain miracle and the comprehensive analysis of the available literary and epigraphic evidence, see: Kovács 2009.
148 Idem, 169–181.
149 Rüpke 1990, 65.
150 Savaria: AÉ 2011, 953: *F(ulgur) d(ivum) c(onditum)*. Apulum, AÉ 1999, 1284: *Iovi / Fulgera(tori) / h(ic) fulg(ur) cond(itum).* See also: Szabó 2018b, 41.
151 AÉ 2008, 1175, AÉ 1973, 445, CIL III 1680, CIL III 1086, CIL III 1596, CIL III 821, CIL III 3953, CIL III 3954.
152 CIL III 7756 = IDR III/5, 136: *I(ovi) O(ptimo) M(aximo) / Aur(elius) Marinus / Bas(s)us et Aur(elius) / Castor Polyd/i circumstantes / viderunt numen / aquilae descidis(s)e / monte supra dracone(m) / res validavit / supstrinxit(!) aquila(m) / hi s(upra) s(cripti) aquila(m) de / periculo / liberaverunt / v(oto) l(ibentes) m(erito) p(osuerunt)*
153 Szabó 2018b, 92–93.
154 The interpretation of his name is problematic. One of the readings argued that Aurelius Castor was son of Polydus, while others read the inscription as 'on the bridge of Lydus'. See: Ando 2010, 46; Lerz *et al.* 2017, 11.
155 Aurelius Bassus is associated in Ampelum and Apulum with the Syrian community: Szabó 2018b, 163.
156 Homer, Il. 12. 219.
157 Aelian *Nature of Animals* 17.37. I am grateful to Professor Daniel Ogden for the reference.
158 Wittkover 1939.
159 Künzl 2008, 87–95.
160 Haynes 1999.
161 Lerz *et al.* 2017.
162 Ando 2010, 45–46.
163 Rüpke 2018, 340.
164 Mistry 2017, 303.
165 Bakker 1999; Ong 2002.
166 Wightman 2015, 171–181.
167 Morgan 1998, 6. See also: Estienne 2015.
168 Virgil, *Aeneid* 6.34. See also: Elsner 1996, 1.
169 Rüpke 2018, 158–163, 329–340.

170 Interpreted as part of Augustus's visual and religious reforms: Alföldy 1991; Rüpke 2018, 183–201.
171 Elsner 1996, 2.
172 Lupa 6282.
173 Lupa 6396.
174 Lupa 6321.
175 Lupa 155.
176 Lupa 442, 827, 1241.
177 Lupa 557.
178 Lupa 3832. See also: Nagy 2013.
179 In Raetia, the major issue was the availablity of stone material, while in Moesia Superior the history of research is still in a problematic phase in the documentation of figurative monuments.
180 Lupa.at. In Roman Dacia, there are only funerary monuments with possible mythological scenes representing the life of Hercules, Icarus, Paris or Polyhymnia. Harl also interpreted the Mithraic iconographies of Dacia as *mythos*, however these 54 reliefs cannot be considered as classical mythological scenes. See also: Ardevan 2013; Ota 2014.
181 See also: Adrych-Dalglish 2020, 84.
182 Novae, AÉ 2008, 1187: *I(ovi) O(ptimo) M(aximo) Dolichen(o) / ubi ferrum na/scit(ur) P(ublius) Aelius Be/nivolus dec(urio) al/ae Com(m)agenor(um) / iussu dei ipsius*; Apulum, CIL III 1128 = IDR III/5, 222: *[I(ovi)? O(ptimo)? M(aximo)?] / Dolicheno [---] / numini et virtutibu[s ---] / nato ubi ferrum exor[itur Iunoni? Reginae? ---?] / naturae boni even[tus pro sal(ute) Imp(eratoris) Caes(aris) T(iti) Ael(i) Hadri]/ ani Antonini Au[g(usti) Pii ---] / Terentiu[s ---]*; Vetoniana, CIL III 11927=AÉ 1889, 68: *I(ovi) O(ptimo) M(aximo) / Duliceno(!) / ubi fer(r)um / [nascit]ur // T(---) // F(---)(?)*. See also: Facella 2013.
183 Nemeti 2019, 238.
184 Țentea 2012, 12–15, 41–48.
185 Noll 1980. A similarly rich inventory was discovered in Brza Palanka (Egeta): Gavrilović Vitas 2020b.
186 Blömer 2017.
187 On the possibility of a central Mithras myth, see: Beck 2002, 283–300.
188 On Persianism in the Mithras cult, see: Gordon 2017.
189 Lupa 10488. See also: Zsidi 2018.
190 Lupa 17291. See also: Szabó 2013.
191 On the problem of Mithraic visual language, see: Adrych *et al.* 2017.
192 For the most important case studies, see: Lupa 5860–5861, Lupa 12826, Lupa 6389, Lupa 22368 Lupa 29799, Lupa 15348, Lupa 17299, Lupa 17466, Lupa 17604, Lupa 17861, Lupa 19314, Lupa 19324.
193 On the problem of a central myth, see also: Nagy 2012.
194 Mastrocinque 2017, 103–104.
195 Arnhold 2018, 126.
196 Faraone 2013.
197 On Christianity as textual religion, see: Rüpke 2018, 348–358.
198 Albrecht *et al.* 2018.
199 Steinhauer 2014.
200 Gosden-Marshall 1999.
201 Idem, 170.
202 For Carnuntum, see: Unterwurzacher *et al.* 2010. For Roman Dacia, see: Müller *et al.* 2011.
203 Unterwurzacher *et al.* 2010, 163, Fig. 1.
204 Idem, 169, Fig. 4.

205 Müller *et al.* 2011, 39–40.
206 Szabó 2012.
207 Lupa 9405.
208 Gordon 1980. See also: CIMRM 1687, 1797, 1816, 1818, 1857, 1973, 2084, 2237.
209 For more examples of glocality in Roman Mithraic visual narratives, see: Dirven-McCarty 2014, Silnović 2018.
210 Szabó 2015.
211 See: Chapter 2.
212 Nemeti 2015.
213 Georgiev 2021. See also: Simón 2018.

5

Religious experience in micro-spaces: housing the gods

In the previous chapters, space sacralisation was associated with large, visible, human-made constructions, geographical areas and natural environments in which human agency is present to a large degree and the maintenance of which requires constant religious, economic and material investment. However, not all the sacralised spaces involved a large amount of human or material agency: probably the most widespread spaces of religious communication in antiquity are those that were related to the individual or a very small number of people (a family, for example) and needed minimal material investment. Dealing with such places is not easy: methodologically, there have been several notions coined for this phenomenon, such as 'home religion' (from the German *Hausreligion*), 'domestic religion', 'family religion' or 'private religion'. All of these reflect a specific, especially social or legal aspect of the religious communication, yet none is useful or sufficient to provide a holistic view or to illustrate all the possible dimensions of the smallest unit of space sacralisation.

Micro-space here is interpreted as the smallest spatial unit in which religious communication between human and divine agency can occur. This can be the human body and its parts (skin marked with tattoos and other stigmata,[1] limbs and other parts of the body decorated with visual markers), a house shrine (commonly known as a *lararium*), private spaces of individuals in domestic or military places, or small road shrines.

The body as active agent in religious communication in the Danubian provinces can be justly presumed based on iconographic features (reliefs, funerary portraits[2]) and in funerary contexts, where the human body was prepared for the Afterlife. A particular case study is the mummified individuals from late antiquity discovered in Pannonia (Brigetio, Intercisa, Aquincum and Carnuntum), which have been interpreted as being among the last surviving pagan elites of the province.[3] Body modifications and religious embodiment can also be observed within the Asclepeia, where individual religious appropriations were reflected and lived through and within the body of the sick person. The presence of the anatomical votives in a few well-attested Asclepeia – such as the one in Colonia Sarmizegetusa or case studies in Pannonia[4] – show that the human body was also used directly and often as a religious agent in communication with the gods. In the Asclepeia in Colonia Sarmizegetusa, three types of anatomical votives were found: ears, hands and forearms.[5] Hands and forearms were also among the most popular anatomical votives in the Greek and Celtic context in Roman times, however the interpretation of this fact is still problematic and doesn't necessarily reflect a medical condition. Instead, it could be related to the embodied communication of the sick with the healing divinities.[6] Since the sick part of the body was in direct and living contact with the entire body and material existence of the patient, the individual who established a religious dialogue with divine powers was rarely alone in the Asklepieia. Aside from the body of the individual him- or herself, which could be modified, appropriated micro-spaces of nature or the human built environment rarely gave the opportunity for private and lonely piety. Micro-spaces, such as incubation chambers or private, domestic bedrooms, could perhaps provide such an opportunity, although in many cases, the former were busy and loud. For the most part, though, incubation chambers are hard to attest archaeologically, especially in the Danubian provinces.[7]

Sacralising the body with decorations and creating an embodied micro-space was usually done with the help of small, portable objects. The most common category of these is the magical gems (amulets, talismans) and votive lead, bronze, gold or perhaps textile (organic) objects used in religious communication (public or private). Unfortunately, most of these objects are discovered without a documented context, although there are some cases with known archaeological context and functionality (especially from Dolichena, where the bronze triangles were used, touched and probably carried in processions).[8] A peculiar case study represents the Egyptian or Egyptianised objects that were used, probably for magical purposes, as portable objects: several Egyptian ushabti and pseudo-ushabti have been discovered in the Danubian provinces, mostly from undocumented contexts or presumably sacralised spaces.[9] Miniature portable bronze and lead objects – plaques and reliefs dedicated to the so-called 'Danubian Riders' (*Domna et Domnus*), lead mirrors[10] and defixiones[11] – have been found in great numbers in the Danubian provinces, which indicates a proportionally unusual amount of materiality of religion used in strict relationship with the human body. These objects were worn and transported by the human body, and often personalised for the owner, and therefore serve as great examples of religious individuation. The very nature of these objects – the material (lead),[12] their embodied relationship with the owners – also represents a glocal aspect of Roman religious communication in the Danubian provinces on the micro-spatial level.

Private and domestic religion was therefore rarely private and not exclusively domestic – two notions that were contested and reinterpreted recently by several important works focusing on spaces of religious communication in houses and villas in both urban and rural environments.[13] Domestic places are traditionally associated as spaces of familial, intimate experiences, with reduced accessibility, limited human agency and material or financial investment in religious communication, but in many cases – especially in urban *domi* and large rural villas – these criteria could easily be changed. As Verity Platt observed in her magistral study on viewing and experiencing gods in Pompeiian houses, communicating with the gods in domestic places was rarely private and hidden, and the visuality of religion was often combined with other communicative aims and forces, such as eroticism, power, intellect or decorative aesthetics.[14]

Urban density in provincial cities was also a significant factor, which in many cases dissolved the public and private dichotomy in urban reality of religious communication, although the role and impact of meso-spaces and macro-spaces and the legal distinction between public and private in the urban context cannot be underestimated.[15] The legal aspects were strictly followed even in the space sacralisation of the *lararia* in private places, which often gained a collective, public legal status when the Lares left the house.[16]

Fig. 5.1 Apollo statuette from Roman Dacia. (Source: Kunsthistorisches Museum Wien, Antikensammlung) Open access: https://www.khm.at/objektdb/detail/66805/

Such details as one can analyse in the case of Pompeii, where the archaeology of religion can be attested in its full methodological depth,[17] cannot be observed in the Danubian provinces. The most spectacular small finds – especially bronze statuettes – discovered in the region (the gods of the so-called 'temple inventory' from Weissenburg I Bay,[18] the bronze Jupiter from Brigetio,[19] the Apollo of Apulum[20] – Fig. 5.1) have no documented provenance and probably represent a later spolia, as the case of the treasure in Weissenburg suggests.

As I highlighted in the previous chapter focusing on urban religion, the cityscapes and urban architectural density is attested in a few cities or larger settlements of the Danubian provinces (Cambodunum, Brigantium, Magdalensberg, Virunum, Aguntum, Cetium, Carnuntum, Aquincum, Gorsium, Sarmizegetusa, Micia, Porolissum, Oescus and Tropaeum Traiani). For the most part, domestic architecture is the least-researched aspect, hence it is one of the major problems of Roman provincial archaeology in the Danubian provinces.[21] In many cases, micro-spaces of religious communication in an urban context have not been preserved and their materiality has been found in secondary positions: this is true of many of the small bronze statuettes in this region of the Roman Empire. The case studies of Brigetio or Aquincum are good examples of the problem of identification of the provenance of the objects and the functionality of the buildings whence they come. Brigetio – one of the most important legionary centres of the Danubian provinces, seat of the I Adiutrix legion from 86 AD – contains more than 100 bronze statuettes representing divine figures.[22] From this significant number, only 11 have a documented archaeological context and known provenance. Most of them were discovered in the Dolichenum of Brigetio [23] and four others have a presumed provenance from the territory of the *canabae* or the fortress. The quality of some of the pieces from Brigetio suggests that these were used to decorate some of the most exquisite *lararia* of the town or the *principia*.[24]

Similar problems can be observed in the case of Aquincum, where the urban cityscape is much better preserved in the civilian town and where numerous urban houses were excavated in the late 19th and 20th centuries.[25] However, few of them were discovered to contain in situ or documented materiality. Most of the bronze statuettes of Aquincum have an unknown provenance or – in cases when the street or the region of modern Budapest was mentioned by the excavators – it is uncertain if the finds were discovered in situ or in a secondary position.[26] The same problem can be observed in Roman Dacia.[27] A particular exception is the beautifully elaborated statuette of Jupiter discovered in one of the private rooms of the *principia*.[28] As most of the domestic environments of the settlements were discovered looted or without major structural features, the materiality of religious communication in such urban and peri-urban micro-spaces (especially *lararia* or house altars) is rarely attested. A case study was documented in Sirmium in a house where aedicular forms were identified in a large room.[29] Although the first publisher identified the chamber as a *lararium* of a private house, there was no material evidence to prove the exact functionality of the place. A similarly problematic case study was carried out in Apulum, Roman Dacia, where a fragmentarily preserved aedicular object was interpreted as a decorated *lararium*, although the provincial analogies suggest the monument more likely had a funerary use.[30] Recently, several houses were identified in the territory of the Municipium Septimium Apulense, but none of them contained a well-documented sacralised space. In one house, just one small fragment of a Venus or Diana statuette was found.[31]

Several miniature altars have been discovered in the last few decades in the territory of Apulum, which might indicate dynamic space sacralisation in the urban system and domestic environments, but these have not yet been published.[32] The case of sacralised micro-spaces in Carnuntum was documented by H. Zabehlicky, but his interpretations in many cases are problematic.[33] In one, for instance, the author interpreted as a *lararium* a place where two altars and several lamps were discovered in the corner of a large, partially preserved rectangular building next to an urban street (Bundestraße no. 9). However, no structural or other forms that might indicate this functionality of the context were discovered. The fragmentarily preserved inscriptions can also be justly identified with Silvanus.[34]

The functionality of the buildings with altars in presumably domestic houses represents one of the great issues of both Roman archaeology and the archaeology of religion.[35] Gabrielle Kremer identified 45 altars in the territory of the civilian settlement of Carnuntum, yet in most of the cases, the exact provenance and archaeological context were not documented.[36] A particular case study from these sites represents the altars dedicated to Silvanus Domesticus. Some of the finds were discovered in buildings associated with domestic use, although again, the excavations from the 19th and early 20th centuries did not confirm the functionality of the buildings.[37] In a place known as 'Burgfeld', west of the *canabae*, three altars dedicated to Silvanus Domestic were found: in this case, too, the major problem is the identification of the functionality of the building.[38] Yet another example was discovered in the corner of a small building, next to the amphitheatre I.[39] Elsewhere in Aquincum, similar problems with the functionality of the buildings and the context of altars dedicated to Silvanus Domesticus can be attested, and few case studies have a documented provenance.[40]

A particular case constitutes the micro-spaces of religious communication in *villae rusticae*. These large, domestic estates – far from the architectural, demographic and religious density of the urban environment – were sites that contained several micro-spaces, where religious communication was established in a highly individual and appropriated manner. In most instances, sacralised spaces were not preserved, but can be presumed based on the discovery of rich material tools used in space sacralisation and religious communication. Such remarkable finds were attested in the Roman villas of Tamási and Nagydém.[41] The *in situ* context of the bronze statuettes was not identified, but the quality of the artefacts suggests a large villa and a *lararium* of a wealthy person, probably of Italic origin.[42] Another particular case study was conducted in Ajka, Pannonia Inferior, where a micro-space dedicated to Hercules was attested outside of the villa.[43] This small space can be interpreted as one of the popular, but rarely attested sacralised spaces near a road, marking the limit between the public and the private. In this case, the micro-space of Hercules could also mark the legal boundary and territory of the family. Such boundary sanctuaries or road shrines were very popular in the Roman Empire, and are especially well attested in the periphery of Rome.[44]

From the Pannonian case studies, probably the most interesting is the villa of Eisenstadt (Kismarton).[45] The partially revealed monumental peristyle villa features an impressive 80 × 65 m planimetry (the north-eastern part is severely damaged) and several (at least 39) rooms and compartments have been identified. The central building had a monumental courtyard with several smaller rooms opening to the central area. The most fascinating are the adjoining so-called rooms nos 26 and 27 in which several altars dedicated to Silvanus, Diana, statues of Fortuna, Aesculapius and most peculiarly, a fragment of a small Mithraic relief were found.[46] The unusual combination of divinities, the apparently private nature of the Mithraic object[47] and the relatively large spaces dedicated to religious communication (the two rooms each measure about 10 × 8 m) makes this case a good example of religious individuation and appropriation.

Similarly to the case studies in Pannonia, Dacia also provides few examples of micro-spaces outside of the urban world. From rural settlements, 27 case studies have been attested (predominantly individual votive inscriptions). Most of the finds are individual inscriptions, often without a well-documented archaeological context.[48] The rural environments of Moesia Inferior, by contrast, were apparently much more densely populated with micro-spaces of religious communication, especially along the major communication routes of the province, often with pre-Roman origins, thugh the archaeological contexts are poorly documented and based especially on antiquarian accounts.[49]

The villa in Meßkirch (Landkreis Sigmaringen/Baden-Württemberg) in Raetia represents a well-documented case study. The small, rectangular sacralised space (approximately 7 × 8 m) was situated in front of the main entrance of the walled villa, 50 m north of the domestic space. The small building hosted an altar dedicated to Diana by Marcus Aurelius Honoratus Pancratius, probably the owner of the villa.[50] The position of this building, which is strictly related to the accessibility and communication routes of the villa, suggests that similar, legally and topographically separated, sacralised spaces might have been present in most of the villas in rural environments. However, their identification is often difficult, especially when employing non-destructive methods, which have nevertheless revealed hundreds of small rectangular annexes in the vicinity of rural villas in the Danubian provinces. These could represent not only a boundary between the sacralised spaces dedicated to the divine agencies, but might also have played a protective role in the domestic area.[51]

A special category of religious micro-spaces is the individual graves and tombs. This is constantly interpreted as being part of the religious communication,[52] yet funeral spaces are first and foremost spaces where the living and the world of the dead communicate. The divine agency in these spaces (*Dii Manes*, demons and divinities of the Underworld evoked in necropoli or individual tombs) is rarely emphasised. Some particular case studies, however, might indicate the presence of the cult of Orcus, Pluto and Proserpina. In addition, an interesting pair of divinities attested especially on terracotta materials in funerary contexts were evoked in necropoli, too.[53]

Micro-spaces of religious communication are special, spatial entities, where social and territorial boundaries are collapsed.[54] Moreover, not only do the social and spatial dimensions become reduced and contested, but also the material density and the very nature of architectural or geographic spatiality of such spaces: the mutilated, used, decorated human body, the dreams of the incubated patients or the dead body itself become micro-spaces used in religious communication. Architectural commonalities and canonical features – which were essential in macro-spaces and even in meso-spaces, such as a Dolichena or Mithraea – are also contested in the micro-level of space sacralisation.[55] Time was also relative in this context: while in macro-spaces and crowded public events the *fasti* played a crucial role, in micro-spaces, timing was a secondary factor. Sacralised spaces discussed in this chapter had no controlled timing aspects, although they were conditioned by time itself: the human body is conditioned by health and age, the micro-spaces of domestic environments by the existence of a family or often changing ownership, and the material resistance of the architectural space itself.

Materiality of religion also represents a much greater, almost impossible-to-quantify variety in micro-spaces: vases, lamps, small finds and miniature ordinary objects can all be transformed into a useful and – for the individual human agent – essential tool in religious communication. This is one of the main reasons why attesting Roman religion in the micro-spaces of the Danubian provinces is so very problematic: materiality of religion in this case doesn't speak the peculiar language of gods, it reflects instead the constantly changing language of communication between the human and the divine.

Notes

1 Bremmer 2015.
2 See Chapter 4 on *instrumenta sacra* of priests and symbols of religious rituals.
3 Póczy 1998b.
4 Gradvohl 2006; Antal-Băeştean 2018.
5 Idem, 322–323, Figs 1 and 2.
6 Hughes 2017, 37, Table 2.2 and 110–116.
7 Renberg 2006, 123.
8 Gavrilović Vitas 2020b, 219–220.
9 Deac 2017b.
10 Bózsa-Szabó 2013.
11 Németh 2015.
12 Németh 2021.
13 On the problematic notion of private religion, see: Ando-Rüpke 2015, 1–11.
14 Platt 2002.
15 Andringa 2009 as AÉ case study for Pompeii. The author distinguishes strictly the public and private sacralised spaces, based especially on legal categories of the cityscape. On the legal aspects of space sacralisation in urban context, see: Noethlichs 2015.
16 Andringa 2021, 97.
17 For AÉ recent approach to urban archaeology of religion, see: Flohr 2020.
18 The material was interpreted as an inventory of AÉ temple; however, the pieces reflect more AÉ collection of rich *lararia* from urban or AÉ representative, but domestic, environment. See also: Kellner-Zahlhaas 1993, 139–141 for the historical interpretation.
19 Bartus 2015, 36–37. The Jupiter now in the British Museum has an unconfirmed provenance, but is probably from the territory of Brigetio.
20 LIMC AÉ 1, 371–373.
21 The best – and still most recent – volume on domestic architecture is: Scherrer-Zabrana 2008.
22 Bartus 2015 lists 106 bronze divinities.
23 Idem, 13–14. See also: Minaroviech 2009.
24 Bartus 2015, 169–173, 187, 214, 228–229.
25 On the domestic architecture of Aquincum, see: Láng 2008.

26 See the short list of bronze statuettes from Aquincum in: Szirmai 1986.
27 Pop-Țeposu-Marinescu 2000.
28 Bărbulescu 2015, 154.
29 Milošević 2008, 373.
30 Băluță 2001. See also: Regep-Timcc 1999–2000, 222.
31 Bounegru 2007b, 166, pl. 7.4. Later, the author interpreted the head as representing Diana: Moga *et al.* 2008, 58, cat. no. 53.
32 The unpublished miniature altars are in the deposit of the National Museum of Union in Alba Iulia.
33 Zabehlicky 2008.
34 Idem, 191–192.
35 Bowes 2015.
36 Kremer 2012, 327.
37 Idem, 210, cat. no. 424.
38 Idem, 210, cat. no. 425.
39 Idem, 214, cat. no. 437.
40 *Tituli Aquincenses* AÉ., 306, 310, 325
41 Thomas 1964, 328. Taf. CCXXII–V.
42 Thomas 1965.
43 Thomas 1964, 14–15.
44 Iara 2015.
45 Thomas 1964, 137–151.
46 Idem, 138.
47 See also: Gordon 2004, 263–266.
48 Gudea 2009, 260–261. See also: Szabó 2018b, 168–175.
49 Tomas 2016, 77–84.
50 CIL AÉ 18893: *Diana[AÉ] / sacrum / M(arcus) Aurel(ius) / Honoratus / Pancratius / v(otum) s(olvit) l(ibens) l(aetus) m(erito)*
51 See also: the case study from Marktoberdorf-Kohlhunden: Czysz-Scholz 2013.
52 Rüpke 2018, 35–48.
53 See also: CIL AÉ 3624 = AÉ 2008, 1144 from Aquincum.
54 Rüpke 2018, 217.
55 Bowes 2015, 210.

6

Conclusion: beyond the materiality of Roman religious communication

Somewhere between the 4th and 3rd centuries BC, a monumental building was dedicated to the Great Mother of Gods in the Greek colony of Dionysopolis, today Balchik, Bulgaria.[1] The elegant blocks of the foundation, the classical facade of Attic columns and cornices and the reliefs in the tympanum representing the frontal, powerful face of Helios in his quadriga evoke the most sophisticated schools of Greek and Hellenistic artistic traditions. The building has a monumental staircase with three doors entering the pronaos, where several altars, statue bases and an eschara are preserved. From the outside, the sacralised space suggests a clean, elegant and – due to the unfinished decorative elements – minimalist, almost painfully empty effect. The facade and the exterior of the building serve as the macro-spaces of urbanity: they reflects the wealth, the power and the architectural density of the city, but also the importance of the cult community within the living urban fabric of Dionysopolis. It dominates the shores of the city and its position close to the sea also has an intentional, well-established visual propaganda: the sacralised space goes beyond the borders of the urban, uniting the city with its essential economic source, the Black Sea and all the maritime routes reaching the city through it.

Entering the pronaos leads the visitor into a radically different, tumultuous space, where statues, altars and beautifully carved artistic masterpieces change the interior of the temple. This small space (5 × 2.5 m) is not for everyone: the material density of tools used in religious communication reflects the repetitiveness, the *longue durée* existence and the ultimate success of the temple as an important urban sacralised space that survived for at least eight centuries. The naos is a larger space, dominated by the louterion and the central altar: as in most of the macro-spaces used in religious communication, centrality plays an important role here, too. This can be even more powerfully observed in the central aedicule of the temple, which served as the house of the Great Mother Goddess, worshipped here as the Pontic Mother.

This local appropriation of a universal god comes from Hellenistic times, long before Romans arrived. At the end of the 1st century AD, when Moesia became an integrated part of the Roman Empire, the monumental, Hellenistic sanctuary had already served for 400 years as a successful sacralised space that defined the urban, social and religious fabric of Dionysopolis. The new administrative, political and social changes caused by the integration of this region within the Roman Empire didn't really affect the strategies and tools of religious communication here. The temple was standing and flourished for four more centuries.

Beautiful statues and reliefs dedicated to the Pontic Mother, Artemis-Diana, Poseidon and the 'Thracian Rider' were erected in the same space, showing the essential power of polytheism and a special network of divine agencies. Religious individualisation and lived religious experiences can, however, be barely attested in such a ceremonial, religiously dense and central macro-space: the monumentality, competitiveness and economic aspects of religious communication here surpasses the sensescape and experience of the individual. Thus the presence of the Roman Empire didn't affect much here, not even the language of the inscriptions: most of the dedications were continuously in Greek. It is possible that the artistic influences and the variety of objects (coins, pottery, lead mirrors) show greater diversification and globalisation, due to the higher mobility of objects, which created further forms of religious appropriations related to the temple. Nevertheless, the impact of the Roman Empire here cannot be compared to Raetia, Noricum, Pannonia or especially Dacia, where pre-Roman religious strategies and forms changed radically in less than two centuries – three generations. The impressive continuity and changeless aspect of these large, public sacralised spaces of the Greek cities in the Pontic area can in turn be compared to some rare cases of *Brandopferplätze* in the Alpine region, where the transformative impact of the Roman Empire had a modest impact.

In the early 3rd century AD, a monumental elaborated relief was dedicated to the Pontic Mother goddess with an album, a member list of a *neomeniastai*, a cult association.[2] The relief represents the central figure of the goddess with her attributes (the throne, a tholos, a lion) accompanied by four figures of various sizes, reflecting the inner hierarchy and fixed roles of the individuals in religious communication and the inner society of the cult association. The inscription names 85 individuals, which beautifully reflects the cultural myriad of ethnic, cultural identities attested in every Roman city, especially in Moesia, where Latin, Greek and Thracian languages were certainly used on a daily basis. The album also shows the continuous use of the space and how inner societies – a micro-world within a macro-space of religious communication – can create reinvented traditions and metahistories of continuities: after the original 72 members, 13 others were later added. Perhaps belonging to the next generation, these members were united in this new, almost timeless third space of religious communication with the Pontic Mother. For these small groups, the temple of the Pontic Mother was not only a monumental macro-space in the urban landscape and an economic or power marker in the region, but also a sacralised space that provided the ultimate opportunity of lived religious experience, as the modest and conventional sacrificial scene from the relief of the album shows.

The sacralised space also gained an Imperial visit in the age of Licinius in the early 4th century AD, although this period marks the last important renaissance of the 800-year-old temple. Probably just a few decades later, the place was slowly abandoned. Without the active, living human agency involved in religious communication, the materiality of religion (statues, reliefs, altars, small finds) became mere passive markers or empty signifiers for the newcomers. Many of the statues were thus mutilated and destroyed. After 800 years of continuous existence, this sacralised space – together with hundreds of others in the Danubian provinces – failed to survive the major changes of the 4th–5th centuries AD. Religious communication ceased to exist: both human and divine agencies actively involved in this place in Dionysopolis changed in the following centuries.

This case study is just one from the 280 sacralised spaces that have been attested archaeologically in the Danubian provinces during the Principate. It is one of the best-preserved, but still, there are countless unanswered questions about the daily life and lived religion that occurred in this sacralised space. There were certainly hundreds of other examples in the Danubian provinces, some of which were preserved through their memorisalisation in epigraphic monuments, others presumed, based only on the concentration of altars, reliefs, small figurative monuments or accidental discoveries that have been made since the Renaissance period.

My intention with this last case study was to unite the major key notions expounded in the previous chapters and to show that space taxonomies of sacralisation (macro-, meso- and micro-spaces)[3] and various facets of religious communication,[4] as well as pre-Roman and Roman reinvented traditions, local and global production and the use of objects and strategies, coexisted in such complex environments. The temple of the Great Pontic Mother is not, however, a typical case study in the Danubian provinces: there are many examples where spaces, facets of religious communication and traditions are much simpler and more one-dimensional. In this volume, several aspects of Roman religious communication have been analysed for the first time through case studies from the Danubian provinces, focusing on the following major issues.

Religion before and after the Romans: continuities and reinvented traditions

For a long time, Central-Eastern European scholarship was influenced by the late-19th century colonialist historiography that affected most prominently Roman religious studies, especially in the works focusing on pre-Roman religiosity. The material evidence and traces of pre-Roman religions were usually presented in strict contrast with the Roman one, focusing on a metahistorical dichotomy and the differences between the two phenomena. The case studies presented in Chapter 2 instead focused on the complex and extremely diverse strategies of religious appropriations and forms of religious bricolage used by settlers and itinerants in the seven provinces analysed.

The chapter proposed a terminological shift, abandoning the notion and dichotomy of continuity and discontinuity, arguing against the relativity of temporality and time perception in antiquity, which was not always and everywhere a linear, evolutionary one, especially in sacralised spaces, where time often gained another organised, special calendar and control.[5] While spatial and even functional continuities can be observed in numerous places, especially in Raetia and Moesia Inferior, the human and divine agencies, as well as the material tools used in the maintenance of these sacralised spaces, changed in a few decades. To facilitate this radical process caused by the globalisation of materiality of religion in this region, I explored numerous cases of glocalisation of religion and reinvented traditions. Both strategies were frequently used in the Danubian provinces, especially in Celtic and Thracian contexts. The case study of the so-called 'Danubian Riders' (*Domna et Domnus*) shows that both glocalisation and the reinvention of traditions could create successful and later even globalised forms or 'dialects' of religious communication.

The case study of Dacia – as has been argued by many authors before me – is a historiographic paradox, which also shows the problematic state of art in local research history, a general issue of provincial archaeology east of Vienna. This chapter also aimed to include the contemporary discussions of Romanisation in Roman religious studies and to deconstruct the old metahistories on the dichotomy of 'Roman' and 'pre-Roman' as qualitative notions. Instead of a historiographic dualism and a comparative approach, I instead a cultural-historical focus on the glocal forms of religion.

Sacralising the spaces: macro-, meso- and micro-spaces of religious communication

The core of this book focused on questions that have often been ignored by researchers of Roman religion, especially in Central-Eastern Europe. How was a part of the natural or human-built, visible geography sacralised and transformed into a sacralised space that was labelled a '*templum*', '*aedes*', '*fanum*', '*spaeleum*' or other denomination? What were the strategies, tools and agencies involved in the process of space sacralisation? How were these sacralised spaces maintained? Why and when did they fail or become desacralised? These questions transform space sacralisation into a lived religious process, in which objects, humans and divine figures interact in natural, human-built and often imagined dimensions of spaces. The innovative aspect of the space taxonomy used in this work consists of the coexistence of temporal layers, multidimensionality and multicentrality of spaces and their active agents.

In Chapter 3, which focuses on space sacralisation, I discussed the role and impact of macro-spaces in religious communication. Macro-spaces here are interpreted as a notion that has a long-term impact on large-scale populations and includes numerous meso- and micro-spaces of religion, too. Although large, geographic, economic, military clusters such as the catchment of the Danube, the Silk Roads, the Amber Road, the *publicum portorii Illyrici* or maritime routes are now analysed in the context of globalisation in the Roman Empire, these macro-spaces have rarely been analysed as direct factors that helped shape Roman religion in the Danubian provinces. I argued that the mobility of objects, the standardisation of visual narratives in religious communication and the institutionalisation (and legalisation) of some forms of religiosity in the Roman Empire created a global aspect of Roman religion, which underwent in most cases a glocal transformation. Among the most important macro-spaces discussed in this book, I focused on the impact of urban systems and the contemporary notion of 'citification' as an important feature in Roman religious communication. The Danubian provinces were never considered to be a highly urbanised area of the Empire. Its urban density and demographic potential were way behind that of the Mediterranean area, but nevertheless the role of the urban settlements here had a *longue durée* effect even beyond the existence of the Empire.

The Danubian area also possesses a unique dichotomy: the catchment of the river united various types of urbanisations, from the Celtic *oppida*-type settlements in the western part as far as the Greek colonies in the Pontic area, and the unique case studies from the Hellenistic-Thracian and Celtic-influenced centres of the Dacians. The book presented the limits of the recently trending aspects of urban religion in antiquity and the traceable aspects of citification in this region of the Empire. This chapter shows – again – that in many instances, contemporary theories and definitions, and methodological approaches formed from recent anthropological traditions cannot explain fully the complex nature of ancient societies, especially where only partially, or badly documented, material evidence is left.

Another macro-space that defined the architectural, built landscape of the Danubian region was the Roman forts (and fortresses). Most of the archaeological evidence from this area of the Empire comes from military contexts, although this notion itself is a problematic one, with numerous aspects and interpretations (legal, social, architectural).

Macro-spaces also include the large, complex sanctuaries and pilgrimage sites, which are the best cases of successfully maintained sacralised spaces and the monumental public buildings of the urban environments. These often push and challenge the limits of 'sacred' and 'profane': the urban fabric united various layers and densities of sacralisation and religious communication, often in the same geography, where apparently non-religious buildings (amphitheatres, hospitals, public squares, fora) were involved directly in religious procedures and festivals. From the 60 urban systems and numerous urban-like settlements, there are few where the architectural fabric and the multidimensionality of space sacralisation can be observed (Cambodunum, Virunum, Carnuntum, Aquincum, Gorsium, Oescus and Sarmizegetusa).

Chapter 4 followed the spatial taxonomy established in the methodological introduction, focusing on sacralised spaces in which architectural, dimensional monumentality, visibility, accessibility and connectivity were limited and the existence and maintenance of such places depended on much smaller religious groups and charismatic individuals, religious founders, and leaders. Small-group religions, elective cults or orientalised Roman cults are contemporary notions that attempt to describe the complexity of those various groupings, which were formed and remained dependent on charismatic religious entrepreneurs and leaders, as well as the assembly houses of these groups. The chapter gives a few well-attested examples from the Danubian provinces, where this category left most of the material evidence of Roman religion. From the 280 archaeologically attested sacralised spaces, at least 80 were dedicated to small-group religions worshiping Mithras, Dolichenus, Isis, Magna Mater or Liber Pater. These sacralised spaces represent, however, a heterogenous group in Roman religious communication, the common feature of which can be understood only through a comparative approach in context with the macro-spaces. A Mithraeum, Dolichenum, Iseum or Bacchium was always a smaller architectural entity than the buildings described in Chapter 3. They could usually accommodate 10–30 people at a time, most of whom had strong personal attachments and bonds. In these spaces, the exterior of the building was rarely important, however in some rare cases – such as the Iseum of Savaria or some of the Palmyrian groups in Sarmizegetusa – they could attain a privileged status in the city, with a monumentalised building in public squares. In most cases, though, the interior of the building played a crucial role and the sacred geography of the Mithraea, the annexed buildings of the Dolichena or other assembly buildings reflects the numerous, probably repetitive banquets and initiations or rituals that were performed in these places. Most of these buildings – especially those dedicated to Mithras and Dolichenus – were maintained in an urban context and were not exclusively used by the military (the Roman army), as was suggested by older literature.

The chapter presents several case studies of religious entrepreneurs, although this feature deserves much more detailed attention in the future. Religious experiences, divinations and local appropriations were also important aspects of these small-group religions. The chapter presents case studies of local appropriations of visual narratives (inventions of new elements in canonised figurative programmes), which can be considered as one of the most powerful and dynamic motors of religious transformation in the Danubian provinces during the Principate. The late formation of these provinces and the ethnic-cultural variety of the populations also accelerated this process.

The most difficult issue in the analysis of the materiality of religion from the Danubian provinces is the question of micro-spaces, the most elementary form of religious experience, which I examined in Chapter 5. The notion includes religious experiences lived within the human body, house shrines, corner shrines of cities, and other small spaces, where the individual has many possibilities for religious individualisation and self-expression. While this topic is flourishing in contemporary religious studies, where numerous case studies and recent experiments and surveys are available, the limitations of a scholar of antiquity here is obvious and painful. Lived religion and most of the facets of Roman religious communication on the level of micro-spaces can be attested only through literary sources or exceptional archaeological case studies, such as Pompeii, Ostia and a few settlements in the

Mediterranean. The heterogenous historiographies of archaeology in Central-Eastern Europe are not helpful in this regard, either: the contemporary state of art in domestic archaeology and ancient micro-history doesn't allow us in most instances to make an in-depth analysis. The case studies presented in this short and, certainly, unsatisfactory chapter reflect optimistic opportunities in urban environments, where this topic is worth exploring.

Roman religion in the digital era: further perspectives

The four major chapters (2–5) reflect the methodological approach established in Chapter 1, which proposed the analysis of the materiality of Roman religion in seven provinces (commonly called the Danubian provinces). The methodology unites the innovative cultural-historical approach of lived ancient religion, established by Jörg Rüpke and his team from Erfurt, with a new space taxonomy, which I used extensively in several of my previous works before 2018. This space taxonomy also enlarged the notion of macro-spaces, including several new spatial factors in religious communication, and highlighted the importance of religious glocalisation in the Danubian provinces. In addition, the methodology opened several new questions and never-before-researched aspects of Roman religion in the Danubian area and questioned successfully the classical, descriptive and object-fetishist provincial archaeological approach. However, in many cases, it turned out to be also self-limiting and unproductive, especially on the level of micro-spaces, individuals and their religious experiences.

As a scholar formed and informed both by Central-East European and Western scholarship, I struggled with the methodological approaches and their limits given that my aim was to explore as much as possible from the unlimited facets of Roman religious communication in such a vast area. Classical methods, such as statistics, big-data analysis of epigraphic sources and catalogues of objects are now being reconsidered in the age of digital humanism, opening new and, perhaps, promising perspectives in Roman studies.[6] This approach is still new in Roman religious studies, but is currently being used especially in projects focusing on theonyms, epigraphic data analysis or network studies.[7]

The first step to use these new methodological approaches is the collection of primary sources. This book and the Digital Atlas of Sanctuaries (DAS) contributed to the systematic collection of the archaeological material and bibliography available (which at present consists of 280 archaeologically attested sacralised spaces[8]). The epigraphic resources are partially digitised by the Epigraphic Database of Heidelberg (EDH) and the Epigraphik-Datenbank Clauss/Slaby (EDCS). The first one lists 5,724 votive inscriptions. The second one – using a different methodology and definition of votive material – contains 7,237 inscriptions in the category of *tituli sacri* for the seven provinces analysed in this book. The non-epigraphic, figurative material and the small finds discovered in the 280 sacralised spaces have not yet been catalogued and are their number is impossible to estimate.[9] The available quantity of material can also serve for several in-depth analyses and studies focusing on the network of human and divine agencies, human and object mobilities, statistical analysis of theonyms, dedicants, objects and spaces (locations). The possibilities of big-data analysis might create numerous combinations of the major actors, spaces and materialities of religious communication.

As the results presented in the Appendices show, this book used only the epigraphic material, with special focus on the divine agencies and spatial aspects (provinces, urban systems). Other, equally important aspects, such as the human agency (the dedicants, their status, their origin, their connectivity and mobility) are occasionally mentioned and analysed in the book, however I am aware that this feature needs a much more detailed focus in the future. Networks studies focusing on human agency in Roman religious communication in the Danubian provinces have already proved their importance in small-scale studies, but such works will need a much larger amount of data from a wider spatial and historical perspective. The chapter focusing on large-scale mobilities has already projected some of the major nodes and central connections attested in the Danubian area.

The analysis of the epigraphic material and the divine agency produced surprising results. From the available epigraphic material in the seven provinces analysed, one-fifth – and sometimes almost one-third – of the sources are *tituli sacri*, votive inscriptions (Fig. A4 in the Appendices). This large proportion demonstrates what the architectural fabric of the settlement systems in the Danubian provinces already suggested: Roman religion was present as a dominant and remarkable feature of society. While in Raetia, Noricum and Moesia Superior the proportion is less than a quarter of the complete epigraphic material, the case study of Pannonia Superior and especially the three Daciae represent fascinating cases, where almost half of the epigraphic material can be associated with religious communication. In this regard, Dacia is also remarkable because of its short existence: in less than 160 years, the population of the province produced more votive inscriptions than Moesia Superior, Moesia Inferior and Noricum put together did in almost 250 years.

Most of the epigraphic materials and the sacralised spaces attested come from the large legionary centres and their complex conurbations, often associated with double urban systems. The cases of Carnuntum, Aquincum and Apulum are exceptional: these three conurbations produced more than a quarter of the total amount of votive material from all of the Danubian provinces (Fig. A3 in the Appendices). The religious impact of these cities in the northern part of the Roman Empire can be compared only to the impact of Rome and Alexandria in the Mediterranean world, although their population probably didn't exceed 100,000–120,000.

As the case studies from Noricum and Moesia Inferior show, most of the inscriptions were dedicated during the 2nd and early 3rd centuries AD, as many other, more general studies focusing on the so-called epigraphic boom suggested, without however analysing the votive material from the Danubian provinces (Figs A13 and A14 in the Appendices).[10] Comparing the so-called 'pantheon' of the provinces, we can also observe clearly the influence of pre-Roman religious traditions and their local appropriations – the reinvention of local traditions through the Roman way of religious communication even among the most popular divine agents (Figs A6–A12 in the Appendices). In all the provinces, Jupiter Optimus Maximus was the most worshipped divinity, associated with the fidelity and centralised institutions of the Roman Empire, especially in military contexts. Some divinities had an obvious popularity in some provinces, such as Mercurius in Raetia, the nymphs in Pannonia or Asclepius in Dacia. These macro-regional differences can be attributed to numerous factors, including ecology, geography and population but also pre-Roman religious traditions. The Danubian provinces are also very rich in divine epithets, especially in Raetia, Noricum (Celtic divinities) and Moesia Inferior (Thracian divinities). This important aspect – together with the human agency and their professional categories – will also need a separate study in the future.

Epilogue

The Danubian provinces represented a culturally extremely heterogeneous world before the Roman conquest, united by the macro-space of the Danube catchment and numerous economic, commercial routes. The world of the Celtic, 'Illyrian', Thracian and numerous other Late Iron Age societies was transformed in less than three centuries into something even more complex and colourful. Their language and self-representation, their material world and their religious communication were marked deeply by the transformative power of the Roman Empire.[11] Roman religion produced new strategies to reach the world of the divine agency, and created successful and remarkable sacralised spaces that featured in the built and natural landscape of this region for centuries, even after the collapse of the Roman Limes in the Danubian area. The urban systems, the Roman roads and the rich material heritage of Roman religion serve as a living heritage of Central-Eastern Europe. The region's Christianity is a direct product of the Roman Empire (at least, the Eastern Empire) and some aspects of Roman religious communication marked for centuries the religious dialects of the changing populations. Roman votive altars built in Christian temples from Bavaria, Austria or Romania reveal the changing faces and rich biographies of objects and material evidence of religion (Fig. 6.1). Some religious strategies, visual narratives or knowledge were transmitted through the local traditions or reinvented and rediscovered in the Renaissance period.

Their presence continues to be important. In the chapel of St George in the village of Zabernovo, Bulgaria, the small relief of the 'Thracian Riders' is used as an exotic visual representation of St George, one of the most important Christian saints of Bulgaria.[12] The rebuilt, monumental Iseum of Savaria frequently serves as a reinterpreted sacralised space for contemporary weddings. The reconstructed Mithraea from Aquincum are sometimes used as reinvented spaces of an imagined

Fig. 6.1 Roman monuments integrated in the Orthodox Church of Densuș, Transylvania. (Source: author)

metahistorical Mithraic liturgy for re-enactment groups. In this manner, Roman religion thus inspires and creates living (religious?) experiences in the 21st century, even if their original human and divine agents are no longer with us.

Notes

1 Lazarenko *et al.* 2013. Cat. no. V.4.
2 IGBulg AÉ^2 14. See also: Lazerenko *et al.* 2013, 55–59.
3 Szabó 2015 (2020), 255–260.
4 Rüpke 2018, 1–20.
5 Gyáni 2016, 70–71.
6 See also: Bagnall-Heath 2018; Szabó 2020d; Szabó 2020h.
7 Bonnet *et al.* 2018; Mazzilli 2018; Varga 2019; Collar 2020b; Glomb 2021.
8 The Digital Atlas will also present the epigraphically attested and presumed sacralised spaces in seven provinces.
9 The number of ceramic fragments discovered just in the Liber Pater shrine from Apulum, Dacia alone is numbered in the thousands. See also: Szabó 2018b, 78–86.
10 MacMullen 1982.
11 Woolf 2012, 289.
12 Kazarow 1938, 294. See also: Dimitrova 2002, 220.

Appendices

1. Sanctuaries in the Danubian provinces

Romans communicated with their gods in various sacralised spaces, creating a large number of material tools during the Principate. The previous chapters presented few of the most well-documented case studies, where materiality of religion was concentrated and used in an intensified manner, contributing to what I call in this work 'space sacralisation'.[1] Although the Danubian provinces contain abundant evidence of the material heritage of Roman religious communication, the attestation, definition and categorisation of sacralised spaces have nevertheless often caused issues, especially in Roman provincial archaeology. In most of the previous works, only public, legally well-defined and limited spaces dedicated to gods (*templa; loca sacra*) were catalogued and presented in the few works focusing on the temples of the Danubian provinces. The paradigmatic series initiated by M. J. Vermaseren (EPRO) opened a special focus on sacralised places in meso-spaces (Mithraea, Dolichena, *collegia* buildings) and recent studies on urban religion reshaped our knowledge about the large variety and strategies of space sacralisation in micro-spaces, especially in the domestic context. Similar changes also occurred in the military context, especially within the forts.

In my previous works focusing on Roman Dacia, I presented in detail the archaeologically, epigraphically attested and presumed sacralised places in macro- and meso-spaces.[2] The uncertain archaeological context of the material of small finds associated with religious communication in domestic contexts didn't allow me to also focus on sacralised places in micro-spaces. For this reason, in the following short list, I deliver only a catalogue of archaeologically attested sacralised places in macro- and meso-spaces of the Danubian provinces. However, the identification of an ancient, sacralised space is not always clear, as explained in the concluding chapter. In numerous instances, the functionality of the building structures, the *in situ* nature of the materiality of religion and the religious experiences and divine agencies associated with the architectural and material evidence are hard for the modern, contemporary mind to perceive.

The list also includes the sacralised spaces within the forts and fortresses (*aedes signorum*). Each item includes a catalogue number (from I.1 to VI.54), which have been cited in the previous chapters of the book. For the 'denomination' column, the list gives the conventional name of the sacralised spaces, usually associated with one or more divinities or ethnic groups, although I am aware that these are modern, historiographic labels for complex spaces of religious communication. Each of the items is accompanied by several bibliographic references: in the case of monographs, I usually cite the monographic study of the sacralised space. If there is no monograph on a site, I mention two or three of the most relevant studies. In the 'further notes' column I include some additional comments relevant to the archaeological context, continuity, further historiographic details or details regarding some of the problematic case studies.

The detailed analysis and further important statistics related to the sacralised spaces listed here are available on the official webpage of the Digital Atlas of Roman Sanctuaries in the Danubian Provinces (DAS).[3]

Archaeologically attested sanctuaries of Roman Raetia

	Catalogue Number	*Denomination*	*Bibliography*	*Further Notes*
Aalen	I.1	*Aedes signorum/ principia*	Farkas 2015, 69.	
Abusina (*Eining-Unterfeld*)	I.2	*Aedes signorum/ principia*	Farkas 2015, 14; Fischer 2016; Lupa 6231	
Abusina (*Eining I*)	I.3	*Aedes signorum/ principia*	Farkas 2015, 33–35.	
Ad Lunam (*Urspring-Lonsee*)	I.4	*Aedes signorum/ principia*	Farkas 2015, 60.	
Biriciana (*Weißenburg*)	I.5	*Aedes signorum/ principia*	Grönke 1997.	
Brigantium (*Bregenz*)	I.6	Capitolium	Trunk 1991, 187–188.	
	I.7	Imperial cult-complex	Ertel *et al.* 2011.	
	I.8	Building 38	CIL III 13542; Brigantium 1985, abb. 1.	
	I.9	Building 39	Brigantium 1985, abb. 1.	
	I.10	Building 40	Brigantium 1985, abb. 1.	
	I.11	Building 41	Brigantium 1985, abb. 1.	
Cambodunum (*Kempten*)	I.12	Capitolium	Trunk 1991, 194–196.	
	I.13	Ara Augusti	Weber 2010, 39–44.	
	I.14–29	'Gallo-Roman Tempelbezirk' (16 sacralised spaces)	Weber 2010, 72–78; CSIR Deutschland I,1 Nr. 203 = Lupa 6660.	
Castra Regina (*Regensburg-Ziegetsdorf*)	I.30	Mercurius sanctuary	Dietz-Fischer 2018, 176; CSIR Deutschland I,1 Nr. 452 = Lupa 6576; Lupa 6580; Lupa 6564; Lupa 6584.	
	I.31	Hercules (?) sanctuary	Gamber 1982.	
Celeusum (*Pförring*)	I.32	*Aedes signorum/ principia*	Farkas 2015, 59.	

(Continued)

	Catalogue Number	*Denomination*	*Bibliography*	*Further Notes*
Dambach	I.33	Spring sanctuary-Aslepeion	Czysz 2009.	
Emerkingen	I.34	*Aedes signorum/ principia*	Farkas 2015, 23.	
Gersthofen	I.35	Mercury sanctuary	Klein 2003; Lupa 6421.	
Iciniacum (*Theilenhofen II*)	I.36	*Aedes signorum/ principia*	Farkas 2015, 67.	
Königsbrunn	I.37	Mithraeum	Czysz 2002.	
Marktoberdorf-Kohlhunden	I.38	Villa sanctuary	Czysz-Scholz 2013.	
Mediana (*Gnotzheim*)	I.39	*Aedes signorum/ principia*	Farkas 2015, 52–53.	
Meßkirch	I.40	Diana sanctuary	Reim 1978.	
Oberstimm	I.41	*Aedes signorum/ principia*	Farkas 2015, 27.	
Phoebiana (*Feimingen*)	I.42	*Aedes signorum/ principia*	Eingartner *et al.* 1993, 14–17.	
	I.43	Apollo Grannus sanctuary	Eingartner *et al.* 1993; Lupa 6422.	
Pons Aeni/Ad Enum (*Pfaffenhofen am Inn*)	I.44	Mithraeum	Garbsch 1985.	
Quintana (*Künzing*)	I.45	*Aedes signorum/ principia*	Farkas 2015, 40–41.	
	I.46	Mithraeum	Schmotz 2000; AÉ 1998, 1007= AÉ 2000, 1140.	
Rainau-Buch	I.47	*Aedes signorum/ principia*	Farkas 2015, 71.	
Riusiava (*Risstissen-Ehingen*)	I.48	*Aedes signorum/ principia*	Farkas 2015, 29–30.	
Schirenhof-Schwäbisch Gmünd	I.49	*Aedes signorum/ principia*	Farkas 2015, 73.	
Scuttarensium (*Nassenfels*)	I.50	*Aedes signorum/ principia*	Rieder 2003, 170–173.	
Sontheim an der Brenz	I.51	Building C–E	Nuber 1994, abb. 101	
Summuntorium (*Mertingen/ Burghöfe*)	I.52	*Aedes signorum/ principia*	Farkas 2015, 21.	

(Continued)

	Catalogue Number	Denomination	Bibliography	Further Notes
Unterböbingen	I.53	*Aedes signorum/ principia*	Farkas 2015, 74.	
		Sanctuary	Planck 1987, 116.	
Vetoniana (*Pfünz*)	I.54	*Aedes signorum/ principia*	Farkas 2015, 65–66.	
	I.55	Dolichenum	Arnold 1889; CCID 479–485.	
Wachstein	I.56	Mithraeum (?)	Schwertheim 1974, 210.	

Archaeologically attested sanctuaries of Roman Noricum

	Catalogue Number	Denomination	Bibliography	Further Notes
Augustianis (*Traismauer*)	II.1	*Aedes signorum/ principia*	Ployer 2013, 76–77.	
Brunn bei Fehring	II.2	Shrine	Schmid 1939.	
Burgstall-St Margarethen	II.3	Latobius Maromogius sanctuary	Groh-Sedlmayer 2007; Groh-Sedlmayer 2011; Sedlmayer 2015, 313–322.	Seven buildings discovered. Functionality of the buildings under discussion.
Cannabiaca (*Zeiselmauer*)	II.4	*Aedes signorum/ principia*	Ployer 2013, 89–90.	The *aedes* today is under a Christian church.
Celeia (*Celje, Zilli*)	II.5	Capitolium	Trunk 1991, 188; Krempuš *et al.* 2007, 43.	
	II.6–9	Sanctuary I–II–III–IV	Krempuš *et al.* 2007	Celtic and Roman spatial continuity.
Colatio (*Stari Trg, Altenmarkt*)	II.10	Sanctuary	Trunk 1991, 216–217.	Associated with Mars, Augustus or Jupiter Optimus Maximus.
Flavia Solva (*Wagna*)	II.11	Nemeseion	Wittenberg 2014, 82.	
Flavia Solva (*Frauenberg bei Leibnitz*)	II.12	Sanctuary	Trunk 1991, 206–227; Groh-Sedlmeyer 2005; Schrettle 2015.	Celtic and Roman spatial continuity.
Gradišče über St Egyden	II.13	Mithraeum	Gleirscher 2011.	Cave sanctuary (*spaeleum*).
Gurina	II.14	'Hercules temple'/ 'ambulatory sanctuary'	Gamper 2007.	Celtic and Roman spatial continuity.
Hochtor	II.15	Sanctuary	Harl *et al.* 2014.	

(Continued)

	Catalogue Number	*Denomination*	*Bibliography*	*Further Notes*
Hohenstein	II.16	'Noreia' sanctuary	Trunk 1991, 193–194; Dolenz 2007, 87–90.	
Immurium (*Moosham-Lungau*)	II.17	Mithraeum	Kovacsovics 1998.	
Ioviacum (*Iovaco, Schlögen*)	II.18	*Aedes signorum/ principia*	Ployer 2013, 18.	
Iuenna (*Globasnitz*)	II.19	Sanctuary	Trunk 1991, 192–193.	The divinity and functionality of the building was not yet confirmed.
Iuvavum (*Salzburg*)	II.20	'Asclepieion'/ sanctuary	Trunk 1991, 214–216.	The building was associated with several divinities.
	II.21	Mithraeum	CIMRM 1402–1403.	
Lauriacum (*Enns; Lorch*)	II.22	*Aedes signorum/ principia*	Flynt 2005, 74; Ployer 2013, 30.	From the numerous buildings identified in the *municipium*, no sacralised spaces were discovered. Flynt presumed a temple under the Saint Laurentius Basilica.
Lendorf	II.23	Mars sanctuary	Seidel 2007; Glaser 2007, 114.	
Lentia (*Linz*)	II.24	Mithraeum	CIMRM 1414–1421; Ployer 2013, 27.	
	II.25–27	Buildings V–VI–IX	Karnitsch 1956.	Uncertain functionality and chronology, identified originally with several Roman divinities based exclusively on the planimetry of the buildings.
Lienz	II.28	Sanctuary	Grabherr 2016; Grabherr-Kainrath 2019.	Celtic-Roman spatial continuity.
Loig (*Wals-Siezenheim*)	II.29	Villa sanctuary/ building C	Glaser 2007, 110.	The functionality of the building is problematic.

(Continued)

	Catalogue Number	*Denomination*	*Bibliography*	*Further Notes*
Magdalensberg	II.30	Sanctuary	Trunk 1991, 207–210.	The functionality of the building is problematic. It was associated with the imperial cult, *Dea Roma* or Augustus.
Mauer an der Url (*Mauer bei Amstetten*)	II.31	Inventory of a Dolichenum	CCID 290–326; Noll 1980.	The building of the inventory was not completely identified, and the context is still under debate.
Ober-Pohanica	II.32	Mithraeum	CIMRM 1457.	
Podkraj bei Hrastnik	II.33	Adsalluta (?) sanctuary	Sedlmayer 2015, 327–331.	Altars for several divinities.
Rabnitz bei Kunberg	II.34	shrine	Schmid 1929.	
Schachadorf	II.35	Mithraeum	CIMRM 1409–1411; Walsh 2019, 108.	
St Michael am Zollfeld	II.36	Sanctuary	Dolenz *et al.* 2019a.	
St Urban	II.37	Mithraeum	CIMRM 1442–1443.	
Teurnia (*St Peter in Holz*)	II.38	Apollo Grannus (?) sanctuary	Glaser 1978–1980; Sedlmayer 2015, 322–327.	The building was identified only based on topographic and antiquarian studies.
Virunum	II.39	Ara Noricorum (?)	Dolenz *et al.* 2019b, 11.	The functionality of the building was recently questioned and reinterpreted.
	II.40	Capitolium (?)/ podium temple I	Trunk 1991, 236–239; Dolenz *et al.* 2019b, 16.	The building was associated with several divinities (Imperial cult, Minerva, Capitoline triad).
	II.41	Podium temple II	Harl 1989, 542; Dolenz *et al.* 2019b, 16.	
	II.42	Podium temple III	Dolenz *et al.* 2019b, 16.	
	II.43	Nemeseion	Barlovits-Gallob 2007; Wittenberg 2014, 96.	
	II.44	Dolichenum	Harl 1989, 543–545; CCID 329–342.	

(Continued)

	Catalogue Number	*Denomination*	*Bibliography*	*Further Notes*
Wabelsdorf	II.45	Spring sanctuaries (I–VI)	Glaser 2007, 113–115.	
Wallsee (*Loco Felicis?/Ad Iuvense*)	II.46	*Aedes signorum/ principia*	Ployer 2013, 40.	

Archaeologically attested sanctuaries of Pannonia Superior and Inferior

	Catalogue Number	*Denomination*	*Bibliography*	*Further Notes*
Ala Nova (*Schwechat*)	III.1	*Aedes signorum/ principia*	Ableidinger 1929.	The building was attested in the early 19th century.
Albertfalva	III.2	*Aedes signorum/ principia*	Visy 1988, 87; Johnson 1987, 152.	
Aquae Iasae (*Varaždinske Toplice*)	III.3–5	Sanctuary of the nymphs (buildings I–II–III)	Špalj 2020.	
Aquincum (*Óbuda, Budapest*)	III.6	Capitolium-Imperial cult temple	Zsidi 2011, 158; Szabó 2019b.	
	III.7	Fortuna Augusta sanctuary	Zsidi 2011, 158.	
	III.8	Nemeseion I	Zsidi 2011, 160; Wittenberg 2014, 75.	
	III.9	Nemeseion II	Wittenberg 2014, 76.	
	III.10	Mithraeum I	CIMRM 1742–1749; Zsidi 2011, 160; Tituli Aquincenses I. 227–230.	
	III.11	Mithraeum II	CIMRM 1750–1757; Zsidi 2011, 158; Tituli Aquincenses I. 231–237.	
	III.12	Mithraeum III	CIMRM 1758–1766; Zsidi 2011, 160; Tituli Aquincenses I. 238–245.	The building was badly documented.
	III.13	Mithraeum IV	CIMRM 1767–1772; Zsidi 2018; Tituli Aquincenses I. 246–248.	
	III.14	Mithraeum V	Kocsis 1991; Tituli Aquincenses I. 249–256.	
	III.15–28	Spring sanctuaries I–XIV	Póczy 1998; Zsidi 2011, 160.	

(Continued)

	Catalogue Number	Denomination	Bibliography	Further Notes
Brigetio (*Ó-Szőny*)	III.29	Mithraeum	CIMRM 1723.	
	III.30	Dolichenum	CCID 236–257; Láng 1941; Minaroviech 2009.	
Campona (*Nagytétény*)	III.31	Mithraeum	CIMRM 1806–1807.	
Carnuntum (*Bad Deutsch-Altenburg*)	III.32	*Aedes signorum/ principia*	Kremer 2012, 351–355.	Several rooms were identified as sacralised spaces in the legionary fortress.
	III.33	Capitol-Forum	Kandler 2003, 38–39.	The interpretation of the finds is problematic and is based exclusively on geophysical measurements.
	III.34	Asclepius sanctuary/ *valetudinarium*	Kremer 2012, 350–351.	
	III.35	Epona shrine (?)	Jobst-Weber 1989.	The functionality of the small compartment is still under debate.
	III.36	Diana sanctuary	Kandler 2003, 39.	
	III.37	Nemeseion I	Kremer 2012, 337–341; Wittenberg 2014, 78.	
	III.38	Nemeseion II	Wittenberg 2014, 79.	
	III.39	Nemeseion III	Wittenberg 2014, 80.	
	III.40	Nemeseion IV	Wittenberg 2014, 81.	
	III.41	Jupiter Heliopolitanus sanctuary	Steigberger-Tober 2013.	
	III.42	Dolichenum	CCID 216–229; Kremer 2012, 345–346.	
	III.43	'aQuadriviae sanctuary'	Kremer 2012, 341–344.	The functionality of the building and the context of the altars are problematic.

(Continued)

	Catalogue Number	Denomination	Bibliography	Further Notes
Carnuntum (*Bad Deutsch-Altenburg*)	III.44	Liber and Libera sanctuary	Kremer 2012, 346.	
	III.45	Silvanus sanctuary	Kremer 2012, 344–345.	
	III.46	Mithraeum I	CIMRM 1664–1680; Kremer 2012, 330–337.	
	III.47	'Mithraeum II'	CIMRM 1681; Kremer 2012, 331–332.	Uncertain functionality of the building.
	III.48	Mithraeum III	CIMRM 1682; Kremer 2012, 332–334.	
	III.49	'Mithraeum IV'	Kremer 2012, 334–335.	Uncertain functionality of the building.
Carnuntum (*Pfaffenberg*)	III.50	Jupiter Karnuntinus sanctuary	Kremer 2004; Piso 2003a.	
	III.51	Antinoos shrine	Šašel Kos 2009.	The functionality of the building and the provenance of the small epigraphic fragment are questioned.
	III.52	Temple III	Jobst 2006, 46.	
Csákvár	III.53	Diana *spelaeum*	Fehér 2012.	
Fertőrákos	III.54	Mithraeum	CIMRM 1636; Tóth 2007.	
Gorsium (*Tác*)	III.55	Imperial cult complex	Fitz 1998, 25–27.	Two small *nymphaea* were part of the forum and the so-called Imperial cult complex. The exact functionality of the buildings is under debate.
	III.56	Sanctuary of the *Dii Magni* (?)	Alföldy 1997.	
Intercisa (*Dunaújváros*)	III.57	*Aedes signorum/ principia*	Paulovics 1951.	
Matrica (*Százhalombatta*)	III.58	*Aedes signorum/ principia*	Kovács 1999b.	

(Continued)

	Catalogue Number	Denomination	Bibliography	Further Notes
Modrić	III.59	Mithraeum	Preloznik-Nestorovic 2018, 277.	
Municipium Iasorum (*Aquae Balissae*)	III.60	Silvanus sanctuary	Schejbal 2004, 110–111.	Partially excavated.
	III.61	Nymph sanctuaries	Schejbal 2004, 110–113.	Natural cavities have been transformed today into modern bath complexes.
Poetovio (*Ptuj*)	III.62	Jupiter sanctuary (?)	Jerala 2011, 80.	
	III.63	Nutrices sanctuary I	Jerala 2011, 80; Šašel Kos 2016.	Spodnja Hajdina area.
	III.64	Nutrices sanctuary II	Jerala 2011, 80; Preloznik-Nestorovic 2018, 278.	Panorama area
	III.65	Silvanus sanctuary	Jerala 2011, 80.	
	III.66	Liber Pater sanctuary	Jerala 2011, 80.	
	III.67	Mithraeum I	CIMRM 1487–1508.	Several small buildings were identified near the first Mithraeum. Their functionality is uncertain.
	III.68	Mithraeum II	CIMRM 1509–1577.	
	III.69	Mithraeum III	CIMRM 1578–1612.	
	III.70	Mithraeum IV (?)	Jerala 2011, 80; Preloznik-Nestorovic 2018, 281–282.	Uncertain context of the finds.
	III.72	Mithraeum V	Jerala 2011, 80.	
Rozanec-Crnomelj	III.73	Mithraeum	CIMRM 1481.	
Ruše	III.74	Mithraeum	Alföldy 1974, 181; Preloznik-Nestorovic 2018, 284–285.	Alföldy argued that the sanctuary was in the territory of Noricum.

(Continued)

	Catalogue Number	Denomination	Bibliography	Further Notes
Savaria (*Szombathely*)	III.75	Iseum	Sosztarits *et al.* 2013.	
	III.76	Mercurius sanctuary (?)	Buócz 1998; Scherrer 2003, 71; Kiss 2014.	
	III.77	Mithraeum	Kiss 2011.	
	III.78	Dolichenum	CCID 271; Vágási 2014, 28–29.	
Sárkeszi	III.79	Mithraeum	Fitz 1957; CIMRM 1809–1817.	
Scarbantia (*Sopron*)	III.80	Capitol temple	Fitz 1998, 64–65.	The building was partially revealed and preserved.
	III.81	Iseum	Mráv-Gabrieli 2011.	
	III.82	Nemeseion	Gömöri 2003, 89.	
Sirmium (*Sremska Mitrovica, Mitrowitz, Szávaszentdemeter*)	III.83	*Beneficiarii* station – sanctuary	Mirković 1991.	
Stix-Neusiedl	III.84	Mithraeum	CIMRM 1655–1662.	
Ulcisia Castra (*Szentendre*)	III.85	*Aedes signorum/ principia*	Visy 1988, 78; Gudea 2013, 506.	
Vetus Salina (*Adony*)	III.86	Dolichenum	CCID 185–192; Bánki 1981.	
Vindobona (*Wien, Vienna*)	III.87	*Aedes signorum/ principia*	Pohanka 1997, 48–49.	
Zgornja Pohanca	III.88	Mithraeum	Preloznik-Nestorovic 2018, 288.	

Archaeologically attested sanctuaries of Moesia Superior

	Catalogue Number	Denomination	Bibliography	Further Notes
Biljanovac (*Kumanovo*)	IV.1	Mithraeum	CIMRM 2201–2205.	
Castrum Novae (*Čezava*)	IV.2	*Aedes signorum/ principia* or Dolichenum	Korać *et al.* 2014, 76.	Gavrilović Vitas 2020a, 101 and 111 argued that in the *principia* there might be a Dolichenum.

(Continued)

	Catalogue Number	Denomination	Bibliography	Further Notes
Egeta (*Brza Palanka*)	IV.3	Dolichenum	CCID 88–97; Gavrilović Vitas 2020b.	The Dolichenum of Diana (Karataš) is questionable: CCID 87; Gavrilović Vitas 2018, 186.
Mediana (*Niš*)	IV.4	Asclepeion	Janković 2012, 34; Vasić 2018.	The archaeological context of the finds is uncertain. It could be a sanctuary from the 4/5th century.
Pojejena	IV.5	Mithraeum	Gudea-Bozu 1977.	The archaeological context of the finds is uncertain.
Ratiaria (*Archar, Vidin*)	IV.6	Diana sanctuary	Topalilov 2017, 292.	The archaeological context of the finds is uncertain.
Singidunum (*Beograd/Београд*)	IV.7	Hekate sanctuary		The archaeological context of the finds is uncertain.

Archaeologically attested sanctuaries of Moesia Inferior

	Catalogue Number	Denomination	Bibliography	Further Notes
Acbunar	V.1	Mithraeum	CIMRM 2288–2294.	
Brestnica (*Loveè region*)	V.2	Thracian hero sanctuary	Boteva 2007, 78.	
Butan (*Vratsa region*)	V.3	Silvanus sanctuary	Hristov 2016.	The building was not excavated, only identified on field by Hristov.
Dionysopolis (*Balchik, Durankulak*)	V.4	Magna Mater/Pontic Mother goddess sanctuary	Lazarenko *et al.* 2013.	The temple shows a continuity from Hellenistic times until the end of the Principate.
Draganovec (*Tãrgoviste region*)	V.5	Thracian hero sanctuary	Boteva 2007, 78.	
Glava Panega (*Loveè region*)	V.6	Asclepeion-'Thracian Riders'	Dimitrova 2002, 219; Boteva 2007, 78.	Some authors argued that the locality was in Thracia.

(Continued)

	Catalogue Number	Denomination	Bibliography	Further Notes
Kreta (*Nikopol area*)	V.7	Mithraeum	CIMRM 2256–2262.	
Lilyache (*Vratsa region*)	V.8	Silvanus sanctuary	Hristov 2016, 133.	Published in the 1950s. Hristov argued that another sanctuary might also be attested in Lehchevo.
Ljublen (*Tãrgoviste region*)	V.9	Sanctuary of the Thracian Hero	Boteva 2007, 78.	
Mejdenska chuka (*Skalsko*)	V.10	*Spaeleum*	Hristov-Barakov 2003.	
Montana (*Kaleto*)	V.11	Sanctuary	Ivanov-Luka 2016, 85–93, 97.	The sanctuary was associated with several divinities (spring cult, Apollo-Diana). It was in continuous use during the pre-Roman and Roman period.
Novae (*Svishtov*)	V.12	*Aedes signorum/ principia*	Sarnowski 1992; Gudea 2005, 420–421; Sarnowski *et al.* 2014.	
	V.13	Mithraeum	CIMRM 2267–2271; Tomas-Lemke 2015; Tomas 2017, 57–60.	
	V.14	Liber Pater sanctuary	Tomas 2015; Tomas 2017, 80–81.	The sanctuary was poorly researched, although the building and the finds clearly suggest a sacralised space.
	V.15	Asclepeion/ *valetudinarium*	Dyczek-Kolendo 2010.	
Oescus (*Pleven*)	V.16–18	Capitolium (I–III)	Kabakchieva 2014, 187.	Three different buildings dedicated to the Capitoline triad.
	V.19	Fortuna temple	Kabakchieva 2014, 187.	
Paskalevec (*Veliko Tãrnovo*)	V.20	Sanctuary of Thracian Hero	Boteva 2007, 78.	

(Continued)

	Catalogue Number	*Denomination*	*Bibliography*	*Further Notes*
Plăstina (*Tărgoviste region*)	V.21	Sanctuary of Thracian Hero	Boteva 2007, 78.	
Sexaginta Prista (*Ruse*)	V.22	Sanctuary (Apollo-Thracian Rider)	Stancev 2006; Varbanov 2013.	Continuity of the sacralised space from pre-Roman to Roman times is attested.
Sostra (*Lomec*)	V.23	*Aedes signorum/ principia*	Eck-Ivanov 2009, 199.	
	V.24	Sanctuary of the so-called 'Thracian Riders'	Hristov *et al.* 2013.	
Târguşor (*Adam's cave*)	V.25	Mithraeum	CIMRM 2303–2306.	
Telerig (*Dobrich*)	V.26	Sanctuary of Hephaestus Dabatopios	Kamenou-Dimitrova 2018.	Continuity of the sanctuary from the 6th century BC until the 4th century AD.
Trănèovica (*Pleven region*)	V.27	Sanctuary of Thracian Hero	Boteva 2007, 78.	
Trimammium (*Stalpishte, Mechka*)	V.28	Rock sanctuary of Thracian Hero	Torbatov 2012, 433–436.	

Archaeologically attested sanctuaries of Dacia

	Catalogue Number	*Denomination*	*Bibliography*	*Further Notes*
Alburnus Maior (*Roşia Montană, Verespatak*)	VI.1	Sanctuary of the kastellum Ansium	See also: Wollmann 1985 –1986, 253–294; Damian *et al.* 2003, 147–190; Szabó 2015 (2020), 277–278.	
	VI.2	Sanctuary of the kastellum Baridustarum/ Galatians?	Damian *et al.* 2003, 253–263; Nemeti 2005, 249–252; Szabó 2015 (2020), 278.	
	VI.3	Sanctuary of the Genius of *collegium sardeatum*	Damian *et al.* 2003, 285–333; Diaconescu 2011,162–167; Szabó 2015 (2020), 278.	
	VI.4	Sanctuary of the Delmatae	Damian *et al.* 2003, 285–333; Diaconescu 2011, 162–167; Szabó 2015 (2020), 278–279.	

(Continued)

	Catalogue Number	*Denomination*	*Bibliography*	*Further Notes*
Apulum (*Alba Iulia, Gyulafehérvár, Karlsburg*)	VI.5	*Aedes signorum/ principia*	Szabó 2015 (2020), 281–282.	
	VI.6	Liber Pater shrine	Szabó 2015 (2020), 282; Szabó 2018b, 78–89.	
	VI.7	Mithraeum	Szabó 2015 (2020), 282–283; McCarty *et al.* 2020.	
	VI.8	*Praetorium consularis*	Szabó 2015 (2020), 283–284; Bolindeț *et al.* 2011	
Arcobadara (*Arcobara?, Ilișua, Alsókosály*)	VI.9	*Aedes signorum/ principia*	Marcu 2009, 78–80; Szabó 2015 (2020), 285.	
Buciumi (*Vármező*)	VI.10	*Aedes signorum/ principia*	Marcu 2009, 38–40; Szabó 2015 (2020), 285.	
Călugăreni (*Mikháza*)	VI.11	*Aedes signorum/ principia*	Szabó 2015 (2020), 285–286.	
Câmpulung-Jidova	VI.12	*Aedes signorum/ principia*	Marcu 2009, 197–198; Szabó 2015 (2020), 286–287.	
Cigmău (*Csigmó*)	VI.13	*Aedes signorum/ principia*	Marcu 2009, 122–126; Szabó 2015 (2020), 287.	
Cumidava (*Râșnov, Barcarozsnyó, Rosenau*)	VI.14	*Aedes signorum/ principia*	Marcu 2009, 218–220; Szabó 2015 (2020), 287.	
Decea Mureșului (*Marosdécse*)	VI.15	Mithraeum	Sicoe 2014, 168: cat. nos 59–61; Szabó 2015 (2020), 287.	
Drobeta (*Drobeta Turnu-Severin, Szörénytornya, Szörényvár*)	VI.16	*Aedes signorum/ principia*	Marcu 2009, 129–133; Szabó 2015 (2020), 288.	
Germisara (*Geoagiu-Băi, Feredőgyógy, Algyógy, Gergesdorf*)	VI.17	Nymphaeum/healing sanctuary	Pescaru-Alicu 2000, 65–74; Szabó 2015 (2020), 288.	
Gilău (*Gyalu, Julmarkt*)	VI.18	*Aedes signorum/ principia*	Marcu 2009, 71–73; Szabó 2015 (2020), 289–290.	

(Continued)

	Catalogue Number	Denomination	Bibliography	Further Notes
Inlăceni (*Énlaka*)	VI.19	*Aedes signorum/ principia*	Marcu 2009, 140–141; Szabó 2015 (2020), 290.	
Micia (*Vețel, Vecel*)	VI.20	Sanctuary of the Commagenian group /Sanctuary of Jupiter Hierapolitanus	Nemeti 2005, 242; Szabó 2015 (2020), 290–291.	
	VI.21	*Templum Dii Patrii Maurorum*	Szabó 2015 (2020), 291–292.	
Porolissum (*Moigrad, Mojgrád*)	VI.22	*Aedes signorum/ principia*	Marcu 2009, 88–91; Szabó 2015 (2020), 293.	
	VI.23	Dolichenum	Gudea-Tamba 2001; Szabó 2015 (2020), 293.	
	VI.24	Templum of Bel/ Palmyrian assembly house	Szabó 2015 (2020), 294.	
	VI.25a	Nemeseion	Szabó 2015 (2020), 294.	
	VI.25b	Sanctuary of the Genius *portorii Illyric*	Gudea 1996; Piso *et al.* 2016.	
Potaissa (*Turda, Torda, Thorenburg*)	VI.26	Aedes signorum/ Principia	Szabó 2015 (2020), 295.	
	VI.27	Sanctuary of Jupiter / Capitolium?	Szabó 2015 (2020), 296.	
Praetorium (*Mehadia, Mehádia, Miháld*)	VI.28	Dolichenum	Benea 2008; Szabó 2015 (2020), 296.	
Racovița (*Jud. Vâlcea, Copăceni, Praetorium?*)	VI.29	*Aedes signorum/ principia*	Szabó 2015 (2020), 296–297.	
Răcari (*Jud. Dolj, Răcari de Jos*)	VI.30	*Aedes signorum/ principia*	Marcu 2009, 217–218; Szabó 2015 (2020), 297.	
Resculum (*Jud. Cluj, Bologa, Sebesvár*)	VI.31	*Aedes signorum/ principia*	Marcu 2009, 28–29; Szabó 2015 (2020), 297.	
Samum (*Jud. Cluj, Ad Samum, Cășeiu, Alsókosály*)	VI.32	*Aedes signorum/ principia*	Marcu 2009, 54–56; Szabó 2015 (2020), 298.	
Sănpaul (*Jud. Cluj, Magyarszentpál*)	VI.55	Silvanus sanctuary	Cupcea *et al.* 2019.	

(Continued)

	Catalogue Number	*Denomination*	*Bibliography*	*Further Notes*
	VI.33	Sacralised spaces in the Forum Vetus	Étienne/Diaconescu/Piso 2006, 143–152; Szabó 2015 (2020), 299.	
	VI.34	Area Sacra in Domus Procuratoris	Schäfer 2007, 245–272, 398–399; Kat. H XII; Szabó 2015 (2020), 299.	
	VI.35	Asclepeion	Schäfer 2007, 64–69, 145–158, 374–376; Szabó 2015 (2020), 300.	
	VI.36	Capitolium	Piso *et al.* 2012; Szabó 2015 (2020), 301.	
	VI.37	Sanctuary of *Domnus et Domna*	Fiedler/Höpken 2010; Szabó 2015 (2020), 302.	
	VI.38	Sanctuary EM 16	Szabó forthcoming: cat. no. I.38; Schäfer 2007, 243–244.	
	VI.39	Sanctuary EM 17	Schäfer 2007, 244; Szabó 2015 (2020), 302.	
Sarmizegetusa (*Jud. Hunedoara, Colonia Sarmizegetusa, Várhely*)	VI.40	Sanctuary EM 18 or the 'Great Temple'	Schäfer 2007, 156–159; Szabó 2015 (2020), 302.	
	VI.41	Sanctuary EM 24	Pescaru-Alicu 2000,104–109; Szabó 2015 (2020), 303.	
	VI.42	Liber Pater and Silvanus sanctuary	Schäfer 2007, 175–190; Szabó 2015 (2020), 303.	
	VI.43	Mithraeum	Király 1886; Szabó 2015 (2020), 304.	
	VI.44	Nemeseion	Schäfer 2007, 163–173; Szabó 2015 (2020), 304.	
	VI.45	Nymphaeum	Bota-Diaconescu 2003; Szabó 2015 (2020), 305.	
	VI.46	Palmyrene sanctuary	Piso-Țentea 2011; Szabó 2015 (2020), 305; Țentea-Olteanu 2020.	
	VI.47	Templum of the Paternal Gods of the Palmyrian tribe of Bene Agrud	Schäfer 2007, 85–93; Szabó 2015 (2020), 306.	
	VI.48	Sanctuary of Silvanus	Pescaru-Alicu 2000, 119–122; Szabó 2015 (2020), 306.	

(Continued)

	Catalogue Number	Denomination	Bibliography	Further Notes
Slăveni (*Jud. Dolj*)	VI.49	*Aedes signorum/ principia*	Marcu 2009, 229–230; Szabó 2015 (2020), 307	
	VI.50	Mithraeum	Petolescu 1976; Szabó 2015 (2020), 307.	
Tibiscum (*Jud. Caraş-Severin, Jupa, Zsuppa/Iaz-Obreja, Obrézsa*)	VI.51	*Aedes signorum/ principia*	Marcu 2009, 162–165; Szabó 2015 (2020), 307–308.	
	VI.52	*Schola* or dining room /Palmyrene sanctuary	Marcu 2009, 168–170; Szabó 2015 (2020), 308.	
	VI.53	*Fanum* of Apollo	Boda-Timoc 2016; Szabó 2015 (2020), 309.	
Vărădia (*Jud. Caraş Severin, Arcidava?*)	VI.54	*Aedes signorum/ principia*	Marcu 2009, 172–173; Szabó 2015 (2020), 309.	

2. Divinities in the Danubian provinces

One of the most relevant – and nowadays, often ignored – aspect of religious communication in the Roman Empire was the divine agencies, commonly known as gods. Evoking the divine agency in macro- meso- and micro-spaces can be attested especially through epigraphic sources, where in most cases, the divine agent is named, often with special epithets. Analysing the names of the gods was a popular research topic in particular in Roman provincial archaeology in the late 19th and early 20th centuries. However, recent trends have opened new perspectives in the analysis of theonyms and their complex role in religious communication, space sacralisation and sociology of religion.[4] Using the names of gods in conjunction with several local and specific, occasional or regional epithets reveals the living and dynamic, constantly changing aspect of religious communication, where bricolage, appropriation and religious individuation were often used as successful strategies to address the divine agencies.

The seven Danubian provinces presented in this book produced in less than three centuries more than 5,700 votive inscriptions[5] naming over 260 divine agents (gods, *genii*, personifications). Many of these divinities are the enduring and most striking evidence of the pre-Roman religious heritage that was reinterpreted and reappropriated numerous times and in various forms during the Principate. The large number of special epithets for divinities, especially in provinces where the pre-Roman, indigenous population can be attested after the Roman conquest (Raetia, Noricum, Pannoniae, Moesia Inferior) shows the dynamic and complex social and religious interactions between the old and new groups who were living together. This list is the result of the analysis of all the 5,724 votive inscriptions available in contemporary digital epigraphic databases. Divinities attested only in non-epigraphic (figurative) monuments are not included. Most of the divine figures attested are present in multiple provinces, and some of them – Jupiter Optimus Maximus, Hercules, Mithras, Silvanus, Apollo, Diana, Fortuna, Nemesis, Dolichenus, Mars, Isis, Iuno – are attested in all the Danubian provinces. There are few divinities, however, which were attested only in one province or even more curiously, on a single known epigraphic monument.

In the following list of divinities, I present only the major divine figures attested in the seven provinces without their numerous epithets. The geographic and social analysis of their epithets will be the topic of future research. A glossary and a much more detailed presentation of all the divine names attested in epigraphic sources is available on the webpage of the project.[6] In the diagrams (Appendix 3), I provide a detailed analysis of the rich material presented below, focusing on divinities and their geographic and chronological distribution.

Name of divinity	*Raetia*	*Noricum*	*Pannonia Superior*	*Pannonia Inferior*	*Moesia Superior*	*Moesia Inferior*	*Dacia*
Acheloos							
Aecorna			2				
Aeracura			1				1
Adonis				1			
Adrastia							1
Adsalluta-Savus		7	2				
Aesculapius et Hygeia		3	8	11	3	16	64
Alounae		3					
Antinoos			1 (?)		1		
Apio Dalmatarum							1
Apollo	2	3	8	3	4	32	27
Apollo Auluzelus						1	
Apollo Grannus	7	2					2
Apollo Pirunenos							1
Aquila			1				
Aquo		1					
Artavis							1
Ata					1		
Atrans		1					
Azizos				1			1
Badones Reginae							1
Baltis			4				

(Continued)

Name of divinity	*Raetia*	*Noricum*	*Pannonia Superior*	*Pannonia Inferior*	*Moesia Superior*	*Moesia Inferior*	*Dacia*
Bedaius		4					
Belenus		3					
Belestis		3					
Bellona					1		
Bona Dea				2			
Bonus Eventus			4	1	1	6	
Bonus Puer							11
Caelestis				1			6
Campestris	1	2	3	1			
Capricornus		1					
Casebonus					1		
Castor		1					3
Casuotanus		1					
Ceres		1	4		2	3	4
Clio					1		
Concordia				1		1	2
Core							1
Dacia							3
Danuvius	3		1	3			
Dea Coryphea			1				
Dea Dardanica					2		1
Dea Orcia					1		
Dea Silvestris					1		
Dea Syria				2	2		4
Dea Vagdavercus				1			
Deus Aeternus			3	3	1	9	21
Deus Andinus					1		
Deus Arimanius				2			
Deus Assallacanus						1	
Deus Attonipal						1	
Deus Dobrates				1			
Deus Harcecius	2						
Deus Mundritus					1		
Deus Saromandus							1
Deus Totovitio						1	

(Continued)

Name of divinity	*Raetia*	*Noricum*	*Pannonia Supericr*	*Pannonia Inferior*	*Moesia Superior*	*Moesia Inferior*	*Dacia*
Deus Zbelsurdos					2		1
Diana	4	3	26	9	10	44	50
Diana Germetitha						1	
Diana Plestrens						1	
Diana Scoptitia						1	
Diana Tifatina				1			
Diana Totobisia						1	
Dii Conservatorii				1			
Dii Maximii	1						
Diis Propitiis							1
Dinithias						1	
Dis Angelis					1		1
Dis Auguralis			1				
Dis Dauadis							2
Dis Deabusque				10			
Dis Immortalibus							1
Dis Itineraris-Itunae et Ituno			2				
Dis Magnis				5			
Dis Maioribus			1			1	
Dis Militarii				2		1	
Dis Omnibus				1			
Dis Pater et Proserpina	2		1	3	1		8
Dis Patris Manapho et Theandrino			1				
Dis Reducibus				1			
Dis Salutaris					1		
Diti Sertius		1					
Domnus et Domna (Danubian rider)			2	1	2	3	6
Dracones					1		
Dravus			1				
Epona	3	6	1	5	2	1	7
Eros			1				
Fates		1	3				

(Cont nued)

Name of divinity	Raetia	Noricum	Pannonia Superior	Pannonia Inferior	Moesia Superior	Moesia Inferior	Dacia
Fons			3				
Fortuna	8	8	21	7	4	1	29
Fortuna Conservatoris				1			
Fortuna Karnuntina			1				
Fortuna Redux				1			
Fortuna Salutaris				1			
Fulgur conditum			2				
Genius	8	32	36	16	10	9	33
Ghesanis							1
Glykon							2
Gontia	1						
Harmogius			1				
Hekate		1			2	3	5
Hephaestus Dabatopios						1	
Hercules	4	26	29	21	15	17	54
Hercules Illyricum				1			
Hercules Magusanus			1			1	4
Honor			1				
Ianus							1
Ianus Geminus		2					3
Iarhibol							5
Jupiter Eraviscus				1			
IOM	22	77	287	274	81	96	246
IOM and Capitoline triad	3	3	8	20	9	4	13
IOM et Celeia et Noricum		2					
IOM et centeris/ dis deabusque	6		12		9	7	15
IOM et Iuno			15			39	14
IOM Ammon			1				1
IOM Appenninus							1
IOM Arubianus		2		1			
IOM Balmarcodes							1
IOM Brigetionis			1				

(Continued)

Name of divinity	*Raetia*	*Noricum*	*Pannonia Superior*	*Pannonia Inferior*	*Moesia Superior*	*Moesia Inferior*	*Dacia*
IOM Bussumarius			1				2
IOM Bussurigius							1
IOM Cimistenus							2
IOM Culminalis			7	3			
IOM Depulsor		6	11	1	2	1	6
IOM Dolichenus	5	48	38	19	18	23	41
IOM Erusenus							1
IOM Exusperantissimus							1
IOM Fulgurator					3		4
IOM Fulminator			3	2			
IOM Heliopolitanus	1		8	1			3
IOM Hierapolitanus							1
IOM Karnuntinus			36				
IOM Melanus					2		
IOM Melcid					1		
IOM Narenos							1
IOM Nundinarius			1				
IOM Olbiopolitanus						1	
IOM Paternus				2	17	1	
IOM Salutaris				1			
IOM Stator							2
IOM Tavianus			1				2
IOM Teutanus			1	29			
IOM Uxlemitanus		1					
Isis	2	2	11	1	1	1	11
Iuno	5	8	7	21	2	1	10
Iuno Populonia							1
Iuno Semlia							1
Laburo			1				
Lares	1	1	4	4	1		
Larunda	1						
Leto						1	1
Liber Pater	1	1	22	37	7	16	51
Luna		1	2			1	
Luna Lucifera							1

(Continued)

Name of divinity	*Raetia*	*Noricum*	*Pannonia Superior*	*Pannonia Inferior*	*Moesia Superior*	*Moesia Inferior*	*Dacia*
Lux			1				
Magna Mater		2	13		1	5	10
Magula			1				
Maia	1						
Malagbel							10
Marimogius			2				
Marmogius		2	1				
Mars	19	7	12	13	6	5	17
Mars et Victoria	5	1					
Mars Gradivus				1			2
Mars Latobius		7					
Mars Toutatis							1
Mars Ultor						1	
Matres	1		1	1			1
Melantonio							1
Men							1
Mercurius	39	5	24	4	3	4	20
Mercurius Censualis	1						
Mercurius Cimicianus	1						
Mercurius Cissonius	1						
Mibricus		2					
Minerva	6	4	7	9	1	3	15
Minerva Supera							1
Mithras	8	51	135	85	22	32	113
Naon							1
Nemesis	1	12	26	10	7	4	35
Neptunus	1	3	9	6	2		5
Nix	1	2	6				
Nocturnus			2				
Noreia	1	8					
Numen Maiestatis				1			
Nundina			1				
Nutrices		1	24				
Nymphs		11	42	3	2	2	20
Obila							1

(Continued)

Name of divinity	*Raetia*	*Noricum*	*Pannonia Superior*	*Pannonia Inferior*	*Moesia Superior*	*Moesia Inferior*	*Dacia*
Omphale					1		
Orcus				1			
Osiris			1				
Parcae	2		4				
Pastores	1						
Pax				1			
Penates							2
Pietas	1						
Pluto	1					3	1
Pollux			1				
Porobonus						2	
Priapus				1			
Primavera							1
Providentia							1
Quadriviae/Triviae	1	1	11		1	4	5
Rhenus	1						
Roma	2						
Rosmerta		1					
Sabasios						3	2
Salus			2	1			1
Saturnus	1		1				3
Savercna			1				
Saxanus		2	1				
Sedatus	1	1	2		1		
Sedes Augusta				1			
Senabus		1					
Serapis		2	12	2	3	6	11
Sideri							1
Signum cohortis				1			
Silvana			5				
Silvanus	4	4	107	30	6	16	39
Silvanus Anticessor				2			
Silvanus Augustus				4			
Silvanus Bellator				1			
Silvanus Conservatoris				1			

(Continued)

Name of divinity	*Raetia*	*Noricum*	*Pannonia Superior*	*Pannonia Inferior*	*Moesia Superior*	*Moesia Inferior*	*Dacia*
Silvanus Deus Pantheus				1			
Silvanus Domesticus			103	30	1		60
Silvanus Herbarius				1			
Silvanus Karnuntinus			1				
Silvanus Magnus			1	4			
Silvanus Silvestris			15	25	1		6
Silvanus Viator			3	3			
Sirona			2				
Sol	3	1	1	1		3	4
Sol Elagabalus	1		2	10			
Sol Invictus	1						2
Sol Socius				3			
Somnus				1	1		
Soranus							1
Spes	4						
Sphinx			2	1			
Sucellus							1
Sulevia	1	1		1			2
Telesphorus				1			
Terminus		2					
Terra Mater			2	7			10
Teurnia		1					
Thracian Rider (Heros)		1			7	40	2
Turmazgades							3
Urbs Roma				2		2	
Venus			4	1	1		7
Vibes		1					
Victoria	3	13	14	2	2	1	8
Vidaso et Thanae			3				
Virtus		1		1			3
Vocretanus		3					
Vulcanus	2	4	6	1	1		4
Zmaragdus							1

3. Diagrams[7]

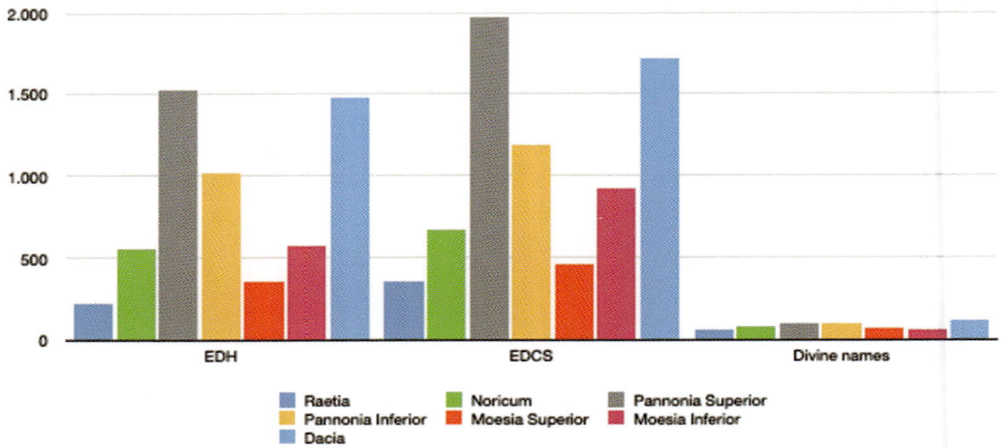

	Raetia	Noricum	Pannonia Superior	Pannonia Inferior	Moesia Superior	Moesia Inferior	Dacia
EDH	223	553	1.524	1.014	354	578	1.478
EDCS	352	667	1.970	1.186	455	918	1.711
Divine names	56	72	98	97	63	60	111

Fig. A1 Votive inscriptions in the Danubian provinces: a holistic analysis from the EDH and EDCS databases.

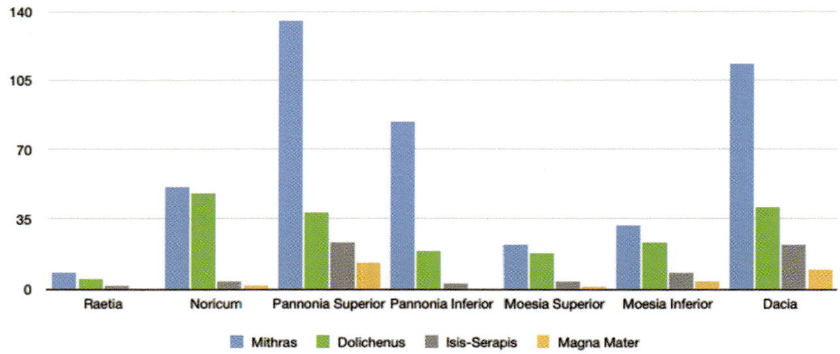

	Mithras	Dolichenus	Isis-Serapis	Magna Mater
Raetia	8	5	2	0
Noricum	51	48	4	2
Pannonia Superior	135	38	23	13
Pannonia Inferior	84	19	3	0
Moesia Superior	22	18	4	1
Moesia Inferior	32	23	8	4
Dacia	113	41	22	10

Fig. A2 Distribution of votive inscriptions dedicated to the mystery cults and small-group religions in the Danubian provinces.

Viminacium	59
Scupi	24
Ratiaria	23
Ulpiana	16
Naissus	30
M.Margum	4
Horreum Margi	0
Singidunum	36
Dardanorum	1
Celegerorum	0
Aureus Mons	0
Histria	33
Tomis	83
Callatis	7
Troesmis	20
Nicopolis ad Istrum	32
Noviodunum	9
Durostorum	16
Novae	114
Tropaeum Traiani	26
Oescus	31
Napoca	41
Romula	18
Apulum	443
Sarmizegetusa	265
Potaissa	109
Porolissum	23
Dierna	6
Ampelum	60
Tibiscum	25

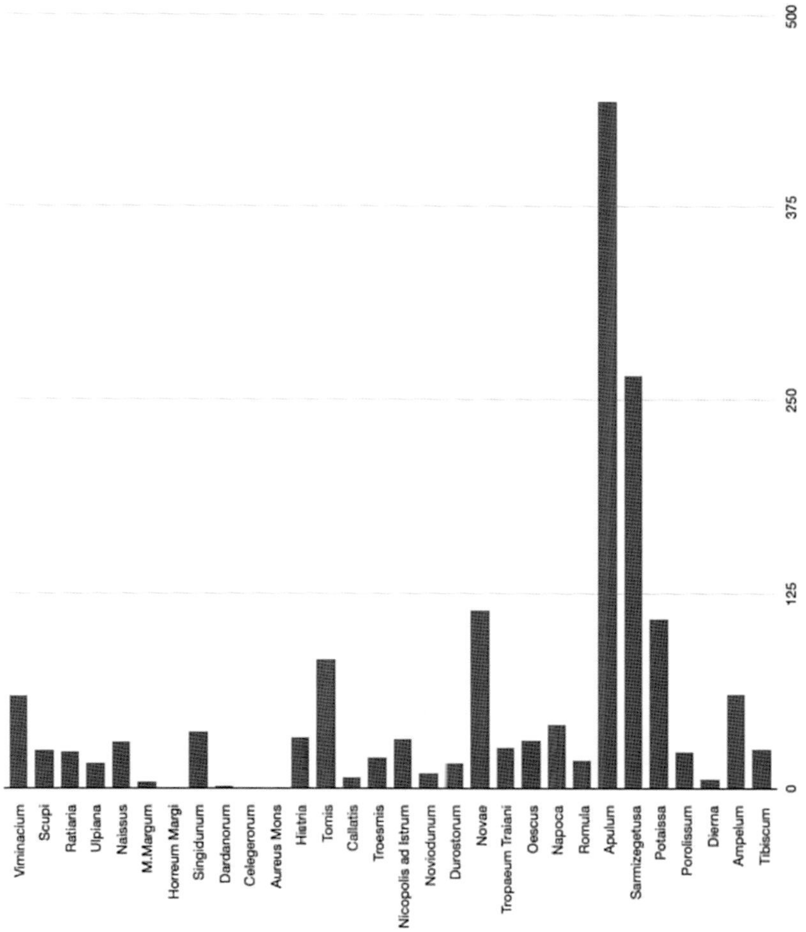

Fig. A3 Distribution of votive inscriptions in the urban settlements (municipia, colonia) of the Danubian provinces.

Augusta Vindelicorum	33
Virunum	144
Celeia	86
Aguntum	3
Teurnia	33
Iuvavum	28
Flavia Solva	48
Cetium	8
Ovilava	6
Lauriacum	57
Neviodunum	30
Andautonia	5
Savaria	84
Siscia	50
Sirmium	117
Scarbantia	38
Poetovio	182
Carnuntum	615
Aquincum	578
Cibalae	5
Bassiana	17
Mogentiana	18
Mursella	0
Salla	11
Brigetio	150
Vindobona	33
Sopianae	20
Iovia	2
M. Iasorum	4
M. Faustinianum	0

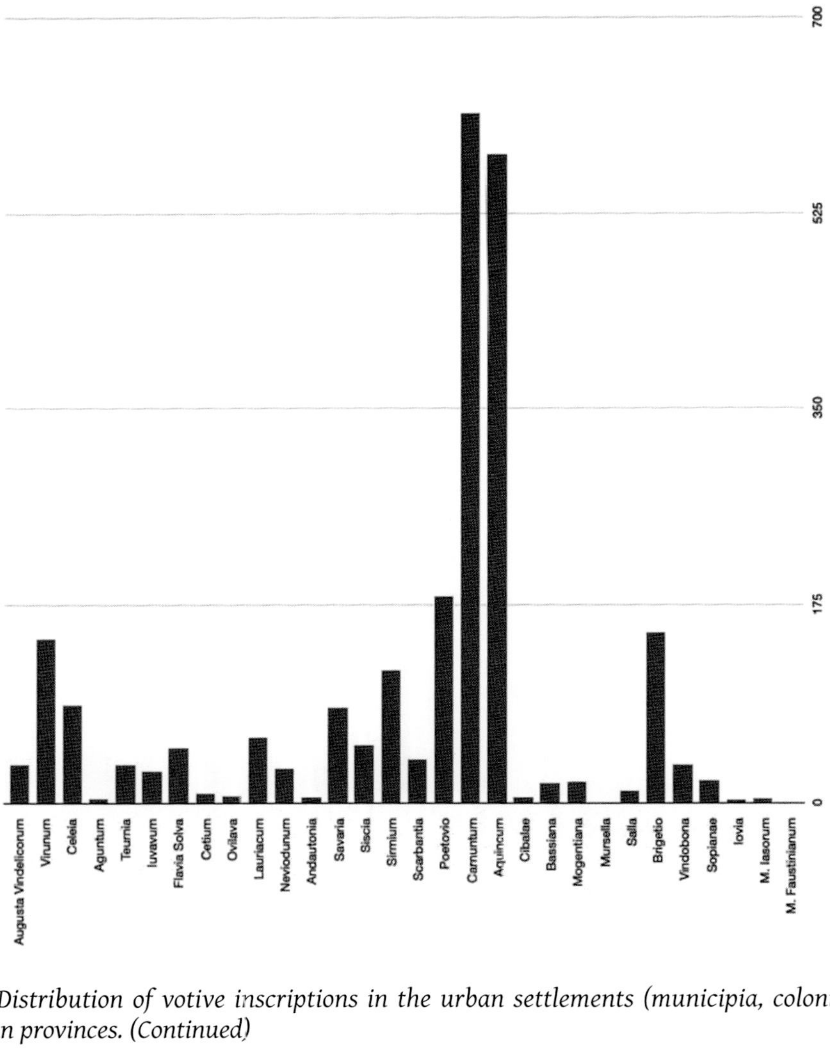

Fig. A3 Distribution of votive inscriptions in the urban settlements (municipia, colonia) of the Danubian provinces. (Continued)

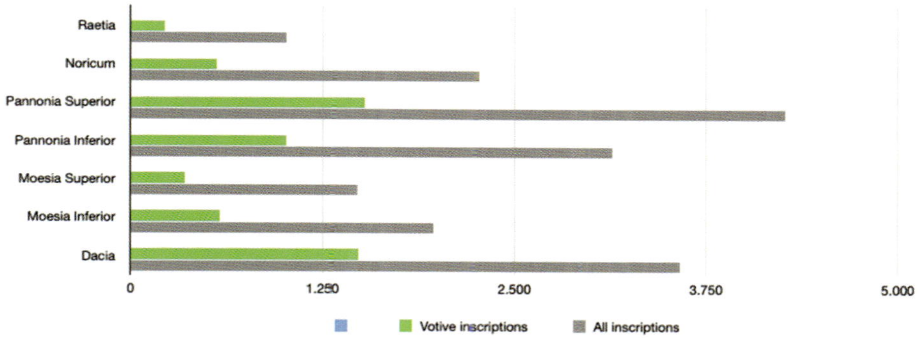

	Votive inscriptions	All inscriptions
Raetia	223	1.012
Noricum	562	2.272
Pannonia Superior	1.524	4.259
Pannonia Inferior	1.015	3.135
Moesia Superior	354	1.476
Moesia Inferior	579	1.973
Dacia	1.482	3.582

Fig. A4 Comparative analysis of votive and all inscriptions attested in the Danubian provinces (based on the EDH database).

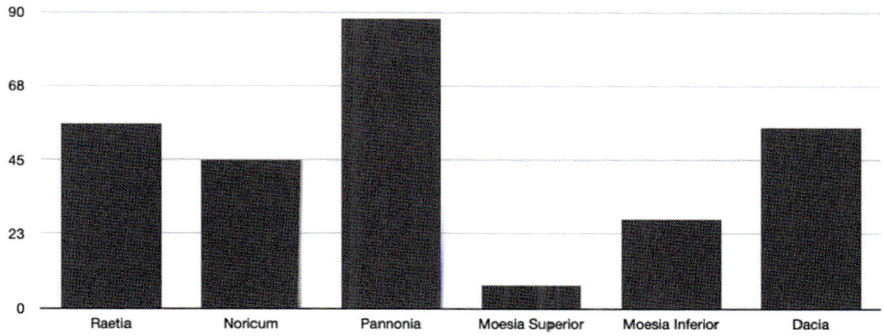

Raetia	56
Noricum	45
Pannonia	88
Moesia Superior	7
Moesia Inferior	27
Dacia	55

Fig. A5 Number of sacralised spaces in macro- and meso-spaces in the Danubian provinces.

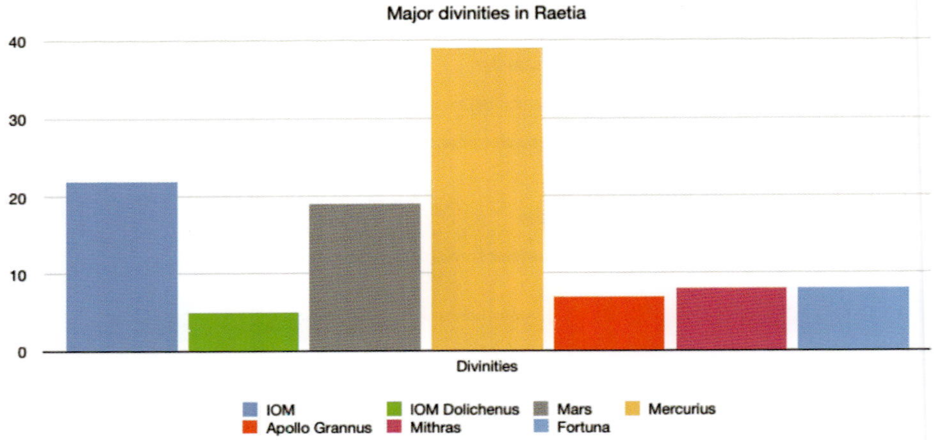

Fig. A6 Major divinities in the province of Raetia.

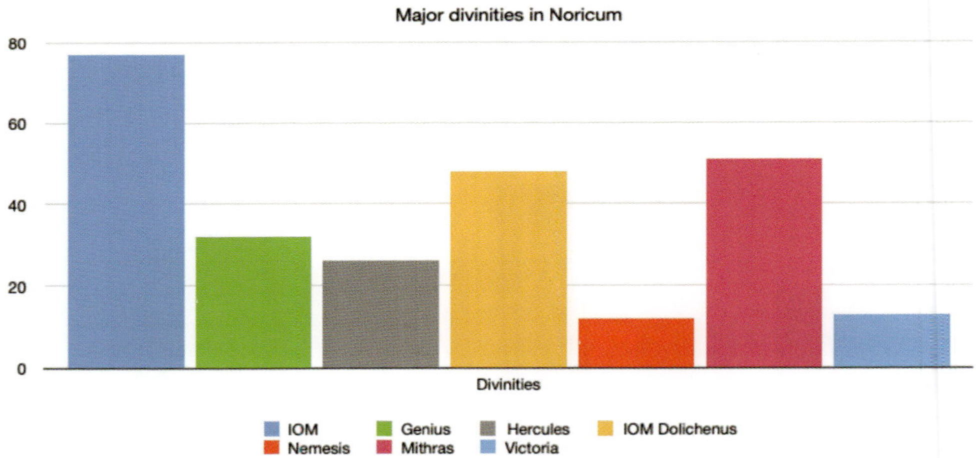

Fig. A7 Major divinities in the province of Noricum.

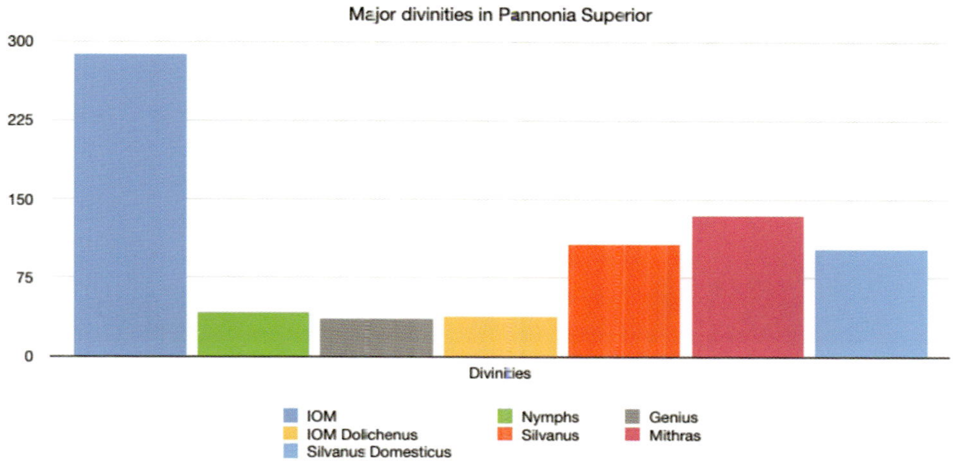

Fig. A8 Major divinities in the province of Pannonia Superior.

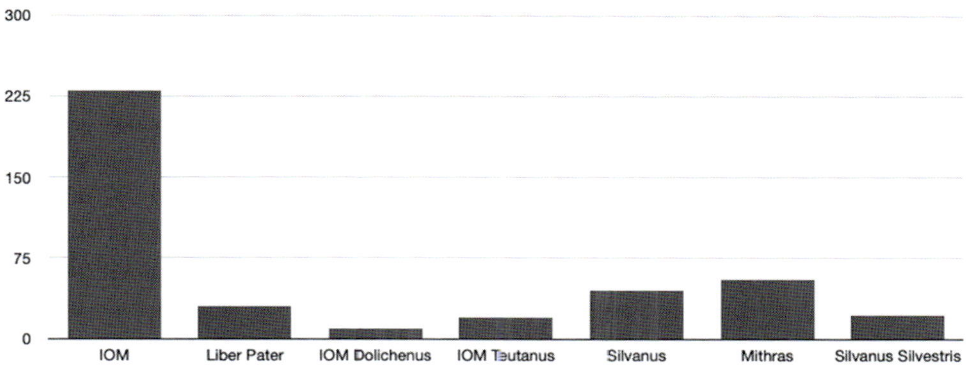

Fig. A9 Major divinities in the province of Pannonia Inferior.

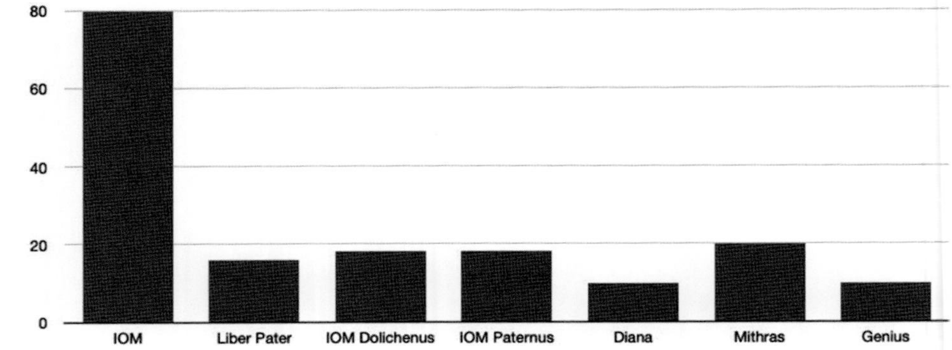

Fig. A10 Major divinities in the province of Moesia Superior.

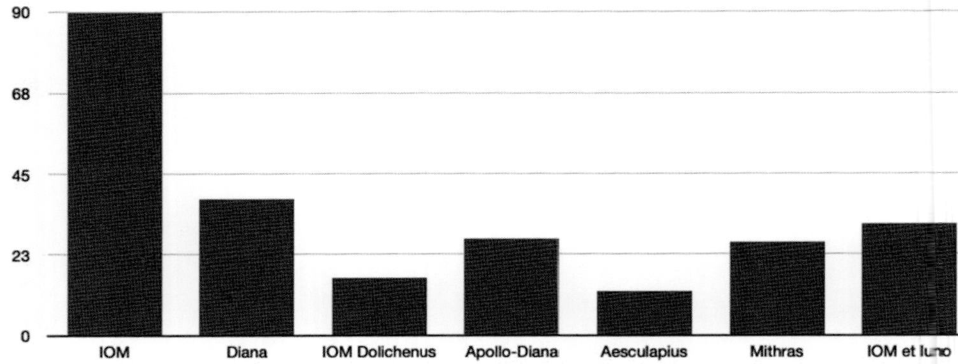

Fig. A11 Major divinities in the province of Moesia Inferior.

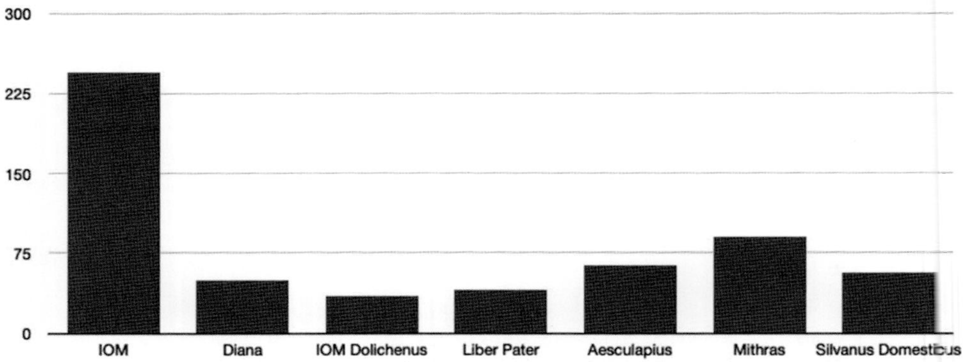

Fig. A12 Major divinities in the province of Dacia.

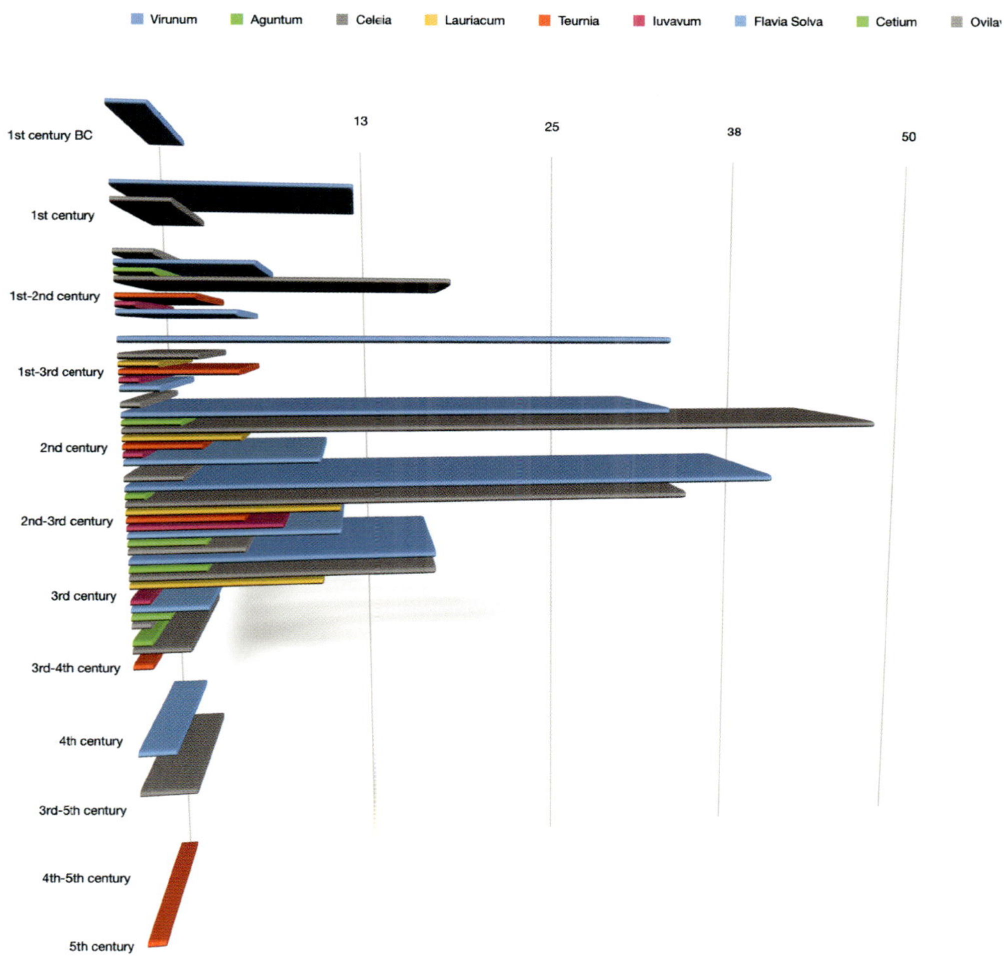

Fig. A13 Chronology of inscriptions from Noricum.

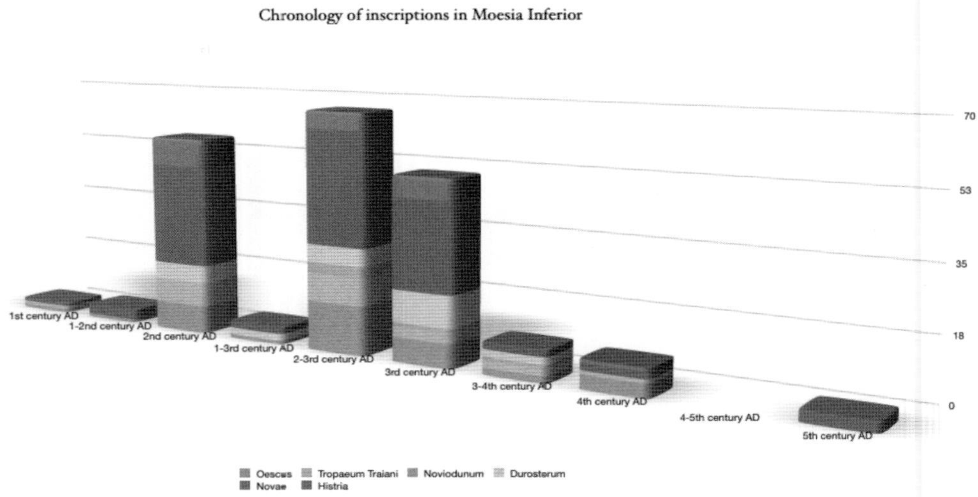

Fig. A14 Chronology of Latin inscriptions from Moesia Inferior.

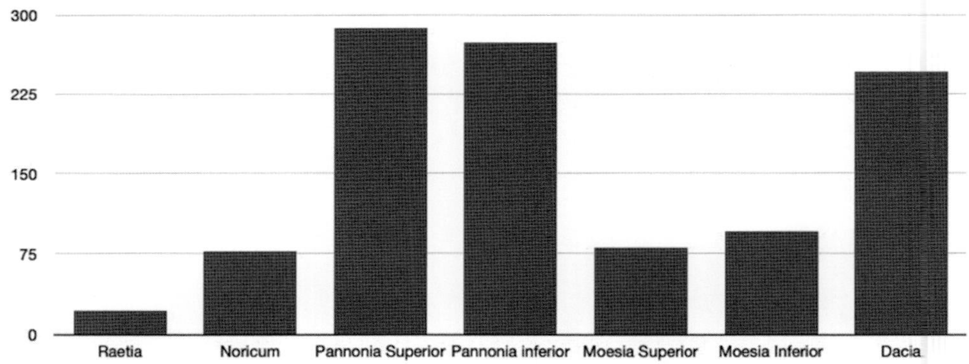

Raetia	22
Noricum	77
Pannonia Superior	287
Pannonia inferior	274
Moesia Superior	81
Moesia Inferior	96
Dacia	246

Fig. A15 Distribution of inscriptions dedicated to Jupiter Optimus Maximus.

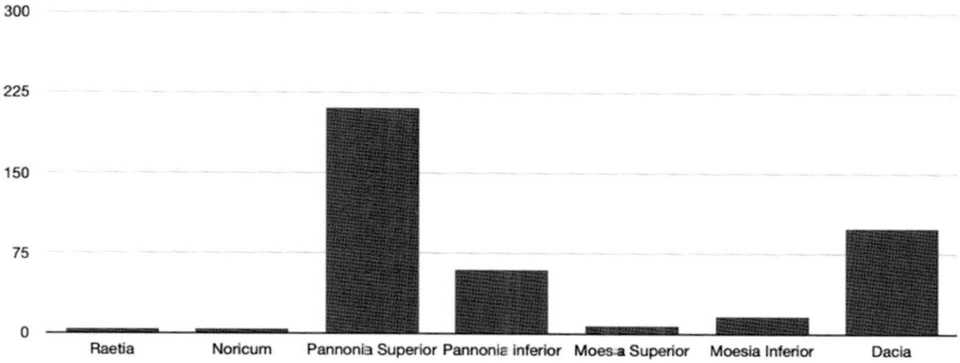

Raetia	4
Noricum	4
Pannonia Superior	210
Pannonia inferior	60
Moesia Superior	7
Moesia Inferior	16
Dacia	99

Fig. A16 Distribution of inscriptions dedicated to Silvanus.

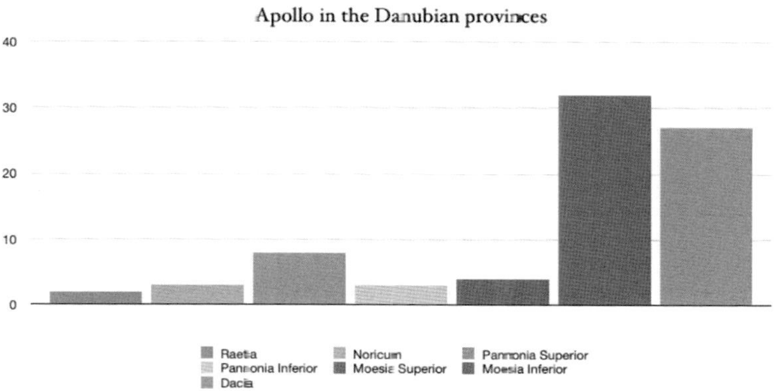

Raetia	Noricum	Pannonia Superior	Pannonia Inferior	Moesia Superior	Moesia Inferior	Dacia
2	3	8	3	4	32	27

Fig. A17 Distribution of inscriptions dedicated to Apollo.

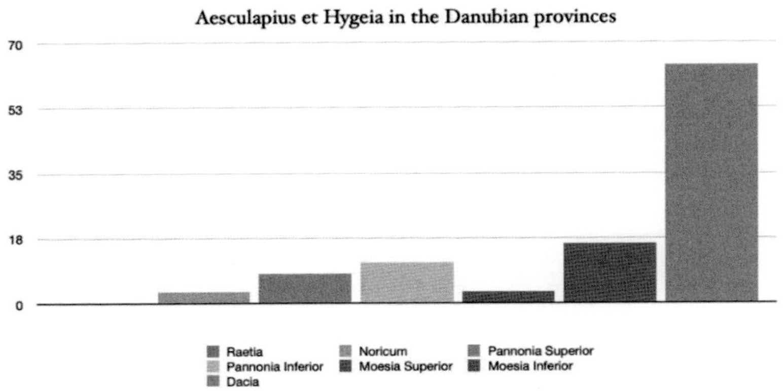

Raetia	Noricum	Pannonia Superior	Pannonia Inferior	Moesia Superior	Moesia Inferior	Dacia
0	3	8	11	3	16	64

Fig. A18 Distribution of inscriptions dedicated to Asclepius.

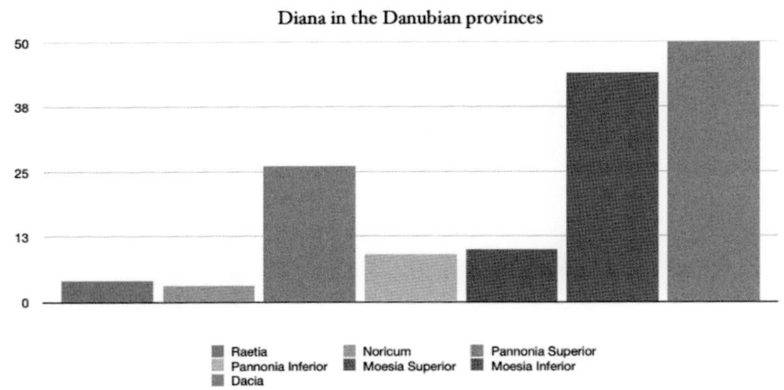

Raetia	Noricum	Pannonia Superior	Pannonia Inferior	Moesia Superior	Moesia Inferior	Dacia
4	3	26	9	10	44	50

Fig. A19 Distribution of inscriptions dedicated to Diana.

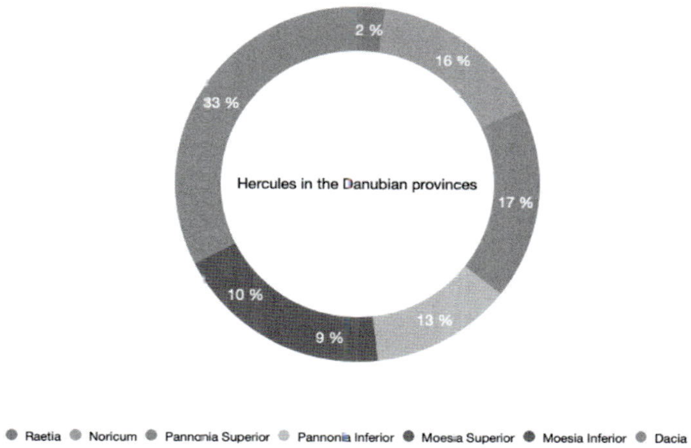

Raetia	Noricum	Pannonia Superior	Pannonia Inferior	Moesia Superior	Moesia Inferior	Dacia
4	26	29	21	15	17	54

Fig. A20 Distribution of inscriptions dedicated to Hercules.

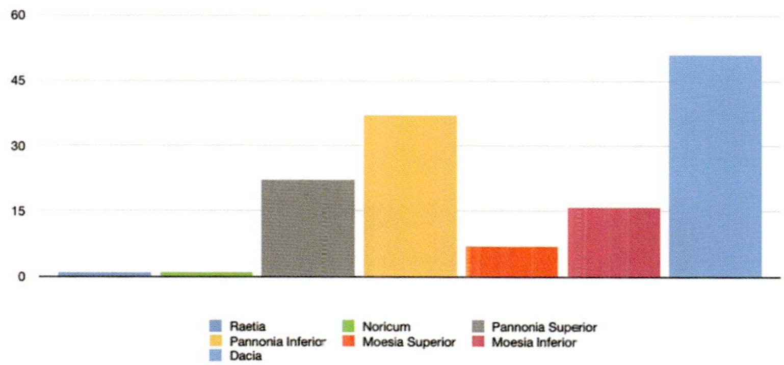

Raetia	Noricum	Pannonia Superior	Pannonia Inferior	Moesia Superior	Moesia Inferior	Dacia
1	1	22	37	7	16	51

Fig. A21 Distribution of inscriptions dedicated to Liber Pater.

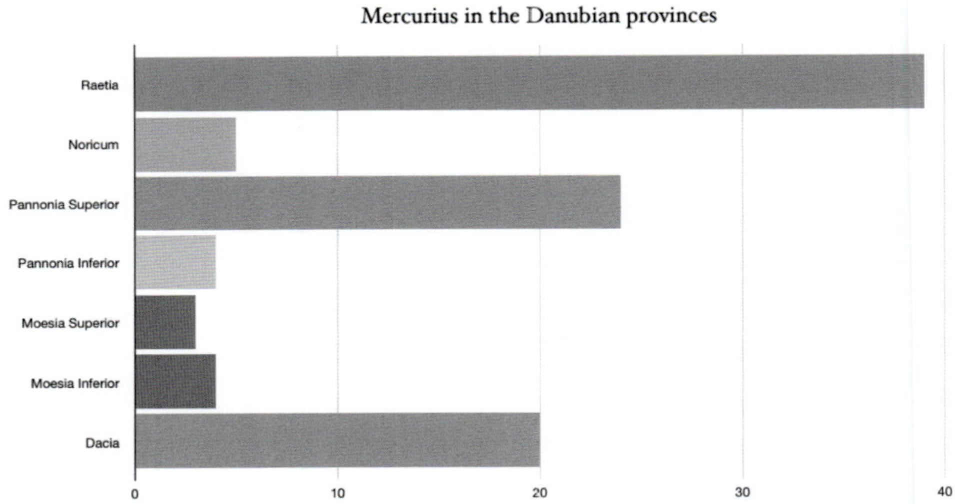

Fig. A22 Distribution of inscriptions dedicated to Mercury.

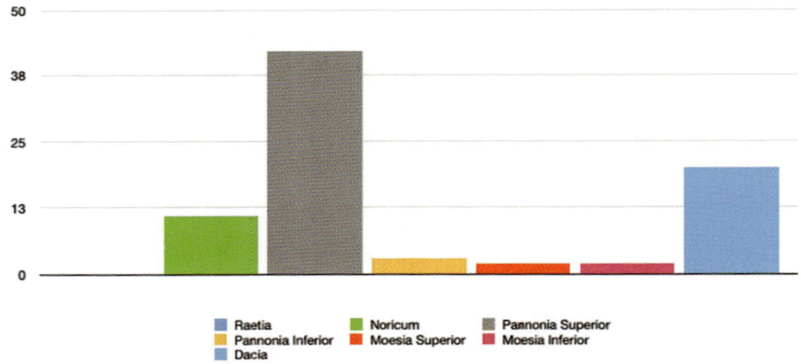

Raetia	Noricum	Pannonia Superior	Pannonia Inferior	Moesia Superior	Moesia Inferior	Dacia
0	11	42	3	2	2	20

Fig. A23 Distribution of inscriptions dedicated to the nymphs.

Notes

1 See also: Rüpke 2016; Raja-Reiger 2021, 61–95.
2 Szabó 2018b; Szabó 2015 (2020).
3 https://danubianreligion.com/atlas-of-roman-sanctuaries-in-the-danubian-provinces/. Last accessed: 15.09.2021.
4 Bonnet *et al.* 2018, 567–569.
5 After the EDH database. In the EDCS database there are 7,300 votive inscriptions, including the Imperial inscriptions (with divine Imperial titles) and defixiones.
6 Gods on the Danube: https://danubianreligion.com/gods-on-the-danube/. Last accessed: 6.10.2021.
7 For the analysis of the charts and diagrams, see also: Chapter 6.

Bibliography

Ableidinger, Johann, *Geschichte von Schwechat*. Verlag der Stadtgemeinde Schwechat. Schwechat, 1929.

Abraham, William, *Divine Agency and Divine Action. Volume I: Exploring and Evaluating the Debate*. Oxford, Oxford University Press, 2017.

Adrych, Philippa – Bracey, Robert – Dalglish, Dominic – Lenk, Stefanie – Wood Rachel, *Images of Mithra*. Oxford, Oxford University Press, 2017.

Adrych, Philippa – Dalglish, Dominic, Writing The Art, Archaeology And Religion Of The Roman Mediterranean. In: Elsner, Jaś (ed.), *Empires of faith in late antiquity – Histories of art and religion from India to Ireland*. Cambridge, Cambridge University Press, 2020, 51–80.

Agócs, Nándor, *Dignitas, Auctoritas, Maiestas és Potestas' Pannoniában – A politikai-, vallási- és gazdasági hatalom ismert pannoniai származású és helyi birtokosai Pannonia térségében Augustustól Iustinianus koráig*. Pécs, Pécsi Tudományegyetem, 2017. Open access.

Alaj, Premtim, *Settlements of the Iron Age in current territory of Kosovo*. Lyon, Université de Lyon, 2019. Dissertation. Open access.

Albrecht, Janiko –Degelmann, Christopher – Gasparini, Valentinc – Gordon, L. Richard – Patzelt, Maik – Petridou, Georgia – Raja, Rubina – Rieger, Katharina – Rüpke, Jörg – Sippel, Benjamin – Urciuoli, Emiliano – Weiss, Lara, Religion in the making: the Lived Ancient Religion approach. In: *Religion*, 48/4, 2018, 568–593.

Alexandrescu, Cristina-Georgeta, On the fate of sculpture in late Antiquity at the Lower Danube. In: Stirling, Lea – Kristensen, Troels Myrup (eds), *The Afterlife of Greek and Roman Sculpture*. Ann Arbor, University of Michigan Press, 2016, 243–262.

Alexandrescu, Cristina-Georgeta – Gugl, Christian – Kainrath, Barbara, *Troesmis I*. Cluj-Napoca, Editura Mega, 2016.

Alexandrescu-Vianu, Maria, Sur la diffusion du culte de Cybele dans le Bassin de la Mer Noire á l'époque archaique. In: *Dacia* 24, 1980, 261–267.

Alföldy, Géza, Aquincum vallási életének története. In: *Budapest Régiségei (Altertümer von Budapest)* 20, 1963, 47–69.

Alföldy, Géza, Augustus und die Inschriften: Tradition und Innovation. Die Geburt der imperialen Epigraphik. In: *Gymnasium* 98, 1991, 289–324.

Alföldy, Géza, Die grossen Götter von Gorsium. In: *Zeitschrift für Papyrologie und Epigraphik* 115, 1997, 225–241.

Alföldy, Géza, Die Romanisierung in den Donauprovinzen Roms. In: Kneissl, Peter – Losemann, Volker (eds), *Alte Geschichte und Wissenschaftsgeschichte. Festschrift für Karl Christ zum 65. Geburtstag*. Darmstadt, Wissenschaftliche Buchgesellschaft 1988, 1–21.

Alföldy, Géza, Egy intercisai feliratról. In: *Archaeologiai értesitő* 84/2, 1957, 214–217.

Alföldy, Géza, *Noricum*. London, Routledge, 1974.

Alföldy, Géza, Pannoniciani augures. In: *Acta Antiqua Academiae Scientiarum Hungariae* 8, 1960, 145–164.

Alföldy, Géza, *Römische Sozialgeschichte*. Stuttgart, Franz Steiner Verlag, 2011.

Alföldy, Géza, Taurisci und Norici. In: *Historia* 15, 1966, 224–241.

Alföldy, Géza, Theodor Mommsen und die römische Epigraphik aus der Sicht hundert Jahre nach seinem Tod. In: *Epigraphica* 66, 2004, 217–245.

Alicu, Dorin, *Micia: Studii monografice. 1. Monumentele de spectacol şi de cult.* Cluj-Napoca, Napoca Star, 2004.

Altheim, Franz, *Römische Religionsgeschichte.* Berlin, De Gruyter, 1931–1933.

Alvar, Jaime, *Romanising oriental gods: Myth, salvation and ethics in the cults of Cybele, Isis and Mithras.* Brill, Leiden-Boston, 2008.

Alvar, Jaime, The 'Romanization' of 'Oriental Cults'. In: Nagel, Svenja – Quack, Joachim Friedrich – Witschel, Christian (eds), *Entangled worlds: religious confluences between East and West in the Roman Empire.* Tübingen, Mohr Siebeck, 2017, 23–46.

Andringa, Van William, *Quotidien des dieux et des hommes: la vie religieuse dans les cites du Vesuve a l'epoque romaine.* Rome, École française de Rome, 2009.

Andringa, Van William, The archaeology of ancient sanctuaries. In: Raja, Rubina – Rüpke, Jörg (eds), *A Companion to the Archaeology of Religion in the Ancient World.* Chichester, John Wiley & Sons, 2015, 29–41.

Ando, Clifford, Praesentia numinis. Part I: The visibility of Roman gods. In: *ASDIWAL. Revue genevoise d'anthropologie et d'histoire des religions* 5/1, 2010, 45–73.

Ando, Clifford – Rüpke, Jörg (eds), *Public and Private in Ancient Mediterranean Law and Religion.* De Gruyter, Berlin-New York, 2015.

Antal, Adriana – Băeştean, Gica, Colonia Dacica Sarmizegetusa Votive Offerings. Hands for the Gods. In: *Acta Archaeologica Academiae Scientiarum Hungariae* 69, 2018, 321–330.

Antal, Adriana, *Venus cult in Roman Dacia.* Cluj-Napoca, Mega Publishing House, 2016.

Anttonen, Veikko, Rethinking the Sacred: The Notions of 'Human Body' and 'Territory' in Conceptualizing Religion. In: Idinopulos, Thomas – Yonan, Edward (eds), *The Sacred and its Scholars Comparative Methodologies for the Study of Primary Religious Data*, Leiden, Brill, 1996, 36–64.

Aparaschivei, Dan, Le culte impérial et les flamines municipaux en Mésie Inférieure et Mésie Supérieure. In: *Archaeologica Bulgarica* 11/3, 2007, 91–100.

Aparaschivei, Dan, *Oraşele Romane de la Dunărea Inferioară (secolele I-III p. Chr.).* Bucuresti, Editura Universitatii Alexandru Ioan Cuza, 2010.

Adrych, Philippa – Dalglish, Dominic, Writing The Art, Archaeology And Religion Of The Roman Mediterranean. In: Elsner, Jaś (ed.), *Empires of faith in late antiquity - Histories of art and religion from India to Ireland.* Cambridge, Cambridge University Press, 2020, 51–80.

Ardagna, Y. – Richier, A. – Vernet, G. – Dutour, O., A case of beheading dating from the celtic period (la Tène B, Sarliève-Grande Halle, France). In: *International Journal of Osteoarchaeology* 15/1, 2005, 73–76.

Ardevan, Radu – Cociş, Sorin, Drei veiteren Votivplättchen aus Dakien. In: Iliescu, Vladimir (ed.), *Graecia, Roma, Barbaricum. In memoriam Vasile Lica.* Galaţi, Editura Muzeului de Istorie Galaţi, 2014, 315–327.

Ardevan, Radu, Die Turranii von Sarmizegetusa. In: Beutler, Franziska (ed.), *Eine ganz normale Inschrift in honorem Ekkehard Weber.* Wien, Österreichische Gesellschaft für Archäologie, 2005, 197–202.

Ardevan Radu, Il fenomeno dell'interpretatio Romana nelle province romane danubiene. In: Zerbini, Livio (ed.), *Culti e religiosità nelle province danubiane. Atti del 2° Convegno internazionale Ferrara, 20–22 novembre 2013.* Ferrara, I Libri di Emi, 2015, 21–37.

Ardevan, Radu, La Rhétorique dans la Société Daco-romaine. In: *Apulum* 50/2, 2013, 111–127.

Ardevan, Radu, *Viaţa municipală in Dacia romană.* Timişoara, Editura Mirton, 1998.

Arneth, Joseph, Studien über Benvenuto Cellini. In: *Philisophisch-historische Classe* 9, 1859, 99–134.

Arnhold, Marlis, Imagining Mithras in Light of Iconographic Standardization and Individual Accentuation. In: Arnhold, Marlis – Maier, Harry – Rüpke, Jörg (eds), *Seeing the God. Image, Space, Performance, and Vision in the Religion of the Roman Empire.* Tübingen, Mohr Siebeck, 2018, 125–147.

Arnhold, Marlis, *Transformationen stadtrömischer Heiligtümer während der späten Republik und Kaiserzeit,* Contextualizing the Sacred, 10. Turnhout, Brepols, 2020.

Arnold, Hugo, Denkmale des Jupiter Dolichenus zu Pfünz und Faimingen. In: *Beiträge zur Anthropologie und Urgeschichte Bayerns*/8, 1889, 179–201.

Arnold, William, *Fire on the Mountain: the Bronze and Iron Alpine Ash Altar Material in the Frankfurth Collection at the Milwaukee Public Museum*. Milwaukee, University of Wisconsin-Milwaukee, 2014. Open access.

Artner, Wolfgang, Opfer, Opfergaben und Heiligtümer der vorrömischen Kelten. In: Leitner, Friedrich (ed.), *Götterwelten. Tempel, Riten, Religionen in Noricum*. Klagenfurt, Landesmuseum Kärnten, 2007, 15–25.

Avram, Alexandru, *Der Vertrag zwischen Rom und Kallatis: ein Beitrag zum römischen Völkerrecht*. Amsterdam, A. M. Hakkert, 1999.

Avram, Alexandru – Hind, John – Tsetskhladze Gocha, The Black Sea Area. In: Hansen, Mogens Herman – Nielsen, Thomas Heine (eds), *An inventory of archaic and classical poleis*. Oxford, Oxford University Press, 2004, 924–973.

Avramova, Mariya, Roman Healing Settlements in Bulgaria: Past Scholarship and Future Perspectives. In: Bassani, Maddalena – Bolder-Boos, Marion – Fusco, Ugo (eds). *Rethinking the concept of ,healing settlements'*. Oxford, Archaeopress, 2019, 95–98.

Babeş, Mircea, Descoperirile funerare şi semnificaţia lor în contextul culturii geto-dace clasice. In: *Studii și Comunicări de Istoria Veche și Archeologie*, 39, 1988, 3-32.

Bagnall, Roger – Heath, Sebastian, Roman Studies and Digital Resources. In: *The Journal of Roman Studies* 108, 2018, 171–189.

Baker, Patricia Anne, *Medical care for the Roman army on the Rhine, Danube, and British frontiers in the first, second, and early third centuries AD*. Oxford, John and Erica Hedges Ltd, 2004.

Bakker, Egbert J., How Oral is Oral Composition? In: MacKay, Anne (ed.), *Signs of Orality*. Leiden, BRILL, 1999, 29–47.

Balla Lajos, *Studia Dacica. Collected papers*. Debrecen, University of Debrecen, 2000.

Ballmer, Ariane, Ritual Practice and Topographic Context. Considerations on the Spatial Forms of Memory in the Central Alps During the Late Bronze Age. In: Bernbeck, Reinhard – Kerstin P. Hofmann – Sommer, Ulrike (eds), *Between Memory Sites and Memory Networks. New Archaeological and Historical Perspectives*. Berlin, Edition Topoi, 2017, 71–90.

Barbuta, Valeria – Ciobanu, Radu, Le port romain d'*Apulum*. In: Bedon, Robert (ed.), *La Loire et les fleuves de la Gaule Romaine et des régions voisines*. Limoges, Pulim, 2000, 257–277.

Barchiesi, Alessandro – Rüpke, Jörg – Stephens, Susan A., *Rituals in ink*. Stuttgart, Franz Steiner Verlag, 2004.

Barlovits, Regina – Gallob, Sebastian, Nemesis und ihr Heiligtum im Amphitheater von Virunum. In: Leitner, Friedrich (ed.), *Götterwelten. Tempel, Riten, Religionen in Noricum*, Klagenfurt. Landesmuseum Kärnten, 2007, 93–103.

Barta Andrea, *Római kori pannoniai átoktáblák és nyelvezetük (Szöveg, nyelv, funkció)*. Doctoral dissertation, Eötvös Lóránd University Budapest, 2015. Open access.

Bartus, Dávid, *Bronzistenek. Római kori figurális bronzplasztika Brigetióban*. Komárom, Komáromi Klapka György Múzeum, 2015.

Bartus Dávid – Borhy László, Topographical research in the canabae of Brigetio in 2014. In: *Dissertationes Archaeologicae*, 3(2), 2014, 451–457.

Bánki, Zsuzsanna, Heiligtum des Iuppiter Dolichenus in Vetus Salina. *Alba Regia* 19. 1981, 95–133.

Băluță, Cloșca, Sanctuarul zeilor Lares de la Apulum. In: *Apulum. Acta Musei Apulensis* 38, 2001, 193–198.

Bărbulescu, Maria – Câteia, Adriana, Pater nomimos în cultul hecatei la tomis. In: *Revista Pontica* 40, 2007, 245–253.

Bărbulescu, Mihai, *Arta romană la Potaissa*, Bucureşti-Cluj. Editura Academiei Române-Editura Mega, 2015.

Bărbulescu, Mihai, *Inscripții din castrul legionar din Potaissa/Inscriptions from the legionary fort of Potaissa*. București, Editura Academiei Române, 2012.
Bărbulescu, Mihai, *Interferențe spirituale în Dacia romană*. Cluj-Napoca, Editura Universitară, 1984.
Bărbulescu, Mihai, *Principia din castrul legionar de la potaissa*. Cluj-Napoca, Editura Mega, 2020.
Beard, Mary, Cicero and Divination: the Formation of a Latin Discourse. In: *Journal of Roman Studies* 76, 1986, 33–46.
Beard, Mary – North, John – Price, Simon, *Religions of Rome: Volume 1: A History*. Cambridge, Cambridge University Press, 1998.
Beattie, Andrew, *The Danube: A Cultural History*. Oxford, Oxford University Press, 2010.
Beattie, William, *The Danube: Its History, Scenery, and Topography*. London, Virtue, 1844.
Beck, Roger, History into fiction: The metamorphoses of the Mithras myths. In: *Ancient Narrative* 1, 2001, 283–300.
Beck, Roger, New thoughts on the genesis of the mysteries of Mithras. In: *Topoi* 11/1, 2001, 59–76.
Beck, Roger, 'Qui Mortalitatis Causa Convenerunt': The Meeting of the Virunum Mithraists on June 26, A. D. 184. In: *Phoenix* 52/3–4, 1998, 335–344.
Beck, Roger, The mysteries of Mithras. In: Kloppenborg, John – Wilson, G. Stephen (eds), *Voluntary Associations in the Ancient World*. London, Routledge, 1996, 176–185.
Belayche, Nicole – Massa, Francesco, *Mystery cults in visual representation in Graeco-Roman antiquity*. Leiden, Boston, Brill, 2021.
Benea, Doina, Câteva observaţii privind depozitul de sare de la Apulum. In: *Apulum. Acta Musei Apulensis* 50, 2013, 119–125.
Benea, Doina, Cu privire la administrarea salinelor din Dacia Romană. In: *Analele Banatului* 15, 2007, 41–46.
Benea, Doina, *Edificiul de cult roman de la Praetorium (Mehadia)*. Timişoara, Editura Excelsior Art, 2008.
Benea, Doina – Lalescu, Ioan, Contribuţii la istoria aşezării de la Ad Mediam (Băile Herculane). In: *Sargetia* 27, 1998, 267–301.
Berciu, Ion – Băluță, Cloșca, O zeitate fluvială la Apulum. In: *Apulum. Acta Musei Apulensis* 12, 1974, 583–587.
Bereczki, Sándor, *Iron Age rites and rituals in the Carpathian Basin*. Târgu Mureş, Editura Mega, 2012.
Bereuter, Alfons – Egle, Helmut – Kneringer, Hermann (eds), *Das römische Brigantium. Ausstellungskatalog*. Bregenz, Vorarlberger Landesmuseum, 1985.
Berthelot, Katell, Philo of Alexandria and the Conquest of Canaan. In: Journal for the Study of Judaism 38.1, *2007*, 39–56.
Beskow, Per, The Portorium and the mysteries of Mithras. In: *Journal of Mithraic Studies III.1-2*, 1980, 1–18.
Bezeczky, Tamás, Amphora types of Magdalensberg. In: *Arheološki vestnik* 49, 1998, 225–242.
Biehl, Peter – Bertemes, Francois, The archaeology of cult and religion. An introduction. In: Biehl, Peter – Bertemes, Francois (eds), *The archaeology of cult and religion*. Budapest, Archaeolingua, 2001, 11–24.
Biehl, Peter, Meanings and Functions of Enclosed Places in the European Neolithic: A Contextual Approach to Cult, Ritual, and Religion. In: *Archaeological Papers of the American Anthropological Association*, 21/1, 2012, 130–146.
Bintliff, John, Sacred Worlds or Sacred Cows? Can we Parameterize Past Rituals? In: T. Meier – P. Tillesen (Hrsg.), *Archaeological imaginations of religion*. Budapest 2014, 249–263.
Birley, Eric, The Governors of Numidia, A.D. 193–268. In: *Journal of Roman Studies* 40/1–2, 1950, 60–68.
Biró, Szilvia, *Die Zivilen Vici in Pannonien*, Mainz, Römisch-Germanisches Zentralmuseum, 2017.
Bishop, C. Mike – Coulston, John, *Roman military equipment: from the Punic wars to the fall of Rome*. Oxford, Oxbow Books, 2006.
Bishop, C. Mike, *Handbook to Roman Legionary Fortresses*. Barnsley, Pen and Sword Books, 2013.

Bîrliba-Mihailescu, Lucrețiu, *Les affranchis dans les provinces romaines de l'Illyricum*, Wiesbaden, Harrassowitz Verlag, 2007.

Bîrliba-Mihailescu, Lucrețiu – Dumitrache, Iulia – Piftor, Valentin, La movilidad local en la Dacia romana según las fuentes epigráficas: I. Dacia Inferior. In: *Studia Historica: Historia Antigua* 28, 2010, 95–108.

Bîrliba-Mihailescu, Lucrețiu, Les salines en Dacie romaine: remarques sur le personnel administratif. In: *Studia Antiqua et Archaeologica* 22/1, 2016, 51–58.

Blăgoi, Olimpia, Navigation facilities on rivers in romania historical travel. In: *Buletinul Institutului Politehnic Din Iași* 64 (68)/17–34, 2018.

Blois, Lukas de, Invasions, Deportations, and Repopulation. In: Lo Cascio, Elio – Tacoma, Laurens Ernst (eds), *The Impact of Mobility and Migration in the Roman Empire*, Brill, 2016, 42–54.

Blömer, Michael – Facellam, Margherita, A New Altar for the God Turmasgade from Dülük Baba Tepesi. In: Winter, Engelbert (ed.), *Vom eisenzeitlichen Heiligtum zum christlichen Kloster*. Bonn, Dr. Rudolf Habelt GmbH, 2017, 99–122.

Blumell, Lincoln H., Petition to a 'Beneficiarius' from Late Third Century A.D. Oxyrhynchus. In: *Zeitschrift für Papyrologie und Epigraphik* 165, 2008, 186–190.

Boda Imola, The sacred topography of Colonia Sarmizegetusa In: *Acta Archaeologica Hungarica* 66, 2015, 281–304.

Boda, Imola – Szabó, Csaba, *The bibliography of Roman Religion in Dacia*. Cluj-Napoca, Mega Publishing House, 2014.

Boda, Imola – Timoc, Călin, The sacred topography of Tibiscum. In: Nemeti, Sorin – Boda Imola – Szabó, Csaba (eds), *New perspectives in the study of Roman religion in Dacia. Studia Historia Universitatis Babes-Bolyai*. Cluj-Napoca, Editura Universitară, 2016, 39–59.

Bodel, John, Religious history in the making. In: *Journal of Roman Archaeology* 33, 2020, 581–591.

Bodenhamer, David – Harris, Trevor M. – Corrigan, John, Spatial narratives and deep maps: a special report. Deep mapping the spatial humanities. In: *International Journal of Humanities and Arts Computing* 7.1–2, 2013, 170–175.

Bolindeț, Rusu Viorica – Cociș, Sorin, Pottery in the Roman vicus Napoca. In: Gaiu, Corneliu – Găzdac, Cristian (eds), *Fontes Historiae. Studia in honorem Demetrii Protase*. Cluj-Napoca-Bistrita, Museum of Bistrita, 2006, 555–586.

Bolindeț, Rusu Viorica, Pottery in funerary context Some aspects of conviviality in Roman Dacia. In: Ruscu, Ligia (ed.), *Banquets of Gods, Banquets of Men.Conviviality in the Ancient World. Studia Universitatis 'Babeș - Bolyai' Historia* Volume 59, 1, 2014, 239–284.

Bonnet, Corinne – Bianco, Maria – Galoppin, Thomas – Guillon, Élodie – Laurent, Antoine – Lebreton, Sylvain – Porzia, Fabio Les dénominations des dieux nous offrent comme autant d'images dessinées (Julien, Lettres 89b, 291 b). Repenser le binôme théonyme-épithète. In: *Studi e materiali di storia delle religioni*, 84/2, 2018, 567–592.

Bonnet, Corinne, *Le 'grand atelier de la science' volumes I et II: Franz Cumont et l'Altertumswissenschaft: Héritages et émancipations. Des études universitaires à la fin de la première guerre mondiale (1888-1923.* Roma, Institut Historique Belge de Rome, 2005.

Bota, Emilian–Diaconescu, Alexandru, La decoration architectonique et sculpturale du 'forum vetus' de Sarmizegetusa: origine, evolution et chronologie. In: *Acta Musei Napocensis* 39–40/I, 2002–2003, 155–196.

Boteva, Dilyana, Dedicators with Roman names and the indigenous cult of the Thracian Horseman. In: *Archaeologia Bulgarica* 11, 2007, 75–89.

Boteva, Dilyana, The 'Thracian Horseman' reconsidered. In: Haynes, Ian (ed.), *Early Roman Thrace: new evidence from Bulgaria*. Portsmouth, Journal of Roman Archaeology Supplementary Series, 82, 2011, 84–105.

Bounegru, George Valentin, Un edificiu de epoca romana descoperit la apulum. In: *Apulum* 44, 2007, 157–173.

Bounegru, Octavian, *Comerț și navigatori la Pontul Stîng și Dunărea de Jos: sec. I-III p. Chr.* Iași, Casa Editorială Demiurg, 2002.

Bounegru, Octavian, Les bureaux du district douanier sur le Bas Danube à l'époque romaine: données épigraphiques. In: *ISTROS* 14/1, 2007, 45–52.

Boutsikas, Efrosyni, *The cosmos in ancient Greek religious experience.* Cambridge, New York, Cambridge University Press, 2020.

Bowes, Kimberly, At Home. In: Raja, Rubina – Rüpke, Jörg (eds), *A Companion to the Archaeology of Religion in the Ancient World.* Chichester, John Wiley & Sons, 2015, 209–219.

Boyanov, Ilian, Oescus – from castra to colonia. In: *Archaeologia Bulgarica* 12/3, 2008, 69–76.

Bozhkova, Delev, Ikonografijata na Ares v provincialnoto monetosečene na gradovete ot Dolna Mizzja i Trakija prez I–III v. In: *Numizmatika, sfragistika i epigrafika* 8, 2012, 9–19.

Bózsa, Anikó – Szabó, Ádám, *'Ajándék a szépnek!' – A Magyar Nemzeti Múzeum római gyűjteményének 'ólomtükrei'.* Budapest, Libelli archaeologici Ser. Nov. No. II, Hungarian National Museum, 2013.

Breeze, David J., The Role of Water in Defining the Limits of the Roman Empire. In: Vagalinski, Liudmil Ferdinandov – Sharankov, Nicolay (eds), *Limes XXII. Proceedings of the 22nd International Congress of Roman Frontier Studies, Ruse, Bulgaria, September 2012.* Sofia, National Archaeological Institute with Museum, 2015, 17–18.

Brelich, Angelo, Aquincum vallásos élete. In: Mahler, Ede (ed.), Laureae aquincenses, memoriae Valentini Kuzsinszky dicatae: aquincumi babérágak Kuzsinszky Bálint emlékének. Budapest, Tudományegyetem, Érem-és Régiségtani Intézet, 1938, 20–142.

Bremmer, Jan, *Initiation into the mysteries of the ancient world.* Berlin-Boston, De Gruyter, 2014.

Bremmer, Jan, Review of Jörg Rüpke, Pantheon, Munich: Beck, 2016. In: *Religion in the Roman Empire* 4/1 (2018), 107–112.

Bremmer, Jan, The Agency of Greek and Roman Statues: from Homer to Constantine. In: *Opuscula* 6, 2013, 7–21.

Bremmer, Jan, *The strange world of human sacrifice.* Leuven, Peeters, 2007.

Bricault, Laurent – Versluys, Miguel John – Müskens, Sander, Epilogue: Eastern provinces with Oriental gods? In: Nikoloska, Aleksandra – Müskens, Sander (eds), *Romanising oriental gods? Religious transformations in the Balkan provinces in the Roman period.* Skopje, Leiden, Macedonian Academy of Sciences and Arts; University of Leiden, 2015, 427–435.

Brîndușa, Manea Elena, *Cultul Afroditei în coloniile grecești din Marea Negră (secolele VII – II d. Hr.).* Summary of PhD thesis. University of Alexandru Ioan Cuza, Iași. Open access.

Brughmans, Tom – Collar, Anna – Coward, Fiona Susan, *The connected past.* Oxford, Oxford University Press, 2016.

Buis, Emiliano J., Ancient Entanglements. In: Duve, Thomas (ed.), *Entanglements in legal history.* Frankfurt am Main, Max Planck Institute for European Legal History, 2014, 151–186.

Buócz, Tibor, Mercurius sanctuary in Savaria. In: Fitz, Jenő (ed.). *Religions and cults in Pannonia,* Székesfehérvár, Museum of Székesfehérvár, 1998, 66–67.

Burkert, Walter, Signs, Commands, and Knowledge: Ancient Divination between Enigma and Epiphany. In: Johnston, Sarah Iles – Struck, Peter (eds), *Mantikê Studies in Ancient Divination.* Leiden-Boston, Brill, 2005, 29–50.

Burns, Thomas, *Rome and the Barbarians, 100 B.C.–A.D. 400.* Baltimore-London, John Hopkins University Press, 2003.

Burton, Paul J., *Rome and the Third Macedonian War.* Cambridge, Cambridge University Press, 2017.

Busch, Alexandra – Versluys, Miguel, Indigenous pasts and the Roman present. In: Busch, Alexandra – Versluys, Miguel (eds), *Reinventing the 'invention of tradition'. Indigenous pasts and the Roman present.* Morphomata 32, Köln, 2015, 7–18.

Butcher, Kevin, Heliopolis: coins, temples, and sight lines. In: *Bulletin of the Institute of Classical Studies* 62/1, 2019, 106–115.

Campbell, Brian, *Rivers and the Power of Ancient Rome*. Chapel Hill, University of North Carolina Press, 2012.

Cancik, Hubert, Rome as sacred landscape. Varro and the end of Republican Religion in Rome. In: *Visible Religion IV – V*, 1986, 250–265.

Cancik, Hubert – Rüpke, Jörg (eds), *Reichsreligion und Provinzialreligion*. Tübingen, Mohr Siebeck, 1997.

Carbó Garcia, Juan Ramón, *Los cultos orientales en la Dacia romana Formas de difusión, integración y control social e ideológico*. Salamanca, Ediciones Universidad de Salamanca, 2010.

Chalupa, Aleš, The Origins of the Roman Cult of Mithras in the Light of New Evidence and Interpretations: The Current State of Affairs. In: *Religio: revue pro religionistiku* 24/1, 2016, 65–91.

Chaniotis, Angelos, Old wine in a new skin. Tradition and innovation in the cult foundation of Alexander of Abonouteichos. In: Dabrowa, E. (ed.), *Tradition and innovation in the ancient world (Electrum 6)*. Krakow, 2002, 67–85.

Chen, Carolyn – Jeung, Russell: Introduction. In: Chen, Carolyn – Jeung, Russell (eds), *Sustaining Faith Traditions: Race, Ethnicity, and Religion among the Latino and Asian American Second Generation*. New York, New York University Press, 2012, 1–24.

Ciglenečki, Slavko, Kontinuität oder Diskontinuität? Höhenbefestigungen von der La-Tene-Zeit bis zum Frühmittelalter. In: Lehner, Manfred – Schrettle, Bernhard (eds), *Zentralort und Tempelberg*. Wien, Phoibos, 2016, 11–23.

Clarke, David, Spatial Information in Archaeology. In Clarke, David (ed.), *Spatial Archaeology*. London, Academic Press, 1977, 1–32.

Clauss, Manfred, Comes tibi so(m) – geheimnisvolle Amulette. In: *Klio* 88, 1, 2006, 216–232.

Clauss, Manfred, Mithras: *Kult und Mysterium*. Darmstadt, Zabern Philipp Von Gmbh, 2012.

Coja, Maria, Terres cuites d'époque hellénistique représentant le Chavalier thrace, trouvées à Histria. In: *Dacia – Revue d'archéologie et d'histoire ancienne* 18, 1974, 283–288.

Collar, Anna, Movement, Labour and Devotion: a Virtual Walk to the Sanctuary at Mount Kasios. In: Collar, Anna – Kristensen, Troels Myrup (eds), *Pilgrimage and economy in the ancient Mediterranean*. Leiden, Boston, Brill, 2020, 33–61.

Collar, Anna, Networks, Connectivity, and Material Culture. In: Cooper, Catherine (ed.), *New Approaches to Ancient Material Culture in the Greek and Roman World*. Leiden-Boston, Brill, 2020, 47–62.

Collar, Anna, *Religious networks in the Roman empire: the spread of new ideas*. Cambridge, Cambridge University Press, 2013.

Conovici, Niculae, The dynamics of trade in transport amphoras from Sinope, Thasos and Rhodos on the Western Black Sea Coast: a comparative approach. In: Stolba, Vladimir F. – Hannestad, Lise (eds), *Chronologies of the Black Sea area in the period, c. 400-100 BC*. Aarhus, Aarhus University Press, 2006, 97–117.

Conrad, Sebastian, *What is Global History?* Princeton, Priceton University Press, 2016.

Conrad, Sven, *Die Grabstelen aus Moesia Inferior: Untersuchungen zu Chronologie, Typologie und Ikonographie Darstellung der römerzeitlichen Grabstelen aus dem Gebiet zwischen Balkan-Gebirge, unterer Donau und westlicher Schwarzmeerküste*. Leipzig, Casa Libri, 2004.

Cook, Arthur B., *Zeus: a study in ancient religion*. Cambridge Cambridge University Press, 1925.

Coulston, Jonathan, Military identity and personal self-identity in the Roman army. In: De Ligt, Luuk – Hemelrijk, Emily (eds), *Roman Rule and Civic Life: Local and Regional Perspectives Proceedings of the Fourth Workshop of the International Network Impact of Empire (Roman Empire, c. 200 B.C. – A.D. 476), Leiden, June 25-28, 2003*. Leiden-Boston, Brill, 2004, 133–152.

Covacef, Zaharia, *Ancient Sculpture in the permanent exhibition of the Museum of National History and Archaeology from Constanța*. Cluj-Napoca, Mega Publishing House, 2011.

Covacef, Zaharia, Cultele orientale în panteonul Dobrogei romane. In: *Pontica* 33–34, 2001, 373–386.

Cristea, Stefana, Serapis/priapus de la micia. In: Forțiu, Sorin – Stavilă, Andrei (eds), *ArheoVest, Nr III: In Memoriam Florin Medeleț*. Szeged, JATEPress, 2015, 993–1000.

Cristilli, Armando, Macellum and Imperium: the relationship between the Roman State and the market-building construction. In: *Analysis archaeologica: an international journal of Western Mediterranean archaeology* 1, 2015, 69–86.

Cumont, V., Franz, *Les religions orientales dans le paganisme romain. Conférences faites au Collège de France en 1905*. Paris, Leroux, 1906.

Cupcea, George, Officium consularis: The Evidence of Dacia. In: *Transylvanian Review* 21/Supplement 3, 2012, 243–254.

Cupcea, George – Rusu-Bolindeț, Viorica – Petiș, Ioniță – Onofrei, Cosmin, A sanctuary of Silvanus in the rural territory of Napoca. In: *Acta Musei Napocensis* 56/147–194, 2019.

Curta, Florin, Ethnic identity and archaeology. In: Smith, Claire (ed.), *Encyclopedia of Global Archaeology*. Dordrecht, London, Springer, 2507–2514.

Czachesz, István, Religious Experience in Mediterranean Antiquity: Introduction to the Special Issue. In: *Journal of Cognitive Historiography* 2/1, 2016, 5–13.

Czysz, Wolfgang, *Die Römer in Bayern*. Stuttgart, Theiss, 1995.

Czysz, Wolfgang, Mithras unter Dach und Fach Stadt Königsbrunn, Landkreis Augsburg, Schwaben. In: *Das archäologische Jahr in Bayern* 2002, 2003, 150–151.

Czysz, Wolfgang – Scholz, Markus, Ein Gastmahl mit Göttern in Notzeiten. In: Schäfer, Alfred – Witteyer, Marion (eds), *Rituelle Deponierungen in Heiligtümern der hellenistisch-römischen Welt*. Mainz, Generaldirektion Kulturelles Erbe, 2013.

Czysz, Wolfgang, Von Holzarmen und Holzbeinen: Ein römisches Quellheiligtum beim Kastell Dambach. In: *Der Limes* 3/1, 2009, 4–6.

Dalby, Andrew, *Empire of Pleasures: Luxury and Indulgence in the Roman World*. London-New York, Routledge, 2000.

Dana, Dan, *Fontes ad Zalmoxin pertinentes. Accedunt fontes alii historiam religionum Thracum Getarum Dacorumque spectantes. Izvoare privitoare la Zalmoxis și alte pasaje referitoare la religia tracilor, geților și dacilor.* Iași, Editura Universității, 2011.

Dana, Dan, Possibles témoignages sur des cultes daces: la documentation épigraphique de la Mésie Inférieure. In: Taufer, Matteo (ed.), *Sguardi interdisciplinari sulla religiosità dei Geto-Daci*. Freiburg im Bresgau-Berlin-Vienna, Paradeigmata 23, Rombach Verlag, 2013, 157–176.

Dana, Dan – Valeriev, Ioto – Moreau, Dominic – M'Barek, Brahim, Un théonyme et des noms thraces nouveau dans une dédicace grecque découverte à Zaldapa (Mésie Inférieure). In: *Zeitschrift für Papyrologie und Epigraphik* 202, 2017, 158–162.

Dana, Dan – Zăgreanu, Radu, Deux dédicaces latines inédites de Porolissum (Dacie romaine). In: *Tyche* 28, 2013, 27–35.

Davies, Wayne K. D., Centrality and the Central Place Hierarchy. In: *Urban Studies* 4/1, 1967, 61–79.

De Ligt, Luuk – Bintliff, John (eds), *Regional Urban Systems in the Roman World, 150 BCE – 250 CE*. Leiden-Boston, Brill, 2020.

Deac, Dan-Augustin, Negotiating with the Dacians: the case of M. Ulpius Celerinus, interpres Dacorum. In: *Ephemeris Napocensis* 23, 2013, 313–321.

Deac, Dan-Augustin, Shabtis and Pseudo-Shabtis from the Roman Provinces of Pannonia, Dacia and Moesia. In: Tomorad, Mladen – Popielska-Grzybowska, Joanna (eds), *Egypt 2015: Perspectives of research*. Oxford, Archaeopress, 2017, 241–256.

Deac, Dan-Augustin – Simion, Mihaela, Isis Miciensis. Isis and religious communication at Micia through a gem depicting the goddess. In: Journal of Roman Archaeology 35. Forthcoming. (With the special permission of the authors).

Deac, Dan-Augustin, *The Egyptian Theophoric Personal Names in the Danubian Provinces of the Roman Empire*. XV. Congressus Internationalis Epigraphiae Graecae et Latinae, Wien, 2017. Open access.

Delev, Peter, Did a 'Late' Odrysian Kingdom ever exist? In: *Studia Archaeologica Universitatis Serdicensis* Supplementum 6/191–196, 2018.

Dészpa, Mihály Loránd, Jupiter Optimus Maximus Dolichenus and the Re-Imagination of the Empire: Religious Dynamics, Social Integration, and Imperial Narratives. In: Nagel, Svenja – Quack, Joachim Friedrich – Witschel, Christian (eds), *Entangled worlds religious confluences between East and West in the Roman Empire*. Tübingen, Mohr Siebeck, 2017, 113–181.

Dészpa, Mihály Loránd, Peripherie-Denken: *Transformation und Adaption des Gottes Silvanus in den Donauprovinzen (1.-4. Jahrhundert n. Chr.)*. Stuttgart, Franz Steiner Verlag, 2012.

Diaconescu, Alexandru, Dacia under Trajan. Some observations on Roman tactics and strategy. In: *Acta Musei Napocensis* 34, 1997, 13–52.

Diaconescu, Alexandru, *Forurile Sarmizegetusei. O plimbare imaginară prin centrul politico-administrativ al micii Rome de la poalele Retezatului*. Deva, Museum of Deva, 2010.

Diaconescu, Alexandru – Schäfer, Alfred – Haynes, Ian, Das Liber Pater Heiligtum von Apulum. In: Cancik, Hubert – Rüpke, Jörg (eds), *Reichsreligion und Provinzialreligion*. Tübingen, Mohr Siebeck 1997, 195–218.

Diaz-Andreu, Margarita, *A History of Archaeological Tourism Pursuing leisure and knowledge from the eighteenth century to World War II*. Dordrecht, London, Springer, 2020. In: When did a *provincia* became a province? On the institutional development of a Republican concept. In: Diaz-Fernández, Alejandro (ed.), *Provinces and Provincial Command in Republican Rome: Genesis, Development and Governance*. Sevilla, Editorial Universidad Sevilla, 2021, 41–70.

Dietz, Karlheinz – Fischer, Thomas, *Regensburg zur Römerzeit*. Regensburg. Verlag Friedrich Pustet, 2018.

Dietz, Karlheinz, Zur vorrömischen Bevölkerung nach den Schriftquellen. In: Hüssen, Clauss-Michael (Hrsg.), *Spätlatènezeit und frühe römische Kaiserzeit zwischen Alpenrand und Donau. Akten des Kolloquiums in Ingolstadt am 11. und 12. Oktober 2001*. Bonn, Habelt, 2004, 1–23.

Dimitrova, Nora, Inscriptions and Iconography in the Monuments of the Thracian Rider. In: *The Journal of the American School of Classical Studies at Athens*, 71, 2, 2002, 209–229.

Dirven, Lucinda – McCarty, Matthew, Local idioms and global meanings: mithraism and Roman provincial art. In: Brody, Lisa – Hoffmann, Gail (eds), *Roman in the provinces: art on the periphery of Empire*. Chestnut Hill, McMullen Museum of Art, Boston College, 2014, 125–141.

Dirven, Lucinda, The Mithraeum as *tableau vivant*. A Preliminary Study of Ritual Performance and Emotional Involvement in Ancient Mystery Cults. In: *Religion in the Roman Empire* vol. 1.1, 2015, 20–50.

Dirven, Lucinda, *The Palmyrenes of Dura-Europos: a study of religious interaction in Roman Syria*. Leiden-Boston, Brill, 1999.

Dise, Robert L., The Beneficiarii Procuratoris of Celeia and the Development of the Statio Network. In: *Zeitschrift für Papyrologie und Epigraphik* 113, 1996, 286–292.

Dise, Robert L., Trajan, the Antonines, and the Governor's Staff. In: *Zeitschrift für Papyrologie und Epigraphik* 116, 1997, 273–283.

Dizdar, Marko – Filipović, Slavica, A Late La Tène Scordiscan Sanctuary from Osijek (Eastern Slavonia, Croatia)? In: Sîrbu, Valeriu – Pețan, Aurora (eds), *Temples and Cult Places from the Second Iron Age in Europe, Proceedings of the 2nd International Colloquium Iron Age Sanctuaries and Cult Places at the Thracians and their Neighbours*. Alun, Editura Dacica, 2020, 87–109.

Dizdar, Marko – Radman-Livaja, Ivan, Continuity of the Late La Tène warrior elite in the Early Roman Period in south-eastern Pannonia. In: Wefers, Stefanie (ed.), *Waffen, Gewalt, Krieg: Beiträge zur Internationalen Tagung der AG Eisenzeit und des Instytut Archeologii Uniwersytetu Rzeszowskiego – Rzeszów 19.-22. September 2012*. Langenweißbach, Beier & Beran, 2015, 209–227.

Dobó, Árpád, Publicum Portorium *Illyrici*. Dissertationes Pannonicae series 2, no. 16, Budapest, University Press, 1940.

Dolenz, Heimo – Ebner-Baur, Desiree – Kall, Andreas – Menne-Fornezza, Marius, Archäologische Untersuchung eines Podiumtempels in der nördlichen Vorstadt des municipium Claudium Virunum im Jahre 2018. In: *Carinthina* I, 209, 2019, 11–30.

Dolenz, Heimo – Ebner-Baur, Desiree – Schindler-Kaudelka, Eleni, Die norisch-römische Siedlung zwischen Willersdorf und St. Michael am Zollfeld (Kärnten/Österreich). In: Strobel, Karl – Dolenz Heimo (eds), *Chronologie und vergleichende Chronologien zum Ausgang der Römischen Republik und zur Frühen Kaiserzeit: Tagungsband des internationalen Kolloquiums anlässlich 70 Jahre Archäologische Ausgrabungen auf dem Magdalensberg: Zugleich Festgabe für Eleni Schindler Kaudelka*. Klagenfurt am Wörthersee, Landesmuseum für Kärnten, 2019, 137–184.

Dolenz, Heimo, Recent studies in Italic temple districts of Noricum. In: Lazar, Irena (ed.), *Religion in public and private sphere. Acts of the 4th International Colloquium The Autonomous Towns of Noricum and Pannonia*. Koper, Univerza na Primorskem, 2011, 87–103.

Dolenz, Heimo, Römische Tempel Zentrum Noricums. Neue Untersuchungen und Feldforschungen im Überblick. In: Leitner, Friedrich (ed.), *Götterwelten. Tempel, Riten, Religionen in Noricum*. Klagenfurt, Landesmuseum Kärnten, 2007, 67–92.

Dolenz, Heimo – Strobel, Karl, Der Magdalensberg: Neue Feldforschungen im Gipfelbereich. In: Zimmer, Stefan (ed.), *Kelten am Rhein: Akten des dreizehnten Internationalen Keltologiekongresses, 23. bis 27. Juli 2007 in Bonn*. Mainz, Philipp von Zabern, 2009, 1–10.

Dolenz, Heimo, Zu spätlatènezeitlichen Wallanlagen am Magdalensberg: Apropos P. Gleirscher, Keltische Baureste am Gipfel des Magdalensbergs? In: *Archäologie Österreichs* 29/2, 2008, 22–24.

Domăneanţu, Catrinel Viorica, Un sanctuaire hellénistique du site de Nuntaşi (comm. d'Histria, dép. de Constanţa). In: *Dacia – Revue d'archéologie et d'histoire ancienne* 37, 1993, 59–79.

Domaszewski, von Alfred, *Abhandlungen zur römischen Religion*. Leipzing-Berlin Teubner, 1909.

Doneus, Michael – Doneus, Nives – Gugl, Christian – Grossmann, Michael (eds), *Die Canabae von Carnuntum – Eine Modellstudie der Erforschung römischer Lagervorstädte: Von der Luftbildprospektion zur siedlungsarchäologischen Synthese (Der römische Limes in Österreich)*. Wien, Verlag der Österreichischen Akademie der Wissenschaften, 2013.

Doneus, Michael – Scharrer, Garbriele, *The city map of ancient Carnuntum – combining archaeological prospection, photogrammetry and gis*. Conference draft. Open access (https://www.cipaheritagedocumentation.org/). Last accessed: 10.10.2021.

Donev, Damjan, *The Busy Periphery: Urban Systems of the Balkan and Danube Provinces (2nd–3rd c. AD)*. Oxford, Archaeopress, 2019.

Donev, Damjan, The top-ranking towns in the Balkan and Pannonian provinces of the Roman Empire. In: Arheološki vestnik 71, 2020, 193–215.

Dorcey, Peter, Saldaecaputenus: God or Toponym? In: *Zeitschrift für Papyrologie und Epigraphik* 72, 1988, 294–296.

Dorcey, Peter, *The cult of Silvanus: a study in Roman folk religion*. Leiden-Boston, Brill 1992.

Drăgan, Andreea, *Living on the River. A Study of the Interactions in the Lower Danube Gorge during the Late Iron Age and Early Roman Times*. Cluj-Napoca, Mega Publishing House, 2020.

Drexler, Wilhelm, *Der Cultus der Aegyptischen Gottheiten in den Donauländern*. Leipzig, Teubner, 1890.

Drinkwater, John, *Roman Gaul (Routledge Revivals): The Three Provinces, 58 BC-AD 260*. Routledge, 1983.

Drnić, Ivan, Water finds of the Late Iron Age from southern Pannonia. Simple stray finds or indicators of possible ritual activities? In: Guštin, Mitja – David, Wolfgang (eds), *The Clash of Cultures? The Celts and the Macedonian World*. Manching, 2014, 201–210.

Duling, Dennis C., The Jesus Movement and Social Network Analysis (Part I: The Spatial Network). In: *Biblical Theology Bulletin: Journal of Bible and Culture* 29/4, 1999, 156–175.

Duller, Eduard, *Die Donauländer: Nebst Wanderungen in Das Baierische Hochland Und Das Salzburgische Hochgebirge*. Leipzig, G. Haendel Verlag, 1849.

Duncan – Jones, Richard, An epigraphic survey of costs in Roman Italy. In: *Papers of the British School of Rome*, 33, 1965, 189–306.

Durand, Aude – Van Andringa, William, To Live or not to Live. In: Berg, Ria – Coralini, Antonella – Koponen, Anu Kaisa – Välimäki, Reima (eds), *Tangible Religion*. Roma, Institutum Romanum Finlandiae, 2021, 85–99.

Dyczek, Piotr – Kolendo, Jerzy, Archaeolcgical and Epigraphical Sources for the Cult to Asclepius and Hygia in the Army Hospital at Novae. In: *Archaeologia* 61, 2010, 35–46.

Dzino, Danijel, *Illyricum in Roman Politics, 229 BC–AD 68*. Cambridge, Cambridge University Press, 2010.

Eck, Werner – Ivanov, Rumen, C. Iulius Victor, senatorischer Legat von Moesia inferior unter Valerianus und Gallienus und das Kastell Sostra-Siosta. In: *Zeitschrift für Papyrologie und Epigraphik*, 170, 2009, 191–200.

Egri, Mariana – Rustoiu, Aurel, The Social Significance of Convivality in the Scordiscian Environment. In: Sîrbu, Valeriu – Vaida, Dan Lucian (eds), *Funerary practices of the Bronze and Iron Ages in Central and South-Eastern Europe*. Cluj-Napoca, Editura Mega, 2008, 83–93.

Egri, Mariana, The role of local elites in economic exploitation of the Danube Provinces. In: *The Lower Danube in antiquity (6th century BC-6th century AD). International Archaeological Conference, Bulgaria-Tutrakan, 6.-7.10.2005*. Sofia, 2007, 103–112.

Egri, Mariana – McCarthy, Matthew – Rustoiu, Aurel, Inel, Constantin, A new mithraic community at Apulum (Alba Iulia, Romania). In: *Zeitschrift für Papyrologie und Epigraphik* 205, 2018, 268–276.

Eichner, Heiner – Istenič, Janka – Lovenjak, Milan, Ein römerzeitliches Keramikgefäß aus Ptuj (Pettau, Poetovio) in Slowenien Ein romerzeitliches KeramikgefaB aus Ptuj (Pettau, Poetovio) in Slowenien mit Inschrift in unbekanntem Alphabet und epichorischer (vermutlich keltischer) Sprache keltischer) Sprache. In: *Arheološki vestnik* 45, 1994, 131–142.

Eingartner, Johannes – Eschbaumer, Pia – Weber, Gerhard, *Der römische Tempelbezirk in Faimingen-Phoebiana*. Mainz am Rhein, Philipp von Zabern, 1993.

Eitler, Josef – Reiter, Johannes, Neue Forschungen am Hemmaberg – überraschende Ergebnisse der Grabung am Gipfelplateau. In: Jerger, Thomas – Brinckmann-Blaha, Ute – Herwirsch, Ilse (eds), *Rudolfinum – Jahrbuch des Landesmuseums für Kärnten 2009/2010*. Klagenfurt, Landesmuseum Kärnten, 2011, 69–72.

Elsner, Jaś, *Art and text in Roman culture*. Cambridge, Cambridge University Press, 1996.

Elsner, Jaś, Excavating Pilgrimage. In: Friese, Wiebke – Kristensen, Troels (eds) *Excavating Pilgrimage. Archaeological Approaches to Sacred Travel and Movement in the Ancient World*. London, Routledge, 2017, 265–274.

Elsner, Jaś, Objects and History. In: Miller, Peter N. (ed.), *Cultural histories of the material world*. Ann Arbor, The University of Michigan Press, 2013, 165–171.

Elsner, Jaś, *Roman eyes: visuality and subjectivity in art and text*. Princeton, Princeton University Press, 2007.

Ersch, Johann Samuel – Gruber, Johann Gottfried (eds), *Allgemeine Encyclopädie der Wissenschaften und Künste*, vol. 24. Leipzig, Friedrich Arnold Brockhaus, 1836.

Ertl, Rudolf Franz, *Donaureiter-Bleivotivtafeln – Versuch einer Typologie*. Petronell-Carnuntum, Publikationen des Museumsvereines Petronell-Carnuntum Auxiliarkastell, 1996.

Ertel, Christine – Hasenbach, Verena – Deschler-Erb, Sabine, *Kaiserkultbezirk und Hafenkastell in Brigantium*. Konstanz, UVK Verlagsgesellschaft, 2011.

Estienne, Sylvia, Images. In: Raja, Rubina – Rüpke, Jörg (eds), *A Companion to the Archaeology of Religion in the Ancient World*. Chichester, John Wiley & Sons, 2015, 379–388.

Facella, Margherita, Ubi ferrum nascitur. In: *Imperium der Götter: Isis – Mithras – Christus. Kulte und Religionen im Römischen Reich*. Karlsruhe, Theiss in Wissenschaftliche Buchgesellschaft, 2013, 284–286.

Fagan, Garrett, *Bathing in Public in the Roman World*. Ann Arbor, Michigan University Press, 2002.

Faraone, Christopher, The Amuletic Design of the Mithraic Bull-Wounding Scene. In: *Journal of Roman Studies* 103, 2013, 96–116.

Farkas, István Gergő, La partecipazione delle truppe del Limes danubiano nella spedizione di Antonino Pio contro i Mauri. In: *Quaderni Friulani di Archeologia* 21, 2011, 189–195.

Farkas, István Gergő, Távolról jött harcosok. A római hadszervezet bemutatása a cohors II és IV Tungrorum ∞ vexillatio dislocatióján keresztül. In: Bene, Krisztián – Dávid, Ferenc – Sarlós István (eds), *Válogatás a Hadtörténeti esték 2006 és 2014 között elhangzott előadásaiból.* Pécs-Budapest Magyar Hadtudományi Társaság, 2014, 69–82.

Farkas István Gergő, *The dislocation of the Roman army in Raetia.* Oxford, BAR International Series 2723, 2015.

Fehér, Bence, Mentula Silvani. In: Bíró, Szilvia – Vámos, Péter (eds), *Firkák II.* Győr, Mursella Régészeti Egyesület, 2012, 47–55.

Fehér, Bence, Syrian Names Given in Pannonia Inferior. In: *Acta Classica Universitatis Scientiarum Debreceniensis* 44, 2008, 95–109.

Fernández-Götz, Manuel, A World of 200 Oppida: Pre-Roman Urbanism in Temperate Europe. In: Ligt, Luuk de – Bintliff, John (eds), *Regional Urban Systems in the Roman World, 150 BCE-250 CE.* Leiden, Boston, Brill, 2020, 35–66.

Fernández-Götz, Manuel, Reassessing the Oppida: The Role of Power and Religion. In: *Oxford Journal of Archaeology* 33/4, 2014, 379–394.

Ferri, Naser, Veneration of Local and Imported Divinities' Cults in Houses and Temples of the Roman Dardania. In: *Histria antiqua* 20/20, 2011, 293–299.

Fiedler, Manuel – Höpken, Konstanze, Micul templu al marilor divinități: Sanctuarul lui Domnus și Domna din Sarmizegetusa. In: Rusu-Bolindeț, Viorica – Sălăgean, Teodor – Varga, Rada (eds), *Studia Archeologica et Historica in Honorem Magistri Dorin Alicu.* Cluj-Napoca, Editura Argonaut, 2010, 319–333.

Filipović, Vojislav – Petrović, Vladimir P., Newly-discovered Traces of the Roman Naissus-Ratiaria Road and the Problem of Locating Two Timacum Stations. In: *Balcanica* 38, 2007, 29–45.

Firth, Josh A. – Hellewell, Joel – Klepac, Petra – Kissler, Stephen – Kucharski, Adam J. – Spurgin, Lewis G., Using a real-world network to model localized COVID-19 control strategies. In: *Nature Medicine* 26/10, 2020, 1616–1622.

Fischer, Thomas, *Das Römerkastell Eining und seine Umgebung.* Regensburg, Pustet, Verlag Friedrich, 2016.

Fischer, Thomas, *Die Armee der Caesaren: Archäologie und Geschichte.* Pustet, Friedrich GmbH, 2014.

Fischl Klára, P., Szertartási edények a bronzkorból. In: *A Herman Ottó Múzeum évkönyve* 38/1, 1999, 129–138.

Fishwick, Duncan, The Sacred Area at Gorsium (Pannonia Inferior). In: *Phoenix* 54/3-4, 2000, 309.

Fitz, Jenő, *A Sárkeszi mithraeum.* Székesfehérvár, Múzeumi Kiadó, 1957.

Fitz, Jenő (ed.), *Religions and cults in Pannonia.* Székesfehérvár, Múzeumi Kiadó, 1998.

Floca, Octavian, Pagus Miciensis. In: *Sargetia* 5, 1968, 49–57.

Floca, Octavian, Un monument sculptural de l'empereur Trajan Decius à Ulpia Traiana-Sarmizegetusa. In: *Latomus* 24/2, 1965, 353–358.

Flohr, Miko, *Spatial archaeologies of religion at Pompeii.* Open access.

Florea, Gelu, Dacii. In: Mitu, Sorin (ed.), *Enciclopedia imaginariilor din România. Vol. III: Imaginar istoric.* Bucuresti, Polirom, 2020, 31–49.

Florea, Gelu, *Dava et Oppidum. Débuts de la genèse urbaine en Europe au deuxième âge du Fer.* Cluj-Napoca, Académie Roumaine, Centre d'Études Transylvaines, 2011.

Florea, Gelu, L'archéologie d'une religion 'anonyme'. In: Taufer, Matteo (ed.), *Sguardi interdisciplinari sulla religiosità dei Geto-Daci.* Berlin-Vienna, Paradeigmata 23, Rombach Verlag, 2013, 123–135.

Flynt, Shannon Rogers, *The military vici of Noricum*. Columbia, University of Missouri-Columbia, 2005. Open access.
Fodorean, Florin, *Pannonia, Dacia and Moesia in the Ancient Geographical Sources*, Stuttgart, Franz Steiner Verlag, 2016.
Fodorean, Florin, Tourism or health necessities? 'Spa' vignettes in Tabula Peutingeriana. Travelling Ad Aquas: thermal water resources in Roman Dacia. In: *Ephemeris Napocensis* 22, 2012, 211–221.
Fontijn, David, Sacrificial landscapes: cultural biographies of persons, objects and 'natural' places in the Bronze Age of the southern Netherlands, *c.* 2300–600 BC. In: *Analecta Praehistorica Leidensia*, 33–34: 1–392.
Fontijn, David, The significance of 'invisible' places. In: *World Archaeology*, 39(1), 2007, 70–83.
Fowler, W. Wardie, *The Religious Experience of the Roman People, from the Earliest Times to the Age of Augustus: The Gifford Lectures for 1909-10*. London, McMillan, 1911.
Frakes, James F. D., Fora. In: Ulrich, Roger B. – Quenemoen, Caroline K. (eds), *A Companion to Roman Architecture*. Oxford, Blackwell Publishing Ltd, 2013, 248–263.
Freeman, Philip, On the Annexation of Provinces to the Roman Empire. In: *Classics Ireland* 5, 1998, 30–47.
Frei-Stolba, Regula, Die Räter in den antiken Quellen. In: Frei, Benedikt – Frei-Stolba, Regula (eds), *Das Räterproblem in geschichtlicher, sprachlicher und archäologischer Sicht*. Chur, Rätisches Museum Chur, 1984, 6–21.
Frei-Stolba, Regula, Die Räter in den antiken Quellen – I reti nelle fonti antiche. In: Metzger, Ingrid R. – Gleirscher, Paul (eds), *Die Räter I Reti*, Bozen, Verlagsanstalt Athesia, 1991, 657–671.
Gabler, Dénes, A belső vámok szerepe a rajnai és a dunai provinciák importált kerámiaspektrumában. In: *Dissertationes Archaeologicae* 3/2, 2014, 45–66.
Gabler, Dénes, Die Siedlungen der Urbevölkerung Unterpannoniens in der frührömischen Zeit. In: Tejral, Jaroslav – Pieta, Karol – Rajtár, Ján (eds), *Kelten, Germanen, Römer im Mitteldonaugebiet. Vom Ausklang der Latène-Zivilisation bis zum 2. Jahrhundert. 7. Internat. Symposium 'Grundprobleme der frühgeschichtlichen Entwicklung im nördlichen Mitteldonaugebiet', Malé Vozokany, 13.-16. Dezember 1994*. Brno, Archeologický ústav Slovenské akademie vied Nitra, 1995, 63–81.
Gabler, Dénes, Le questioni cronologiche del tempio di Iside a Savaria. In: Zerbini, Livio (ed.), *Culti e Religiosità nelle Province Danubiane*. Bologna I Libri di Emil, 2015, 247–266.
Gabler, Dénes, Utak Pannonia és Dacia között a 'Barbaricumon' át. In: *Dolgozatok az Erdélyi Múzeum Érem- És Régiségtárából* 3–4, 2010, 43–54.
Gáll, Erwin – Dobos, Alpár – Petruț, Dávid – Kapcsos, Norbert –Wanek, Ferenc – Piroska, Eszter – Nagy, Szabolcs – Iván, András, *'Daciától Ultrasilvaniáig' A Kis-Szamos medencéjének településtörténeti változásai. 3/4-12/13. Század*. Kolozsvár, Erdélyi Múzeum Egyesület, 2017.
Gallego Franco, Henar, Dependencia personal y romanizacion: los Sabinii y los Barbii de la provincia romana de Noricum. In: *Florentia Iliberritana* 8, 1997, 149–168.
Gamber, Klaus, Die St. Emmeramskirche in Regensburg. Geht ihr ein gallo-römisches Hercules-Heiligtum voraus? In: Gamber, Klaus (eds), *Sarmannina: Studien zum Christentum in Bayern und Österreich während der Römerzeit*. Regensburg, Pustet, 1982, 38–57.
Gamper, Die heilige Kuppe auf der Gurina Topographie und Forschungsgeschichte zur Gurina. In: Leitner, Friedrich (ed.), *Götterwelten. Tempel, Riten, Religionen in Noricum*. Klagenfurt, Landesmuseum Kärnten, 2007, 25–30.
Garbsch, J. – Kellner, H. J., Das Mithraeum von Pons Aeni 50, 1985, 355–462.
Gasparini, Valentino – Gordon, L. Richard, Egyptianism. Appropriating 'Egypt' in the 'Isiac Cults' of the Graeco-Roman World. In: *Acta Antiqua Academiae Scientiarum Hungaricae*, 58 /1–4, 2018, 571–606.

Gasparini, Valentino – Patzelt, Maik – Raja, Rubina – Rieger, Anna-Katharina – Rüpke, Jörg – Urciuoli, Emiliano (eds), *Lived Religion in the Ancient Mediterranean World Approaching Religious Transformations from Archaeology, History and Classics.* Berlin-New York, De Gruyter, 2020.

Gasparini, Valentino, Religious Agency and Time Regimes in the Roman Empire: The Cult of Anubis as a Case Study. In: *Numen* 68/1, 2020, 39–76.

Gasparini, Valentino, Renewing the past: Rufinus' appropriation of the sacred site of Panóias (Vila Real, Portugal). In: Gasparini, Valentino – Begemann, Elisabeth (eds), *Lived religion in the ancient Mediterranean world.* Berlin, Boston, De Gruyter, 2020, 319–350.

Gasparini, Valentino, Tracing Religious Change in Roman Africa. In: Raja, Rubina – Rüpke, Jörg (eds), *A Companion to the Archaeology of Religion in the Ancient World.* Chichester, John Wiley & Sons, 2015, 478–489.

Gavrilović-Vitas, Nadežda, A Contribution to the Study of the Cultof God Mercury in Moesia Superior. In: *Archaeologia Bulgarica* 14/1, 2010, 57–79.

Gavrilović-Vitas, Nadežda, Dolicheneum and Dolichenus' cult objects from the locality Brza Palanka – Egeta: contribution to the study of the cult of Iuppiter Dolichenus. In: Radman-Livaja, Ivan – Bilić, Tomislav (eds), *Monumenta marmore aereque perenniora.* Zagreb, The Archaeological Museum in Zagreb, 2020, 204–223.

Gavrilović-Vitas, Nadežda, *Ex Asia et Syria. Oriental Religions in the Roman Central Balkans.* Oxford, Archaeopress, 2021.

Gavrilović-Vitas, Nadežda, *Kult Herkula i Merkura u Gornjoj Meziji. The Cult of Hercules and Mercury in Moesia Superior.* Belgrade, 2014. Open access.

Gavrilović-Vitas, Nadežda, Roman religion and cults on the Danube Limes in Serbia. In: Golubović, Snežana – Mrđić, Nemanja (eds), *Vivere Militare Est: From Populus to Emperors – Living on the Frontier. Volume I.* Belgrade, Institute of Archaeology, 2018, 167–194.

Gawlikowski, Michel, Theoi Synnaoi. In: Balty, Jean Charles (ed.), *Lexicon iconographicum mythologiae classicae: LIMC. 8,1 Thespiades – Zodiacus et supplementum Abila – Thersites.* Zürich, München, Artemis Verlag, 1997, 1205–1206.

Geertz, W. Armin, Religious bodies, minds and places. A cognitive science of religion perspective. In: Carnavale, Laura (ed.), *Spazi e luoghi sacri. Espressioni ed esperienze di vissuto religioso.* Bari, Edipuglia, 2017, 35–52.

Gentile, Michael – Tammaru, Tiit – van Kempen, Ronald, Heteropolitanization: Social and spatial change in Central and East European Cities. In: *Cities* 29/5, 2012, 291–299.

Georgiev, Petür, *The mysteries of Mithra or The mysteries of Sabazios.* Sofia, Bulga Media Publishing House, 2016.

Gerov, Boris, Zur epigraphischen Dokumentation des publicum portorii Illyrici et ripae Thraciae. In: *Epigraphica* 42, 1980, 119–130.

Ghey, Eleanor, Empty spaces or meaningful places? A broader perspective on continuity. In: King, C. Anthony – Haeussler, Ralph (eds), *Continuity and innovation in religion in the Roman West I.* Portsmouth, Journal of Roman Archaeology Supplement, 2007, 19–30.

Glaser, Franz, Der Bronzejüngling vom Magdalensberg 1502–2002. In: Jerger, Thomas – Brinckmann-Blaha, Ute – Herwirsch, Ilse (eds), *Rudolfinum – Jahrbuch des Landesmuseums für Kärnten 2002.* Klagenfurt, Landesmuseum Kärnten, 2003, 89–98.

Glaser, Franz, Ein Heiligtum des Grannus Apollo in Teurnia. In: *Jahreshefte des Österreichischen Archäologischen Institutes in Wien* 52, 1978, 121–127.

Glaser, Franz, Heiligtümer im östlichen Alpenraum als Ausdruck lokaler Identität. In: Schmidt-Colinet, Andreas (ed.), *Lokale Identitäten in Randgebieten des Römischen Reiches.* Wien, Phoibos, 2004, 91–100.

Glaser, Franz, Ländliche Heiligtümer und Quellkult. In: Leitner, Friedrich (ed.), *Götterwelten. Tempel, Riten, Religionen in Noricum.* Klagenfurt, Landesmuseum Kärnten, 2007, 103–120

Gleirscher, Paul, Archäologische Untersuchungen am Förker Laas-Riegel. In: Jerger, Thomas – Brinckmann-Blaha, Ute – Herwirsch, Ilse (eds), *Rudolfinum – Jahrbuch des Landesmuseums für Kärnten 2005*. Klagenfurt, Landesmuseum Kärnten, 2007, 39–44.

Gleirscher, Paul, Eine Mithrashöhle auf der Gradišče über St. Egyden. In: *Rudolfinum- Jahrbuch des Landesmuseums für Kärnten* 2011, 15–18.

Gleirscher, Paul – Nothdurfter, Hans – Schubert, Eckehart, *Das Rungger Egg*. Mainz am Rhein, Philipp von Zabern, 2002.

Gleirscher, Paul, Review of Der spätlatène- und römerzeitliche Brandopferplatz im Forggensee (Gde: Schwangau). In: *Germania* 79, nr. 2, 2001, 467–469.

Gleirscher, Paul, Vorrömerzeitliche Naturheiligtümer und die Frage Jhres Fortwirkens in die Römerzeit. In: Sporn, Katja – Ladstätter, Sabine – Kerschner, Michael (eds), *Natur - Kult - Raum*. Wien, Österreichisches Archäologisches Institut, 2015, 127–151.

Gleirscher, Paul, Zur antiken Bebauung auf dem Gipfel des Magdalensbergs. Zwischen Oppidum, Königsburg und Heiligtum. In: *Bonner Jahrbücher,* 207, 2007, 103–120.

Glodariu, Ioan, Asezari dacice si daco-romane la *Slimnic*. Bucuresti, Editura Academiei, 1983.

Glodariu, Ioan – Hampartumian, Nubar, *Dacian trade with the hellenistic and Roman world*. Oxford, BAR, 1976.

Glomb, Tomáš, The spread of the cult of Asclepius in the context of the Roman army benefited from the presence of physicians: A spatial proximity analysis. In: PloS ONE 16 (8), 2021. Open access: https://doi.org/10.1371/journal.pone.0256356

Gočeva, Zlatozara, Specific features in the iconography of Silvanus in Moesia Inferior. In: Chmielewski, Waldemar – Lipska, Anna – Niezgoda, Ewa – Ząbecka, Maria (eds), *Studia Aegaea et Balcanica in honorem Lodovicae Press*. Warszawa, Wydawn, Uniwersytetu Warszawskiego, 1992, 183–189.

Gojkovič, Mojca Vomer, Mithraea in Poetovio and the new discovery. In: *Acta Antiqua Academiae Scientiarum Hungariae* 58, 2018, 263–273.

Golubović, Snežana, Viminacium Necropolis: Observing Acculturation Process. In: Zerbini, Livio (ed.), *Culti e religiosità nelle province danubiane*. Bologna, I libri di Emil, 2015, 473–483.

Gömöri, János, Municipium Flavium Scarbanta. In: Pavan, Massimiliano (ed.), *La Venetia nell'area padano-danubiana: Le vie di comunicazione: convegno internazionale, Venezia, 6-10 aprile 1988*. Padova, Giunta regionale del Veneto 1990, 401–417.

Gömöri, János, Scarbantia. In: Šašel Kos, Marjeta – Scherrer, Peter (eds), *The autonomous towns of Noricum and Pannonia: Situla = Die autonomen Städte in Noricum und Pannonien, vol. Pannonia I*. Ljubljana, Narodni Muzej Slovenije, 2003, 81–92.

Gordon, Richard L., Coming to Terms with the 'Oriental Religions of the Roman Empire'. In: *Numen* 61/5–6, 2014, 657–672.

Gordon, Richard L., Institutionalised religious options: Mithraism. In: Rüpke, J. (ed.), *The Companion of Roman Religion*. Blackwell-Wiley, 2007, 392–405.

Gordon, Richard L., Mithras. In: Dölger, Franz (ed.), *Recllexikon für Antike und Christentum* vol.24/ Lfg. 193, 2012, 964–1009.

Gordon, Richard L., Projects, performance and charisma: Managing small religious groups in the Roman Empire. In: Gordon, Richard – Petridou, Georgia – Rüpke, Jörg (eds), *Beyond priesthood*. Berlin, De Gruyter, 2017, 277–316.

Gordon, Richard L., (Re-)modelling religious experience: some experiments with hymnic form in the imperial period. In: Gasparini, Valentino – Begemann, Elisabeth (eds), *Lived religion in the ancient Mediterranean world*. Berlin, Boston, De Gruyter, 2020, 23–48.

Gordon, Richard L., Small and miniature reproductions of the Mithraic icon: reliefs, pottery, ornaments and gems. In: Martens, Marleen – De Boe, Guy (eds), *Roman mithraism: the evidence of*

the small finds (papers of the international conference, Tienen, 7-8 November 2001). Bruxelles, Institute of Archaeological Heritage, 2004, 259–283.
Gordon, Richard L., The date and significance of CIMRM 593 (British Museum, Townley Collection). In: *Journal of Mithraic Studies* 2, 1978, 148–174.
Gordon, Richard L., The Roman Army and the Cult of Mithras: a critical view. In: Le Bohec, Yann – Wolff, Catherine (eds), *L'armée romaine et la religion*. Paris, De Boccard, 2009, 379–450.
Gosden, Chris – Marshall, Yvonne, The cultural biography of objects. In: *World Archaeology* 31/2, 1999, 169–178.
Gostencnik, Kordula, Die Stadt auf dem Magdalensberg und ihre Eliten. In: *Carinthia* I/208, 2018, 11–38.
Gostencnik, Kordula – Schindler, Eleni, Magdalensberg Bibliographie 2018. In: *Kärntner Museumsschriften* 87, 2019, 525–602.
Grabherr, Georg, Biodiversity in the high ranges of the Alps: Ethnobotanical and climate change perspectives. In: *Global Environmental Change* 19/2, 2009, 167–172.
Grabherr, Gerald, Die Via Claudia Augusta in Nordtirol - Methode, Verlauf, Funde. In: Walde, Elisabeth – Grabherr, Gerald (eds), *Via Claudia Augusta und Römerstrassenforschung im östlichen Alpenraum*. Innsbruck, Innsbruck University Press, 2006, 35–336.
Grabherr, Gerald – Kainrath, Barbara, Zinn- und Bleivotive aus dem römerzeitlichen Heiligtum auf dem Klosterfrauenbichl in Lienz in Osttirol. In: *Archäologisches Korrespondenzblatt* 49/3, 2019, 393–411.
Grabherr, Gerald, Vom Feuerbock zu den Aposteln – Ein antikes rurales Heiligtum in Lienz. In: Lehner, Manfred – Schrettle, Bernhard (eds), *Zentralort und Tempelberg*. Wien, Phoibos, 2016, 25–37.
Gradvohl, Edina, Votive uteri in the Hungarian National Museum. In: Zsidi, Paula – Németh, György (eds), *Ancient medicine and Pannonia*. Budapest, Pro Aquinco Foundation, 2006, 33–38.
Grammer, Benedikt, Stadtentwicklung in Pannonien während der Soldatenkaiserzeit. In: *Carnuntum Jahrbuch* 1, 2015, 11–70.
Grand-Clément, Adeline, Sensorium, Sensescapes, Synaesthesia, Multisensoriality: A New Way of Approaching Religious Experience in Antiquity? In: Alvar Nuño, Antón – Alvar Ezquerra, Jaime – Woolf, Greg (eds), *SENSORIVM*. Leiden, Boston, Brill, 2021, 141–159.
Gray, Patrick, *Varieties of Religious Invention*. New York, Oxford University Press, 2016.
Grbic, Dragana, The Thracian hero on the Danube new interpretation of an inscription from Diana. In: *Balcanica* 44, 2013, 7–20.
Gregoratti, Leonardo, North Italic settlers along the 'Amber Route'. In: *Studia Antiqua et Archaeologica* 19/1, 2013, 133–153.
Gregoratti, Leonardo, 13 Roman Traders as a Factor of Romanization in Noricum and in the Eastern Transalpine Region. In: Roselaar, Saskia T. (ed.), *Processes of cultural change and integration in the Roman world*. Leiden, Boston, Brill, 2015, 239–252.
Groh, Stefan – Láng, Orsolya – Sedlmayer, Helga – Zsidi, Paula, Neues zur Urbanistik der Zivilstädte von Aquincum-Budapest und Carnuntum-Petronell. In: *Acta Archaeologica* 65/2, 2014, 361–403.
Groh, Stefan – Sedlmayer, Helga, Contextual Archaeology: the Late Antique Fort and Vicus Favianis / Mautern. Methods and Results. In: *Late Antique Archaeology* 9/1, 2012, 483–509.
Groh, Stefan – Sedlmeyer, Helga, *Der norisch-römische Kultplatz am Frauenberg*. Montagnac, M. Mergoil, 2005.
Groh, Stefan – Sedlmeyer, Helga, *Forschungen Im Romischen Heiligtum Am Burgstall Bei St. Margarethen in Lavanttal (Noricum) (Zentraleuropaische Archaologie)*. Vienna, Austrian Academy of Sciences Press, 2011.
Groh, Stefan – Sedlmeyer, Helga, Späteisenzeitliche und Frührömische Kulte auf dem Frauenberg bei Leibniz. In: Leitner, Friedrich (ed.), *Götterwelten. Tempel, Riten, Religionen in Noricum*. Klagenfurt, Landesmuseum Kärnten, 2007, 31–35.

Grönke, Eveline, *Das römische Alenkastell Biricianae in Weissenburg i. Bay: Die Grabungen von 1890 bis 1990*. Mainz am Rhein, Verlag Philipp von Zabern, 1997.

Grottanelli, Cristiano, Ideologie del sacrificio umano. Roma e Cartagine. In: *Archiv für Religionsgeschichte* 1, 1999, 41–58.

Grüll, Tibor, *A Római Birodalom gazdasága*. Budapest, Gondolat Kiadó, 2017.

Grüll, Tibor, Jewish presence in the Danubian provinces of the Roman Empire. In: Hrbácsek, Magdaléna (ed.), *Židovský kultúrny fenomén v stredoeurópskom kontexte = Zsidó kultúra közép-európai kontextusban*. Nitra, Univerzita Konštantía Filozofa v Nitre, 2016, 9–18.

Grünewald, Martin, Roman healing pilgrimage north of the Alps. In: Friese, Wiebke – Kristensen, Troels (eds) *Excavating Pilgrimage. Archaeological Approaches to Sacred Travel and Movement in the Ancient World*. London, Routledge, 2017, 130–152.

Grünewald, Martin, Studien zur Bevölkerungsdichte und Migration in Obergermanien und Raetien. Ein Überblick anhand ausgewählter Gräberfelder. In: *Germania* 96/1–2, 2018, 159–208.

Gudea, Nicolae, *Aşezări rurale în Dacia Romană: 106-275 p. Chr: schiţă pentru o istorie a agriculturii şi satului daco-roman*. Oradea, Primus, 2008.

Gudea, Nicolae – Bozu, O., A existat un sanctuar mithraic la Pojejena?. Banatica IV, 1977, 117–130.

Gudea, Nicolae, *Christiana minora: Studii, articole si note în legatura cu crestinismul timpuriu din Dacia romana, Dacia postramana si unele provincii vecine*. Cluj-Napoca, Mega Publishing House, 2011.

Gudea, Nicolae, Der Dakische Limes. Materialien zur seiner Geschichte. In: *Jahrbuch des Römisch-Germanischen Zentralmuseums Mainz*, 44.2 Mainz, 1997, 497–609.

Gudea, Nicolae, Der untermoesische Donaulimes und die Verteidigung der moesischen Nord- und Westküste des Schwarzen Meeres: Limes et litus Moesiae Inferioris (86–275 n. Chr.). In: *Jahrbuch des Römisch-Germanischen Zentralmuseums Mainz* 52/2, 2005, 317–566.

Gudea, Nicolae, Die Nordgrenze der römischen Provinz Obermoesien. Materialien zu ihrer Geschichte (86–275 n. Chr.). In: *Jahrbuch des Römisch-Germanischen Zentralmuseums Mainz* 48/2, 2001, 3–118.

Gudea, Nicolae, Ländliche Siedlungen in den dakischen Provinzen (106–275 n. Chr.). Archäologische Beitrage zur Geschichte des Dorfes und der Landwirtschaft in der Romerzeit. In: J *Jahrbuch des Römisch-Germanischen Zentralmuseums Mainz*, 58, 2009, 187–319.

Gudea, Nicolae, *Porolissum: un complex daco-roman la marginea de Nord a Imperiului Roman. II, Vama romanăna: monografie arheologică, contribuţii la cunoasterea sistemului vamal din provinciile dacice*. Cluj-Napoca, Muzeul Naţional de Istorie a Transilvaniei, 1996.

Gudea, Nicolae, *Porolissum. X, Un focar al crestinismului timpuriu în provincia Porolissensis (secolele II-III p. Chr.) şi î epoca post aureliană (secolele IV-VI p. Chr) = Ein Zentrum des frühen Christentums in der Provinz Dacia Porolissensis (2.-3. Jahrhundert n. Chr.) und in der nachaurelianischen Zeit (4.-6. Jahrhundert n. Chr)*, Cluj-Napoca, Mega Publishing House, 2016.

Gudea, Nicolae – Tamba, Dan, *Porolissum: Un complex daco-roman (3) la marginea de nord a imperiului roman. Despre templul zeului Iupiter Dolichenus din municipium Septimium. (Über ein Iupiter Dolichenus Heiligtum in der municipium Septimium Porolissensum)*. Cluj-Napoca, Napoca Star, 2001.

Gudea, Nicolae, The Limes in the province of Pannonia inferior (AD 106–294). In: *Jahrbuch des Römisch-Germanischen Zentralmuseums Mainz* 60/2, 2013, 459–658.

Gugl, Christian, Das Umland Teurnias vo 2. Jahrhundert v. Chr. bis ins 1. Jahrhundert n. Chr: Eine Studie zur Siedlungskontinuität von der Latene- zur Romerzeit im oberen Drautal. In: *Arheološki Vestnik*, 52, 2001, 303–349.

Gugl, Christian – Kastler, Raimund, *Legionslager Carnuntum: Ausgrabungen 1968–1977*. Wien, Verlag der Österreichischen Akademie der Wissenschaften, 2007.

Gugl, Christian – Wallner, Mario – Neubauer, Wolfgang – Doneus, Michael – Löcker, Klaus, Die militärischen Anlagen in Carnuntum. In: Beutler, Franziska – Farka, Christa – Gugl, Christian – Humer, Franz – Kremer, Gabrielle – Poilhammer, Eduard (eds), *Der Adler Roms: Carnuntum und die Armee der Caesaren*. Mainz, Nünnerich-Asmus Verlag & Media, 2017, 76–85.

Gyáni, Gábor, *A történelem mint emlék(mű),* Pozsony, Kalligram, 2016.

Gyurka, Orsolya – Szebenyi, Tamás, Ókori leletek a Debreceni Egyetem Klasszika-filológiai és Ókortörténeti Tanszékének régészeti gyűjteményéből. In: *Történeti tanulmányok* 24, 2016, 114–135.

Haeussler, Ralph, Interpretatio Indigena. Re-inventing local cults in a global world. In: *Mediterraneo Antico* 15, 2012, 143–174.

Haeussler, Ralph, The dynamics and contradictions of religious change in Gallia Narbonensis. In: King, C. Anthony – Haeussler, Ralph (eds), *Continuity and innovation in religion in the Roman West I*. Portsmouth, Journal of Roman Archaeology Supplement, 2007, 81–103.

Hainzmann, Manfred, Aesculapius et Hygeia als Dii Maiores? In: *Studia Europaea Gnesenсia* 16, 2017, 259–280.

Hainzmann, Manfred, *Fontes epigraphici religionum Celticarum antiquarum. I Provincia Noricum. Fasciculus 1 und 2*. Wien, Verlag der Österreichischen Akademie der Wissenschaften, 2020.

Hainzmann, Manfred, Roman influence in Noricum. Review of (M.) Zimmermann Romanisation und Repräsentation in Noricum. (Antiquitas. Reihe 1, Abhandlungen zur Alten Geschichte 71.) Pp. xii + 465, ill., maps. Bonn: Dr. Rudolf Habelt, 2017. Cased, €93. ISBN: 978-3-7749-4080-2. In: *The Classical Review* 69/1, 2019, 243–245.

Handy, Markus, Bemerkungen zum Belenus Kult in Noricum. In: *Römisches Österreich* 41, (2018) 2019, 58–66.

Handy, Markus, Das Regnum Noricum und seine 'formative Periode' unter Caesar und Augustus. In: Lehner, Manfred – Schrettle, Bernhard (eds), *Zentralort und Tempelberg Siedlungs-und Kultentwicklung am Frauenberg bei Leibnitz im Vergleich*. Wien, Phoibos Verlag 2016, 49–60.

Hanson, Jon William – Ortman, Scott – Lobo, José, Urbanism and the division of labour in the Roman Empire. In: *Journal of The Royal Society Interface*, 14(136), 20170367. doi:10.1098/rsif.2017.0367. Open access.

Harding, D. W., *The archaeology of Celtic art*. London, Routledge, 2007.

Harl, Ortolf, Der Stadtplan von Virunum nach Luftaufnahmen und Grabungsberichten. In: *Jahrbuch des Römisch-Germanischen Zentralmuseums Mainz*, 36, 1/2, 1989, 521–598.

Harl, Ortolf – Günther, Dembski – Gschwantler, Kurt – Càssola Guida, Paola, *Hochtor und Glocknerroute. ein hochalpines Passheiligtum und 2000 Jahre Kulturtransfer zwischen Mittelmeer und Mitteleuropa*. Wien Österreichisches Archäologisches Institut, 2014.

Harrisson, Juliette, *Dreams and dreaming in the Roman Empire*. London, Bloomsbury, 2013.

Haynes, Ian, Characterising cult communities in the Roman provinces: some observations on small finds from the sanctuary of Liber Pater from Apulum. In: Collins, Rob – McIntosh, Frances (eds), *Life in the Limes: Studies of the people and objects of the Roman frontiers*. Oxford, Oxbow Books, 2014, 87–95.

Haynes, Ian, Introduction: the Roman army as a community. In: Goldsworthy, Adrian – Haynes, Ian (eds), *The Roman army as a community*. Portsmouth, JRA, 1999, 7–14.

Haynes, Ian, The shrine of Liber. In: *Current World Archaeology* 10, 2005, 38–45.

Haupt, Peter – Zanier, Werner, Der Spätlatène- und frühkaiserzeitliche Opferplatz auf dem Döttenbichl südlich von Oberammergau. In: *Bonner Jahrbücher* 216, 2017, 399–402.

Haverfield, Francis, *The Romanisation of Roman Britain. Papers on Roman Britain, Volume 11*. London Published for the British Academy by H. Frowde, 1889.

Hechelheim, Friedrich, Árpád Dobó: Publicum Portorium Illyrici. (Dissertationes Pannonicae, Ser. II, Fasc. 16.) Pp. 52, Budapest: Institut für Münzkunde u. Archaeologie der P. Pázmány Universität, 1940. In: *The Classical Review*, Volume 56, 2, July 1942, 93–94.

Heidenreich, Christophe Schmidt, *Le Glaive et l'Autel*. Camps et piété militaires sous le Haut-Empire romain. Rennes, Presses universitaires de Rennes, 2013.

Heiss, Andreas, Speisen, Holz und Räucherwerk. Die verkohlten Pflanzenreste aus dem jüngereisenzeitlichen Heiligtum von Ulten, St. Walburg, im Vergleich mit weiteren alpinen

Brandopferplätzen. In: Steiner, Hubert (ed.), *Alpine Brandopferplätze: Archäologische und naturwissenschaftliche Untersuchungen = Roghi votivi Alpini: archeologia e scienze naturali.* Bozen, Abteilung Denkmalpflege, Amt für Bodendenkmäler, 2010, 787–813.

Hervás, Rocio Gordillo, Antinous and the Games of the Koinon of the Achaeans and the Arcadians in Mantinea. In: *Hermes*, 148, 2, 2020, 218–231.

Herzog, Johann Jakob, *Real-encyklopädie für protestantische theologie und kirche, vol. XIV.* Gotha, Verlag von Rudolf Hesser, 1861.

Hijmans, Steven, Material Matters: Object, Authorship, and Audience in the Arts of Rome's Empire. In: Alcock, Susan E. – Egri, Mariana – Frakes, James F. D. (eds), *Beyond boundaries.* Los Angeles, Getty Publications, 2016, 84–101.

Hirt, Alfred Michael, *Imperial mines and quarries in the Roman world: organizational aspects 27 BC – AD 235.* Oxford, Oxford University Press, 2010.

Hodder, Ian, *Religion, History, and Place in the Origin of Settled Life.* Louisville, University of Colorado Press, 2018.

Hódi, Attila, Apuleius Savariensis II. In: *Ókor* 11/4, 2012, 63–68.

Hofeneder, Andreas, Apollon Grannos – Überlegungen zu Cassius Dio 77, 15,5–7. In: Hofeneder, Andreas – Bernardo Stempel, Patrizia de (eds), *Théonymie celtique, cultes, interpretatio = Keltische Theonymie, Kulte, interpretatio.* Vienna, Verlag der Österreichischen Akademie der Wissenschaften, 2013, 101–111.

Hofeneder, Andreas, Die Gründungslegende von <em>Virunum</em>. In: Stüber, Karin – Zehnder, Thomas – Bachmann, Dieter (eds), *Akten des 5. Deutschsprachigen Keltologensymposiums, Zürich, 7. – 10. September 2009.* Vienna, Praesens, 2010, 123–136.

Holzer, Veronika, Das keltische Zentrum Roseldorf – ein neuer Siedlungstyp. In: Prammer, Johannes – Sandner, Ruth – Tappert, Claudia (eds), *Siedlungsdynamik und Gesellschaft, Beiträge des internationales Kolloquiums zur keltischen Besiedlungsgeschichte im bayrischen Donauraum.* Österreich und der Tschechischen Republik, 2008, 393–410.

Horváth, Tünde, Kelta szarvasáldozatok Balatonőszöd-Temetői-dűlő (M7/S10 lelőhely) La Tene D településen. In: Ilon, Gábor – Bartosiewicz, László (eds), *Mikroszkóppal, feltárásokkal, mintavételezéssel, kutatásokkal az archeometria, a geoarcheológia és a régészet szolgálatában.* Szeged, SZTE TTIK Földrajzi és Földtani Intézet, 2019, 115–133.

Höck, Anton – Zemmer-Plank, Liselotte – Sölder, Wolfgang, Der Fundplatz 'Südwestecke Innsbruck-Wilten-VELDIDENA', ein rätischer Brandopferplatz der frühen Kaiserzeit? In: *Veröffentlichungen des Tiroler Landesmuseum Ferdinandeum,* 75/76 (1995/96), 1997, 167–218.

Hristov, Ivan – Barakov, Venelin, Thracian rock sanctuary in the vicinity of Discoduratere. In: *Thracia* 15, 2003, 691–698.

Hristov, Ivan, Newly discovered sanctuary of the god Sylvanus in the village of Butan, Vratsa province. In: *Yearbook of* нацИонален ИсторИческИ музей - соФИя tome 28, 2016, 130–134.

Hristov, Ivan – Torbatov, Sergey – Ivanova, Bilyana – Ivanov, Stiliyan – Lazar Nino, *The sanctuary of the Thracian horseman by Sostra.* Sophia, Unicart, 2013.

Hughes, Jessica, *Votive Body Parts in Greek and Roman Religion,.* Cambridge, Cambridge University Press, 2017.

Hübner, Johann, *Kurtze Fragen aus der Neuen und Alten Geographie.* Regensburg, Emerich Baders Verlag, 1746.

Husar, Adrian, *Din istoria Daciei romane.* Cluj-Napoca, Presa Universitară Clujeană, 2002.

Hye, Simon, Materiali datanti. In: De Simone, Carlo – Marchesini, Simona, La lamina di Demlfeld. Roma-Pisa, Fabrizio Serra Editore, 2013, 23–31.

Iacob, Mihaela, Culte şi zeităţi în Moesia Inferior. Demetra, evidenţa numismatică. In: *Pontica* 33–34, 2000–2001, 355–371

Iara, Kristine, Moving In and Moving Out: Ritual Movements between Rome and its Suburbium. In: Östenberg, Ida – Malmberg, Simon – Bjørnebye, Jonas (eds), *The Moving City*. London, Bloomsbury Academic, 2015, 125–132.

Ibarra, Álvaro, Dacian riders: transcultural expressions of religious identity in Roman Dacia in the midst of war. In: Brody, Lisa – Hoffmann, Gail (eds), *Roman in the provinces: art on the periphery of Empire*. Chestnut Hill, McMullen Museum of Art, Boston College, 2014, 167–179.

Ilić, Olivera – Golubović, Snežana – Mrđić, Nemanja, Supplying and transport along Danube Limes in the upper Moesia. In: *Archaeology and Science* 6, 2010, 61–76.

Ilon, Gábor – Sosztarits, Ottó – Oross, Katalin – Molnár, Antal, Előzetes jelentés a Sé–Doberdón 1998-ban végzett leletmentésről. Preliminary report of the rescue excavations conducted at Sé–Doberdó in 1998 (Vas County). In: *Régészeti kutatások Magyarországon*. Budapest, Magyar Nemzeti Múzeum, 2001, 63–75.

Israelowich, Ido, The Authority of Physicians as Dream Interpreters in the Pergamene Asclepieion. In: Michaeilides, Demetrios (ed.), *Medicine and Healing in the Ancient Mediterranean World*. Oxford/Philadelphia, Oxbow Books, 2014, 291–296.

Ivanov, Rumen – Luka, Krassimira, *Montana. Praesidium, Raegio, Municipium*. Sofia, s.n. 2016.

Jackson, Ralph, The Senuna treasure and shrine at Ashwell (Herts). In: King, C. Anthony – Haeussler, Ralph (eds), *Continuity and innovation in religion in the Roman West I*. Portsmouth, Journal of Roman Archaeology Supplement, 2007, 37–54.

Jankovic, M., The Social Role of Roman Baths in the Province of Moesia Superior. In Zuchowska, M. (ed.) The Archeology of Water Supply. Oxford, 2012, 34.

Jerala, M., The topography of ritual monuments of Poetovio. In: Lazar, Irena (ed.), *Religion in public and private sphere. Acts of the 4th International Colloquium The Autonomous Towns of Noricum and Pannonia*, Koper, Univerza na Primorskem, 2011, 75–87.

Jeremić, Miroslav, *Sirmium: Grad na Vodi: razvoj urbanizma i arhitekture od I do VI veka*. Belgrade Archaeological Institute, 2016.

Jobst, Werner, *11. Juni 172 n. Chr.: der Tag des Blitz- und Regenwunders im Quadenlande*. Wien, Verlag der Österreichische Akademie der Wissenschaften, 1978.

Jobst, Werner, *Der römische Tempelbezirk auf dem Pfaffenberg/Carnuntum: Ausgrabungen – Funde – Forschungen = The Roman temple district of Pfaffenberg/Carnuntum: excavations – findings – research*. Klagenfurt JOBSTMedia Präsentation Verl. 2006.

Jobst, Werner – Piras, Rita, Il Tempio II del Santuario di Giove sul Pfaffenberg/Carnuntum. In: *Carnuntum Jahrbuch* 1, 2018, 25–46.

Jobst, Werner – Piso, Ioan – Kremer, Gabrielle, *Das Heiligtum des Jupiter Optimus Maximus auf dem Pfaffenberg/Carnuntum, Band 2: Die rundplastischen Skulpturen*. Wien, Verlag der Österreichischen Akademie der Wissenschaften, 2003.

Jobst, Werner – Weber, Ein Heiligtum der Pferdegöttin Epona in Carnuntum? In: *Acta archaeologica Academiae Scientiarum Hungaricae*. 41, 1989, 349–358.

Johannsen, Dirk – Kirsch, Anja, Narrative Strategies. In: Koch, Anne – Wilkens, Katharina (eds), *The Bloomsbury handbook of the cultural and cognitive aesthetics of religion*. London, Bloomsbury Academic, 2019, 143–154.

Johnson, Anne, (deutsche Bearbeitung von Dietwulf Baatz): *Römische Kastelle*. Verlag Philipp von Zabern, Mainz, 1987.

Johnston, David, *Roman Law in Context*. Cambridge, Cambridge University Press, 1999.

Jones, Christopher, *New Heroes in Antiquity: From Achilles to Antinoos*, London-Cambridge MA, Harvard University Press, 2010.

Jones, Siân, *The Archaeology of Ethnicity. Constructing identities in the past and present*. London, Routledge, 1997.

Jovanović, Alexandar, *Ogledi iz antičkog kulta i ikonografije*, Beograd, Filozofski fakultet, Centar za arheološka istraživanja, 2007.

Juhász, Lajos, The Pannonian wars of Aelius Caesar and Antoninus Pius. A fiction of modern scholars? In: *Acta Numismatica Pannonica* I, 2019, 45–55.

Jung, Julius, *Römer und Romanen in den Donauländern: historisch-ethnographische Studien*, Innsbruck, Wagnerischen Verlag, 1877.

Kabakčieva, Gergana, Oescus under Emperor Trajan's Rule: From Legionary Camp to Roman Colony. In: Piso, Ioan – Varga, Rada (eds), *Trajan und seine Städte: Colloquium Cluj-Napoca, 29. September - 2. Oktober 2013.* Cluj-Napoca, Mega Publishing House, 2014, 181–193.

Kádár, Zoltán, Gyógyitó istenségek kultusza Pannóniában topográfiai adatok tükrében. In: *Orvostörténeti Közlemények* 93–96, 1981, 63–78.

Kaizer, Ted, *The Religious Life of Palmyra: a Study of the Social Patterns of Worship in the Roman Period.* Stuttgart, Franz Steiner, 2002.

Kamenou, Marios – Dimitrova, Alina, Hephaestus Dabatopios and the divine patronage of metallurgy in Moesia Inferior and Thracia. In: Pavúk, Peter – Klontza-Jaklová, Věra – Harding, Anthony (eds), *ΕΥΔΑΙΜΩΝ. Studies in honour of Jan Bouze.* Prague, Faculty of Arts, Charles University, 423–438.

Kandler, Manfred, Bilddokumente zum Forum von Brigantium. In: *Archäologie in Gebirgen. Festschrift E. Vonbank.* Bregenz 1992, 131–136.

Kappie, Lawrence, *Legions and veterans: Roman army papers, 1971-2000.* Stuttgart, Franz Steiner Verlag, 2000.

Karnitsch, Paul, Der heilige Bezirk von Lentia. In: *Historisches Jahrbuch der Stadt Linz* 1, 1956, 177–210.

Katsiardi-Hering, Olga – Maria A. Stassinopoulou (eds). *Across the Danube: Southeastern Europeans and Their Travelling Identities (17th-19th C.).* Leiden-Boston, Brill, 2017.

Kaul, Flemming, The Gundestrup Cauldron: Thracian Art, Celtic Motifs. In: *Etudes Celtiques* 37/1, 2011, 81–110.

Kazarow, Gawril, The Thracian Rider and St. George. In: *Antiquity*, 12(47), 1938, 290–296.

Kellner, Hans-Jörg – Zahlhaas, Gisela, *Der römische Tempelschatz von Weissenburg i.Bay,* Mainz, von Zabern, 1993.

Kemkes, Martin – Willburger, Nina, *Der Soldat und die Götter. Römische Religion am Limes.* Stuttgart, Theiss 2004.

Kenner, Hedwig, Die Masken von der Mautern an der Donau. In: *Jahreshefte des Österreichischen Archäologischen Institutes in Wien*, 38, 1950, 162–180.

Kenner, Friedrich von, *Noricum und Pannonien: Eine Untersuchung über die Entwickelung, Bedeutung und das System der römischen Verteidigungsanstalten in den mittleren Donauländern.* Wien, Verlag des Altertumsvereins, 1870.

Khondker, Habibul, Globalisation to Glocalisation: A Conceptual Exploration. In: *Intellectual Discourse* 13, nr. 2, 2005, 181–199.

Kiernan, Philip, *Roman Cult Images: The Lives and Worship of Idols from the Iron Age to Late Antiquity.* Cambridge, Cambridge University Press, 2020.

Kindt, Julia, Oracular Shrines as Places of Religious Experience. In: Raja, Rubina – Rüpke, Jörg (eds), *A Companion to the Archaeology of Religion in the Ancient World.* Chichester, John Wiley & Sons, 2015, 268–278.

King, Anthony, Romano-Celtic temples in Britain: Gallic influence or indigenous development? In: King, Anthony – Haeussler, Ralph (eds), *Continuity and innovation in religion in the Roman West: 1.* Portsmouth, 2007, 13–18.

Király Pál, A sarmizegetusai Mithraeum. In: *Archeológiai Közlöny* 15, 1886, 1–95.

Kiss, Péter, Mithras altäre aus Savaria. In: Lazar, Irena (ed.), *Religion in public and private sphere. Acts of the 4th International Colloquium The Autonomous Towns of Noricum and Pannonia.* Koper, Univerza na Primorskem, 2011, 183–192.

Klein, Michael J., 'Von den Göttern verehren sie am meisten Merkur': Heiligtümer, Götterbilder und Inschriften aus Obergermanien und Raetien. In: Klein, Michael J. (ed.), *Die Römer und ihr Erbe*. Mainz, Philipp von Zabern, 2003, 107–128.

Kloppenborg, John, Social Networks and the Dissemination of Elective Cults. In: *Early Christianity* 10, nr. 2, 2019, 121–156.

Knibbe, Kim – Kupari, Helena, Theorizing lived religion: introduction. In: *Journal of Contemporary Religion* 35/2, 2020, 157–176.

Knittler, Herbert, Die Donaumonarchie 1648–1848. In: Kellenbenz, Hermann – Mieck, Ilja (eds), *Handbuch der europäischen Wirtschafts- und Sozialgeschichte. Bd 4, Europäische Wirtschafts- und Sozialgeschichte von der Mitte des 17. Jahrhunderts bis zur Mitte des 19. Jahrhunderts*. Stuttgart, Klett 1993, 880–915.

Knott, Kim, *The location of religion. A spatial analysis*. London, Routledge, 2005.

Knott, Kim, From locality to location and back again: A spatial journey in the study of religion. In *Religion* 39, 2009, 154–160.

Kocsis, László, A Tribunus Laticlaviusok háza az aquincumi 2–3. sz-i legiotáborban: előzetes jelentés. In: *Budapest Régiségei* 28, 1991, 117–121.

Kohler-Schneider, Marianne – Caneppele, Anita – Heiss, G. Andreas, Land use, economy and cult in late Iron Age ritual centres: an archaeobotanical study of the La Tène site at Sandberg-Roseldorf, Lower Austria. In: *Vegetation History and Archaeobotany* 24, 2015, 517–540.

Koortboijan, Michael, *Crossing the Pomerium: The Boundaries of Political, Religious, and Military Institutions from Caesar to Constantine*. Princeton, Princeton University Press, 2020.

Köpeczy, Béla (ed.), *Erdély Története I*. Budapest, Akadémiai Kiadó, 1986.

Korać, Miomir – Golubović, Snezana – Mrdić, Nemanja – Jeremić, Gordana – Lazić-Pop, Stefan, *Frontiers of the Roman Empire. Roman Limes in Serbia*. Belgrade, Digital Art, 2014.

Kovács Péter, A pomérium régészete. In: Szabó, Ádám – Fehér Bence (eds), *Studia Epigraphica Pannonica II*. Budapest, Történelmi Ismeretterjesztő Társulat Egyesület, 2010, 129–142.

Kovács, Péter, Civitas Eraviscorum. In: Vaday Andrea (ed.), *Pannonia and beyond: studies in honour of László Barkóczi*. Budapest, Archaeological Institue of the Hungarian Academia of Sciences, 199[illegible], 278–295.

Kovács, Péter, *History of Pannonia during the Principate*. Bonn, Rudolf Habelt, 2014.

Kovács, Péter, Iuppiter Optimus Maximus Paternus and the cohors milliaria Maurorum. In: *Acta Antiqua Academiae Scientiarum Hungariae* 40/1-4, 2000, 239–246.

Kovács Péter, *Marcus Aurelius' Rain Miracle and the Marcomannic Wars*. Boston-Leiden, Brill, 2009.

Kovács, Péter, Notes on the 'Jewish' Inscriptions in Pannonia. In: *Journal of Ancient Judaism* 1/2, 2010, 159–180.

Kovács, Péter, Oppidum Scarbantia Iulia. In: *Antik Tanulmányok* 46/1-2, 2002, 147–191.

Kovács, Péter, Some Notes on the Division of Illyricum. In: Piso, Ioan (ed.), *Die Römischen Provinzen. Begriff und Gründung, Colloquium ClujNapoca, 28th September – 1 Oktober 2006*. Cluj-Napoca, Mega Publishing House, 2008, 237–248.

Kovács, Péter, Territoria, pagi and vici in Pannonia. In: Eck, Werner – Kovács Péter – Fehér Bence (eds), *Studia epigraphica in memoriam Géza Alföldy*. Bonn, Rudolf Habelt, 2013, 131–164.

Kovács, Péter: The principia of Matrica. In: Communicationes archeologicae Hungariae 1999 Magyar Nemzeti Muzeum. Népművelési Propaganda Iroda, Budapest 1999, S. 49–74.

Kovács, Péter, Újabb római sírkő Somogy megyéből. In: Fehér, Bence – Kovács, Péter (eds), *Epigráfiai tanulmányok Alföldy Géza emlékére*. Budapest, TITE, 2017, 67–70.

Kovacsovics, Wilfried K., Das Mithrasheiligtum von Immurium-Moosham. In: Fleischer, Robert – Kovacsovics, Wilfried K. – Moucka-Weitzel, Veronika (eds), *Die römische Strassenstation Immurium-Moosham im Salzburger Lungau*. Salzburg, Amt der Salzburger Landesregierung (Landesarchäologie), 1998, 287–297.

Kremer, Gabrielle, *Das Heiligtum des Jupiter Optimus Maximus auf dem Pfaffenberg/Carnuntum, Band 2: Die rundplastischen Skulpturen*. Wien, Verlag der Österreichischen Akademie der Wissenschaften, 2003.
Kremer, Gabrielle, Der Kaiser als Pharao oder Antinoos? In: *Carnuntum Jahrbuch* 2015, 71–80.
Kremer, Gabrielle, *Götterdarstellungen, Kult- und Weihedenkmäler aus Carnuntum*. Wien, Österreichische Akademie der Wissenschaften, 2012.
Kremer, Gabrielle, Some remarks about Domnus-Domna and the ,Danubian Riders'. In: Nemeti, Sorin – Beu-Dachin, Eugenia – Nemeti, Irina – Dana, Dan (eds), *The Roman Provinces. Mechanisms of integration*. Cluj-Napoca, Mega Publishing House, 2019, 275–291.
Krempuš, G. – Gaspari, A. – Novšak, M , Die neuen spätkeltischen und frühkaiserzeitlichen Heiligtümer von Celeia. In: Leitner, Friedrich (ed.), *Götterwelten. Tempel, Riten, Religionen in Noricum*. Klagenfurt, Landesmuseum Kärnten, 2007, 39–45.
Kristensen, Troels Myrup, The Life Histories of Roman Statuary and Some Aspects of Sculptural Spoliation in Late Antiquity. In: Altekamp, Stefan – Marcks-Jacobs, Carmen – Seiler, Peter (eds), *Perspektiven der Spolienforschung. 1, Spolierung und Transposition*. Berlin, De Gruyter, 2013, 23–46.
Kritzinger, Peter, Das römische Zollsystem bis in das 3. Jh. n. Chr. In: Kritzinger, Peter – Schleicher, Frank – Stickler, Timo (eds), *Studien zum römischen Zollwesen*. Duisburg, Wellem, 2015, 11–57.
Kusan, Dora – Bilić, Tomislav – Spahić, Nina Pirnat (eds), *Aquae Iasae- nova otkrića iz rimskog razdoblja na području Varaždinskih Toplica (katalog izložbe)/Aquae Iasae-recent discoveries of roman remains in the region of Varaždinske Toplice (exibition catalogue)*. Zagreb, Arheološki muzej u Zagrebu, 2015.
Künzl, Ernst, Aesculapius im Valetudinarium--oder warum die bisherige Interpretation der römischen Lazarette weiter gilt. In: *Wurzburger medizinhistorische Mitteilungen* 24, 2005, 99–109.
Künzl, Ernst, Der Adler und die Kobra – Ein seltenes Motiv im römischen Waffendeko. In: *Archäologisches Korrespondenzblatt* 38/1, 2008.
Laet, Siegfried. de, *Portorium: étude sur l'organisation douanière chez les romains, surtout à l'époque du Haut-Empire*. Brugge, De Tempel, 1949.
Lăscoiu, Mirela Elena, Observaţii asupra unei inscripţii de la 'Sub Cununi'. In: Stavilă, Andrei (ed.), *Arheovest I. In memoriam Liviu Măruia: interdisciplinaritate în Arheologie şi Istorie: Timişoara, 7 decembrie 2013*, Szeged, 2013, 373–380.
Laurence, Ray – Trifiló, Francesco, The global and the local in the Roman Empire: Connectivity and mobility from an Urban perspective. In: Pitts, Martin – Versluys, Miguel (eds), *Globalisation and the Roman World: Archaeological and Theoretical Perspectives*. Cambridge, Cambridge University Press, 2015, 99–122.
Lazar, Irena (ed.), *Religion in public and private sphere. Acts of the 4th International Colloquium The Autonomous Towns of Noricum and Pannonia*, Koper, Univerza na Primorskem, 2011.
Lazarenko, Igor – Mircheva, Elina – Encheva, Radostina – Stoyanova, Daniela – Sharankov, Nicolay, *The temple of the Pontic Mother of gods in Dionysopolis*. Varna, Slavena Publishing House, 2013.
Láng, Nándor, Das Dolichenum von Brigetio. In: *Dissertationes Pannonicae* II. No 11, 141, 165–181.
Láng, Orsolya, Functions and Phases: The 'Peristyle – House' in the Civil Town of Aquincum. In: Scherrer, Peter – Zabrana, Lilli (eds), *Domus: das Haus in den Städten der römischen Donauprovinzen: Akten des 3. Internationalen Symposiums über römische Städte in Noricum und Pannonien*. Wien, Österreichisches Archäologisches Institut, 2008, 271–284.
László, Levente – Nagy, Levente – Szabó, Ádám, *Mithras misztériumai I–II*. Budapest, Kairosz, 2005.
László, Péter, Nympháknak szentelt oltár Kékkútról. In: *Veszprém Megyei Múzeumok Közleménye*, 15, 1980, 73–76.
Le Bohec, Yann, La fondation de Timgad (100 après J.-C.). In: Piso, Ioan – Varga, Rada (eds), *Trajan und seine Städte: Colloquium Cluj-Napoca, 29. September – 2. Oktober 2013*. Cluj-Napoca, Mega Publishing House, 2014, 91–99.
Lefebvre, Henri, *The Production of Space*. Oxford-Cambridge, Blackwell, 1991.

Leitner, Friedrich (ed.), *Götterwelten. Tempel, Riten, Religionen in Noricum*. Klagenfurt, Landesmuseum Kärnten, 2007.

Lerz, Antonietta – Henig, Martin – Hayward, Kevin, The Minories Eagle: A New Sculpture from London's Eastern Roman Cemetery. In: *Britannia* 48, 2017, 19–35.

Lichtermann, Paul – Raja, Rubina – Rieger, Katharina – Rüpke, Jörg: Grouping Together in Lived Ancient Religion. In: *Religion in the Roman Empire* 3/1, 2017, 3–10.

Liska, Igor, Managing an International River Basin Towards Water Quality Protection: The Danube Case. In: Liska, Igor (ed.), *The Danube River Basin*. Dordrecht, London, Springer, 2015, 1–19.

Lőrincz, Barnabás, *Zur Militärgeschichte der Donauprovinzen des Römischen Reiches: Ausgewählte Studien, 1975-2009*. Hungarian Polis Studies Nr. 19, Budapest-Debrecen, 2011.

Luchesi, Brigitte, Cult images. In: Koch, Anne – Wilkens, Katharina (eds), *The Bloomsbury handbook of the cultural and cognitive aesthetics of religion*. London, Bloomsbury Academic, 2019, 207–218.

Luginbühl, Thierry, Ritual activities, processions and pilgrimages. In: Raja, Rubina – Rüpke, Jörg (eds), *A Companion to the Archaeology of Religion in the Ancient World*. Chichester, John Wiley & Sons, 2015, 41–59.

Lungarova, Pepa, *Rimskite kultove v provincija Dolna Mizija: katalog na pametnicite*. Veliko Tărnovo, Universitetskop Izdatelstvo, 2012.

Luschin, Edgar Markus, Das Stadtzentrum von Virunum. In: *Jahreshefte des Österreichischen Archäologischen Institutes in Wien* 1/72, 2004, 149–175.

Maier, Bernhard, *Die Religion der Kelten*. München, C. H. Beck, 2004.

Mantzilas, Dimitris, Mater Matuta: an overview of her cult. In: Mantzilas, Dimitris (ed.), *Myrema (Mythology-Religion-Magic). 30 Articles and Essays*. Ioannina, Carpe Diem Publications, 2018, 487–542.

Maráz, Borbála, Budapest-Gellérthegy és környékének késő latène-kori településtörténete (2., A gellérthegyi kelta oppidum és a romanizált őslakosság települései a Gellérthegy körüli síkságon). In: *Budapest Régiségei* 40, 2006, 31–44.

Marchesini, Simona, Considerazioni storico-linguistiche. In: De Simone, Carlo – Marchesini, Simona, *La lamina di Demlfeld*. Roma-Pisa, Fabrizio Serra Editore, 2013, 73–90.

Marchesini, Simona, La ricezione di elementi cultuali allogeni in ambito celtico: Taranis in Val di Fiemme (TN). In: Regoli, Carlo (ed.), *Mode e Modelli. Fortuna e insuccesso nella circolazione di cose e idee*. Roma, Officina Etruscologia 7, 2012, 177–190.

Marchesini, Simona – Roncador, Rosa, *Monumenta Linguae Raeticae*. Roma, Scienze e Lettere, 2015.

Marchesini, Simona – Rosa, Roncador, Celts and Raetians in the Central-Eastern Alpine Region during the Second Iron Age: multidisciplinary research. In: Armit, Ian – Potrebica, Hrvoje – Črešnar, Matija – Mason, Philip – Büster, Lindsey (eds), *Cultural encounters in Iron Age Europe*. Budapest, Archaeolingua Alapítvány, 2016, 267–284.

Marcu, Felix – Cupcea, George – Bajusz, Mátyás – Petiş, Ioniţă – Cociş, Horaţiu – Zăgreanu, Radu Iustinian, Frontiera Daciei Porolissensis între castrele de la Tihău şi Căşeiu (Samum). In: *Limes* 2, 2017, 20–24.

Marcu, Felix, Places of worship in forts. In: *Acta Musei Napocensis* 41–42, 2005 75–105.

Marcu, Felix, *The internal planning of roman forts of Dacia*. Cluj-Napoca, Mega Publishing House, 2009.

Mărgineanu-Cârstoiu, Monica, Der Theos Megas Tempel von Histria. Die Arkitectur. In: *Dacia – Revue d'archéologie et d'histoire ancienne* 33, 1989, 79–110.

Margolis, Robert – Elifson, Kirk, A Typology of Religious Experience. In: *Journal for the Scientific Study of Religion*, 18, No. 1 1979, 61–67.

Marsh, G. D., Three ,Theatre' Masks from London. In: *Britannia* 10, 1979, 263–265.

Martin, H. Luther, *The Mind of Mithraists: Historical and Cognitive Studies in the Roman Cult of Mithras*. London, Bloomsbury, 2014.

Marzatico, Franco, I Reti e i popoli delle Alpi orientali. In: Lanzinger, Michele (ed.), *Preistoria Alpina*. Trento, Museo delle Scienze, 2019, 73–82

Marzatico, Franco, Paesaggi del culto nelle Alpi centro-orientali. In: Negroni Catacchio, Nuccia (ed.), *Paesaggi cerimoniali. Ricerche e scavi*. Milano, Centro studi di preistoria e archeologia, 2014, 315–332.

Marzatico, Franco, Testimonianze figurative nel bacino dell'Adige fra l'età del Bronzo e l'età del Ferro. In: *Preistoria Alpina* 46/2, 2012, 309–332.

Maschek, Dominik, Architekturlandschaften. Eine phänomenpologische Analyse spätrepublikanischer Heiligtümer. In: Bolder-Boss, Marion – Maschek, Dominik (eds), *Orte der Forschung, Orte des Glaubens: neue Perspektiven für Heiligtümer in Italien von der Archaik bis zur Späten Republik. Akten der internationalen Tagung in Darmstadt am 19 . und 20 . Juli 201.*, Bonn, Rudolf Habelt Verlag 2016, 131–147.

Mastrocinque, Attilio, *The Mysteries of Mithras: A Different Account*. Tübingen, Mohr Siebeck, 2017.

Mateescu, Răzvan, *Istoriile unui templu*. Cluj-Napoca, Mega Publishing House, 2012.

Matei-Popescu, Florian, (Dii) Maiores at Histria (ISM I 298). In: Cosnean Nistor, Letitia – Apostol, Virgil – Popescu, Mariana Cristina – Bâlici, Ştefan – Toma, Natalia (eds), *Arhitectură - restaurare - arheologie: in honorem Monica Mărgineanu Cârstoiu*. Bucureşti, Editura ARA, 2021, 282–289.

Matei-Popescu, Florian, The Dacians from Moesia Inferior. In: Mihailescu-Bîrliba, Lucrețiu (ed.), *Migration, Kolonisierung, Akkulturation im Balkanraum und im Osten des Mittelmeerraumes (3. Jh. v. Chr.- 6 Jh. n. Chr.)*. Konstanz, artung-Gorre Verlag, 2017, 139–159.

Matei-Popescu, Florian, *The Roman Army in Moesia Inferior*. Bucharest, Conphyus Publishing House, 2010.

Matei-Popescu, Florian, Tropaeum Traiani. In: Piso, Ioan – Varga, Rada (eds), *Trajan und seine Städte: Colloquium Cluj-Napoca, 29. September - 2. Oktober 2013*. Cluj-Napoca, Mega Publishing House, 2014, 205–223.

Matijević, Krešimir, Epigraphische Anmerkungen zum so genannten 'Caracalla-Altar' in Abusina/ Eining-Raetia (CIL III 5935). In: *Frankfurter elektronische Rundschau zur Altertumskunde* 17, 2012, 1–11.

Maumené, Claude, The Gundestrup Cauldron: Is This The Key To The Enigma? In: *Mediterranean Archaeology and Archaeometry* 16/4, 2016, 351–358.

Mayer, Anton, Vidasus, der illyrische Silvanus. In: *Vjesnik Hrvatskog arheološkog društva*, 22–23, 1942, 187–191.

Mazzilli, Francesca, *Rural Cult Centres in the Hauran: Part of the broader network of the Near East (100 BC – AD 300)*. Oxford, Archaeopress, 2018.

McCarty, Matthew M. – Egri, Mariana – Rustoiu, Aurel, The archaeology of ancient cult: from foundation deposits to religion in Roman Mithraism. In: *Journal of Roman Archaeology* 32, 2019, 279–312.

McClure, Laura K., *Women in Classical Antiquity: From Birth to Death*. Hoboken, Wiley-Blackwell, 2019.

McGuire, Meredith, *Lived Religion. Faith and practice in everyday life*. Oxford, Oxford University Press, 2008.

MacMullen, Ramsay, Tertullian and ,national' gods. In: *The Journal of Theological Studies* 26/2, 1975, 405–410.

MacMullen, Ramsay, The Epigraphic Habit in the Roman Empire. In: *The American Journal of Philology* 103, No. 3 1982, 233–246.

Méa, Corentin, Le salariarius: un contractuel del'armeé romaine. In: *Zeitschrift für Papyriologie und Epigraphik*, 181, 2012, 207–213.

Meier, Thomas – Tillessen, Petra, Archaeological imaginations of religion: an introduction from an Anglo-German perspective. In: Meier, Thomas – Tillessen, Petra (eds), *Archaeological imaginations of religion*. Budapest Archaeolingua 2014, 11–247.

Melhard, Gyula, A nagy-berki-i (Somogy megye) leletről. In: *Archaeologiai értesítő* 20/4-5, 1900, 386–390.

Meneghini, Roberto, Il foro di Traiano alla luce dei nuovi scavi et studi. In: Piso, Ioan – Varga, Rada (eds), *Trajan und seine Städte: Colloquium Cluj-Napoca, 29. September – 2. Oktober 2013*. Cluj-Napoca, Mega Publishing House, 2014, 69–85.

Metzner-Nebelsick, Carola, Creativity versus Taboo in Late Bronze Age Central and South Eastern Europe. In: Sofaer, Joanna (ed.), *Considering Creativity: Creativity, Knowledge and Practice in Bronze Age Europe*. Oxford, Archaeopress, 2018, 39–53.

Metzner-Nebelsick, Carola – Lang C. Amei – Sommer, Sebastian – Steidl, Bernd, Transalpine Mobility and Trade since the Mesolithic. In: Grupe, Gisela – Grigat, Andrea – McGlynn, George C. (eds), *Across the Alps in Prehistory Isotopic Mapping of the Brenner Passage by Bioarchaeology*. New York, Springer, 2017, 1–26.

Mihăilescu, Sorin – Praporgescu, Gabriel, About the Mureş-Tisa-Danube waterway. In: *Annals of the University of Petroşani, Mechanical Engineering*, 13, 2011, 89–96.

Mihaljević, Maria – Dizdar, Marko, The late La Tène bronze helmet from the Sava at Stara Gradiška. In: *Vjesnik Arheolo kog muzeja u Zagrebu*, 40, 2007, 117–146.

Mihajlović, Vladimir D., Dea Dardanica: pre-rimska plemenska boginja ili rimska imperijalna tvorevina? In: *Issues in Ethnology and Anthropology* 11/3, 2016, 679–710.

Mihajlović, Vladimir D., *The Scordisci between Ancient and Modern Interpretations: A Question of Identity in (Proto)History*. Novi Sad, Filozovski Fakultet, 2019.

Miklós, Domokos, History and Results of the Hydrological Co-operation of the Countries Sharing the Danube Catchment (1971–2008). In: Brilly, Mitja (ed.), *Hydrological Processes of the Danube River Basin Perspectives from the Danubian Countries*. Dordrecht, London, Springer, 2010, 1–25.

Miklós, Domokos – Neppel, Ferenc, Palaeogeography of the Danube and Its Catchment. In: Brilly, Mitja (ed.), *Hydrological processes of the Danube River Basin*. Dordrecht, London, Springer, 2010, 79–124.

Miloševič, Gordana, Domus and villae urbanae in Serbia. In: Scherrer, Peter (ed.), *Domus: Das Haus in den Städten der römischen Donauprovinzen*. Wien, Österreichisches Archäologisches Institut, 2008, 367–386.

Mirković, Miroslava, Beneficiarii consularis and the new outpost in Sirmium. In: Maxfield, Valerie – Dobson, Michael John (eds), *Roman frontier studies 1989: proceedings of the XVth International Congress of Roman Frontier Studies*, Exeter, University of Exeter Press, 1991, 252–256.

Mirković, Miroslava, Die Anfänge der Provinz Moesia. In: Piso, Ioan (ed.), *Die römischen Provinzen: Begriff und Gründung: (Colloquium Cluj-Napoca, 28. September-1. Oktober 2006)*. Cluj-Napoca, Mega Publishing House, 2008, 249–270.

Mirković, Miroslava, *Moesia Superior. Eine Provinz an der mittleren Donau*. Mainz, Von Zabern, 2007.

Miŝić, Blanka, *Cults and religious integration in the Roman cities of the Drava valley (Southern Pannonia)*. PhD dissertation, Royal Holloway University of London, 2013. Open access.

Mistry, Amreen, The art of storytelling: cognition and action through stories. In: *International Journal of Arts & Sciences* 9/4, 2016, 301–324.

Mitthof, Franz – Schreiner, Peter – Schmitt, Oliver Jens (eds), *Handbuch zur Geschichte Südosteuropas Volume 1: Dominance and Politics in Southeastern Europe before 1800 Band 1: Herrschaft und Politik in Südosteuropa von der römischen Antike bis 1300*. Berlin-New York, De Gruyter, 2019

Mladenović, Dragana, *Urbanism and settlement in the Roman province of Moesia Superior*. Oxford, Archaeopress, 2012.

Mócsy, András, *Pannonia a korai császárság idején*. Budapest, Akadémiai Kiadó, 1974.

Mócsy, András, *Pannonia and Upper Moesia: a history of the middle Danube provinces of the Roman Empire*. London-Boston, Routledge & K. Paul, 1974.

Moga, Vasile – Timofan, Anca – Bounegru, George – Ota, Radu – Bălan, Gabriel – Lascu, Ilie, *Descoperă arheologia Urbană! Apvlvm 2007, Catalog de expoziţie*. Alba Iulia, Muzeul National Al Unirii Alba Iulia, 2008.

Mommsen, Theodor, *Römische Geschichte. Fünfter Band. Die Provinzen von Caesar bis Diocletian*. Berlin, Weidmann, 1885.

Monteix, Nicolas, The Archaeological Perception of Capital and its Transformations in Urban Occupations. In: Erdkamp, Paul – Verboven, Koenraad – Zuiderhoek, Arjan (eds), *Capital, investment, and innovation in the Roman world*. Oxford, Oxford University Press, 2020, 195–222.

Moser, Claudia – Feldman, Cecelia (eds), *Locating the Sacred*. Oxford, Oxbow Books, 2014.

Moser, Claudia, Linear Reflections. In: Moser, Claudia – Feldman, Cecelia (eds), *Locating the Sacred*. Oxford, Oxbow Books, 2014, 13–34.

Moser, Claudia, *The Altars of Republican Rome and Latium Sacrifice and the Materiality of Roman Religion*. Cambridge, Cambridge University Press, 2019.

Morgan, David, *Images at Work: The Material Culture of Enchantment* Oxford, Oxford University Press, 2018.

Morgan, David, *Visual piety*. Berkeley, University of California Press, 1999.

Mráv, Zsolt, Considerations on the archaeological and natural contexts of cult places and sanctuaries in the Pannonian provinces. In: *Carnuntum Jahrbuch* 2016 (2017), 101–108.

Mráv, Zsolt – Gabrieli, Gabriella, A scarbantiai Iseum és feliratos emlékei. In: *Arrabona* 49/1, 2011, 201–238.

Mráv, Zsolt, Graves of auxiliary soldiers and veterans from the first century AD in the northern part of Pannonia. In: Sanader, Mirjana (ed.), *Proceedings of the XVIIth Roman Military Equipment Conference: Weapons and military equipment in funerary context*. Zagreb, Filozofski fakultet: Arheološki muzej, 2013, 87–116.

Mráv, Zsolt, Nagybronz szoborleletek pannoniában – Rövid áttekintés. In: *Communicationes Archaeologicae Hungariae*, 2016, 173–203.

Mráv, Zsolt – Ottományi, Katalin, A pagus Herculius és vicusainak Terra Mater oltára Budaörsről. In: *Specimina Nova* 19, 2005, 71–118.

Mráv, Zsolt, Római-kori feliratok és faragott kőemlékek Pátyról. In: *Studia Comitatensia* 30, 2007, 403–423.

Mráv, Zsolt, Septimius Severus and the cities of the middle Danubian provinces. In: Eck, Werner – Fehér, Benedictus – Kovács, Péter (eds), *Studia epigraphica in memoriam Géza Alföldy*. Bonn, Dr Rudolf Habelt GmbH, 2013, 205–240.

Mráv, Zsolt, The Roman Amy along the Amber Road between Poetovio and Carnuntum in the 1 st Century A.D. – Archaeological Evidence. A Preliminary Research Report. In: Communicationes Archaeologicae Hungariae 2010–2013, 49–100.

Munteanu, Claudiu, *Transportul de mărfuri pe căile navigabile interioare din provinciile române renane şi dunărene: (secolul I-III p. Chr.)*, Sibiu, Editura Muzeului Brukenthal, 2015.

Mussini, Elena, La rappresentazione del dio fluviale Acheloo in area Slovena. In: *Arheološki vestnik* 49, 1998, 261–270.

Müller, Harald – Schweighofer, Bernd – Piso Ioan – Benea, Marcel, *Der Marmor im Römischen Dakien*. Cluj-Napoca, Mega Publishing House, 2011.

Mylonopoulos, Joannis, *Divine Images and Human Imaginations in Ancient Greece and Rome*. Leiden, BRILL, 2010.

Nagy, Lajos, Les symboles astraux sur les monuments funeraires de la population indigene de la Pannonie. In: *Dissertationes Pannonicae* II, 11, 1941, 232–250.

Nagy, Levente, Die Lage der Erforschung des frühen Christentums in Ungarn im Spiegel eines neuen Projekts. In: Pillinger, Renate (ed.), *Neue Forschungen zum frühen Christentum in den Balkanländern*. Vienna, Austrian Academy of Sciences Press, 2015, 19–36.

Nagy, Levente, Ein Alkestis Relief aus Intercisa und die Ikonografie einiger verstorbenen mythischen Gestalten in der kaiserzeitlichen Grabkunst. In: *Specimina Nova* 21–22, 2013, 145–158.

Nagy, Levente, Gondolatok Tóth István Pannoniai vallástörténetéről: Tóth István Pannoniai vallástörténet. L'Harmattan, Budapest, 2015. 251 oldal. In: *Korall* 17/63, 2016, 158–174.
Nagy, Levente, The Short History of Time in the Mysteries of Mithras: The Order of Chaos, the City of Darkness, and the Iconography of Beginnings. In: *Pantheon* 7, 2012, 37–58.
Nagy, Tibor, Vallási élet Aquincumban. In: Szendi Károly – Alföldi, András – Nagy, Lajos (eds), *Budapest története I. Budapest az ókorban*. Budapest, 1942, 386–463.
Nash-Williams, V. E. – Praschniker, C. – Kenner H., Der Bäderbezirk Von Virunum (Österreichisches Archäologisches Institut). Wien: Rudolf M. Rohrer Verlag, 1947. Pp. 243, with 10 plates (4 coloured), and 222 text illustrations. In: *Journal of Roman Studies* 40/1-2, 1950, 170.
Nedelea, Luciana, Pontic sigillata at potaissa. New data regarding the import of fine ware in romandacia at Castra legionis v macedonicae. In: *Acta Musei Napocensis* 53/1, 2016, 185–202.
Negula, Dana Iulia – Moise, Cristian – Lazăr, Andi Mihai – Rișcuța, Nicolae Cătălin – Cristescu, Cătălin – Dedulescu, Andreea Luminița – Mihalache, Cristina Elena – Badea, Alexandru, Satellite Remote Sensing for the Analysis of the Micia and Germisara Archaeological Sites. In: *Remote Sensing* 12/12, 2020, 2003.
Nelis-Clément, Jocelyne, *Les beneficiarii. Militaires et administrateurs au service de l'Empire (ier s. a.C.-vie s. p.C)*. Paris, Ausonius Éditions, 2000.
Német, György, Why lead? In: Baratta, Giulia (ed.), *Instrumenta inscripta VIII. Plumbum litteratum studia epigraphica Giovanni Mennella oblata*. Roma, Scienze e lettere, 2021, 447–454.
Nemeth, Eduard, *Politische und militärische Beziehungen zwischen Pannonien und Dakien in der Römerzeit: Relații politice și militare între Pannonia și Dacia în epoca romană*. Cluj-Napoca, Editura Tribuna, 2007.
Németh, György, Neueste Ergebnisse der Magieforschung in Dacien. In: Zerbini, Livio (ed.), *Culti e religiosità nelle province danubiane*. Bologna, I libri di Emil, 2015, 393–401.
Németh, Margit, Die Militäranlagen von Óbuda. In: Zsidi, Paula (ed.), *Forschungen in Aquincum 1969–2002*. Budapest, Budapest Történeti Múzeum, 2003, 85–93.
Nemeti, Sorin, *Dialoguri păgâne*. Iași, Presa Universitară Alexandru Ioan Cuza, 2012.
Nemeti, Sorin, Finding Arcobadara: Essay on the geography and administration of Roman Dacia. Cluj-Napoca, Mega Publishing House, 2014.
Nemeti, Sorin, I rilievi dei Cavalieri Danubiani: Spunti per l'interpretazione diacronica delle varianti regionali. In: Alexandrescu, Cristina (ed.), *Cult and votive monuments in the Roman provinces: proceedings of the 13th International Colloquium on Roman Provinical Art, Bucharest, Alba Iulia, Constanța, 27th of May - 3rd of June 2013: within the framework of Corpus Signorum Imperii Romani*. Cluj-Napoca, 2015, 129–138.
Nemeti, Sorin, La religione dei Daci in età romana. In: Taufer, Matteo (ed.), *Sguardi interdisciplinari sulla religiosità dei Geto-Daci*. Freiburg im Bresgau-Berlin-Vienna, Paradeigmata 23, Rombach Verlag, 2013, 137–155.
Nemeti, Sorin, *Le syncrétisme religieux en Dacie Romaine*. Cluj-Napoca, Mega Publishing House, 2019.
Nemeti, Sorin, Magical Practices in Dacia and Moesia Inferior. In: Alexandrescu, Cristina (ed.), *Jupiter on your side: gods and humans in antiquity in the Lower Danube area: accompanying publication for the thematic exhibitions in Bucharest, Alba Iulia and Constanta, May – September 2013*. Bucuresti Masterprint Super Offset, 2013, 143–156.
Nemeti, Sorin – Marcu, Felix, The historiography of religions in Roman Dacia. A brief account. In: Boda, Imola – Szabó, Csaba, *The bibliography of Roman Religion in Dacia*. Cluj-Napoca, Mega Publishing House, 2014, 9–20.
Nemeti, Sorin, *Sincretismul religios în Dacia romană*. Cluj-Napoca, Presa Universitară Clujeană, 2005.
Nemeti, Sorin, Society and Religion in Ilisua. In: *Classica et Christiana* 5/2, 2010, 395–433.

Nenninger, M., Der Kult der Kybele in der römischen Provinz Moesia Inferior. In: Conrad, Sven – Oppermann, Manfred (eds), *Pontos Euxeinos. Beiträge zur Archäologie undGeschichte des antiken Schwarzmeer- und Balkanraumes.* Langenweissbach, Beier & Beran 2006, 199–212

Nesselhauf, Herbert, Publicum portorii Illyrici utriusque et ripae Thraciae. In: *Epigraphica* 1, 1939, 331–338.

Neubauer, W. – Eder-Hinterleitner, A. – Seren, S. – Melichar, P., Georadar in the Roman civil town Carnuntum, Austria: an approach for archaeological interpretation of GPR data. In: *Archaeological Prospection* 9/3, 2002, 135–156.

Neusch, Marcel, *Le sacrifice dans les religions.* Paris, Beauchesne, 1994.

Niederwanger, Günther, *Burgstall am Schlern - ein alpiner Brandopferplatz.* Bozen, Athesia, 2002.

Nielsen, I., Buildings of religious communities. In: Raja, Rubina – Rüpke, Jörg (eds), *A Companion to the Archaeology of Religion in the Ancient World.* Chichester, John Wiley & Sons, 2015, 279–293.

Nielsen, Inge, *Housing the chosen: the architectural context of mystery groups and religious associations in the ancient world.* Turnhout, Brepols, 2014.

Nikolova, Stella, Hold Your Horses – Animals in Ancient Thrace. In: Kaercher, Kyra – Arntz, Monique – Bomentre, Nancy – Hermoso-Buxán, Xosé L. – Kay, Kevin – Ki, Sabrina – Macleod, Ruairidh – Muñoz-Mojado, Helena – Timbrell, Lucy – Wisher, Izzy (eds), *New Frontiers in Archaeology: Proceedings of the Cambridge Annual Student Archaeology Conference 2019.* Oxford, Archaeopress Access Archaeology, 2020, 164–179.

Nock, Arthur Darby, *Conversion: the old and the new in religion from Alexander the Great to Augustine of Hippo.* Oxford: Claredon Press, 1933.

Noethlichs, Karl, The Legal Framework of Religious Identity in theRoman Empire. In: Rebillard, Éric – Rüpke, Jörg (eds), *Group Identity and religious individuality in Late Antiquity.* Washington, D.C., The Catholic University of America Press, 2015, 13–30.

Noll, Rudolf, *Das Inventar des Dolichenusheiligtums von Mauer an der Url (Noricum).* Wien, Österreichischen Akademie der Wissenschaften, 1980.

North, John, The development of religious pluralism. In: Lieu, Judith – North, John – Rajak, Tessa (eds), *The Jews among pagans and Christians in the Roman Empire.* London, Routledge, 1992, 174–193.

Nuber, Hans Ulrich – Seitz, Gabriele, Strassenstation Sontheim/Brenz-'Braike', Kreis Heidenheim. In: *Archäologische Ausgrabungen in Baden-Württemberg* 1994, 1995, 156–164.

Oberrauch, Hanns, Zum Ursprung der Brandopferplätze. In: Hye, Simon – Töchterle, Ulrike (ed.), *UPIKU:TAUKE Festschrift für Gerhard Tomedi zum 65. Geburtstag.* Bonn, Dr. Rudolf Habelt GmbH, 2019, 435–456.

Olson, Kenneth R. – Krug, Edward, The Danube, an Empire Boundary River: Settlements, Invasions, Navigation, and Trade Pathway. In: *Journal of Water Resource and Protection* 12/10, 2020, 884–897.

Oltean, Ioana, *Dacia: Landscape, Colonisation and Romanisation.* London, Routledge, 2007.

Oltean, Ioana A. – Fonte, João, GIS Analysis and Spatial Networking Patterns in Upland Ancient Warfare: The Roman Conquest of Dacia. In: *Geosciences* 11/1, 2021, 17.

Oltean, Ioana – Hanson, William, Conquest strategy and political discourse: new evidence for the conquest of Dacia from LiDAR analysis at Sarmizegetusa Regia. In: *Journal of Roman Archaeology*, 30, 2017, 429 – 446.

Oltean, Radu, *Dacia. Războaiele cu romanii. Sarmizegetusa.* București, Humanitas, 2019.

Olteanu, Florian – Amon, Lucian, Horothesia Histriei, un Dosar Istoric. In: *Revista de Stiinte Juridice*, 2008, 168.

Ong, Walter J., *Orality and Literacy: The Technologizing of the Word.* London – New York, Routledge, 2002.

Onofrei, C., Maurii în Dacia. In: *Revista Bistriței* 21/1, 2007, 269–282.

Oprea, Emanuel George – Oprea, Cristiana, Dacian Temples and Ancient Astronomical Research in Sarmizegetusa. In: *Dialogo* 2/1, 2015, 226–230.

Opreanu, Coriolan Horațiu, Arhitectura epocii Latene din Munții Șureanu (Sebeșului). O analiză metodologică, Analele Banatului 23, 2015, 151–186.

Opreanu, Coriolan Horațiu, Castrul roman de la Grădiștea Muncelui (Sarmizegetusa Regia). Cronologia și semnificația sa istorică. In: *Ephemeris Napocensis* 9–10, 2000, 151–168.

Opreanu, Coriolan Horațiu, Profan vs. sacru la Sarmizegetusa Regia & Profane vs. Sacred at Sarmizegetusa Regia. In: *Analele Banatului* 24, 2016, 233–254.

Opreanu, Coriolan H., The Enigmatic Dacian Architecture at Sarmizegetusa Regia. Profane vs. Sacred Purpose. In: *Ephemeris Napocensis* 29, 2019, 177–192.

Opriș, Ioan Carol – Rațiu, Alexandru, Roman customs station from Capidava. Statio for publicum portorii Illyrici in the 2nd century AD and ahypothetical model for interactions with Barbaricum in the 4th century AD. In: Bârcă, Vitalie (ed.), *Orbis Romanus and Barbaricum*. Cluj-Napoca, Mega Publishing House, 2016, 89–110.

Ørsted, Peter, *Roman imperial economy and Romanization: a study in Roman imperial administration and the public lease system in the Danubian provinces from the first to the third century A.D.* Copenhagen, Museum Tusculanum Press, 1985.

Ota, Radu, O statuetă a lui Icarus descoperită la Apulum. In: *Terra Sebus: Acta Musei Sabesiensis* 6, 2014, 253–257.

Ottományi, Katalin, A római kor emlékei Pest megyében (őslakosság, településszerkezet, temetkezés, vallás, betelepített barbárok). In: Fancsalszky, Gábor (ed.), *Pest Megye Monográfiája I/1. A kezdetektől a honfoglalásig. Pest megye régészeti emlékei*. Budapest, Pest Megye Monográfia Közalapítvány, 2007.

Ottományi, Katalin, *Római vicus Budaörsön: régészeti tanulmányok*. Budapest, Archaeolingua Alapítvány, 2012.

Owen, Suzanne, *The Appropriation of Native American Spirituality*. London, Bloomsbury, 2011.

Pallasmaa, Juhani, Space, place and atmosphere. Emotion and peripherical perception in architectural experience. In: *Lebenswelt. Aesthetics and philosophy of experience* 4, 2014, 230–245.

Panagiotidou, Olympia – Beck, Roger, *The Roman Mithras Cult A Cognitive Approach*. London, Bloomsbury, 2017.

Panaite, Adriana, Protective Deities of Roman Roads. In: Alexandrescu, Cristina (ed.), *Jupiter on your side: gods and humans in antiquity in the Lower Danube area: accompanying publication for the thematic exhibitions in Bucharest, Alba Iulia and Constanta, May – September 2013*. Bucuresti, Masterprint Super Offset, 2013, 133–142.

Paturel, Simone, *Baalbek-Heliopolis, the Bekaa, and Berytus from 100 BCE to 400 CE. A Landscape Transformed*. Leiden-Boston, Brill, 2019.

Patzelt, Maik, About servants and flagellants: Seneca's Capitol description and the variety of 'ordinary' religious experience at Rome. In: Rigotti, Eddo – Greco, Sara (ed.), *Inference in Argumentation*. Dordrecht, London, Springer, 2019, 117–136.

Paulovics, István: Eine Inschrift des Fahnenheiligtums von Dunapentele. In: *Archaeologiai Értesítő* 78, 1951, S. 21–23.

Pazmany, Karolien, *Between mountains and frontiers: the Roman settlement system in the provinces of Germania Superior, Raetia and Noricum*. Leiden, Universiteit Leiden, 2019. Open access.

Pârvan, Vasile, *Dacia: An Outline of the Early Civilizations of the Carpatho-Danubian Countries*. Cambridge, Cambridge University Press, 1928.

Perinić, Ljubica, *The Nature and Origin of the Cult of Silvanus in the Roman Provinces of Dalmatia and Pannonia*. Oxford, Archaeopress, 2016.

Pescaru, Adriana – Alicu, Dorin, *Templele romane din Dacia*. Deva, Astra, 2000.

Pescaru, Adriana, *Sanctuarele Daciei*. Deva, Astra, 2005

Petculescu, Liviu – Mitar, Cristina, The Civilian Settlement at Micia. Topography, Chronology and Legal Status. In: *Limes* 23, 2015, 95–101.

Petres, Éva, On celtic animal and human sacrificies. In: *Acta Archaeologica Academiae Scientiarum Hungariae* 24, 1972, 365–383.

Petres, Éva, The late pre-Roman age in Hungary with special reference to Oppida. In: Cunliffe, Barry – Rowley, Trevor (eds), *Oppida in Barbarian Europe. Papers Presented to a Conference at Oxford, 10-12 October 1975* British archaeological reports; Supplementary series 11. Oxford, BAR, 1976, 51–80.

Pețan, Aurora, Omonimele Istrului II. Istrul Argonauților. In: Pețan, Aurora – Bîtrănoiu, Raluca (eds), *Arheologie și Studii Clasice* 2. Bucuresti, Editura Dacica, 2012, 176–239.

Pețan, Aurora, Șapte temple și un sanctuar. Opinii pe marginea unei cărți recente despre zona sacră a Sarmizegetusei Regia. In: *Rapoartele Centrului de Studii a Fundației Dacica,* 4, 2015, 60–83.

Peter, Ulrike, Religious-cultural identity in Thrace and Moesia Inferior. In: Howgego, Chris – Heuchert, Volker – Burnett, Andrew (eds), *Coinage and identity in the Roman provinces,* Oxford, Oxford Univerity Press, 2005, 107–114.

Petraccia, Maria, Magistrati municipali uccisi da latrones. In: Olivé, Marc Mayer – Baratta, Giulia – Guzmán Almagro, Alejandra (eds), *XII Congressus internationalis epigraphiae graecae et latinae: provinciae imperii romani inscriptionibus descriptae: Barcelona, 3-8 Septembris 2002: acta.* Barcelona, Institut d'estudis catalans, 2007, 1139–1146.

Petridou, Georgia, Aelius Aristides as Informed Patient and Physician. In: Leira, Bernt J. (ed.), *Optimal Stochastic Control Schemes within a Structural Reliability Framework.* Cham, Springer, 2016, 451–470.

Petridou, Georgia, *Divine Epiphany in Greek Literature and Culture.* Oxford, Oxford University Press, 2016.

Petridou, Georgia, Healing Shrines. In: Irby, Georgia (ed.), *Companion to Greek Science, Medicine, and Technology.* Chichester, Wiley-Blackwell, 2016, 434–449.

Petrikovits, von Harald, *Die Innenbauten römischer Legionslager während der Prinzipatszeit.* Opladen, Westdeutscher Verlag, 1975.

Petrovic, Petar, Novi votivni natpisi iz južne Srbije. In: *Starinar* 15–16, 1966, 245–251.

Petrović, Vladeta, Terrestrial Communications in the Late Antiquity and the Early Middle Ages in the Western Part of the Balkan Peninsula. In: Živkovic, Tibor – Rudic, Srđan (eds), *The world of the Slavs: studies on the East, West and South Slavs: civitas, oppidas, villas and archeological evidence (7th to 11th centuries AD),* Belgrade, The Institute of history, 2013, 235–286.

Petrović, Vladimir P., The Aquae Station on the Roman Danube Limes Road in Upper Moesia. In: *Open Archaeology* 4/1, 2018, 386–393.

Petrović, Vladimir P., The cult of Jupiter Dolichenus in Moesia Superior: mining aspects. In: Bitrakova Grozdanova, Vera – Bricault, Laurent – Versluys, Miguel John – Nikoloska, Aleksandra – Müskens, Sander (eds), *Romanising oriental gods? Religious transformations in the Balkan provinces in the Roman period: new finds and novel perspectives.* Skopje, Leiden, Macedonian Academy of Sciences and Arts: University of Leiden, 2015, 323–332.

Pfahl, Stefan, Requisit oder Dekor? Bruchstücke einer lebensgroßen Tonmaske aus dem gallo-römischen Vicus von Taberna-Tawern. In: *Funde und Ausgrabungen im Bezirk Trier: Aus der Arbeit des Rheinischen Landesmuseums Trier* 31, 1999, 20–29.

Phillips, C. Robert, *Approaching Roman religion: the case for Wissenschaftgeschichte.* In: Rüpke, Jörg (ed.), *A Companion to Roman Religion.* Chichester, Wiley-Blackwell, 2007, 10–29.

Pilipović, Sanja, *Kult Bahusa na centralnom Balkanu. I-IV vek / The Cult of Bacchus in the Central Balkans.* Belgrade, Institute de Études Balkaniques, 2009.

Pines, Yuri – Biran, Michal – Rüpke, Jörg (eds), *The Limits of Universal Rule: Eurasian Empires Compared.* Cambridge, Cambridge University Press, 2021.

Pippidi, Dionisie M., Dionysische Inschriften aus Histria aus dem II – III Jh.u.Z. In: *Dacia – Revue d'archéologie et d'histoire ancienne* 3, 1959, 391–414.

Piso, Ioan, *Das Heiligtum des Jupiter Optimus Maximus auf dem Pfaffenberg, Carnuntum, 1. Die Inschriften.* Wien, Akademie Verlag, 2003.

Piso, Ioan – Deac, Dan – Opreanu, Coriolan Horatiu, Das Heiligtum der Zollstation von Porolissum. In: *Zeitschrift für Papyrologie und Epigraphik* 200, 2016, 544–548.
Piso, Ioan, Die Inschrift aus Albertirsa. In: Eck, Werner – Kovács Péter – Fehér Bence (eds), *Studia epigraphica in memoriam Géza Alföldy*. Bonn, Rudolf Habelt, 2013, 275–285.
Piso, Ioan, Die Inschriften vom Pfaffenberg und der Bereich der Canabae legionis. In: *Tyche* 6, 1991, 131–160.
Piso, Ioan, Die Trajansfora: Politische Botschaft. In: Piso, Ioan – Varga, Rada (eds), *Traian und seine Städte: Colloquium Cluj-Napoca, 29. September - 2. Oktober 2013*. Cluj-Napoca, Mega Publishing House, 2014, 255–273.
Piso, Ioan, Ein Gebet für die Nymphen aus Germisara. In: *Acta Musei Napocensis* 52, 2015 (2017), 47–68.
Piso, Ioan, *Fasti provinciae Daciae I, Die senatorischen Amtsträger*. Bonn, Rudolf Habelt, 1993.
Piso, Ioan, *Fasti provinciae Daciae II, Die ritterlichen Amtsträger*. Bonn, Rudolf Habelt, 2013.
Piso, Ioan, Gli Illiri ad Alburnus Maior. In: Urso, Gianpaolo (ed.), *Dall'Adriatico al Danubio. Illirico nell'età greca e romana (Atti del convegno internazionale Cividale del Friuli, 25–27 settembre 2003)*. Pisa, Convegni della Fondazione Niccolò Canussio, ETS, 2004, 271–307.
Piso, Ioan, *Le forum vetus de Sarmizegetusa*. București, Editura Academiei, 2006.
Piso, Ioan, Les légions dans la province de Dacie. In: Le Bohec, Yann – Wolff, Catherine (eds), *Les légions de Rome sous le Haut-Empire*. Paris, De Boccard, 2000, 205–225.
Piso, Ioan, L'urbanisation des provinces danubiennes. In: Reddé, Michel Dubois, Laurent – Briquel, Dominique (eds), *La naissance de la ville dans l'Antiquité*. Paris, De Boccard, 2003, 285–298.
Piso, Ioan – Moga, Vasile, Un bureau du publicum portorium Illyrici à Apulum. In: *Acta Musei Napocensis* 35, 1998, 105–108.
Piso, Ioan – Țentea, Ovidiu – Marcu, Felix, Das Kapitol von Sarmizegetusa. In: *Dacia* 56, 2012, 119–123.
Piso, Ioan – Țentea, Ovidiu, Un nouveau temple Palmyrénien à Sarmizegetusa. In: *Dacia* 55, 2011, 111–121.
Piso, Ioan, The Trajan's Forum (Forum Vetus). In: Țentea, Ovidiu – Rațiu, Alexandru (eds), *Sarmizegetusa - The beginings of Roman Dacia*. Bucharest, National Museum of Romanian History, 2017, 20–32.
Piso, Ioan, Un nouveau conductor salinarum en Dacie. In: *Acta Musei Napocensis* 41–42, 2007, 179–182.
Pitts, Martin – Versluys, Miguel John, *Globalisation and the Roman World*. New York, Cambridge University Press, 2014.
Planck, Dieter – Beck, Willi, *Der Limes in Südwestdeutschland*. Stuttgart, Konrad Theiss Verlag, 1987
Platt, Verity, Viewing, Desiring, Believing: confronting the divine in a Pompeian house. In: *Art History* 25/1, 2002, 87–112.
Plemić, Bojana, *Roman and Autochthonous Goddess: Diana's Cult in the Provinces of Western and Centra Balkans (English summary of the Serbian PhD thesis)*. Belgrade, 2015. Open access.
Ployer, René, *Der norische Limes in Österreich*. Wien, Bundesdenkmalamt, 2013.
Pohanka, Reinhard, *Das römische Wien*. Wien, Pichler, 1997.
Polleres, J., Isis-Noreia. Ägiptisch- einheimischer Synkretismus in der Provinz Noricum. In: Leitner Friedrich (ed.), *Götterwelten. Tempel, Riten, Religionen in Noricum*. Klagenfurt, Landesmuseum Kärnten, 2007, 61–66.
Pop, Cosntantin – Țeposu-Marinescu, Lucian, *Statuete de bronz din Dacia Romană*. București, Muzeu Național al României, 2000.
Popescu, Mihai, *La religion dans l'armée romaine de la Dacie*. București, Editura Academiei Române, 2004
Popović, Ivana, The Židovar treasure and Roman jewellery from the Balkan provinces of the empire In: Guštin, Mitja – Jevtić, Miloš (eds), *The Eastern celts*. Koper-Beograd, Univerza na Primoerskem 2011, 179–188.

Porozhanov, Kalin, The Relations between Thracian States and Coastal Poleis along the Western Black Sea Coast: 3rd Century BC – 1st Century AD, According to Epigraphic Data. In: *ORPHEUS. Journal of Indo-European and Thracian Studies* 23–24, 2017, 32–38.

Posth, Cosimo *et al.*, The origin and legacy of the Etruscans through a 2000-year archeogenomic time transect. In: *Science Advances* 4 Sep 2021, 7, Issue 39. Open access.

Potrebica, Hrvoje – Dizdar, Marko, Changing Identities of the Iron Age Communities of Southern Pannonia. In: Popa, Cătălin Nicolae – Stoddart, Simon (eds), *Fingerprinting the iron age*. Oxford, Oxbow Books, 2014, 123–141.

Póczy, Klára, A pannóniai késő császárkori múmiatemetkezések néhány tanulsága. In: *Budapest Régiségei* 32, 1998, 59–75.

Póczy, Klára, Eraviskersiedlungen in Raum Aquincum. In: Zsidi, Paula (ed.), *Forschungen in Aquincum 1969-2002*. Budapest, Budapest Történeti Múzeum, 2003, 73-81.

Póczy, Klára, Healing deities. In: Fitz, Jenő (ed.), *Religions and cults in Pannonia*. Székesfehérvár, Fejér Megyei Múzeumok Igazgatósága, 1998, 33–36.

Póczy, Klára, Iuppiter Optimus Maximus Teutanus Aquincumban. In: Gaál, Attila (ed.), *Pannóniai kutatások*. Szekszárd, Wosinsky Múzeum, 1999, 201–207.

Póczy, Klára, Szent kerületek Aquincum és Brigetio aqueductusánál. In: *Archaeológiai Értesitő* 107, no. 1, 1980, 3–26.

Preiser-Kapeller, Johannes – Daim, Falko, *Harbours and maritime networks as complex adaptive systems*. Mainz, Verlag des Römisch-Germanischen Zentralmuseums, 2015.

Preložnik, Andrej – Nestorović, Aleksandra, Between Metropolis and Wilderness: The Topography of Mithraea in Ager Poetoviensis. In: *Acta Antiqua Academiae Scientiarum Hungariae* 58/1–4, 2018, 275–290.

Price, Simon, Religious Mobility in the Roman Empire. In: *The Journal of Roman Studies* 102, 2012, 1–19.

Protase, Dumitru, Dacia romană. In: Protase, Dumitru (ed.), *Istoria Românilor. vol. II. Daco-romani, romanici, alogeni,* București, Editura Academiei Române, 2010, 35–296.

Proudfoot, Wayne, *William James and a science of religions*. New York, Chichester, Columbia University Press, 2004.

Putzer, Andreas, Ein Beitrag zur Erforschung der Steinkegelaltäre vom Typ Rungger Egg Vorbericht über die Ausgrabungen am Wallnereck in der Gemeinde Ritten (Südtirol). In: *Germania* 89, 2011, 39–77.

Quinn, C. Josephine – Wilson, Andrew, Capitolia. In: *Journal of Roman Studies* 103, 2013, 117–173.

Rabadjiev, Kostadin, Theoi Samothrakes at Pontos Euxeinos. In: *Archaeologia Bulgarica* 21, no. 2, 2017, 11–25.

Rady, Martin, *The Habsburg Empire: A very short introduction*. Oxford, Oxford University Press, 2017.

Raja, Rubina, Complex sanctuaries in the Roman period. In: Raja, Rubina – Rüpke, Jörg (eds), *A Companion to the Archaeology of Religion in the Ancient World*. Chichester, John Wiley & Sons, 2015, 307–319.

Raja, Rubina – Rieger, Anna-Katharina, Sanctuaries – places of communication, knowledge and memory in Roman religion. In: Rüpke, Jörg – Woolf, Greg (eds), *Religion in the Roman Empire*. Stuttgart, Kohlhammer Verlag, 2021, 61–106.

Raja, Rubina – Rüpke, Jörg (eds), *A Companion to the Archaeology of Religion in the Ancient World*. Chichester, John Wiley & Sons, 2015.

Raja, Rubina – Sindbæk, Søren (eds), *Urban network evolutions: towards a high-definition archaeology*. Aarhus, Aarhus University Press, 2018.

Raja, Rubina – Weiss, Lara, The Significance of Objects: Considerations on Agency and Context. In: *Religion in the Roman Empire 2*, no. 3, 2016, 297–306.

Rankin, H. D., *Celts and the classical world*. London, Routledge, 1987.

Rapin, Claude, Les Alpes dans la cartographie antique: table de Peutinger, Strabon, Ptolémée. In: Dell'Era – Gregori, Gian Luca (ed.), *Romani nelle Alpi: storia, epigrafia e archeologia di una presenza: atti del convegno internazionale, Losanna, 13-15 maggio 2019.* Roma, Sapienza Università Editrice, 2021, 105–155.

Ratimorská, Priska – Minaroviech, Jana, Roman Sanctuary of Jupiter Dolichenus in Brigetio and its Hypothetical Reconstruction. In: *Anodos. Studies of the Ancient World* 9, 2009, 119–132.

Rebillard, Éric – Rüpke, Jörg (eds), *Group Identity and religious individuality in Late Antiquity.* Washington, D.C., The Catholic University of America Press, 2015.

Reddé, Michel – Barral, Philippe – Favory, François – Guillaumet, Jean-Paul – Marc, Jean-Yves – Nouvel, Pierre – Nuninger, Laure – Petit, Christophe, *Aspects de la Romanisation dans l'Est de la Gaule : Volume 2.* Glux-en-Glenne, Bibracte, 2011.

Reeves, M. Barbara, *The 'Feriale Duranum', Roman military religion, and Dura -Europos: A reassessment.* Buffalo, State University of New York, 2005. Open access.

Regep, Simona – Timoc, Călin, Despre vasele de cult din piatră descoperite în Dacia romană. In: *Cuprins Sargetia* 28–29/1, 1999, 221–230.

Reid, James Smith, Human Sacrifices at *Rome* and Other Notes on *Roman* Religion. In: Journal of Roman Studies 2, *1912*, 34–52.

Reim, Hartmann, Ein römisches Tempelgebäude bei Meßkirch, Kreis Sigmaringen. In: Gesellschaft für Vor- und Frühgeschichte in Württemberg und Hohenzollern (eds), *Archäologische Ausgrabungen 1978. Bodendenkmalpflege in den Regierungsbezirken Stuttgart und Tübingen.* Stuttgart, Gentner, 1979, 66–68.

Remus, Harold, Aelius Aristides at the Asclepeion in Pergamum. In: Kloppenborg, John – Wilson, Stephen (eds), *Voluntary associations in the ancient world.* London, Routledge, 1996, 146–175.

Renberg, Gil H., The Role of Dream-Interpreters in Greek and Roman Religion. In: Weber, Gregor (ed.), *Artemidor von Daldis und die antike Traumdeutung.* Berlin, De Gruyter, 2015, 233–262.

Renberg, Gil H., Was Incubation Practiced in the Latin West? In: *Archiv für Religionsgeschichte* 8/1, 2006, 105–147.

Renberg, Gil, H., *Where Dreams May Come: Incubation Sanctuaries in the Greco-Roman World.* Leiden-Boston, Brill, 2017.

Rendić-Miočević, A. – Šegvić, M., Religions and cults in South Pannonian regions. In: Fitz, Jenő (ed.), *Religions and cults in Pannonia.* Székesfehérvár, Fejér Megyei Múzeumok Igazgatósága, 1998, 7–16.

Renfrew, Colin, The archaeology of ritual, of cult and of religion. In: Kyriakidis, Evangelos (ed.), *The archaeology of ritual,* Los Angeles: Costen Institute, 2007, 109–122

Rieckhoff-Pauli, Sabine (ed.), *Die Römer in Schwaben: Jubiläumsausstellung 2000 Jahre Augsburg,* München, Bayerisches Landesamt für Denkmalpflege, 1985.

Rieder, Karl Heinz, Nassenfels: römisches Kastell mit Vicus und mittelalterliche Burg. In: *Führer zu archäologischen Denkmälern* 42, 2003, 170–173.

Rieger, Anna-Katharina, *Heiligtümer in Ostia. Architektur, Austattung und Stellung öffentlicher Heiligtümer in einer römischen Stadt.* München, Pfeil, 2004.

Rieger, Anna-Katharina, This god is your god, this god is my god: local identities at sacralized places in Roman Syria. In: Rigotti, Eddo – Greco, Sara (eds), *Inference in Argumentation.* Cham, Springer, 2019, 351–384.

Riesebrodt, Martin, Charisma in Max Weber's Sociology of Religion. In: *Religion* 29/1, 1999, 1–14.

Rives, James B., Graeco-Roman Religion in the Roman Empire: Old Assumptions and New Aproaches. In: *Currents in Biblical Research* 8, 2010, 240–299.

Rives, James B., Imperial Cult and Native Tradition in Roman North Africa. In: *The Classical Journal* 96/4, 2001, 425–436.

Rives, James B., Religion in the Roman provinces. In: Bruun, Christer – Edmondson, Jonathan (eds), *The Oxford Handbook of Roman Epigraphy.* Oxford, Oxford University Press, 2015, 420–445.

Robertson, Roland, Globalisation or glocalisation? In: *Journal of International Communication*, 1, no. 1., 1994, 33–52.
Roscoe, Will, Priests of the Goddess: Gender Transgression in Ancient Religion. In: *History of Religions* 35/3, 1996, 195–230.
Roselaar, Saskia T., State-Organised Mobility in the Roman Empire: Legionaries and Auxiliaries. In: Ligt, Luuk de – Tacoma, Laurens Ernst (eds), *Migration and mobility in the early Roman Empire.* Leiden, Brill, 2016, 138–157.
Rösler, Eduar Robert, *Zur Geschichte der unteren Donauländer.* Wien, Gerold's Sohn, 1864.
Roudometof, Victor, Glocal Religions: An Introduction. In: *Religions* 2018, 9, 294–302.
Roymans, Ton – Derks, Nico (eds), *Ethnic Constructs in Antiquity: The Role of Power and Tradition.* Amsterdam, Amsterdam University Press, 2009.
Rusu, Adriana, Marcus Statius Priscus la Germisara. Marcus Statius Priscus à Germisara. In: *Sargetia* 21–24, 1991, 653–656.
Ruscu, Ligia, 'Personal' external relations of the Western Pontic cities in pre-Roman period. In: Panova, S. (ed.), *Cerno More mezhdu istoka i zapada. Reka Dunav most mezhdu narodi i kultury.* Varna, 2004, 144–160.
Ruscu, Ligia, Relaţiile apoikiilor vest-pontice cu vecinii lor greci şi barbari în epocile elenistică şi romană. In: Panait Bîrzescu, Florina – Bîrzescu, Iulian – Matei-Popescu, Florian – Robu, Adrian (eds), *Poleis în Marea Neagră.* Bucureşti, Humanitas, 2013, 11–44.
Rustoiu, Aurel – Babeş, Mircea, The Carpathian and Danubian area. In: Colin Haselgrove, Colin – Rebay-Salisbury, Katharina S. – Wells Peter (eds), *The Oxford Handbook of the European Iron Age.* Oxford, Oxford University Press, Open access.
Rustoiu, Aurel – Egri, Mariana, The Celts from the eastern Carpathian Basinand their connections with the Mediterranean. In: Guštin, Mitja – David, W. (eds), *The Clash of Cultures? The Celts andthe Macedonien World.* Manching, Kelten-Römer-Museums Manching, 2014, 117–128.
Rustoiu, Aurel, *Războinici și artizani de prestigiu în Dacia preromană.* Cluj-Napoca, University 'Babeş-Bolyai' Cluj-Napoca, Fac. de Teologie Greco-Catolică, 2002.
Rustoiu, Aurel, The Carpathian and Danubian area. In: Haselgrove, Colin – Rebay-Salisbury, Katharina – Wells, Peter S. – Rustoiu, Aurel (eds), *The Oxford Handbook of the European Iron Age.* Oxford, Oxford University Press, 2018.
Rüpke, Jörg (ed.), *A Companion to Roman Religion.* Leiden-Boston, Brill, 2007.
Rüpke, Jörg, *Domi militiae: die religiöse Konstruktion des Krieges in Rom.* Stuttgart, Franz Steiner, 1990.
Rüpke Jörg, *From Jupiter to Christ: on the history of Religion in the Roman imperial period.* Oxford, Oxford University Press, 2014.
Rüpke, Jörg, Individual Appropriation of Sacred Space. In: *Espaces sacrés dans la Méditerranée antique.* Rennes: Presses universitaires de Rennes, 2016, 69–80.
Rüpke, Jörg, Individual choices and individuality in the archaeology of religion. In: Raja, R. – Rüpke, Jörg (eds), *A Companion to the Archaeology of Religion in the ancient World.* Leiden-Boston, 2015, 437–451.
Rüpke, Jörg, Individualization and individuation as concepts for historical research. In: Rüpke, Jörg (ed.), *The individual in the religions of Ancient Mediterranean.* Oxford, Oxford University Press, 2013, 3–40.
Rüpke, Jörg, Lived Ancient Religions. In: Rüpke, Jörg (ed.), *Oxford Research Encyclopedia of Religion.* Oxford University Press, 2019.
Rüpke, Jörg, Lived Ancient Religion: Questioning 'Cults' and 'Polis Religion'. In: *Mythos* 5, 2011 (2012), 191–204.
Rüpke, Jörg, *Pantheon. A new history of Roman religion.* Princeton, Princeton University Press, 2018.
Rüpke, Jörg, *Religion and its History A Critical Inquiry.* London, Routledge, 2021.

Rüpke, Jörg – Santangelo, Federico, Public priests and religious innovation in imperial Rome. In: Gordon, Richard L. – Petridou, Georgia – Rüpke, Jörg (eds), *Beyond Priesthood.* De Gruyter, 2017, 15–48.

Rüpke, Jörg, *Urban Religion. A Historical Approach to Urban Growth and Religious Change.* New-York-Berlin, De Gruyter, 2020.

Rustoiu, Aurel – Egri, Mariana, Danubian kantharoi – almost three decades later. In: Bereczki, Sándor (ed.), *Iron Age chronology in the Carpathian Basin.* Cluj-Napoca, Editura Mega, 2010, 217–287.

Sage, Michael, Marcus Aurelius and « Zeus Kasios» at Carnuntum. In: *Ancient Society* 18, 1987, 151–172.

Sage, Michael, *Septimius Severus and the Roman Army.* South Yorkshire, Pen and Sword, 2020.

Sanader, Mirjana, Novi aspekti kulta božice Terra Mater. In: *Opvscvla archaeologica* 20, 1, 1996, 119–130.

Sarnowski, Tadeusz, Das Fahnenheiligtum des Legionslagers Novae. In: Chmielewski, Waldemar – Lipska, Anna (eds), *Studia Aegaea et Balcanica in honorem Lodovicae Press.* Warszawa, Wydawn, Uniwersytetu Warszawskiego, 1992, 221–233.

Sarnowski, Tadeusz, Iuppiter und die legio I Italica. In: Zerbini, Livio (ed.), *Culti e religiosità nelle province danubiane.* Bologna, I libri di Emil, 2015, 507–524.

Sarnowski, Tadeusz, Statio publici portorii in novae (niedermoesien) und eine neue statuenbasis aus dem stabsgebäude der 1. Italischen legion. In: *Studia Europaea Gnesnensia* 16, 2017, 71–89.

Sarnowski, Tadeusz – Tomas, Agnieszka – Kowalevskaja, Ludmiła – Zakrzewski, Piotr – Dziurdzik, Tomasz – Jęczmienowski, Emil, Preliminary Report on the Excavations and Prospection Surveys of the University of Warsaw Archaeological Expedition. In: *Archeologia* 65, 2014, 177–203.

Sarnowski, Tadeusz – Tomas, Agnieszka – Zakrewski, Piotr – Dziurdzik, Tomasz – Jęczmienowski, Emil, Legionary defences and Headquarters building. In: *Światowit. Rocznik Instytutu Archeologii. Uniwersytetu Warszawskiego* 11, 2014, 179–188.

Šašel Kos, Marjeta, Adsalluta and Magna Mater – is there a link? In: Arenas-Esteban, J. Alberto (ed.), *Celtic religion across space and time.* Toledo, Junta de Comunidades de Castilla-La Mancha, 2010, 242–256.

Šašel Kos, Marjeta, Antinous in Upper Moesia: the introduction of a new cult. In: Bertinelli Angeli, Maria Gabriella – Donati, Angela (eds), *Opinione pubblica e forme di comunicazione a Roma.* Faenza, Fratelli Lega, 2009, 177–188.

Šašel Kos, Marjeta, Autochthonous cults between Emona and Poetovio. In: Fitz, Jenő (ed.), *Religions and cults in Pannonia.* Székesfehérvár, Fejér Megyei Múzeumok Igazgatósága, 1998, 17–22.

Šašel Kos, Marjeta, Illyria and Illyrians. In: Bagnall, Roger S. – Brodersen, Kai – Champion, Craige Brian – Erskine, Andrew – Huebner, Sabine R. (eds), *The encyclopedia of ancient history.* Chichester, Wiley-Blackwell, 2012, 1–3.

Šašel Kos, Marjeta, Nutrices: the most popular goddesses at Poetovio. In: Lehner, Manfred – Schrettle, Bernhard (eds), *Zentralort und Tempelberg.* Wien, Phoibos, 2016, 167–174.

Šašel Kos, Marjeta, Pannonia or Lower Illyricum? In: *TYCHE – Contributions to Ancient History, Papyrology and Epigraphy* 25/1, 2011, 123–130.

Šašel Kos, Marjeta, Poetovio before the Marcomannic Wars: From Legionary Camp to Colonia Ulpia. In: Piso, Ioan – Varga, Rada (eds), *Trajan und seine Städte: Colloquium Cluj-Napoca, 29. September – 2. Oktober 2013.* Cluj-Napoca, Mega Publishing House, 2014, 139–165.

Šašel Kos, Marjeta, *Pre-Roman divinities of the eastern Alps and Adriatic.* Ljubljana, Narodni Muzej Slovenije, 1999.

Šašel Kos, Marjeta, Savus and Adsalluta. In: *Arheološki vestnik* 45, 1994, 99–122.

Šašel Kos, Marjeta, The Roman conquest of Illyricum (Dalmatia and Pannonia) and the problem of northeastern border of Italy. In: *Studia Europaea Gnesnensia*/7, 2013, 169–200.

Šašel, Jaroslav, Zur Erklärung der Inschrift am Tropaeum Alpium (Plin. n. h. 3, 136–137. cil v 7817). In: *Živa antika. Antiquité vivante*, 22,1972, 135–144.

Săsărman, Mihai, *Onomasticon Provinciae Daciae*. PhD-Thesis, Babeş-Bolyai University, Cluj-Napoca, 2013. Open access.

Schalles, Hans-Joachim, Urbanisierung an der Nordgrenze des Imperium Romanum: Die Ausstattung der Colonia Ulpia Traiana mit öffentlichen Bauten, ihr Gründungsdatum und die Präsenz des Kaisers. In: Piso, Ioan – Varga, Rada (eds), *Trajan und seine Städte: Colloquium Cluj-Napoca, 29. September – 2. Oktober 2013*. Cluj-Napoca, Mega Publishing House, 2014, 111–137.

Schallmayer, Egon – Eibl, Kordula – Ott, Joachim – Preuss, Gerhard – Wittkopf, Esther, *Der römische Weihebezirk von Osterburken I. Forschungen und Berichte zur Vor- und Frühgeschichte in Baden-Württemberg Band 40*. Stuttgart, Landesamt für Denkmalpflege im Regierungspräsidium, 1990.

Schäfer, Alfred, *Tempel und Kult in Sarmizegetusa. Eine Untersuchung zur Formierung religiöser Gemeinschaften in der Metropolis Dakiens*. Padaberg, Verlag Scriptorium, 2007.

Schäfer, Felix, *Praetoria. Paläste zum Wohnen und Verwalten in Köln und anderen römischen Provinzhauptstädten*. Mainz, Verlag Nünnerich-Asmus, 2014.

Scheid, John, Epigraphy and Roman Religion. In: Wilkes, John – Davies, James (eds), *Epigraphy and the historical sciences*. Oxford, Oxford University Press, 2012, 31–44.

Scheid, John, Natur und Religion: zu einigen Missverständnissen. In: Sporn, Katja – Kerschner, Michael (eds), *Natur, Kult, Raum: Akten des internationalen Kolloquiums Paris-Lodron-Universität Salzburg, 20.-22. Jänner 2012*. Wien, Österreichisches Archäologisches Institut, 2015, 303–312.

Scheid, John, Sacrifices for Gods and Ancestors. In: Rüpke, Jörg (ed.), *A Companion to Roman Religion*. Leiden-Boston, Brill, 2007, 265–272.

Scheid, John, *The Gods, the State, and the Individual: Reflections on Civic Religion in Rome*. Philadelphia, University of Pennsylvania Press, 2015.

Scheidel, Walter, *Debating Roman demography*. Leiden, Boston, Brill, 2001.

Schejbal, Berislav, Municipium Iasorum (Aquae Balissae). In: Šašel Kos, Marjeta – Scherrer, Peter (eds), *The autonomous towns of Noricum and Pannonia: Situla = Die autonomen Städte in Noricum und Pannonien, vol. Pannonia II*. Ljubljana, Narodni Muzej Slovenije, 2004, 99–130.

Schels, Johann Baptist, *Geschichte der Lander des ostreichischen Kaiserstaates*. Wien, J. B. Heubner Verlag, 1820.

Scherrer, Peter, Das Bild der Gottheit in südlichen Noricum. In: Leitner, Friedrich (ed.), *Götterwelten. Tempel, Riten, Religionen in Noricum*. Klagenfurt, Landesmuseum Kärnten, 2007, 45–60.

Scherrer, Peter, Savaria. In: Šašel Kos, Marjeta – Scherrer, Peter (eds), *The autonomous towns of Noricum and Pannonia: Situla = Die autonomen Städte in Noricum und Pannonien, vol. Pannonia I*. Ljubljana, Narodni Muzej Slovenije, 2003, 53–80.

Scherrer, Peter, *Vom Regnum Noricum zur römischen Provinz*. Ljubljana, Narodni Muzej Slovenije, 2002.

Scherrer, Peter – Zabrana, Lilli (eds), *Domus: das Haus in den Städten der römischen Donauprovinzen: Akten des 3. Internationalen Symposiums über römische Städte in Noricum und Pannonien*. Wien, Österreichisches Archäologisches Institut, 2008.

Scheuermann, Leif, *Religion an der Grenze: provinzialrömische Götterverehrung am Neckar- und äußeren obergermanischen Limes*. Rahden, Leidorf, 2013.

Schmid, Walter, Der heilige Bezirk von Brunn bei Fehring in Steiermark. In: *Jahreshefte des Österreichischen Archäologischen Institutes in Wien* 31, 1939, 81.

Schmid, Walter, Ein ländliches Heiligtum in Rabnitz bei Kumberg, Oststeiermark. In: *Jahreshefte des Österreichischen Archäologischen Institutes in Wien* 25, 1929, 91.

Schmidts, Thomas, The Raetian frontier and its changes. In: https://www2.rgzm.de/transformation/. Open access.

Schmotz, Karl, Der Mithrastempel von Künzing, Lkr. Deggendorf. Ein Vorbericht. In: *Vorträge des Niederbayerischen Archäologentages* 18, 2000, 111–143.

Schneider, Gerwulf – Daszkiewicz, Malgorzata, Imported and local Firmalampen in Aquileia. Chemical analyses by WD-XRF. In: *Aquileia Nostra* 82, 2011, 261–282.

Schrettle, Bernhard, Frauenberg bei Leibnitz – Die Transformation eines Heiligtums von der spätlatènezeitlichen Kultstelle zum außerstädtischen Heiligtum. In: Lohner-Urban, Ute – Scherrer, Peter (eds), *Der obere Donauraum 50 v. bis 50 n. Chr. von Ute Lohner-Urban*. Berlin, Frank & Timme, 2015, 291–312.

Schrettle, Bernhard, *Neue Forschungen im römischen Heiligtum auf dem Frauenberg bei Leibnitz: Grabungsergebnisse 2013 - 2016*. Wien, Phoibos, 2019.

Schultz, Celia E., Roman Sacrifice, Inside and Out. In: *Journal of Roman Studies* 106, 2016, 58–76.

Schwertheim, Elmar, Iupiter Dolichenus. In: Vermaseren, Maarten J. (ed.), *Die orientalischen Religionen im Römerreich*. Brill, 1981, 193–212.

Schwertheim, Elmar, Raetia. In: Schwertheim, Elmar (ed.), *Die Denkmäler orientalischer Gottheiten im römischen Deutschland*. Brill, 1974, 210–223.

Sedlmayer, Helga, *Die Fibeln vom Magdalensberg. Funde der Grabungsjahre 1948–2002 und Altfunde des 19. Jahrhunderts*, Klagenfurt am Wörthersee, Verlag des Landesmuseums Kärnten, 2009.

Sedlmayer, Helga, Römische Kultplätze in Flusslandschaften – die südnorischen Heiligtümer von Teurnia/St. Peter in Holz, Burgstall/St. Margarethen im Lavanttal und Podkraj bei Hrastnik. In: Sporn, Katja – Ladstätter, Sabine – Kerschner, Michael (eds), *Natur - Kult - Raum*. Wien, Österreichisches Archäologisches Institut, 2015, 313–334.

Seidel, Yvonne, Funde aus dem Marsheiligtum in Lendorf. In: Jerger, Thomas – Brinckmann-Blaha, Ute – Herwirsch, Ilse (eds), *Rudolfinum - Jahrbuch des Landesmuseums für Kärnten 2007*. Klagenfurt, Landesmuseum Kärnten, 2009, 55–60.

Selheimer, Matthew, Urban network evolutions: towards a high-definition archaeology. In: *Bryn Mawr Classical Review* 2020.05.12, 2020.

Sellar, William Young, *The Roman Poets of the Republic*. Edinburgh, Edmonston and Douglas, 1863.

Shopova, Irina, The Cult of Dionysos in Lower Moesia According to the Latin Inscriptions. In: *Thracia* 17, 2017, 419–421.

Sicoe, Gabriel, *Die mithräischen Steindenkmäler aus Dakien*. Cluj-Napoca, Mega Publishing House, 2014.

Simón, Francisco Marco, A Place with Shared Meanings: Mithras, Sabazius, and Christianity in the 'Tomb of Vibia'. In: *Acta Antiqua Academiae Scientiarum Hungariae* 58/1–4, 2018, 225–242.

Sîrbu, Valeriu, *Credințe și practici funerare, religioase și magice în lumea geto-dacilor: pornind de la descoperiri arheologice din Câmpia Brăilei*. Galati, Porto-Franco, 1993.

Sîrbu, Valeriu – Dăvîncă, Diana, Dog skeletons-remains found in the Getae-Dacian settlements (3rd c. BC – 1st c. AD): Ritual inhumation, corpse riddance and consumption. In: Sîrbu, Valeriu – Pețan, Aurora (eds), *Temples and Cult Places from the Second Iron Age in Europe, Proceedings of the 2nd International Colloquium 'Iron Age Sanctuaries and Cult Places at the Thracians and their Neighbours'*. Alun, Editura Dacica, 2020, 209–236.

Sîrbu, Valeriu – Florea, Gelu, *Imaginar şi imagine în Dacia preromană: Imaginaire et image dans la Dacie préromaine. Imagery and image in pre-Roman Dacia*. Brăila, Editura Istros, 1997.

Sîrbu, Valeriu – Pețan, Aurora (eds), *Temples and Cult Places from the Second Iron Age in Europe, Proceedings of the 2nd International Colloquium 'Iron Age Sanctuaries and Cult Places at the Thracians and their Neighbours'*. Alun, Editura Dacica, 2020.

Sîrbu, Valeriu, Sanctuaires et lieux de culte chez les Géto-Daces (2e siècle av : J.-C.-1er siècle J.-C.). In: Barral, Philippe (ed.), *L'âge du Fer dans l'arc jurassien et marges. Dépôts, lieux sacrés et territorialité à l'âge du Fer. Actes du 29e colloque international de l'AFEAF, Bienne, 5-8 mai 2005*. Besançon, Presses universitaires de Franche-Comté, 2007, 855–869.

Sireix, Christophe – Sireix, Michel – Gomez de Soto, José – Pernot, Michel, La tête janiforme à double feuille de gui de la Tène ancienne de Lacoste à Mouliets-et-Villemartin (Gironde, France). In: *Archäologisches Korrespondenzblatt* 32, 2002, 81–89.

Smith, Jonathan Z., *Map is not Territory: Studies in the History of Religions*. Leiden, Brill, 1978.

Smith, Jonathan Z., *To take place. Toward theory of ritual*. Chicago, Chicago University Press, 1987.

Smith, Melanie, Glocalization. In: *The Blackwell Encyclopedia of Sociology*. Wiley Online Library. Open access.

Somervell, Brehon, Navigation Problems on the Danube. In: *The Military Engineer* 18/100, 1926, 301–310.

Sommer, C. Sebastian, Die Anfänge der Provinz Raetien. In: Piso, Ioan (ed.), *Die römischen Provinzen: Begriff und Gründung (Colloquium Cluj-Napoca, 28. September-1. Oktober 2006)*. Cluj-Napoca, Mega Publishing House, 2008, 207–224.

Sostarits, Ottó – Balázs, Péter – Csapláros, Andrea (eds), *A savariai Iseum*. Szombathely, Iseum Savariense Régészeti Műhely, 2013.

Špalj, Dora Kušan, Roman settlement Aquae Iasae – recent discoveries in the sanctuary area. In: *Acta Musei Tiberiopolitani* 3, 2020, 171–184.

Spânu, Daniel, Pre-Roman divinities in Dacia – appearances and identities. In: Alexandrescu, Cristina-Georgeta (eds), *Jupiter on your side: Gods and humans in Antiquity in the Lower Danube area*. Bucharest, Masterprint Super Offset, 2013, 13–22.

Speidel, Michael, A Thousand Tracian Recruits for Mauretania Tingitana. In: *Antiquités africaines* 11/1, 1977, 167–173.

Speidel, Michael, *The religion of Iuppiter Dolichenus in the Roman army*. Leiden, Brill, 1978.

Spickermann, Wolfgang, Aspekte einer 'neuen' Religion und der Prozess der 'interpretatio' im römischen Germanien, Rätien und Noricum. In: Cancik, Hubert – Rüpke, Jörg (eds), *Reichsreligion und Provinzialreligion*. Tübingen, Mohr Siebeck, 1997, 145–167.

Spiridon, Olivia (ed.), *Die Donau und ihre Grenzen Literarische und filmische Einblicke in den Donauraum*. Bielefeld, Transcript, 2019.

Srejović, Dragoslav, *Rimska skulptura u Srbiji = Roman sculpture in Serbia*, Beograd, Srpska akademija nauka i umetnosti, 1987.

Stancev, Dimitar, Ein Heiligtum des thrakischen Heros in Sexaginta Prista. In: Conrad, Sven, *Pontos Euxeinos: Beiträge zur Archäologie und Geschichte des antiken Schwarzmeer- und Balkanraumes*. Langenweißbach, Beier & Beran, 2006, 237–253.

Stark, Rodney, Why religious movements succeed or fail: A revised general model. In: *Journal of Contemporary Religion* 11/2, 1996, 133–146.

Staudt, Markus, Ein rätisches Haus in Wenns, Tirol. In: *Fundberichte aus Österreich* 49, 2010, 145–162.

Stănescu, Florin, Astronomical Orientation in the Ancient Dacian Sanctuaries of Romania. In: Ruggles, Clive L. N. (ed.), *Handbook of archaeoastronomy and ethnoastronomy*. Dordrecht, London, Springer, 2014, 1365–1375.

Ştefănescu-Oniţiu, Atalia, *Religia militarilor în Dacia romană*. Excelsior Art, Timişoara, 2009.

Steigberger, Eva – Tober, Barbara, The sanctuary of Iuppiter Heliopolitanusat Carnuntum – Destruction or demolition? A case study. In: Driessen, Jan (ed.), *Destruction*. Louvain-La-Neuve, Presses Universitaires de Louvain, 2013, 435–448.

Steinacher, Roland, Das Tiroler Inntal in vor- und frührömischer Zeit. In: Zanier, Werner (ed.), *Kulturwandel um Christi Geburt. Spätlatène- und frühe römische Kaiserzeit in den mittleren Alpen zwischen Südbayern und Gardasee, vol. II*. München, C. H. Beck, 2019, 590–608.

Steinhauer, Julietta, *Religious Associations in the Post-Classical Polis*. Stuttgart, Franz Steiner, 2014.

Stempel, Bernardo, Patrizia – Hainzmann, Manfred, *Fontes Epigraphici Religionum Celticarum Antiquarum I. Provincia Noricum Faszikel 1. Die Gottheiten in ihren sprachlichen und kultischen Erscheinungsfomen. Mit einem Beitrag von Gerhard Bauchhenß. Faszikel 2: Die epigraphischen Testimonien*. Wien, Verlag der Österreichischen Akademie der Wissenschaften, 2020.

Stewart, Peter, *Statues in Roman society: representation and response*. Oxford, Oxford University Press, 2003.

Stewart, Peter, *The social history of Roman art*. Cambridge, Cambridge University Press, 2008.

Stiefelhagen, Ferdinand, *Geschichte des Volkes Israel, zugleich mit den Umrissen der Geschichte des klassischen Alterthums*, vol. 3. Köln, L. Schwann, 1854.

Ştirbulescu, Christina, Il culto d'Ercole nella provincia Mesia Inferiore. I bassorilievi votivi. In: Anghelescu, Mircea – Achim, Irina (eds), *Antiquitas Istro-Pontica: mélanges d'archéologie et d'histoire ancienne offerts à Alexandru Suceveanu*. Cluj-Napoca, Mega Publishing House, 2010, 453–492.

Stöger, Johanna, *Rethinking Ostia: a spatial enquiry into the urban society of Rome's imperial port-town*. Leiden, Leiden University Press, 2011.

Stojić, Milorad, *Veliki vetren*. Belgrade, Arheološki institut, 2003.

Stoyanov, Totko, The Getic Capital at Sboryanovo (North-Eastern Bulgaria). In: *TALANTA – Proceedings of the Dutch Archaeological and Historical Society* 32–33, 2000–2001, 207–221.

Strobel, Karl, Augustus und die Annexion des Alpenbogens Die Einrichtung der Provinzen Raetia und Noricum. In: *Germania* 89, 2009, 437–509.

Strobel, Karl, Das Regnum Noricum, die sogenannte Norische Münzprägung und Rom: Frühe Kontakte als Vorspiel von Annexion und Romanisierung – Fiktion oder Realität? Mit einem Appendix zur Noreia-Frage. In: *Archaeologia Austriaca*, 96, 2012, 11–34.

Strobel, Karl, Die Noreia-Frage. Neue Aspekte und Überlegungen zu einem alten Problem der historischen Geographie Kärntens. In: *Carinthia* 193, 2003, 25–71.

Swift, Cathy, Celts, Romans and the Coligny Calendar. In: Carruthers, Martin – van Driel-Murray, Carol – Gardner, Andrew – Lucas, Jason – Revell, Louise – Swift, Ellen (eds), *TRAC 2001*. Oxford, Oxbow Books, 2002, 83–95.

Syme, Ronald, *Danubian papers*. Bucharest, Association internationale d'études du sud-est européen, 1971.

Szabó, Ádám, A daciai Publius Aelius Antipater főpapi címe. In: *Acta: a Csíki Székely Múzeum és a Székely Nemzeti Múzeum évkönyve* 1, 1999, 167–172.

Szabó, Ádám, Aesculapius és az álom általi gyógyítás Dáciában. In: Németh, György (ed.), *A gyógyító számok. Források és tanulmányok a számok szerepéről az antik gyógyászatban*. Szeged, Lectum, 2008, 99–111.

Szabó, Ádám, Contributions to the religious life of Pannonian auxiliary units – the religious inscriptions of the alae. In: Visy, Zsolt (ed.), *Limes XIX. Proceedings of the XIXth International Congress of Roman Frontier Studies held in Pécs, Hungary, September 2003*. Pécs, University of Pécs, 2005, 457–462.

Szabó, Ádám, *Daciai papság*. Budapest, Martin Opitz, 2007.

Szabó, Ádám, Dedicatio Pannoniában. In: Kovács, Péter – Szabó, Ádám (eds), *Felirattani közlemények és tanulmányok 2019-ből*. Budapest, MTA, 2020, 195–238.

Szabó, Ádám, Der 'Locus' von Apulum. In: Ardevan, Radu – Ciongradi, Carmen – Găzdac, Cristian – Ruscu, Ligia (eds), *Orbis Antiquus. Studia in Honorem Ioannis Pisonis*. Cluj-Napoca, Nereamia Napocae Press, 2004, 787–801.

Szabó, Ádám, *Domna et Domnus. Contributions to the cult-history of the 'Danubian riders' religion*. Wien, Phoibos Verlag, 2017.

Szabó, Ádám, Formális és nem formális kultuszhelyek a Római Birodalom tartományaiban. In: *Történeti tanulmányok* 24, 2016, 50–71.

Szabó, Ádám, Forum Provinciae in Sarmizegetusa. In: *Acta Musei Napocensis* 55/1, 2018, 175–187.

Szabó, Ádám, *Noricumi papság: a feliratos források katalógusa = Priests of Noricum: catalogue of epigraphic sources*. Budapest, Eötvös Loránd University, Department of Ancient History, 2010.

Szabó, Ádám, *Pannoniciani Sacerdotes. A szervezett vallási élet principatuskori vezetői*. Pécs, Bornus Nyomda, 2006.

Szabó, Ádám, Special ceremonial square in Aquincum. In: Visy, Zsolt – Farkas, István Gergő – Neményi, Réka – Szabó, Máté (eds), *Visy 75. Artificem commendat opus – studia in honorem Zsolt Visy*. Pécs, CLIR Kutatóközpont, 2019, 494–508.

Szabó, Csaba, A dunai provinciák régészete. In: *Erdélyi Krónika*. 2020-05-06. Open access.
Szabó, Csaba, Danubian provinces: history of a notion. In: *Revista Transilvania* 5/2020, 88–96.
Szabó, Csaba, Gods and cities: Roman religion in urban context in the 2nd–3rd centuries AD. A methodological overview. In: Farkas Gergő István – Neményi Réka – Szabó Miklós (eds), *Visy 75. Artificem commendat opus. Studia in honorem Zsolt Visy*. Pécs, Kontraszt Plusz, 2019, 511–533.
Szabó, Csaba, Mapping Roman religion. A methodological approach. In: *European Journal of Science and Theology* 16/5, 2020, 183–195.
Szabó, Csaba, Notes on a new Cautes statue from Apulum. In: *Archaeologische Korrespondenzblatt* 2/2015, 237–247.
Szabó, Csaba, Notes on a new salariarius from Apulum. In: *Apulum* 51, 2014, 533–544.
Szabó, Csaba – Ota, Radu – Marius Ciută, Artemis from Ephesus in Apulum: notes on a recently discovered bronze statuette. In: *Acta Archaeologica Hungarica*, 67, vol. 2., 2016, 231–243.
Szabó, Csaba, Pannonian religion or religions of Roman Pannonia? Review-article. In: *Journal of Roman Archaeology* 31, 2018, 883–890.
Szabó, Csaba, Párbeszéd Róma isteneivel. A római vallások kutatásának jelenlegi állása és perspektívái. In: *Orpheus Noster*, 2017, 2, 151–163.
Szabó, Csaba, Pilgrimage and healing sanctuaries in the Danubian provinces. In: *Studia Universitatis Cibiniensis. Seria Historica*, 2020, 83–99.
Szabó, Csaba, Religious appropriations and the Antonine Plague. In: *Brukenthal. Acta Musei Brukenthalia* Nr. 10, 2020, 807–820.
Szabó, Csaba, Review of Zerbini, L. (ed.), *e Religiosità nelle Province Danubiane*. Bologna 2015. In: *Acta Archaeologica Academiae Scientiarum Hungariae* 67, 2016, 480–483.
Szabó, Csaba, Roman Dacia in the digital era. In: *Journal of Ancient History and Archaeology* 7/2, 2020, 185–190.
Szabó, Csaba, Roman Religious Communication in the Danubian Provinces. Historiography and New Perspectives. In: Petković, Sofija – Gavrilović Vitas, Nadezda (eds), *Ancient Cult in Balkans through Archaeological Findings and Iconography*. Belgrade, Serbian Archaeolgical Society, 2020, 159–172.
Szabó, Csaba, Roman religious studies in Romania. Historiography and new perspectives. In: *Ephemeris Napocensis*, 24, 2014, 195–208.
Szabó, Csaba, Sanctuaries in Roman Dacia. A catalogue of sacralised places in shared and secondary spaces. In: *Jahrbuch der Römisch-Germanisches Museum* 62, 2015 (2020), 255–340.
Szabó, Csaba, *Sanctuaries in Roman Dacia: materiality and religious experience*. Oxford, Archaeopress, Roman Archaeology Series 49, 2018.
Szabó, Csaba, Searching for the lightbearer: notes on a Mithraic relief from Dragu. In: *Marisia* 32, 2012, 135–145.
Szabó, Csaba, The cult of Mithras in Apulum: communities and individuals. In: Zerbini, Livio (ed.), *Culti e religiosità nelle province danubiane. Atti del 2° Convegno internazionale Ferrara, 20–22 novembre 2013*. Ferrara, I Libri di Emi, 2015, 407–422.
Szabó, Csaba, The Mithraic statue of Secundinus from Apulum. In: *Revista Doctoranzilor de Istoria Veche si Arheologie* 1, 2013, 45–65.
Szabó, Máté – Fábián, Boglárka – Fodor, Fanni, Research on Roman temporary camps near Brigetio (Komárom-Szőny). Results of the excavations conducted on the BRI V, VI(–VII), X–XI, XIII–XIV, XIX, XXII–XXIII, XXX and XXXII archaeological sites. In: Farkas, Gergő István – Neményi, Réka – Szabó, Máté (eds), *The Danube Limes in Hungary - Archaeological research conducted in 2015-2020*. Pécs, Kontraszt Plusz, 2020, 77–112.
Szabó, Miklós, A badacsony-lábdi kettősfej kérdéséhez. In: *Archaeologiai Értesítő* 90/1, 1963, 69–74.
Szabó, Miklós, *A keleti kelták - A késő vaskor a Kárpát-medencében - A késő vaskor a Kárpát-medencében*. Budapest-Párizs, L'Harmattan, 2005.

Szabó, Miklós – Borhy, László, *Magyarország története az ókorban: Kelták és rómaiak* Budapest, L'Harmattan, 2015.
Szabó, Miklós, Pannonia a római foglalás előtt. In: Fitz, Jenő – Mócsy, András (eds), *Pannonia régészeti kézikönyve*, Budapest, Akadémiai Kiadó, 1990, 15–31.
Szilágyi, János György, András Alföldi and Classical Studies in Hungary. In: Richardson, James – Santangelo, Federico (eds), *Andreas Alföldi in the twenty-first century*. Stuttgart, Franz Steiner, 2015, 23–36.
Szilágyi, Magdolna, Római utak a középkori Dunántúlon. Az utak nevei és szerepük a középkori térszervezésben. In: *Történelmi szemle* 56, 2014, 1–25.
Szirmai, Krisztina, *Aquincumi bronzszobrocskák*. Budapest, Budapest Történeti Múzeum, 1986.
Tacheva-Hitova, Margarita, *Eastern cults in Moesia Inferior and Thracia (5th century BC-4th century AD)*. Leiden, Brill, 1983.
Talbert, Richard, Urbs Roma to Orbis Romanus: Roman Mapping on the Grand Scale. In: Talbert, Richard (ed.), *Ancient Perspectives Maps and Their Place in Mesopotamia, Egypt, Greece, and Rome*. Chicago, Chicago University Press, 2012, 163–192.
Taves, Ann, *Religious Experience Reconsidered: A Building-Block Approach to the Study of Religion and Other Special Things*. Princeton, Princeton University Press, 2009.
Taves, Ann, *Revelatory Events: Three Case Studies of the Emergence of New Spiritual Paths*. Princeton, Princeton University Press, 2016.
Tecchiati, Umberto, Jenseits der Brandopferplätze – Kultformen und Kultplätze der Bronze- und Eisenzeit im südlichen Alpenraum. Einige methodologische und kritische Fragestellungen. In: Kreiner, Ludwig (ed.), *Opfer- und Festplätze von der Bronze- zur Latènezeit – Symposium 27.02.-01.03.2014*. Rahden/Westf., Verlag Marie Leidorf, 2018, 205–231.
Teichner, Felix – Drăgan, Andreea, A 'Rider' between the East and the West? Old and New Finds from Municipium Ulpianum (Kosovo). In: Uhač, Ida Koncani (ed.), *Akti XII. međunarodnog kolokvija o rimskoj provincijalnoj umjetnosti*. Pula, Arheoloski muzej istre, 2014, 95–100.
Teichner, Felix, From Aquileia to Carnuntum: Geographical Mobility Along the Amber Road. In: *VELEIA* 30, 2013, 47–73.
Téglás, Gábor (ed.), *Hunyad Vármegye földjének története az őskortól a honfoglalásig*. Budapest, Athenaeum, 1902.
Țentea, Ovidiu, *Bath and bathing in Alburnus Maior*. Cluj-Napoca, Mega Publishing House, 2015.
Țentea, Ovidiu, *Ex Oriente ad Danubium: the Syrian units on the Danube frontier of the Roman Empire*. București, Mega, 2012.
Țentea, Ovidiu – Olteanu, Bianca, Decorating Overlapping Buildings: A Domus and Palmyrene Temple at Colonia Dacica Sarmizegetusa. In: *Theoretical Roman Archaeology Journal* 3, 1:6, 1–17.
Țeposu-Marinescu, Lucia, O gemă de la Micia cu reprezentarea lui Harpocrate. In: *Studii si Cercetari de Istoria Veche si Arheologie* 15.2, 1964, 257–264.
Thomas, Edit, *A nagydémi lararium (Bakonyi Múzeum, 1965) - antikvarium.hu*. Veszprém, Bakonyi Múzeum, 1965.
Thomas, Edit, Ornat und Kultgeräte einer Sol- und Luna-Priesterin aus Pannonien. In: *Acta Antiqua Academiae Scientiarum Hungariae* 11, 1963, 49–80.
Thomas, Edit, Religion. In: Lengyel, Alfonz – Radan, T. B. George (eds), *The archaeology of Roman Pannonia*. Lexington, University of Kentucky, 1980, 177–206.
Thomas, Edit, *Römische Villen in Pannonien. Beiträge zur pannonischen Siedlungsgeschichte*. Budapest, Akadémiai Kiadó, 1964.
Timoc, Călin, Contribuţii la navigaţia fluvială pe râul Mureş în secolele II – III p.Chr. şi portul de la Apulum. In: *Apulum* 43, 213–218.
Timotin, Andrei, Paleocreştinismul carpato-danubian. In: *Archaevs* 2, 1998, 43–172.

Tomas, Agnieszka, Civil settlement at Novae (Moesia inferior). In: Sommer, Sebastian – Matešić, Suzana (eds), *Limes XXIII. Proceedings of the 23rd International Congress of Roman Frontier Studies Ingolstadt 2015*. Mainz, Nünnerich-Asmus Verlag, 2018, 748–755.

Tomas, Agnieszka, Dionysus or Liber Pater? The Evidence of the Bacchic Cult at Novae (castra et canabae legionis) and in its Hinterland. In: Tomas, Agnieszka (ed.), *Ad fines Imperii Romani: studia Thaddaeo Sarnowski septuagenario ab amicis, collegis discipulisque dedicata*. Varsaviae, Institute of Archaeology, 2015, 257–276.

Tomas, Agnieszka, *Inter Moesos et Thraces: The Rural Hinterland of Novae in Lower Moesia (1st - 6th Centuries AD)*. Oxford, Archaeopress, 2016.

Tomas, Agnieszka – Lemke, Martin, The Mithraeum at Novae Revisited. In: Tomas, Agnieszka (ed.), *Ad fines imperii Romani*. Warszawa, Instytut Archeologii UW, 2015, 227–247.

Tomas, Agnieszka, *Living with the Army I. Civil Settlements near Roman Legionary Fortresses in Lower Moesia*. Warsaw, Institute of Archaeology University of Warsaw, 2017.

Tomedi, Herhard, South and southeast Central-Europe. In: Nasso, Alessandro (ed.), *Etruscology*, vol. I, Berlin-New York, De Gruyter, 1585–1607.

Tomorad, Mladen, Various manifestations of Isis cult in the region of Istria, Illyricum and Pannonia and its diffusion to the Central European Region (2nd c. B.C.–4th c. A.D.). In: *Shodoznanvstvo* 81, 2018, 58–99.

Tomović, Miograd, *Roman sculpture in upper Moesia*. Beograd, Archaelogical Institute, 1992.

Topalilov, Ivo, A New Governor of Moesia Superior. In: *Zeitschrift für Papyrologie und Epigraphik* 201, 2017, 292–296.

Topál, Judit, Connection between funerary rites and ethnic groups in the cemeteries of north-eastern Pannonia. In: Pearce, John – Millet, Martin – Struck, Manuela (eds), *Burial, Society and Context in the Roman World*. Oxford, Oxbow Books, 2000, 197–203.

Torbatov, Sergey, Trimammium – a Roman castellum and civitas on the Lower Danube. In: Vagalinski, Lydmil – Torbatov, Sergey (eds), *The Lower Danube Roman Limes (1st - 6th c. AD)*. Sofia, National Archaeological Institute and Museum, Bulgarian Academy of Sciences, 2012, 429–460.

Tóth, Endre, A császárkultusz főoltára Pannonia Superiorban. In: *Archaeologiai Értesítő* 126/1, 2001, 5–33.

Tóth, István, A Dacian 'Apostle' of the cult of Mithras? In: *Specimina Nova* 1992/8, 1994, 153–160.

Tóth, István, *A fertőrákosi Mithraeum*. Budapest, Pan, 2007.

Tóth, István, *Das lokale System der Mithraischen Personifikationen im Gebiet von Poetovio*. In: *Archeološki Vestnik* 28, 1977, 385–392.

Tóth, István, Destruction of the sanctuaries of Iuppiter Dolichenus at the Rhine and in the Danube Region (235–238). In: *Acta Archaeologica Hungarica* 25/1–2, 1973, 109–116.

Tóth, István, Egy mithraikus főpap sírja Pannoniából? In: *Ókor: folyóirat az antik kultúrákról* 5/2, 2006, 3–6.

Tóth, István, *Mithras, a misztériumok istene?* In: *Ókor. folyóirat az antik kultúrákról* 2/1, 2003, 26–30.

Tóth, István, *Pannóniai vallástörténet*, Pécs-Budapest, L'Harmattan, 2015.

Tóth, István, Sacerdotes Iovis Dolicheni. In: Veliky, János (ed.), *Studium II*. Debrecen, Kossuth Lajos Tudományegyetem, 1971, 23–28.

Trunk, Markus, *Römische Tempel in den Rhein- und westlichen Donauprovinzen: ein Beitrag zur architekturgeschichtlichen Einordnung römischer Sakralbauten in Augst*. Augst, Römermuseum, 1991.

Unruh, Frank, Werner Zanier, Der spätlatène- und römerzeitliche Brandopferplatz im Forggensee (Gde. Schwangau). Mit Beiträgen von Angela von den Driesch, Hansjörg Küster und Willy Tegel. Münchner Beiträge zur Vor- und Frühgeschichte 52 (C.H. Beck Verlag, München 1999) 202 S., 34 Abb., 8 Tab., 46 Taf., 4 Beilagen. Leinen, 88,- DM. In: *Trierer Zeitschrift* 63, 2020, 447–449.

Unterwurzacher, Michael – Uhlir, Christian – Kremer, Gabrielle, La procedencia de artefactos de mármol de la metrópoli Romana 'Carnuntum', Austria. In: *Geología Colombiana* 35, 2010, 162–174.

Urban, Otto H., Ausgewählte latènezeitliche Eisendepotfunde aus Österreich. In: Bataille, Gérard – Guillaumet, Jean-Paul (eds), *Les dépôts métalliques au second âge du Fer en Europe tempérée*. Glux-en-Glenne, Bibracte, 2006, 83–100.

Urciuoli, Emiliano, Citification of Religion: A Proposal for the Historical Study of Urban Religion. In: *Religion and Urbanity Online*. Open access.

Vágási, Tünde, *A pannoniai katonaság vallási élete a principátus korában. Mithras és Jupiter Dolichenus feliratos emlékei*. Budapest, Eötvös Loránd Tudományegyetem, 2014. Open access.

Van Alten, David, Glocalization and Religious Communication in the Roman Empire: Two Case Studies to Reconsider the Local and the Global in Religious Material Culture. In: *Religions*, 8, 2017, 1–20.

Van der Leeuw, Gerardus, *Religion in Essence and Manifestation*. Princeton, Princeton University Press, 1986.

Van der Ploeg, Ghislaine, *The Impact of the Roman Empire on the Cult of Asclepius*. Leiden-Boston, Brill, 2018.

Van Oyen, Astrid – Pitts, Martin (eds), *Materialising Roman Histories*, Oxford, Oxbow Books, 2017.

Varbanov, Varbin, Roman sanctuary in Sexaginta Prista. In: Alexandrescu, Cristina (ed.), *Jupiter on your side: gods and humans in antiquity in the Lower Danube area: accompanying publication for the thematic exhibitions in Bucharest, Alba Iulia and Constanta, May – September 2013*. Bucuresti, Masterprint Super Offset, 2013, 55–63.

Varga, Rada, A Quantitative Approach on Latin Occupational Epigraphy. In: *Journal of Ancient History and Archaeology* 6.4/2019, 78–109.

Varga, Rada, Locuri de cult ale zeilor taumaturgi in Dacia romana. In: *Chronos – revista de istorie* 3, 2005, 5–8.

Várhelyi, Zsuzsanna, Political murder and sacrifice: from Roman Republic to Empire. In Várhelyi, Zsuzsanna – Knust, Jennifer Wright (eds), *Ancient Mediterranean sacrifice*. Oxford, Oxford University Press 2011, 125–142.

Várhelyi, Zsuzsanna, The Specters of Roman Imperialism: The Live Burials of Gauls and Greeks at Rome. In: *Classical Antiquity* 26, 2007, 277–304.

Vasáros, Zsolt – Havas, Zoltán, Revision of the architectural reconstruction of the Aquincum Governor's Palace. In: Havas, Zoltán (ed.), *Authenticity and experience: Governor's palaces of Roman imperial period and the limes; proceedings of the international conference, Budapest, 5-6 November 2018*. Budapest, Budapest History Museum, 2019, 77–96.

Vasić, Miloje, Sculptures and 'the sanctuary of Aesculapius' in Mediana. In: *Starinar* 68, 2018, 89–109.

Velkov, Velizar, Kulte und religionen in thrakien und Niedermösien. In: *ANRW* II 18.2, 1989, 1317–1361.

Veres, Madalina Valeria, Review: Andrew Beattie, The Danube: A Cultural History. Oxford, Oxford University Press, 2010. In: *Austrian History Yearbook* 43, 2012, 191–192.

Vermaseren, Maarten, *Corpus Inscriptionum et Monumentorum Religionis Mithriacae II*. Hague, Martinus Nijhoff Publishers, 1960.

Versluys, Miguel, Orientalising Roman Gods. In: Bricault, Laurent – Bonnet, Corinne (eds), *Panthée: religious transformations in the Graeco-Roman Empire*. Leiden-Boston, Brill, 2013, 239–259.

Versluys, Miguel, Understanding objects in motion: an archaeological dialogue on Romanization. In: *Archaeological Dialogues* 21.1, 2014, 1–20.

Visy, Zsolt, *Dacia ... diuturno bello Decibali viris fuerat exhausta*: András Alföldi and the Continuity of Dacia. In: Richardson, James – Santangelo, Federico (eds), *Andreas Alföldi in the twenty-first century*. Stuttgart, Franz Steiner, 2015, 269–290.

Visy, Zsolt, *Der pannonische Limes in Ungarn*. Stuttgart, Theiss, 1988.

Visy, Zsolt (ed.), *The Roman army in Pannonia: An archaeological guide of the ripa Pannonica*. Pécs, Pro Minoritate Foundation, 2003.

Vivas, García Gustavo Alberto, Géza Alföldy and Ronald Syme: A Case Study. In: *Studia Europaea Gnesnensia* 16 2017, 529–551.

Von Schnurbein, Siegmar, Die Besetzung des Alpenvorlandes durch die Römer. In: Rieckhoff-Pauli, Sabine (ed.), *Die Römer in Schwaben: Jubiläumsausstellung 2000 Jahre Augsburg*. München, Bayerisches Landesamt für Denkmalpflege, 1985, 17–24.

Vout, Caroline, Antinous, Archaeology and History. In: *The Journal of Roman Studies* 95, 2005, 80–96.

Vucović-Bogdanović, Sonja – Jovović, Mladen, Dog Burials from the Cemeteries of the Roman City of Viminacium (Moesia Superior, Kostolac, Serbia). In: Ferdinandov Vagalinski, Luidmil – Sharankov, Nikolaĭ (eds), *Proceedings of the 22nd InternationalCongress of Roman Frontier Studies, Ruse, Bulgaria, September 2012*, Sofia, National Archaeological Institute with Museum Bulgarian Academy of Sciences, 2015, 687–702.

Walsh, David, *The Cult of Mithras in Late Antiquity. Development, Decline and Demise ca. A.D. 270–430*. Leiden-Boston, Brill, 2019.

Walsh, David, The Fate of Temples in Noricum and Pannonia. In: *American Journal of Archaeology* 120/2, 2016, 221–238.

Wamser, Ludwig, *Die Römer zwischen Alpen und Nordmeer*. Düsseldorf, Albatros im Patmos Verlag, 2004.

Watkins, Thomas H., Colonia Marciana Traiana Thamugadi: Dynasticism in Numidia. In: *Phoenix* 56/1–2, 2002, 84–108.

Weber, Gerhard, *Cambodunum-Kempten – Erste Hauptstadt der römischen Provinz Raetien?* Mainz am Rhein, Philipp von Zabern, 2000 *Becoming Roman: the origins of provincial civilization in Gaul*. Cambridge, 1998.

Weber, Gerhard, Kempten – Cambodunum, erste Hauptstadt in der römischen Alpenprovinz Rätien? In: *Zeitschrift des Historischen Vereins für Schwaben* 102, 2010, 39–83.

Weber, Gerhard, Träume und Visionen im alltag der römischen Kaiserzeit. Das Zeugnis der Inscriften und Papyri. In: *Quaderni Catanesi*, 4–5, 2005–2006, pp. 55–121.

Webster, Jane, A Dirty Window on the Iron Age? Recent Developments inthe Archaeology of Pre-Roman Celtic Religion. In: Ritari, Katja – Bergholm, Alexandra (eds), *Understanding Celtic religion: Revisiting the pagan past*. Cardiff, University of Wales Press, 2015, 121–176.

Weddle, Candace, The Sensory Experience of Blood Sacrifice in the Roman Imperial Cult. In: Day, Jo (ed.), *Making sense of the past: Toward a sensory archaeology*. Carbondale, Center for Archaeological Investigations, 2013, 137–159.

Wendling, Holger, Manching Reconsidered: New Perspectives on Settlement Dynamics and Urbanization in Iron Age Central Europe. In: *European Journal of Archaeology*, 16, 2013, 459–490.

Weiss, Lara, Perpetuated Action. In: Raja, Rubina – Rüpke, Jörg (eds), *A Companion to the Archaeology of Religion in the Ancient World*. Chichester, John Wiley & Sons, 2015, 60–70.

Wells, Peter, Indigenous Forms, Styles, and Practices in Provincial Roman Europe. Continuity, Reinvention, or Refashioning? In: Busch, Alexandra – Versluys, Miguel (eds), *Reinventing the 'invention of tradition'. Indigenous pasts and the Roman present*. Morphomata 32, Paderborn, Wilhelm Fink, 2015, 161–188.

Wightman, Gregory J., *The origins of religion in the Paleolithic*. Lanham, Rowman & Littlefield Publishers, 2015.

Wilkes, John, *Dalmatia*. London-New York, Routledge, 1969.

Wilkes, John, Die Donauprovinzen. In: Lepelley, Claude (ed.), *Rom und das Reich. 44 v. Chr. - 260 n. Chr. Die Regionen des Reiches*. Hamburg, Nikol Verlaggeselschaft, 2006, 247–309.

Wilkes, John, The Danubian and Balkan provinces. In: Bowman, Alan – Champlin, Edward – Lintott, Andrew (eds), *Cambridge Ancient History* 10, vol. 2. Cambridge, Cambridge University Press, 1996, 545–585.

Wilkes, John, The Roman Danube: An Archaeological Survey. In: *Journal of Roman Studies* 95, 2005, 124–225.

Williamson, George, Mucianus and the touch of the Miraculous: Pilgrimage and tourism in Roman Asia Minor. In: Elsner, Jas – Rutherford, Ian (eds) *Pilgrimage in Graeco-Roman and Early Christian Antiquity: Seeing the Gods.* Oxford, Oxford University Press, 2005, 219–253.

Wilson, Andrew – Flohr, Miko, *Urban craftsmen and traders in the Roman world.* New York, Oxford University Press, 2016.

Wissowa, Georg, *Religion un Kultus der Römer*. München, C. H. Beck, 2nd edition, 1902.

Wittenberg, Tim, *Kult bei der Arena: Nemesis-Heiligtümer im Kontext römischer Amphitheater*. Oxford, British Archaeological Reports 2615, 2014.

Wittkower, Rudolf, Eagle and Serpent. A Study in the Migration of Symbols. In: *Journal of the Warburg Institute* 2/4, 1939, 293–325.

Wollmann, Volker, *Mineritul metalifer, extragerea sării și carierele de piatră în Dacia romană = der Erzbergbau, die Salzgewinnung und die Steinbrüche in römischen Dakien.* Cluj-Napoca, s.n. 1996.

Woolf, Greg, *Becoming Roman: the origins of provincial civilization in Gaul.* Cambridge, Cambridge University Press, 1998.

Woolf, Greg, Beyond Romans and Natives. In: *World Archaeology*, Vol. 28, No. 3, 339–350.

Woolf, Greg, Diasporas and colonization in Classical Antiquity. In: Ness, Immanuel – Bellwood, Peter S. (eds), *The encyclopedia of global human migration.* Chichester, Wiley-Blackwell, 2013, 1–14.

Woolf, Greg, Global deities: gods on the move in the ancient mediterranean world. In: *Journal of the Spanish Association for the Sciences of Religions* 11, 2019, 111–128.

Woolf, Greg, Only connect? Network analysis and religious change in the Roman World. In: *Hélade*, 2, 2, 2016, 43–58.

Woolf, Greg, Representation as cult: the case of the Jupiter columns. In: Spickermann, Wolfgang – Cancik, Hubert – Rüpke, Jörg (eds), *Religion in den germanischen Provinzen Roms.* Tübingen, Mohr Siebeck 2001, 117–134.

Woolf, Greg, Ritual Traditions of Non-mediterranean Europe. In: Raja, Rubina – Rüpke, Jörg (eds), *A Companion to the Archaeology of Religion in the Ancient World.* Chichester, John Wiley & Sons, 2015, 465–477.

Woolf, Greg, Romanization 2.0 and its alternatives, *Archaeological Dialogues* 21,1, 2014, 45–50.

Woolf, Greg, Roman Things and Roman People: A Cultural Ecology of the Roman World. In: Van Oyen, Astrid – Pitts, Martin (eds), *Materialising Roman Histories.* Oxford, Oxbow Books, 2017, 211–216.

Woolf, Greg, *Rome. An Empire's Story.* Oxford, Oxford University Press, 2012.

Woolf, Greg, *Tales of the barbarians: ethnography and empire in the Roman West.* Chichester/Malden, Wiley-Blackwell, 2011.

Woolf, Gregory Duncan, The Formation of Roman Provincial Cultures. In: Metzler, Jeannot – Millett, Martin – Roymans, Nico – Slofstra, Jan (eds), *Integration in the early Roman west: the role of culture and ideology*. Luxembourg, Musée National d'Histoire et d'Art, 1995, 9–18.

Woolf, Greg, *The life and death of ancient cities. A natural history*. Oxford, Oxford University Press, 2020.

Woolf, Greg, The Present State and Future Scope of Roman Archaeology: A Comment. In: *American Journal of Archaeology* 108, No. 3, 2004, 417–428.

Zabehlicky, Heinrich, Hausheiligtümer in städtischen Wohnhäusern in Pannonien und Noricum, Fallbeispiel Carnuntum. In: Scherrer, Peter – Zabrana, Lilli (eds), *Domus: das Haus in den Städten der römischen Donauprovinzen: Akten des 3. Internationalen Symposiums über römische Städte in Noricum und Pannonien*. Wien, Österreichisches Archäologisches Institut, 2008, 185–203.

Zaccaria, Claudio, Dall'Aquileiense portorium al'publicum portorii Illyrici: revision e aggiornamento della documentazione epigrafica. In: Zerbini, Livio (ed.), *Culti e Religiosità nelle Province Danubiane.* Bologna I Libri di Emil, 2015, 53–79.

Zaccaria, Claudio, Testimonianze epigrafiche dei rapporti tra Aquileia e l'Illirico in età imperiale romana. In: *Antichità Altoadriatiche* 26, 1985, 85–120.

Zajac, Józef, Die keltischen Elemente in der Religion Noricums in der Zeit des frühen Römischen Kaiserreiches (I.–III. Jh. uZ). In: *Acta Universitatis Nicolai Copernici* 96, 1979, 59–94.

Zanier, Werner, *Der spätlatène- und frühkaiserzeitliche Opferplatz auf dem Döttenbichl südlich von Oberammergau*. München, C. H. Beck, 2016.

Zanier, Werner, *Der spätlatène- und römerzeitliche Brandopferplatz im Forggensee (Gde. Schwangau): Münchner Beiträge zur Vor- und Frühgeschichte.* München, C. H. Beck, 1999.

Zakrzewski, Piotr, Reconstructing the phases of the fortifications of the legionary fortress at Novae (Moesia Inferior). In: *Journal of Roman Archaeology* 33, 2020, 432–447.

Zerbini, Livio (ed.), *Culti e Religiosità nelle Province Danubiane.* Bologna I Libri di Emil, 2015.

Zerbini, Livio (ed.), Roma e le province del Danubio. Soveria Mannelli, Pisa, 2010.

Zhuravlev, Denis, Western Sigillata in the Northern Pontic Region. In: *Ancient Civilizations from Scythia to Siberia* 14/1–2, 2008, 85–121.

Zimmermann, Markus, *Romanisation und Repräsentation in Noricum*. Bonn, Rudolf Habelt, 2017.

Zimmermann, Tanja. Die Donau: Identitäten im Strom. In: Spiridon, Olivia (ed.), *Die Donau und ihre Grenzen Literarische und filmische Einblicke in den Donauraum.* Bielefeld, Transcript, 2019, 217–231.

Zotović, Radmila, *Greek Cult Votive Monuments in the Territory of Central Serbia.* 11th International Scientific Conference 'Science and Higher Education in Function of Sustainable Development' 24–25 May 2019, Mećavnik – Drvengrad, Užice, Serbia. 9–23.

Zsidi, Paula, Die Geographie Aquincums In: Zsidi, Paula (ed.), *Forschungen in Aquincum 1969-2002.* Budapest, Budapest Történeti Múzeum, 2003, 43–48.

Zsidi, Paula, Kultstätten in der Topographie der Zivilstadt von Aquincum. In: Lazar, Irena (ed.), *Religion in public and private sphere. Acts of the 4th International Colloquium The Autonomous Towns of Noricum and Pannonia.* Koper, Univerza na Primorskem, 2011, 157–182.

Zsidi, Paula, *Mithras in Aquincum: The Mithraeum of Symphorus.* Budapest, Archaeolingua, 2018.

Zugravu, Nelu, Divinităţi şi experienţe onirice în Dacia. In: *Ephemeris Napocensis,* 14–15, 2005, 101–122.

Żyromski, Marek, The army as an important factor of social mobility in Roman Empire. In: *Tyragetia (Serie Nouă)* 2/1, 2008, 287–292.

Index

I Adiutrix 193
II Adiutrix 113
V Macedonica 70, 155, 274
VII Gemina 60
XIII Gemina 97
XIV Gemina 120

Abusina 167, 186, 209
Ad Herculis 103, 105
Ad Mediam 103, 250
Adriatic Sea 45, 107, 117
Adsalluta 55, 96, 213, 226
Aecorna 65, 85, 105, 226
aedes signorum 124, 125, 208, 209, 210, 211, 212, 214, 215, 216, 218, 220, 221, 222, 223, 225
Alexander of Abonoteichus 105, 153, 155
Alexandria 105, 205
Alföldi, Andreas 8
Alföldy, Géza 9, 23, 34, 37, 64, 78, 79, 82, 83, 85, 87, 88, 138, 141, 144, 145, 149, 188, 216, 217
Alps, Alpine 2, 4, 12, 27, 28, 29, 36, 45, 46, 48, 52, 64, 77, 90, 98, 117, 169, 199, 249, 262
Amber Road 12, 19, 38, 39, 58, 99, 102, 105, 117, 141, 142, 160, 201
Ampelum 122, 162, 163, 187
amphitheatre 62, 104, 113, 114, 115, 123, 132, 194, 202
Anatolia 62, 118, 163, 175
anatomical votive 190, 191
Antinoos 62, 84, 117, 216, 226
Antoninus Pius 106, 130, 178
Apollo 56, 61, 64, 70, 102, 103, 170, 183, 192, 210, 213, 220, 221, 225, 226, 247
Apulum 76, 91, 92, 93, 96, 97, 104, 105, 108, 115, 117, 122, 125, 139, 144, 150, 154, 155, 157, 159, 162, 163, 164, 169, 170, 171, 172, 173, 176, 177, 181, 182, 183, 185, 186, 187, 188, 192, 193, 205, 207, 222
Aquae Iasae 40, 65, 102, 103, 130, 148, 214
Aquileia 12, 35, 36, 52, 90, 99, 102, 105, 117, 138
Aquincum 4, 41, 61, 64, 90, 93, 96, 102, 103, 108, 109, 110, 112, 113, 114, 115, 116, 117, 128, 144, 145, 147, 159, 160, 176, 182, 186, 190, 192, 193, 194, 196, 197, 202, 205, 206, 214
Ara Augusti 59, 89, 104, 110, 115, 166, 209
architecture, architectural atmosphere 9, 17, 19, 37, 38, 41, 53, 54, 56, 59, 60, 63, 67, 68, 69, 72, 79, 81, 86, 98, 102, 104, 108, 109, 111, 113, 118, 121, 122, 123, 126, 130, 132, 134, 137, 146, 150, 152, 169, 182, 192, 194, 195, 196, 198, 202, 203, 205, 208
Asclepius 75, 99, 103, 115, 125, 126, 159, 170, 183, 186, 206, 215, 244
Asia Minor 99, 104, 105, 106, 123, 155, 161, 169
augur, *augures* 64, 82, 85, 135, 140, 15[illegible], 168, 169
Augustus 4, 8, 27, 28, 35, 46, 56, 57, 70, 105, 120, 188, 211, 213, 232
Austria 5, 9, 12, 36, 48, 78, 206
auxiliary fort 68, 94, 96, 108, 111, 120, 121, 122, 123, 135, 147, 162
Attis 56, 162

Baalbek 118, 119, 122
Bacchium 76, 153
Barbaricum 4, 44, 61, 96, 99, 105, 117, 122
Bavaria 5, 12, 206
Belenus 37, 49, 64, 227
beneficiarius 94, 95, 102, 140, 218
Black Sea 27, 43, 44, 95, 105, 106, 107, 198
Brandopferplatz, Brandopferplätze 12, 31,32, 34, 47, 48, 82, 199
Brigantium 31, 128, 130, 192, 209
Brigetio 108, 111, 115, 121, 144, 190, 192, 193, 196, 215, 229
brooch, brooches 33, 36, 48, 83
Bronze Age 27, 29, 31, 32, 33, 34, 36, 39, 41, 42, 45, 47, 48, 80, 88, 99, 122, 172, 175, 176, 191, 194, 196
Bulgaria 1, 5, 13, 44, 198, 206
Burgstall 38, 47, 53, 54, 83, 211

Cambodunum 93, 110, 111, 117, 144, 192, 202, 209
Capitolium, Capitolia 36, 59, 113, 125, 128, 130, 131, 132, 149, 209, 211, 213, 214, 220, 223, 224, 229
Caracalla 102, 103, 131, 170, 186
Carnuntum 2, 4, 12, 41, 59, 61, 62, 65, 76, 88, 90, 96, 103, 105, 108, 112, 117, 118–122, 124, 125,

128, 144–146, 149, 160, 161, 167, 179, 182, 184, 188, 190, 192–194, 202, 205, 215, 216
Celeia 38, 55, 56, 57, 94, 96, 140, 211, 229
Celts, Celtic 8, 12, 27, 28, 29, 33, 34–44, 47, 49–54, 60–63, 65, 66, 76, 79, 82, 96, 98, 106, 107, 112, 128, 139, 191, 201, 202, 206, 211, 212
cemetery, cemeteries 13, 32, 40, 60, 65, 82
Central-Eastern Europe 1, 2, 5, 8, 9, 11, 14, 15, 22, 67, 143, 200, 201, 204, 206
Cernunnos 40
Christianity, Christians 11–15, 23, 25, 35, 56, 68, 153, 161, 178, 183, 188, 206, 211
Cimbri 29
citification 18, 83, 108–110, 171, 202
cognitive studies 126, 127, 149, 153, 154, 167, 168, 169, 171, 173, 186
coin, coins 2, 16, 25, 39, 80, 81, 103, 146, 190, 199
collegium, collegia 76, 92, 96, 97, 108, 132, 135, 139–141, 152, 158, 179, 208, 221
colony, colonialization 2, 20, 43–44,48, 75, 92, 93, 104–105, 107, 108, 111, 113, 115, 119, 128, 137, 141, 143, 144, 168, 171, 190–191, 200, 202, 224, 235, 236
colonia deducta 107, 111, 144
Commagene 122, 162, 163, 175, 223
conductor 90, 92–94, 97, 137, 139, 157
Constantine 102
Cumont, Franz 10, 11, 23
curia 150
Curia 31

Dacia, Dacian 2, 3, 4, 8, 13, 14, 15, 23, 24, 27, 32, 38, 39, 42, 43–45, 58, 61, 63, 67–71, 73, 75, 78, 86, 90–93, 96, 99, 102–108, 115, 121, 122, 135, 137–139, 143, 144, 147, 150, 159–161, 168–172, 179–181, 188, 192, 195, 199, 201, 202, 205–208, 221, 226–231, 240
Dalmatia 8, 9, 23, 56, 90, 99, 105
Danube, Danubius 1–15, 20, 22–30, 32–34, 36, 38, 40–46, 48, 50, 52, 54, 56–58, 60, 62, 64, 66, 68, 70–76, 80, 82, 84, 100–160
Danubian Riders 73–76, 88, 93, 99, 144, 161, 181–182, 191, 201, 228
Dardania 42, 71
Decebalus 68
defixio, defixiones 191, 246
demography 108, 109, 161
Delos 35, 78
Deus Aeternus 172, 227
Diana 72, 99, 103, 146, 193–195, 197, 199, 210, 215–216, 219, 220, 226, 228, 244
digital humanities 204–206
Dionysopolis 43, 198, 199, 200, 219
dislocation 2, 9, 41, 58, 60, 94, 106, 107, 112, 118, 140, 144, 155, 161
divination 62, 118, 126, 152, 154–155, 166, 168–171, 186, 203
Doliche 162, 163, 175
Dolichenum 104, 147, 153, 162, 163, 193, 203, 211, 213, 215, 218, 219, 223
domestic religion 10, 12, 19, 31, 33, 41, 63, 65, 68, 70, 73, 109, 115, 117, 140, 154, 167, 169, 174, 190–192, 194, 196, 204, 208
Domnus et Domna: see Danubian Riders
Domus 224
Dragu 179, 180
Drava 40, 42, 58, 80, 95, 96
Durostorum 108

Edessa 118
Egypt 15, 84, 106, 117, 122, 134, 169, 171, 183, 191
Emona 40, 59, 105,
emporium 35–37, 78
Ephessos 99
epiphany 154, 168, 171–173
Eravisci 38, 40, 60, 61, 112

flamen 92, 93, 135, 150, 151
Flavia Solva 54, 211
Fortuna 17, 40, 53, 112, 113, 130, 132, 138, 154, 191, 194, 214, 220, 226, 229
forum, fora 56, 89, 94, 113–115, 126–133, 137, 149, 166, 172, 215–216, 224
Frauenberg 38, 53–55, 211

Gallia, Gallic 28, 37, 66, 78, 81, 90
Genius, genii 5, 71, 73, 75, 91, 92, 97, 103, 138, 187, 221, 223, 229
Germania Superior 95, 181
Germanic, Germans 22, 29, 33, 62, 98, 102, 117, 176
Germisara 103, 104, 222
glocalisation 3, 14, 20, 21, 22, 50, 73, 90, 201, 204
Glycon 105, 183
Gorsium 75, 130, 192, 202, 216
governor, governors 62, 69, 94, 95, 97, 104, 105, 113, 117, 120, 121, 131–132, 143
Gurina 34, 211

haruspex 135, 150, 170, 171, 187
Hellenism, Hellenistic 41, 43–44, 72, 76, 106, 107, 118, 143, 157, 172, 176, 183, 198, 202, 219
Hercules 28, 52, 63, 103, 174, 177, 188, 194, 209, 211, 226, 229, 245

Hispania 60
historiography 10, 11, 38, 42, 45, 46, 47, 56, 57, 72, 76, 78, 89, 120, 124, 143, 144, 153, 200
Histria 43, 157
hoard, hoards 42, 94, 99
Hochtor 38, 52, 211
Hohenstein 49, 51, 126
Hungary 5, 9, 39, 40, 41, 59, 102, 109
Hygeia 75, 99, 103, 104, 115, 125, 126, 169–170, 186, 226

Illyricum 5, 9, 11, 27, 56, 57, 76, 88, 229
incubatio 99, 102, 169, 191
indigenous population 36, 38, 40, 45–48, 54, 59–62, 67, 72, 225
interpretatio indigena 37, 46, 49, 53
interpretatio Romana 24, 45, 46, 49, 66, 70, 73, 144
Iouenat 35
Iron Age 5, 10, 17, 19, 27–29, 31, 33, 35, 40–44, 52, 53, 62, 65, 67, 68, 75, 76, 80, 94, 97, 103, 06, 107, 109, 112, 121, 130, 152, 154, 163, 169, 173, 190, 191, 194, 195, 196, 200, 202, 204, 206
Iseum 100–102, 122, 123, 132, 134, 153, 168, 203, 206, 218
Isis 102, 104, 132, 134, 165, 167, 170, 174, 203, 226, 230
Isis Noreia 34, 35, 37, 49, 50, 51, 53, 78, 149, 212, 231
Iuvavum 169, 170, 212

Judaism 15, 178
Julio-Claudian dynasty 27, 48, 56, 58, 59, 70, 83, 84, 108
Juno-Iuno, Hera 102, 132, 176, 226, 229, 230
Jupiter Dolichenus 62, 71, 92, 118, 135, 155, 161–163, 165, 170, 174–176, 203, 226, 230
Jupiter Heliopolitanus 12, 117–120, 122, 123, 146, 161, 215, 230
Jupiter Karnuntinus 41, 61, 62, 64, 112, 216, 230, 233
Jupiter Optimus Maximus 62, 71, 75, 94, 120, 162, 167, 170, 171, 206, 211, 226, 242
Jupiter Paternus 71, 230
Jupiter Teutanus 41, 61, 62, 64, 80, 84, 112, 230
Jupiter Turmazgades 163, 164, 233

La Tène 35, 38, 39, 41, 47, 52, 53, 56, 63, 65, 80, 102
Lambesis 159
lararium, lararia 2, 190–194, 196
legionary fortress 46, 61, 96, 97, 108, 111, 112, 115, 117, 123–126, 148, 193, 215

Liber Pater-Bacchus 71, 76, 93, 135, 160, 167, 174, 180, 203, 207, 217, 220, 222, 224, 230, 245
libertus, liberti 36, 71, 92, 139, 160
limes, Limesforschung 5, 8, 9, 12, 13, 44, 46, 58, 95, 96, 122, 124, 144, 206
Lived Ancient Religion 11, 14–17, 21, 22, 25, 26, 103, 111, 141, 152, 166, 204
Londinium, London 52, 93, 132, 173

macro-spaces 89–152, 166, 167, 172–174, 181, 182, 186, 192, 195, 198–204, 206, 208, 225, 237
Magdalensberg 35–37, 49, 54, 78, 107, 161, 192, 213
magic, magical practices 10, 12–14, 171, 191
Magna Mater-Cybele 43, 55, 56, 97, [illegible], 135, 150, 162, 165, 174, 203, 219, 231
Marcus Aurelius 22, 94, 106, 150, 155, 171, 172, 195
Marcomannic Wars 113, 138, 145, 171
Maros 91, 96, 141, 172, 222
Mars 37, 53, 83, 125, 132, 179, 188, 211, 212, 226, 231
Mars Latobius 37, 53, 211, 231
Mauer an der Url 176, 183, 213
Mediana 99, 210, 219
memory, memorialisation 19, 27, 31, 32, 35, 60, 62, 64, 67, 69, 70, 76, 85, 94, 121, 126, 127, 131, 132, 150, 154, 158, 168, 171, 173, 184, 200
Mercurius 37, 64, 91, 92, 123, 170, 206, 209
meso-spaces 14, 19, 20, 43, 76, 89, 109, 110, 115, 117, 120, 122, 132, 152–190, 192, 195, 200, 201, 208, 225, 237
Mesopotamia 107, 167
Micia 92, 93, 118, 121–123, 147, 163, 164, 192, 223
micro-spaces 19, 20, 41, 63–65, 89, 107, 115, 117, 120, 166, 167, 173, 174, 190–198, 200, 201, 203, 208, 225
Minerva 102, 128, 132, 213, 231
Mithraeum 93, 115, 116, 122, 123, 132, 133, 147, 153, 157, 158, 164, 167, 168, 180, 184, 203, 210–222, 225
Mithras 2, 73–75, 88, 91–93, 97, 139, 156, 157,159, 164, 167, 170, 174, 176, 180–182, 188, 203, 226, 231
mobility 2, 5, 8, 14, 21, 29, 32, 41, 44, 47, 53, 70, 89, 90, 91, 94–97, 105, 106, 111, 112, [illegible], 135, 142, 144, 153, 164, 175, 199, 202, 205
Mócsy, András 9, 13, 38, 66, 99, 108
Moesia Inferior 3, 13, 24, 43, 44, 69, 70, 72, 73, 75, 90, 95, 96, 105, 106, 112, 125, 135, 138, 140, 144, 150, 155, 169, 170, 174, 195, 201, 205, 206, 219, 242

Moesia Superior 3, 13, 41, 42, 62, 70, 71, 73, 75, 87, 90, 95, 96, 99, 100, 105, 107, 112, 137, 150, 163, 169, 174, 188, 205, 218, 226, 240
Mommsen, Theodor 8, 10, 23, 142
Monumentum Ancyranum 4, 5, 56
mountain archaeology 12, 44
Morava 43, 95
mythology, mythological 68, 88, 154, 174, 188

Naissus 71, 72, 105
Nemesis 123, 226, 231
Nemeseion 113, 115, 211, 213–215, 218, 223, 224
Neptunus 97, 130, 231
Nero 1, 156
Noricum 1–3, 8, 12, 23, 27, 34–38, 46, 48–50, 52, 53, 58, 61, 76, 82, 90, 96, 105, 107, 135, 142, 150, 160, 169, 170, 174–176, 199, 205, 206, 211, 217, 225, 238, 241
North Africa 16, 106, 111, 118, 123
Novae 1, 2, 90, 96, 108, 111, 124–126, 144, 148, 157, 158, 175, 186, 188, 218, 220
Numidia 106
Nutrices 49, 54, 65, 66, 161, 217, 231

Oescus 70, 128, 132, 133, 137, 170, 192, 202, 220
Olt 95
oppidum, *oppida* 33, 35, 36, 39, 59, 77, 106, 107, 112, 143, 202
ordo decurionum 104
Oriental, orientalism 10, 11, 13, 14, 36, 62, 118, 153, 157, 162, 167, 172, 182, 203
Ostia 105, 109, 111, 203

Pákozd 40
Palmyra, Palmyrian 106, 109, 131, 135, 161, 203, 223, 224, 225
Pannonia Inferior 3, 12, 24, 60, 63, 75, 90, 96, 103, 105, 112, 135, 145, 150, 158, 160, 169, 174, 194, 195, 205, 206, 214, 225
Pannonia Superior 3, 12, 39, 41, 42, 57, 62, 63, 75, 90, 96, 99, 100, 103, 105, 107, 112, 120, 137, 150, 157, 159, 160, 169, 174, 179, 205, 214, 226, 239
pater 135, 151, 158, 160, 168, 184
Pergamon 104, 132, 169
Pfaffenberg 61, 62, 117, 145, 216
pilgrimage 19, 65, 76, 98–104, 126, 141, 169, 186, 202
Pliny the Elder 4, 22, 28
podium, podium temple 36, 53, 54, 131, 213
Poetovio 5, 24, 40, 54, 59, 65, 66, 88, 91, 93, 99, 102, 108, 137, 138, 143, 157, 157–161, 157, 176, 217
Pompeii 109, 111, 128, 192, 196, 203
pontifex 135, 151, 170, 171
Porolissum 5, 91–93, 105, 162, 163, 192, 223
pottery 29, 34, 36, 45, 52, 56, 60, 63, 68, 105, 199
priesthood, priests 12, 14, 24, 37, 39, 45, 61, 109, 132, 134, 135, 137, 150, 162, 166, 168–171, 179, 184, 196
principia 124–126, 166, 193, 210–216, 218, 220–223, 225
Procopius 4
publicum portorii Illyrici 5, 9, 19, 90, 91, 93, 94, 99, 123, 137, 157, 164, 201

Quadriviae 215, 232

Raetia 2, 3, 8, 12, 23, 27–31, 34, 38, 45, 46, 47, 48, 61, 76, 81, 90, 95, 107, 140, 142, 144, 150, 160, 167, 170, 174, 179, 186, 188, 195, 199, 201, 205, 206, 209, 238
Ratiaria 105, 132, 137, 219
religio militum 120
religio castrensis 120, 125
religious agency 17, 18, 31, 32, 40–42, 49, 52, 59, 63–68, 71, 72, 76, 89, 90, 96, 103, 109, 112, 113, 122, 125–128, 132, 153, 154, 161, 165–171, 185, 190, 195, 200, 205, 206, 225
religious communication 2, 3, 9, 10, 12–22, 27, 29, 31, 34, 35, 38, 40–46, 47, 49, 50, 53, 56, 58–63, 65, 71–73, 75, 89, 90, 93, 98, 102, 106–109, 127, 128, 132, 134, 137, 150, 152, 162, 165, 166–168, 170, 173, 174, 179, 182, 185, 190–196, 200–205
religious experience 2, 10, 11, 18, 19, 22, 62, 64, 65, 68, 102, 112, 121, 127, 132, 137, 149, 152, 156, 165–171, 185, 186, 190, 193, 195, 199, 203, 207, 208
religious founder 19, 152–159, 163, 164, 176–178, 183, 202
religious identity 68, 73, 125
religious networks 12, 18, 32, 94, 105, 111, 155, 161–165, 182, 184, 205
Rhine 29
Roman citizenship 1, 71, 90, 105, 171
Romania 5, 9, 13, 14, 42, 67, 69, 103, 121, 122, 147, 206
Romanisation 12, 20, 26, 38, 46, 66, 69, 82, 106, 144, 174, 201
Rome 5, 8, 15, 35, 44, 45, 48, 49, 67, 69, 81, 99, 105, 111, 112, 117, 130, 132, 145, 162, 170, 171, 175, 178, 194, 205
rural religion 19, 31, 35, 44, 52, 53, 59, 62, 63, 65, 69, 70, 75, 90, 121, 143, 160, 179, 180, 191

Rüpke, Jörg 11, 15, 16, 23–26, 81, 121, 161, 166, 173, 179, 204

Sabazios 71, 73, 88, 170, 174, 182, 184
sacerdos, sacerdotes 93, 135, 137, 150, 160, 162, 185
sacrifice, sacrificial 32, 35, 40, 41, 45, 52, 69, 77, 86, 97, 98, 135, 157, 166, 167, 182, 185, 199
Salona 99, 105
Sandberg 35
Sarmatians 4
Sarmizegetusa, colonia 75, 92, 93, 104, 105, 107, 110, 111, 115, 128, 130, 131, 132, 137, 139, 143, 144, 158, 168, 169, 176, 190–192, 202, 203, 224
Sarmizegetusa Regia 35, 61, 67, 77, 86, 121, 172
Sava 38, 40–43, 55, 95, 96
Savaria 12, 59, 64, 65, 93, 100, 101, 102, 105, 108, 110, 132, 134, 143, 161, 168, 187, 203, 206, 218
Scarbantia 59, 128, 218
Scordisci 38, 39, 42–44, 70–72, 80
Septimius Severus 5, 22, 63, 94, 113, 118, 119, 120, 131, 143
Serapis 102, 104, 232
Serbia 5, 9, 42, 99
Silk Roads 19, 201
Silvanus 63–65, 71, 115, 170, 194, 216, 217, 219, 220, 223, 224, 226, 232, 233, 243
Singidunum 13, 72, 105, 108, 143, 161, 219
Sirmium 13, 73, 76, 94, 95, 105, 107, 108, 137, 143, 161, 193, 218
Slovenia 5
small group religions 12, 19, 21, 73, 89, 93, 105, 106, 109, 110, 122, 123, 134, 137, 144, 153–156, 159, 161, 162, 164, 168, 173, 176, 178, 180, 182, 202, 203, 234
Sol, Helios 39, 74–75, 92, 176, 198
space sacralisation 3, 14, 16, 17, 18–22, 29, 31–35, 40, 49, 50, 52, 53, 59, 63, 64, 67, 72, 75, 78, 90, 94, 103, 107, 109, 117, 120–122, 124–127, 134, 152, 159, 161, 165, 167, 171, 173, 175, 177, 179, 183, 185, 189, 192–196, 201, 202, 208, 225
spelaeum 19, 216
spring, springs 19, 40, 56, 65, 102, 103, 104, 115, 126, 142, 209, 210, 214, 220
statio, stationes 5, 61, 90, 94, 95, 120
statue, statues 2, 34, 36, 37, 40, 45, 53, 78, 91, 92, 97, 99, 103, 113, 118, 120, 122, 125, 130–132, 137, 138, 149, 155, 157, 158, 163, 164, 170–173, 176, 179, 192–194, 197–200
statuette 2, 34, 40, 122, 126, 179, 192–194, 197
Strabo 28, 46, 76, 79
St Lorenzen bei Knittelfeld 35
Syria 15, 106, 118, 123, 138, 143, 156, 162, 167, 187, 227

Taurisci 34, 40, 105
tauroctony 180
territorium, territoria 55, 59, 60, 61, 62, 105, 144
third space 19, 31, 102–104, 121, 169, 199
Thrace, Thracian 13, 23, 43, 44, 70–73, 87, 90, 99, 105–107, 141, 149, 162, 169, 180, 184, 199, 201, 202, 206, 219, 220, 221, 233
Tiberius 1, 56, 57, 59, 60, 81, 105, 150
Tibiscum 92, 93, 139, 170, 225
Tisza 95, 147
Tomis 105, 132, 135, 137, 154, 155, 158
Tóth, István 12, 24, 38–40, 61–64, 73, 75, 79, 83–86, 91, 92, 112, 139, 216
Trajan 4, 22, 61, 69, 97, 100, 107, 112, 113, 118, 130, 131, 146, 157, 158, 173
Troesmis 95, 108, 111, 144
Tropaeum Alpium 28, 46
Tropaeum Traiani 192

urbanisation 21, 49, 107, 108, 113, 123, 135, 202
Urbs Roma 125, 233

valetudinarium 103, 125, 126, 215, 220
Veldidena 48
Venus, Aphrodite 43, 160, 193, 233
Vergilius, Virgil 28, 76, 187
Vespasian 1, 145
veteran, veterans 2, 59, 60, 111, 184
Via Claudia 29, 31, 46, 48, 54, 59, 99
Victoria, Niké 61, 69, 70, 84, 138, 157, 177, 178, 231, 233
villa 63, 75, 99, 178, 191, 194–196, 210, 212
Viminacium 13, 72, 73, 90, 97, 149, 176
Vindelici 28, 29, 33, 46
Virunum 1, 2, 35, 37, 83, 117, 126, 128–130, 132, 158, 160, 168, 170, 171, 176, 192, 202, 213
Vitruvius, Vitruvian 36, 128, 130, 134, 146

Wilkes, John 9, 11, 23, 24
Wissowa, Georg 10, 23, 64, 144

Zollfeld 38, 160, 213